OXFORD STUDIES IN AFRICAN POLITICS AND INTERNATIONAL RELATIONS

General Editors

NIC CHEESEMAN, PEACE MEDIE, AND RICARDO SOARES DE OLIVEIRA

Oxford Studies in African Politics and International Relations is a series for scholars and students working on African politics and International Relations and related disciplines. Volumes concentrate on contemporary developments in African political science, political economy, and International Relations, such as electoral politics, democratization, decentralization, gender and political representation, the political impact of natural resources, the dynamics and consequences of conflict, comparative political thought, and the nature of the continent's engagement with the East and West. Comparative and mixed methods work is particularly encouraged. Case studies are welcomed but should demonstrate the broader theoretical and empirical implications of the study and its wider relevance to contemporary debates. The focus of the series is on sub-Saharan Africa, although proposals that explain how the region engages with North Africa and other parts of the world are of interest.

The Railpolitik

Leadership and Agency in Sino-African Infrastructure Development

YUAN WANG

OXFORD
UNIVERSITY PRESS

OXFORD
UNIVERSITY PRESS

Great Clarendon Street, Oxford, OX2 6DP,
United Kingdom

Oxford University Press is a department of the University of Oxford.
It furthers the University's objective of excellence in research, scholarship,
and education by publishing worldwide. Oxford is a registered trade mark of
Oxford University Press in the UK and in certain other countries

Published in the United States of America by Oxford University Press
198 Madison Avenue, New York, NY 10016, United States of America

British Library Cataloguing in Publication Data

Data available

Library of Congress Control Number: 2023942196

ISBN 9780198873037

DOI: 10.1093/oso/9780198873037.001.0001

Printed and bound by
CPI Group (UK) Ltd, Croydon, CR0 4YY

Contents

Acknowledgements

In writing this book I have incurred many debts. This book could not have been completed without the interviewees' generous sharing in Angola, China, Ethiopia, and Kenya. Their rich practical experiences are valuable sources of knowledge for me academically. At a personal level, I was constantly inspired by their strong determination to proceed despite obstacles. I was extremely saddened to hear the news that three of my former interviewees had passed away. Dr Newai, José Patrocínio, and Solomon Ouna were deeply passionate and knowledgeable about their work and were generous and kind in sharing their experience with me. Many of my interviewees' quotes must remain anonymous, but without their goodwill I never could have collected enough empirical evidence to finish this book.

During the writing of this manuscript, Ricardo Soares de Oliveira was always the first reader of each chapter draft and was a constant source of advice and constructive criticism. Ricardo himself represents the highest level of research in the political economy of Angola and African politics, and is also an accomplished writer. I have been fortunate in receiving his supervision for my MSc and DPhil studies at Oxford, and our collaboration has continued since I left Oxford. Ezequiel González Ocantos and Miles Larmer provided extremely valuable comments for this manuscript, saved me from many errors, and made my argument clearer and sharper. I was inspired by the thought leadership of Deborah Bräutigam to pursue Sino-African relations academically. She has always been a rich source of inspiration, support, and encouragement.

The book has benefited from conversations and advice about African politics, global China, and China–Africa infrastructure cooperation. Chris Alden, Emmanuel Akyeampong, Jamie Monson, Folashadé Soulé-Kohndou, Tom Christensen, Iain Johnston, and Min Ye have all, on at least one occasion, provided significant insight for the development of this manuscript. The China and the World Program (CWP) alumni's perceptive comments and criticism at the CWP Workshop in April 2022 were tremendously helpful for developing this book. In particular, Dawn Murphy and Zoe Zhongyuan Liu read my sample chapters and provided extremely helpful suggestions for revision. I am also particularly grateful for the insightful comments and criticism from three anonymous reviewers of my book proposal at Oxford University Press, as well as the editorial support from Dominic Byatt and Vicki Sunter.

Other individuals that generously lent their support to my fieldwork in Angola, Ethiopia, Kenya, and China deserve mentioning here. My fieldwork in Angola could not have been completed without the generous sharing of connections and advice from Manuel Alves da Rocha, Ana Duarte, Luísa Rogério, Regina Santos, Francisco Miguel Paulo, Allan Cain, Miguel Gomes, Rafael Marques de Morais, Edmilson Angelo, Victor Morais, and Nelson Pestana, among many others. Argument development about Angola also benefited from discussions with Lucy Corkin, Jesse S. Ovadia, Rebecca Elisabeth Husebye Engebretsen, Jacob Hansen, and Ricardo Soares de Oliveira, and from reading their works. My fieldwork and later development of the argument around Ethiopia benefited from advice from and works by Jason Mosley, Biruk Terrefe, Alexandra Zeitz, Harry Verhoeven, Yunnan Chen, Weiwei Chen, Maria Repnikova, Berihu Assefa, Mulu Yesus, Girum Abebe Tefera, and Zizhu Zhang, among others. The title of this book, *The Railpolitik*, is inspired by Yunnan Chen's excellent working paper: 'Railpolitik: Ethiopia's Rail Ambitions and Chinese Development Finance'. In Kenya, Lin Qi, Zhengli Huang, Xin Zhang, Peng Liu, Jiao Hu, Jinghao Lu, and Tong Wu, among others, generously shared their connections and goodwill to support my fieldwork. In China, I am grateful to Li Anshan, Liu Haifang, Xu Liang, He Wenping, Tang Xiaoyang, Zhou Jinyan, Zheng Yu, Xu Xiuli, and Wang Yalin for their kind introduction to informants and intellectual advice.

My cohort of fellow former graduate students and postdoctoral fellows continues to be a source of friendship and support. Different chapters of this manuscript have been passed and presentations made among colleagues at Oxford, SOAS, and Columbia-Harvard CWP, and I have benefited beyond estimation from the discussions as well as innumerable suggestions and criticisms that I have received. I am grateful to Clara Voyvodic Casabo, Hang Zhou, Biruk Terrefe, Filip Bubenheimer, Mikael Hiberg Naghizadeh, Alexandra Zeitz, Yutao Huang, Barnaby Dye, Naosuke Mukoyama, Danny Hatem, Hangwei Li, and Weidi Zheng for their discussions and comments. During writing and revising this manuscript, Blen Taye, Emile Mathieu, Liyang Han, Danny Hatem, Xuanyi Sheng, Marina Eriksson, and Rustem Yeshpanov have been constant sources of friendly support. My postdoctoral life in New York was significantly enriched by the friendship and intellectual companionship of

Hong Zhang, Justin Key Canfil, Daniel Suchenski, Chi Zhang, Junyan Jiang, Austin Strange, and Yue Hou. My thanks also goes to Zhen Yang and Ken Bosire who provided valuable insights in the final editorial stage.

My DPhil experience would have been completely different without the professional and caring support of Elizabeth Brenner. Hugh Petter helped create the channel to connect my emotions and music; those small episodes of piano lessons ignited colourful sparkles in my Oxford life. My friends in China, Molly Huazheng Guan, Wen Xu, and Xia Shen, as well as my parents, grandma, and other members of my extended family, are constant sources of strength and love.

The China Scholarship Council and China Oxford Scholarship Fund generously funded my DPhil and MSc studies. The Department of Politics and International Relations and Mansfield College at Oxford, my CWP office at Riverside Church in New York, and my office at Duke Kunshan University provided ideal venues for me to complete this work. Parts of this book appear in the following two articles: Wang, Y. (2022). Executive agency and state capacity in development: Comparing Sino-African railways in Kenya and Ethiopia. *Comparative Politics*, *54*(2), 349–73; Wang, Y. (2022). Presidential extraversion: Understanding the politics of Sino-African mega-infrastructure projects. *World Development*, *158*, 105976.

Kunshan, China
October 2022

List of figures

List of tables

Introduction

Kenyan President Uhuru Kenyatta (in office 2013–22) was proud to achieve the impossible. 'Today will be marked as a great day in the history of our Republic', said President Kenyatta when he addressed the inauguration ceremony of the Chinese-financed and -constructed Standard Gauge Railway (SGR) on 31 May 2017. Kenyatta intentionally selected this inauguration date to be two months before the presidential elections in August when he was seeking a second term, shortening the contracted schedule by half. Originally contracted to be completed in five years, the project took only two and a half years to finish, making this the first project to be completed ahead of schedule in Kenyan history. The SGR crossed two national parks, opposed by politicians, and was involved in hundreds of court cases, yet politics, courts, civil society, and even nature did not delay its construction. The railway operation also boasted no accident since the onset of its operation, which started on 1 June 2017, a day after the inauguration ceremony.

The trajectory of the Chinese-sponsored Kenyan railway was not shared by its Ethiopian and Angolan counterparts. In 2019, I visited two other Chinese-sponsored railways in Africa: the Angolan Caminho de Ferro de Benguela (CFB) and the Addis Ababa–Djibouti railway (ADR). Their development trajectory was not as smooth as the Kenyan railway: the Ethiopian railway experienced a fourteen-month delay from completion to operation, and the first six months of operation were interrupted by two accidents. The Angolan railway, contracted to finish within twenty months, took as long as eleven years to complete with frequent accidents during operation.

Africa in the twenty-first century has witnessed the rising of buildings, the stretching of roads and railways connecting urban centres and rural areas, and the establishment of increasingly sophisticated electricity networks. Much of this hard infrastructure development has been facilitated by China. Starting from the early 2000s, Chinese policy banks and state-owned enterprises (SOEs) have completed many infrastructure projects in Africa and worldwide. China has helped African countries build and upgrade over 10,000 kilometres of railway, 100,000 kilometres of highway, 1,000 bridges, and 100 ports, as well as power plants, hospitals, residential apartments, and schools.[1] Yet Chinese-financed and -constructed projects demonstrate starkly

[1] Vine (2022).

The Railpolitik. Yuan Wang, Oxford University Press. © Yuan Wang (2023). DOI: 10.1093/oso/9780198873037.003.0001

different trajectories in different countries, and even in the same country across different times.

Why do Chinese-sponsored projects that are similar in nature develop along very different trajectories in different African states? And relatedly, what explains the variation of African state effectiveness in public goods delivery? Existing explanations focus on either structural or institutional factors. The structural explanation emphasizes the imbalanced relationship between Africa and external powers, emphasizing how external agency, rather than African agency, determines the effectiveness of African states to achieve developmental projects.[2] The institutional explanation concentrates on the host country's state characteristics, notably bureaucratic capability, in public goods delivery.

My book argues that it is the salience of the African political leadership that determines Sino-African railway development, and I term it *political championship theory*. This political championship theory emphasizes the personalistic, idiosyncratic, and unpredictable aspect of state effectiveness—the agency of the political leaders, a phenomenon that has yet to receive due academic emphasis. Instead of undermining the role of institutions, my approach focuses on how political institutions shape the incentives of leaders, and how, in consequence, these leaders choose policies.

1 China in Africa

China's economic expansion, together with its domestic economic growth, represents a major transformation in the international political economy. As it has evolved into a superpower over the past two decades, China has increased its global economic engagement through investment, trade, completed contracts, and development aid. China maintained an average annual GDP growth rate of 9.5 per cent from 1978 to 2018.[3] Even with the effects of Covid-19 containment measures on economic activities, China achieved 3.2 per cent annual growth in 2020, higher than any other country.[4] The country's outbound foreign direct investment, trade, and aid show a steep upward trajectory since the early 2000s. Take, for instance, the number of contracts completed by Chinese companies overseas. With Beijing's announcement of the 'going global' policy in the early 2000s, which was further institutionalized by the Belt and Road Initiative in 2013, Chinese policy banks and state-owned

[2] Taylor and Zajontz (2020); Taylor (2016, 2020); Carmody (2020).
[3] Data Commons (n.d.).
[4] OECD (14 September 2020).

companies have increasingly cooperated with developing countries to finance and complete infrastructure projects. According to China's Bureau of Statistics, Chinese companies completed US$173 billion in contracts in 2019, 90 per cent of which were completed in Asia, Africa, and Latin America. In Africa alone, from 2000 to 2018, Chinese banks issued 1,076 loans totalling US$148 billion.[5] Figure 0.1 shows Chinese companies' completed contracts from 2000 to 2019 in Asia, Africa, Latin America, and developed countries, respectively.

This exponential expansion of China's global engagement has elicited varied opinions from international and host country commentators. Optimistic views welcome China as an alternative choice for developing countries. Financial sources from China and other emerging donors allowed African states to reduce their reliance on traditional donors;[6] the ability of African countries to leverage competition between the West and China could reduce the recipient countries' dependence on Beijing.[7] Beijing's portrayal of China's economic engagement with developing countries as a 'win-win' cooperation was mirrored by many host countries, where Chinese companies need work and host countries need infrastructure. Resource-for-infrastructure deals enhanced China's resource security on the one hand, and provided financial and technical assistance to infrastructure construction in the host countries on the other.[8]

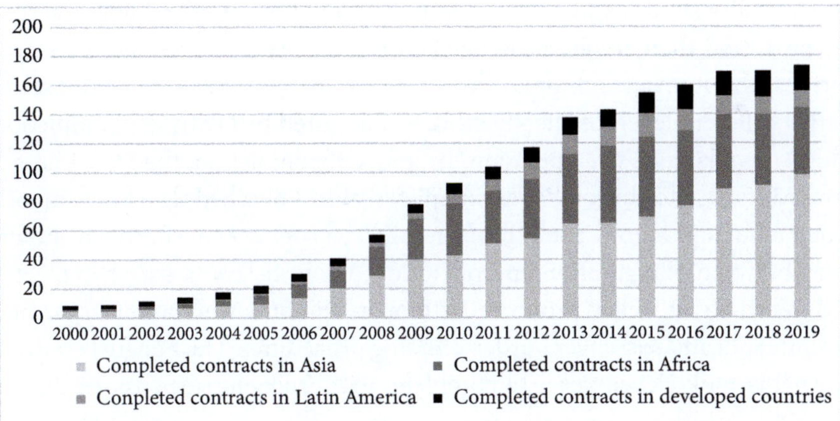

Figure 0.1 Chinese companies' completed contracts by year (2000–19) in US$ billion

[5] Brautigam, Hwang, Link, and Acker (2019).
[6] Greenhill, Prizzon, and Rogerson (2013); Zeitz (2019, 2021).
[7] Taylor and Zajontz (2020); Ellis (2009); Brautigam (2011); Wise (2020).
[8] Alves (2013).

China's rising global influence has also raised concerns regarding the political and developmental implications of Chinese economic activities. Some commentators see the seeds of a new form of dependency or 'neo-colonialism' in the relationship between Chinese natural resource interests and the debt sustainability of African nations. They particularly note that a large portion of these debts were accumulated through Chinese loans for infrastructure construction.[9] The concept of a predatory or even 'neo-colonial' China is also widespread among African and Western intellectuals, media, and in the policy sphere.[10] The influx of Chinese manufactured goods, given China's low labour costs and subsidized credits, made it difficult for developing countries' industrial firms to compete.[11] Chinese corporate practices have also raised local and international concerns on environmental impact,[12] labour practices,[13] and corruption.[14]

Instead of following the majority of these analyses that perceive China as a consistent and homogenous entity, I take a different approach and investigate how Chinese-financed and -constructed projects that are similar in nature demonstrate starkly different trajectories in different African countries. Take, for instance, the three recently launched Chinese-sponsored railways: the ADR, the SGR in Kenya, and the CFB in Angola. The three railway projects have important similarities: they are financed through loans from China Export and Import Bank (EximBank) and contracted to Chinese SOEs for feasibility studies and construction; they link the countries' hinterland to the port; and their routes all follow colonial railways. Yet despite such similarities, the Kenyan, Ethiopian, and Angolan railway projects demonstrate starkly different levels of effectiveness, as measured by (1) timely completion and (2) regular and safe operation. In terms of completion, the SGR Phase 1 from Mombasa to Nairobi[15] was completed ahead of schedule with a smooth transition to operation. The Ethiopian railway experienced a fourteen-month delay between inauguration and operation due to delays in supplying water and electricity, as well as protracted Ethiopia–Djibouti negotiations regarding revenue split and passenger border-crossing procedures. The Benguela railway in Angola took eleven years to complete, with frequent suspensions during

[9] Taylor and Zajontz (2020); Tarrósy (2020); Taylor (2016, 2020); Gallagher and Porzecanski (2010); Stallings (2020).
[10] Sanusi (11 March 2013).
[11] Gallagher and Porzecanski (2010).
[12] Ray, Gallagher, López, and Sanborn (2017); Shinn (2015).
[13] Oya and Schaefer (2019).
[14] Solomon and Frechette (2018).
[15] The SGR from Mombasa to Nairobi is Phase 1; it then extended from Nairobi to Naivasha (Phase 2A).

construction. Regarding operation, the Kenyan railway's safety performance and operation figures humbled its Ethiopian and Angolan counterparts. This book explains why Chinese-sponsored projects that are similar in nature develop differently in different African states. This requires an understanding of African state effectiveness first and foremost.

2 Understanding state effectiveness

State effectiveness refers to the effectiveness of states to achieve official policy objectives.[16] Large infrastructure projects have both material and symbolic functions, and therefore they are frequently instrumentalized politically as state-building and power projection tools.[17] Transport infrastructure, such as roads and railways, facilitates connectivity, shapes the movements of people and goods, connects sites of production and consumption, enhances international trade, and promotes national economic growth. Beyond these material functions, infrastructure projects are also state-sponsored imaginaries of modernity, transformation, and development.[18] Precisely because of their material and ideological functions, mega-infrastructure projects are often instrumentalized by the state to fulfil specific political agendas. Famously, Herbst argues that transport infrastructure served as colonial tools of power projection in Africa, enabling state administrations to exercise control over a large but less populous landscape and enhance policy reach.[19] Some historians have proposed a notion of 'railway imperialism' and argue that colonial railways carried the symbols of imperialism and modernization.[20] Mega-infrastructure cannot be apolitical, and examining the politics of infrastructure is a way to unpack state effectiveness.

Railway projects are particularly politically salient and railway effectiveness serves as a strong indication of state effectiveness. *Effectiveness* is measured the fundamental purpose that the railway is designed and expected to fulfil, including: (1) timely completion: whether the railway was completed within the contracted and politically assigned schedule and (2) regular and safe operation: whether the cargo and passenger services operate regularly and safely. Although narrowly defined, railway effectiveness assumes broader political and economic implications: the construction and operation of railways involve

[16] Centeno, Kohli, and Yashar (2017); Fukuyama (2013); Skocpol (1985).
[17] Monson (2009).
[18] Harvey and Knox (2015); Dye (2020).
[19] Herbst (2014).
[20] Davis, Wilburn, and Robinson (1991).

a set of changes to their surrounding social, economic, and environmental landscape. These changes include, most prominently, land acquisition and compensation, labour employment and disputes, corruption, modifications to livelihoods and the environment, and a readjustment of the logistics industry. Railway effectiveness captures the immediate project results while leaving aside the longer-term project expectations, such as repaying loans, boosting economic growth and industrialization, and facilitating regional and international trade and connectivity. I focus on short-term outcomes because having an operating railway is a precondition for loan repayment and any long-term economic and social implications. Furthermore, successful completion of railway construction and initiating operations are within the control of the state, making it a more direct proxy for state effectiveness than the long-term developmental impacts of the railway, which are determined by a wide range of other factors.

The dominant explanations of state effectiveness emphasize either bureaucratic capacity or external determination. Bureaucracy has been at the centre of discussions on the politics of public service delivery in developing countries, divided into two main streams of literature: the Weberian bureaucracy and 'pockets of effectiveness' (POEs) theories. Drawing on the original insights of Weber, researchers of the East Asian developmental states argue that a professional state bureaucracy, characterized by meritocratic recruitment and long-term career rewards, is essential to explaining the economic 'miracles' in these states.[21] In the study of bureaucratic capacity in developing countries, many scholars focus on a single capable bureaucratic agency within a generally ineffective state. This 'pocket of efficiency' is a 'public organization that is relatively effective in providing public goods and services that the organization is officially mandated to provide, despite operating in an environment in which effective public service delivery is not the norm'.[22] African railway corporations, usually under the management of the Ministry of Transport and sometimes directly supervised by the executive, are the owners of the railway projects. They are the bureaucrats that engage with Chinese SOEs on a daily basis and implement the project across multiple levels of domestic politics. According to the bureaucratic capacity explanation, the capable management and strong political leverage of a railway corporation is the central factor that led to high railway effectiveness.

[21] Evans (1995); Weber (1968); Johnson (1982).
[22] Roll (2014, p. 24).

Another explanation for the divergent state effectiveness is the external agency argument. According to this argument, it is the variation in the commitment and capacity of the external actors, in this case Chinese contractors, that determines the different project outcomes. Many scholars depict African states as weak and passive, shaped by external forces since the colonial era. In this view, Africa has never ceased to exchange goods and ideas with Europe, Asia, and later with America, and this relationship has been characterized by the unevenness and asymmetry between Africa on the one hand, and Europe and Asia on the other.[23] China–Africa economic relations also conform to this dependency paradigm, which is characterized by structural asymmetry, with Africa once again situated in a marginal position within the global economic system and defined by its limited value as a provider of mineral resources.[24] The 'Chinese agency' version of the external agency theory argues that variation in capacity across Chinese SOEs determines the different outcomes of Chinese-sponsored projects. The Chinese SOEs are crucial actors in China's engagement overseas, alongside Chinese government actors, including the Ministry of Foreign Affairs, the Ministry of Commerce, and the EximBank. The same Chinese government actors are involved in all railway projects, but the Chinese SOEs involved differ. According to this argument, the central causal factor that shapes the trajectories of the projects is the agency of the Chinese SOEs. Chinese SOEs with higher technical strength and political connection could deliver railway projects more successfully in Africa.

3 The argument

This book seeks to explain the variation in the outcomes of railway projects between Kenya, Ethiopia, and Angola which reflects their variation in state effectiveness; that is, the effectiveness of states to achieve official policy objectives.[25] Drawing on existing studies of leadership, I introduce a theory of political championship to explain variance in railway effectiveness, and more broadly in African states' effectiveness to achieve infrastructural outcomes. Despite the visibility and centrality of political leaders, the study of leadership in state effectiveness and political economy of development is scarce. Existing studies focus either on the psychology of leaders and followers,[26] 'crisis

[23] See a recapture of this view and its critique in Bayart (2000); Clapham (1996).
[24] Taylor and Zajontz (2020); Taylor (2016, 2020); Tarrósy (2020); Carmody (2020).
[25] Centeno, Kohli, and Yashar (2017); Fukuyama (2013); Skocpol (1985).
[26] Bell (2014).

leadership',[27] or the study of dictatorship, largely because many scholars believe that the phenomenon of leadership is incompatible with the practice of democracy.[28] The leadership–development nexus has also received some scholarly attention, with mixed evidence for whether leadership can be an explanatory factor for economic growth.[29] While the study of politics in advanced economies with strongly institutionalized systems has tended to focus on institutions, individual personalities have retained the largest possible role in weakly institutionalized political systems such as those found in many African countries.[30] The way in which Africa's core political dynamics closely revolve around national presidents is further articulated through the notion of 'personal rule'[31] and the somewhat more wide-ranging idea of 'big-man politics'.[32] Political leaders in Africa are understood to be more likely to override institutional constraints and act largely autonomously.[33] However, 'personal rule' and 'big-man politics' theories put more emphasis on how leaders pursue personal enrichment and maintain patronage system to remain in power, but less, if any at all, on the leaders' role in achieving policy objectives. Political championship theory advances this literature by recognizing personal rule in policy and project implementation, and emphasizing the efficacy of informal politics without understating the importance of bureaucracy.

I propose a political championship theory to explain variation in state effectiveness to deliver mega-infrastructure projects and development policies. *Political championship* is the actions of individuals in top political positions (usually the executive) who endeavour to solve or circumvent the obstacles that beleaguer the efforts of less senior actors in processes of public goods delivery.[34] My argument is two-fold. The perceived threats from competitive elections engineer strong political commitment to developmental projects from the state's leadership; that is, the political champion. When the leader has strong authority, they build a coalition for project implementation, generating bureaucratic ambitions and tempering resistance from their subordinates, leading to better project outcomes. This is an endeavour to 'bring the individual back in' to the study of the state without discounting the role of collective entities such as bureaucracy.[35]

[27] Weber (1968); Lodge and Wegrich (2012).
[28] Beerbohm (2015).
[29] Besley and Case (1995); Jones and Olken (2005); Brown (2020); Carbone and Pellegata (2020).
[30] Carbone and Pellegata (2020); Rotberg (2012).
[31] Jackson and Rosberg (1982).
[32] Price (1974); Hyden (2012).
[33] Rotberg (2012).
[34] This definition is derived from the definition of leadership in Young (1991).
[35] Evans, Peter, Rueschemeyer, and Skocpol (1985).

Political commitment refers to political leaders' decision to prioritize a project. Rulers' interests have significant influence on policy choices. By making a conspicuous display of their concern for a particular project or policy, the ruler is able to keep their subordinates alert to their wishes and desires, and bureaucrats, whose primary incentive is their career advancement, will think long and hard before sabotaging them. *Perceived threats from electoral competition* engineer political commitment. This is achieved in two ways. In competitive regimes, political commitment increases prior to elections when the incumbent seeks another term, and decreases when the incumbent's priority shifts to power consolidation.[36] In less competitive states, contentious elections may lead to legitimacy threats to the incumbent, and thus the leader's commitment to developmental policies or projects increases after an election as the leader seeks to demonstrate their stewardship to the people. Apart from elections, leadership commitment is also contingent on other factors such as ongoing crises, natural resources, and foreign leverage.

Leader's authority is the leader's ability to build a coalition of key actors on the project or policy and push the delivery agenda forward. Coalition-building requires the leader's capacity to identify, mobilize, and motivate the right people.[37] The leader's authority is broader than the constitutional power attached to the presidency or premiership. It emphasizes the leader's ability to go beyond formal institutions and utilize informal ones to push the policy or project agenda forward. Ranging from bureaucratic and legislative norms to clientelism and patrimonialism, informal institutions shape political behaviours and outcomes, and in some contexts more strongly than formal political institutions.[38] The leader may employ various stratagems to secure cooperation to guarantee project or policy delivery. Common stratagems may include coopt opposition leaders,[39] bypassing bureaucracies, increased monitoring, provision of rewards and the threat of sanctions to induce higher effort in subordinates,[40] and generating a sense of mission and ideology.[41]

Why do African rulers choose to engage with China to initiate and champion these projects? I argue that foreign-sponsored mega-infrastructure projects have coincided with African rulers' political survival strategies and been used effectively by the ruler. Internationally, African rulers have strategized amongst their available choices to ensure foreign finance and services on the most

[36] Nordhaus (1975); Dubois (2016); Guo (2009).
[37] Khan (2018, p. 645); Bueno de Mesquita, Smith, Siverson, and Morrow (2003).
[38] Helmke and Levitsky (2004, p. 727).
[39] Jackson and Rosberg (1982, p. 25).
[40] Dixit (2002).
[41] Weber (1968).

favourable terms. Domestically, they have instrumentalized foreign funding and foreign-sponsored projects both to demonstrate performance legitimacy and to maintain rulership through provision of patronage.

The political championship theory emphasizes the personalistic, idiosyncratic, and unpredictable characters of politics, an aspect that has yet to receive due academic emphasis. This theory also highlights the informality in political decision-making and policy implementation. By emphasizing African agency, the political championship theory raises an important aspect which is overlooked by scholars who emphasize structural asymmetry between Africa and the external powers, and whose focus has been on external agency. By disaggregating African states, differentiating the executive from the bureaucracy, and analysing the imbricated formal and informal powers of the presidency, the political championship theory captures the volatile characteristics of state effectiveness in policy and project delivery that cannot be explained by the institutional and structural theories, thus shedding light on a previously understudied area in state effectiveness—the agency of the political leaders.

The political championship theory also challenges the conventional belief that electoral competition produces short-term survival incentives for elites, which is supposedly not as effective for development as centralized, long-term rent management. This research shows that short-term electoral institutions can be as effective as long-term centralized ones in generating leadership commitment to and intervention in developmental projects or policies.

4 Evaluating competing arguments

To empirically evaluate the political championship theory and alternative explanations, I trace the process of three Chinese-financed and constructed railways in three African countries: the SGR in Kenya, the ADR in Ethiopia, and the CFB in Angola. Through in-depth examination of case studies, I not only test existing theories on state effectiveness but also serve a theory-generating purpose by proposing a new leadership explanation—that is, the political championship theory—and explore its causal mechanism. This book seeks to establish causality primarily through within-case process tracing. Process tracing uses the evidence from within a case to make inferences about causal explanations for outcomes in that case.[42] The process-tracing exercise uses a combination of inductive and deductive study. The political

[42] Goertz and Mahoney (2012, p. 4).

championship explanation was primarily derived inductively from the Kenyan railway Phase 1 case through 'soaking and poking', as this case was not well explained by existing theories. During desk research and fieldwork, I immersed myself in the details of this case and was open to all kinds of possible explanations, and selected the hypotheses that became plausible and worthy of more rigorous testing.[43] After the political championship theory was developed inductively from the Kenyan SGR-1 case, process tracing was followed deductively to test the validity of this theory against two alternative theories; that is, the external agency and bureaucratic capacity theories, derived from existing literature. Examining the political championship theory against alternative theories can reduce confirmation bias.[44] Evidence from fieldwork is considered against each explanation. The political championship theory inducted from this case was then tested deductively with different pieces of evidence from the same case as well as from other cases.[45] This deductive process tracing implicitly follows the Bayesian logic, which provides a way to use evidence to update one's beliefs in the likelihood of truth of alternative explanations.[46]

This research complements within-case process tracing with structured and controlled comparisons across cases. This comparison is 'structured' in that data collection for each case is guided and standardized by the same interview themes, questions, and groups of interviewees, thereby making systemic comparison and cumulation of the findings of the cases possible.[47] The comparison is strictly controlled in the sense that the cases are comparable in every respect but one. This controlled comparison is achieved by dividing single longitudinal cases into two—the 'before' case and the 'after' case that allows observation of a discontinuous change in an important variable.[48] Key to this type of design is to hold before/after cases similar on variables other than the variable of interest. This can be strengthened by process tracing to assess whether differences other than those in the main variable of interest might

[43] Ibid.

[44] George and Bennett (2005). Section 2 of Appendix 1 lists the case-specific observable implications of all three theories in question.

[45] Methodologists differ in terms of whether the same evidence that was used for inductive theory-generating can be used for deductive tests. Bennett and Checkel (2015) and Mahoney (2012) propose that although a theory derived inductively from a case does not necessarily need to be tested against a different case, it should be tested against different and independent evidence in the case from which it was derived. Fairfield and Charman (2017) proved, using Bayesian logic, that even the same evidence used for inductive theory-generating can be used to test the same theory. In this book I follow the former proposal.

[46] Bennett and Checkel (2015); Fairfield and Charman (2022).

[47] George and Bennett (2005).

[48] Ibid.

account for the differences in the outcomes.[49] Instead of establishing causality through cross-case comparison, the multiple cases in Kenya, Ethiopia, and Angola are selected to investigate whether the theory holds for different political contexts.[50]

I disassemble the Kenyan, Ethiopian, and Angolan railways temporally into multiple subcases, generating seven subcases in total. Kenyan SGR Phase 1 (completed in May 2017) and Phase 2A (commenced in September 2017) are divided by the Kenyan presidential election on 8 August 2017. After the election, the president's commitment to the railway project reduced, and I use process tracing to show that all other variables either remain constant or their changes are spurious, not causal determinants of the change in outcome. The Ethiopian ADR is divided into three subcases: the ADR under Prime Minister Meles Zenawi, the ADR under Prime Minister Hailemariam Desalegn before the eruption of political crisis in November 2015, and the ADR-Hailemariam after 2016. The three Ethiopian subcases are divided by Meles' sudden death in August 2012 and the eruption of political crisis in November 2015. The change of political leaders changes the leader's authority variable while all other variables remain constant,[51] and the political crisis changes the political commitment variable. The Angolan CFB is divided into two subcases: CFB under the Office of National Reconstruction (GRN) and CFB under the Ministry of Transport. The two cases are divided by the presidential directive in 2010 to dissolve the GRN and transfer the project from the GRN to the Ministry of Transport. Across the two subcases, the Angolan president's commitment to the project remained minimal. Figure 0.2 shows the seven subcases.

The cases are selected to fill in the two-by-two Figure 0.3 with different values on the two factors: political commitment and leader's authority. The Kenyan SGR-1 case and the Ethiopian-Meles case demonstrate high

[49] Ibid.

[50] Despite many similarities in the Chinese-sponsored railways in Kenya, Ethiopia, and Angola, cross-country comparison is still challenging, as there are many factors that could potentially explain why Kenyan railway develops better than Ethiopian and Angolan ones. For instance, some may argue that both Ethiopian and Angolan railways are cross-national ones and therefore may require extra efforts for cross-country coordination; others may argue that the topography of the areas where Kenyan railways pass through are more enabling than Ethiopian and Angolan ones, etc. By adopting the 'before/after' design, I can evade these questions on the comparability of railways. In other words, I am not comparing Kenyan railways to Ethiopian and Angolan railways; I am comparing different phases of the same railways, thereby controlling for many other factors to isolate the effect of the political leadership.

[51] The sudden death of a political leader is used by Jones and Olken (2005) as an exogenous change to leadership that is unrelated to economic conditions or any other factors that may influence subsequent economic performance.

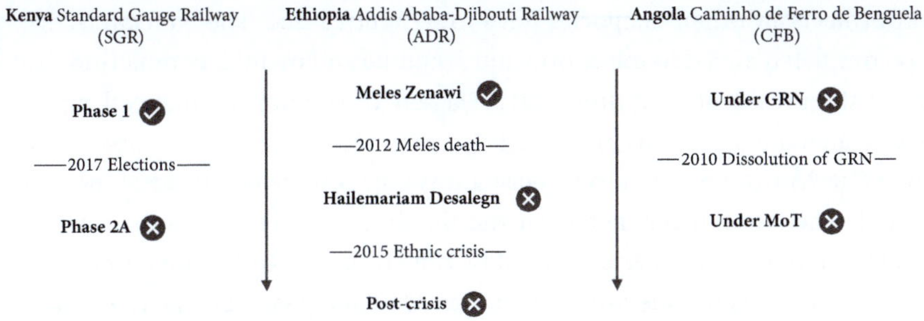

Figure 0.2 Temporal division of three railways into seven subcases
Source: China's Bureau of Statistics.

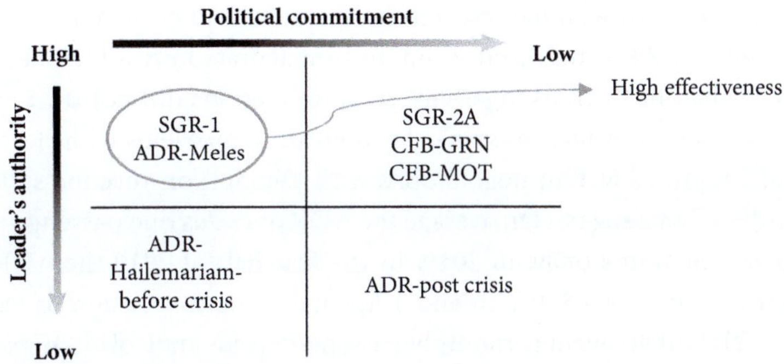

Figure 0.3 Subcase variation by independent variables

political commitment and high leader's authority. After the Kenyan 2017 election, President Kenyatta's priority changed; his commitment to the SGR-2A reduced although the leader's authority remained high under Kenyatta. In Ethiopia, when Hailemariam took the premiership from Meles, political commitment remained high, but the leader's authority was significantly reduced. When Ethiopian political crisis erupted in 2015, political commitment to the railway project dropped, the ADR-Hailemariam-2016 onwards thus had low leader's authority under Hailemariam, and low political commitment from the prime minister under the state of emergency. Political commitment to the Angolan CFB remained low before and after the transition of supervising bureaucracy, as the elite was sustained by its resource endowment. Although the leader's authority under President José Eduardo dos Santos was high, it did not set the project on a successful trajectory.

The cases selected for this study demonstrate stark variation in effectiveness, which is defined by (1) timely completion and (2) regular and safe operation. Only projects in the upper-left corner of Figure 0.3 exhibit high effectiveness, and projects in other categories have low effectiveness. The Kenyan SGR-1 was completed ahead of the contracted schedule and met the completion date set by the president on 1 June 2017. Passenger service commenced immediately after inauguration and freight service started on 1 December 2018. The SGR-2A from Nairobi to Naivasha was also completed ahead of the contracted schedule but did not meet the timeline set by the president, which was December 2018—a delay caused by difficulties in land acquisition. SGR-2A was finally inaugurated on 16 October 2019 and passenger service started immediately, while cargo service commenced on 18 December 2019. On average the SGR operates six passenger trains and seventeen freight trains per day, with average monthly occupancy of passenger services over 90 per cent as of June 2022.[52] At the time of the research no accidents had occurred.

The Ethiopian ADR was completed and inaugurated on 5 October 2016 in Addis Ababa but the passenger and cargo operations did not start until 1 January 2018. This fourteen-month delay was due to problems with electricity and water supply, as well as negotiations with Djibouti on revenue split and cross-border of passengers. On average the ADR operates one passenger train and four freight trains daily, in 2019. In the first half of 2019 the ADR had two major accidents, on 8 March and 4 April, causing suspension of service. In 2019, ADR had an average monthly passenger occupancy of 7,335 passengers.[53] Because I could not observe railway construction and operation results in the three cases, I use the efficiency of obstacle resolution, especially land acquisition and compensation, as a proxy for the dependent variable in each of the ADR cases.

The 1,344-kilometre Angolan CFB was contracted to complete in twenty months but took eleven years with frequent suspension of construction. The major suspension was in 2009–11 when, because of the financial crisis, the government of Angola could not issue payment to the Chinese contractor. Operation started immediately after construction, but the operational figures remained low: in 2019, the CFB operated five passenger and two cargo trains daily, with an average monthly occupancy of 12,466 passengers. My informants from CFB-Public Enterprise (CFB-EP) and China Railway 20th Bureau (CR20) refused to reveal the total number of accidents on the CFB, but as I picked up from casual discussions with Chinese managers in CR20, the CFB has more frequent accidents than the ADR, and there were reported casualties of Chinese train drivers in one of the accidents.

[52] State Council Information Office (2022).
[53] CCECC (April 2019).

Table 0.1 Variation in dependent variable: railway effectiveness

	Effectiveness **Timely completion and smooth transition to operation**	**Effectiveness** **Regular and safe operation**
Kenya SGR-1	Halved contracted schedule Met president's schedule	6 passenger trains/day 17 freight trains/day 0 accidents
Kenya SGR-2A	Met contracted schedule Failed president's schedule	6 passenger trains/day 17 freight trains/day 0 accidents
Ethiopia ADR	Met contract schedule 14 months' delay in operation	1 passenger trains/day 4 freight trains/day 2 accidents in the first half of 2019
Angola CFB	A decade's delay in construction Smooth transition to operation	5 passenger trains/day 1.5 freights trains/day Multiple accidents (data unavailable)

Data updated as of August 2019.

Similar to the Ethiopian railway, as I cannot observe effectiveness in two cases of the CFB, I use the efficiency of resolving the biggest challenges during construction and operation; that is, financial and technical difficulties as proxies. Table 0.1 summarizes the variation in completion and operation among the railway cases.

This book also briefly investigates two shadow cases: the Hawassa Industrial Park project in Ethiopia and the Kilamba Kiaxi social housing project in Angola. Both cases were led by capable political champions and demonstrated relatively high effectiveness. The Hawassa Industrial Park was contracted to China Civil Engineering Construction Corporation (CCECC), one of the contractors on the Ethiopian railway. Construction started in July 2015 and the park opened in July 2017, with PVH, a leading international apparel company, establishing a factory in the park. The park was championed by Arkebe Oqubay, former minister and advisor to Prime Minister Hailemariam. The Kilamba Kiaxi project was constructed by CITIC construction, a Chinese SOE, and financed through the same 'oil-for-infrastructure' arrangement with EximBank as the CFB. Championed by President José Eduardo dos Santos, Kilamba is the largest housing project ever built in Angola. The project initially involved the construction of 20,000 apartments, with support infrastructure, at a value of US$3.5 billion. Phase 2 of the project included an additional 5,000 units that were completed in 2015, in addition to the construction of service-related infrastructure. A third phase of the project foresees the construction of a total of 70,000 apartments.[54] Initially referred to as 'ghost town' because of its low occupancy, now Kilamba is fully occupied, hosting over 80,000 residents.[55] The Kilamba project has multiple issues in real estate service and the apartments are too expensive to fulfil its initial purpose as a social housing project. Using the Kilamba project as a shadow case does not mean I claim it a 'success'. Instead, in comparison with the Benguela railway, the Kilamba project demonstrated relatively higher effectiveness; that is, it was completed in time and is fully occupied by residents. These two shadow cases were under the patronage of capable political champions while the railway projects in their respective countries did not receive similar political commitment. The comparison between the relatively higher effectiveness of the shadow cases compared to the railway projects demonstrates that the failure of the railways was largely due to the lack of political commitment.

The empirical evidence of this book is collected from extensive field research in Kenya, Ethiopia, Angola, and China from 2014 to 2019. Empirical analysis is based on 250 in-depth interviews with African and Chinese government officials, corporate managers, civil society leaders, journalists, citizens, and scholars, in combination with short episodes of participatory observation with Chinese railway contractors in Africa. I was resident in Kenya when the Chinese-sponsored railway was widely publicized in 2014 and visited the Kenyan railway on a yearly basis from 2015 to 2019. I had two visits to the Ethiopian railway, in 2017 and 2019, respectively, and stayed in Angola from October 2018 to March 2019 to study the CFB. The repeated visits guarantee a time-sensitive documentation of project development, granting this book a unique cross-temporal perspective. This large amount of highly detailed and original information is supported by a wide body of multilingual documentary material, including policy and media reports, and non-traditional and restricted sources such as legal documents, Chinese companies' internal publications, corporate contracts, and communications between Chinese companies and African and Chinese government agencies acquired via investigative journalists. Navigating through languages, the primary and secondary data of this book presents a balanced view that presents perspectives from both China and Africa instead of relying overly on one side.[56]

During research design, fieldwork, and particularly at the write-up stage, I frequently reflected on my positionality. Throughout the research design and

[54] Croese (2017).
[55] China-Africa Research Initiative (2 April 2014).
[56] Appendix 1 provides a detailed documentation of my data collection methods; Appendix 3 is a list of interview questions; and Appendix 4 includes a list of interviewees.

data collection, I constantly asked how power dynamics are involved in my interactions with African, Chinese, and Western interviewees and subjects as a female, Chinese researcher based at a UK institute. I also note how my Chinese identity and research funding from a Chinese government scholarship might affect the way I design this research and present my findings. Given the hard-to-access nature of Chinese companies and government, the Chinese perspective on the ground is frequently missing in academic research. My identity and funding source did grant me better access to and trust from Chinese interviewees. With careful judgement of the evidential value of interview data, this research is an important step towards completing the picture with the Chinese perception of African politics and Sino-African relations. This book contains a detailed reflexive analysis in Appendix 2, and I hope that this transparency might permit readers to make a more informed analysis of how the conclusions were reached based on the cases and evidence.

5 Outline

The rest of this book proceeds as follows. In Chapter 1, I introduce a theory to explain variation in state effectiveness with reference to existing theoretical debates on leadership, African politics, and Sino-African relations. I propose a political championship theory that centres on African political leadership, a theory that emphasizes individual agency within structural and institutional constraints. In this chapter, I also elaborate on two competing theories: an explanation that emphasizes the structural asymmetry of African states with international powers and how external agency, rather than African agency, determines the capability of African states' effectiveness; and an institutional explanation that underscores institutional characteristics, particularly the effectiveness of African bureaucracy as the defining feature of state effectiveness. I design a series of process-tracing tests to empirically examine the three theories. These tests and the observable implications provide guidance to the empirical chapters.

Chapter 2 presents the Kenyan SGR. I trace the process of the initiation, implementation, and operation of the SGR Phase 1 (from Mombasa to Nairobi) and Phase 2A (Nairobi to Naivasha). I show that the political championship from President Uhuru Kenyatta in SGR-1 led to high effectiveness of this phase, and missing Kenyatta's championship in SGR-2A resulted in delays. I explain how Kenyatta's initial commitment to the SGR-1 was inspired by the 2013 election, and the railway served as campaign capital for Kenyatta's

2017 electoral campaign. The president directly intervened in SGR-1 by setting timelines for its completion date, making frequent site-visits, issuing directives to bypass bureaucratic hurdles, and co-opting opposition leaders. The president's commitment to the SGR faded away after the 2017 election. In SGR-2A, losing Kenyatta's championship resulted in delays in Phase 2A despite the experience that had been gained by the Kenyan railway corporation and the Chinese contractor. I also show that external agency and bureaucratic capacity explanations cannot account for the success of SGR-1 and delay in SGR-2A.

In Chapter 3, I trace the process of the rise and fall of political championship in the ADR project in Ethiopia. The ADR project was divided into three subcases: (1) the ADR-Meles (initiation), (2) the ADR-Hailemariam pre-2016 (construction), and (3) the ADR-Hailemariam post-2016 and ADR-Abiy (operation). I show that the ADR was highly salient to the Ethiopian People's Revolutionary Democratic Front's (EPRDF's) legitimacy to rule. Prime Minister Meles initiated and championed the ADR, making his time the 'golden era' of railway development. I also illustrate that exogenous leverage from bureaucratic and Chinese actors were not the sources of Meles' championship. During 2012–16, under Hailemariam, the ADR was still the priority of the government, but with the deteriorating security situation in the country, the priority of the EPRDF gradually diverted to maintaining security and stability. Even at the beginning of Hailemariam's time in power, he lacked the charisma and political acuteness to 'fill Meles' shoes', and so the development of the ADR gradually slowed down, despite the clear efforts of the Chinese contractors and government. I also briefly investigate the relative success of the Hawassa Industrial Park under the championship of Arkebe in 2015–16. This industrial park promised 10,000 employment positions and aligned well with the survival incentive of the government to maintain security and stability shortly prior to and during the state of emergency.

In Chapter 4, I trace the process of the Angolan CFB's trajectory from its initiation between 2003 to 2006, through its construction from 2006 to 2017, to its present operation. I show how low political championship led to a less effective project. Weak bureaucratic capacity and minimal Chinese extra-contractual intervention were consequential but not causal to the low level of project effectiveness. Angola's rich resource endowment allows it to develop and maintain a highly coherent centralized state. The CFB was not strategically salient to the dominant party Movimento Popular de Libertação de Angola (MPLA) administration, whose survival was dependent on the cohesion and loyalty of the elites combined by their resource endowment and patronage systems. Neither President José Eduardo dos Santos nor other key political actors in the MPLA committed to the CFB, demonstrating weak political championship. The railway corporation and the Ministry of Transport were ineffective bureaucracies, and these technicians were not involved in the decision-making process, and so CFB implementation experienced suspensions and the railway is struggling to operate. I also briefly show that with similar bureaucratic and Chinese factors, the Kilamba Kiaxi project, which provided housing for ministerial employees and MPLA loyalists, was protected from failure thanks to the championship of the president.

Chapter 5 ties together the three empirical cases and situates these cases in the broader scholarly debate on Sino-African relations. I explain *how* and *why*, despite the China–Africa power asymmetry, African actors, particularly political leaders, were able to effectively exercise their agency and shape the project trajectory. This chapter starts with a discussion of the dependency–extraversion debate. Building on the classic African extraversion theory, I argue that African rulers, benefiting from their dependent position in relation to external powers, actively participate in the process of framing their societies as a dependent partner in the world economy. Internationally, they strategize their available choices to ensure that the state receives the largest amount of foreign funding and in the most favourable terms. Domestically, they instrumentalize the Chinese-sponsored projects and Chinese loans that came along to demonstrate their performance legitimacy and feed the patronage machines. Instead of dealing with a powerful and coherent China, African actors work with a plethora of Chinese actors that sometimes disagree with each other. The fragmented nature of Chinese actors in Africa helped balance the asymmetric relationship by diluting China's power and enhancing African agency.

The final chapter concludes. I recapitulate my argument and discuss the theoretical and practical contributions of this book, its generalizability and limitations, its policy implications, and the normative implication of the African agency argument.

1

The railpolitik

Agency of African leaders in Sino-African relations

My task in this book is to explain an empirical puzzle and a theoretical one: why do African states demonstrate different effectiveness when managing foreign-sponsored projects that are similar in nature? What explains differential African state effectiveness? State effectiveness refers to the effectiveness of states to achieve official policy objectives. This book seeks to explain the variance among trajectories of Chinese-financed and -constructed railways in Africa, as a reflection of the variance in state effectiveness.

Large infrastructure projects have both material and symbolic functions and are frequently politically instrumentalized as tools of state-building and power projection, as demonstration of 'high modernism' ideology (Scott 1999), or as informal tools of colonial empire-building. Railways are particularly politically salient, and success in railway development is an indication of strong state effectiveness. I use railway effectiveness as an operationalization of state effectiveness, and provide two measurements of railway effectiveness: (1) timely completion and (2) frequent and safe operation.

Since the state was 'brought back in',[1] researchers have sought to explain what the state can and cannot do, how well the state does it, and why. In this process, scholars have introduced a variety of concepts relating to the state and its capacity or have used the same name for different meanings. They vary from state capacity to state strength, infrastructural power, state performance, effectiveness, and state power. These various concepts may refer both to what states *can* do and what they actually *achieve*. In this book, I will not engage in a prolonged discussion of various concepts related to state capacity as researchers have already taken steps to clarify them.[2] I define state effectiveness simply as the *effectiveness* of states to achieve official policy objectives and define state capacity as the *ability* of states to achieve these objectives.[3] State effectiveness emphasizes what states *actually do*, whereas state capacity focuses

[1] Evans, Rueschemeyer, and Skocpol (1985).
[2] Soifer and vom Hau (2008).
[3] Centeno, Kohli, and Yashar (2017); Fukuyama (2013); Skocpol (1985).

The Railpolitik. Yuan Wang, Oxford University Press. © Yuan Wang (2023). DOI: 10.1093/oso/9780198873037.003.0002

on what states *can do*. State effectiveness is operationalized as infrastructure delivery. State capacity, a major dimension of which is the professionalization (or 'Weberian-ness') of its bureaucracy,[4] is an explanatory variable in the alternative argument.

The study of state capacity and effectiveness frequently neglects the role of political will.[5] Soifer and vom Hau (2008) categorized the two major dimensions of studies of state capacity as the relative autonomy of the state from societal pressures[6] and Weberian bureaucracy.[7] A third dimension is often called state reach or power. Along this dimension, for instance, Herbst (2014) explores African states' power projection over distance, and Skocpol (1979) argues that civil administration's grip over a country contributes to fiscal crisis and ultimately leads to its collapse. In their study of state–society relations, a frequently overlooked variable is the 'political will'. In fact, researchers often assume political will in their analysis of the state. For example, in Enriquez and Centeno's (2012) study of state capacity to development, they write: 'this paper is based on the assumption that the states analysed are interested in providing basic services to their people as defined by the United Nations' Millennium Development Goals'.[8] But in reality this is not always the case. Holland (2016) challenges the capacity-based approach and argues that the lack of political will may play a critical role in law enforcement in developing countries.[9] A contribution of this book to the state capacity and effectiveness literature is to emphasize the commitment of the political leaders in successful infrastructure delivery, a previously understudied factor.

This chapter starts by detailing historical-political implications of railway infrastructure in Africa, and lays out this often overlooked factor in state effectiveness of infrastructure delivery from historical to contemporary Africa; that is, the championship of political leaders. It also discusses why Sino-African structural asymmetry and institutional explanations of African bureaucratic capacity fall short in explaining the personalistic and volatile nature of infrastructure delivery and state effectiveness in Africa. By introducing three competing explanations of state effectiveness—the structural, institutional, and individual agency explanations—this chapter establishes the theoretical foundation for the subsequent empirical analysis.

[4] Evans and Rauch (1999); Geddes (1994); Skowronek (1982); Weber (1968).
[5] Centeno (2003, pp. 3–4, 8); Enriquez and Centeno (2012).
[6] Bates (1981); Evans (1995); Nordlinger (1981); Skocpol (1979); Waldner (1999).
[7] Carpenter (2001); Evans and Rauch (1999); Geddes (1994); Skowronek (1982); Weber (1968).
[8] Enriquez and Centeno (2012, p. 133).
[9] Holland (2016).

1.1 Political implications of railway infrastructure

Mega-infrastructure projects are material and symbolic expressions of state power.[10] Transport infrastructure such as roads and railways create connectivity, hold the potential to control the movements of people and goods and the locations of production and consumption, enhance international trade, promote national economic growth, and provide economic opportunities for those with access to the roads and railways. Researchers have reviewed the material functions of other types of infrastructure: providing irrigation, electricity, and alternating the physical landscape through dam construction;[11] offering physical shelters to the urban poor through housing projects;[12] and fulfilling industrial purpose via constructing oil pipelines.[13] Beyond their material functions, infrastructure projects also embody state-sponsored imaginaries of modernity, transformation, and development.[14] The development of the interstate highway network in the United States in the 1950s to 1960s was a demonstration of an American vision: it not only represented the height of American technology but also, as Lewis put it, suggested 'all our dreams for what America might become—one nation, indivisible, bound for all time by concrete and asphalt strands.'[15] Harvey and Knox examined the promise of political freedom manifest by roads in Peru: 'roads offers a means of rectifying this history of inequality based on the limited social and physical mobility of peasant communities.'[16]

Precisely because of their materialist and ideological functions, mega-infrastructure projects are often instrumentalized by the state to fulfil certain political agendas. Mohamud and Verhoeven examined the role of dam construction on state- and nation-building. In Sudan, dam-building played a role in the construction, consolidation, and expansion of states, as well as restructuring local and regional political economies, and as objects of contention and possible cooperation in transboundary waterscapes.[17] Dam-building in Rwanda was adopted as a symbol of the 'high-modernist' ideology that overemphasized in a simplified manner science and technology as drivers of modernization while ignoring context-specific knowledge.[18] Famously, Herbst

[10] Monson (2009).
[11] Mohamud and Verhoeven (2016); Verhoeven (2002).
[12] Holston (2009).
[13] Barry (2013).
[14] Harvey and Knox (2015).
[15] Lewis (2013).
[16] Harvey and Knox (2015).
[17] Mohamud and Verhoeven (2016).
[18] Dye (2016).

argues that transport infrastructure such as railways and roads served as tools of colonial power projection in Africa, to administer the state and exercise control over a large but less populous landscape and enhance policy reach.[19] Mega-infrastructure cannot be apolitical. Examining the politics of infrastructure is a way to appraise state effectiveness.

More specifically concerning railways, variation in project effectiveness is a reflection of variation in state effectiveness. *Railway effectiveness* captures the fundamental purpose that the project is designed and expected to fulfil; that is, timely completion as well as regular and safe operation. Although narrowly defined, railway effectiveness assumes broader political and economic implications. The construction and operation of railways involve a set of changes to the social, economic, and environmental landscape. These changes include land acquisition and compensation, labour employment and disputes, the emergence of business opportunities through local procurement and subcontracting, corruption, modification to environment and livelihood, readjustment of the logistics industry, and improvements in the mobility of people and products. Project effectiveness captures the immediate project results and leaves aside long-term expectations of railways such as paying back the loans, boosting economic growth and industrialization, and facilitating regional and international trade and connectivity. This short-term outcome is selected because an operating railway is the prerequisite for loan repayment and any long-term economic and social implications. Furthermore, successful completion of railway construction and initiating operations are within the control of the state, making it a more direct proxy for state effectiveness than the long-term developmental impacts of the railway, which are determined by a wide range of other factors.

Like all mega-infrastructure projects, railways always have political significance, whether intentionally crafted by politicians or as an unintended consequence. Railways have unique characteristics that make them especially subject to politicization. First, railway planning, construction, operation, and maintenance are heavily dependent on state investment. Compared with road transport, development and maintenance of railway infrastructure require state involvement because of the technical rigidity and centralization of its operation.[20] The uninterrupted function of a railway also requires a complementary set of infrastructure, such as stable electricity and water supplies, signalling and communications systems, route security against the intrusion

[19] Herbst (2014).
[20] African Development Bank (2015).

of people and animals, and the construction of inland container terminals and dry ports. The provision and maintenance of such complementary infrastructure requires extensive state involvement.

Second, during colonial times, railways were symbols of imperialism and modernization. Robinson and other historians coined the term 'railway imperialism' to describe the political functions of railways in Africa.[21] They perceive railway-building from a Eurocentric viewpoint and argue that railway served as an instrument for power projection and political control by the metropole. 'Steel rails had a capacity for transforming the societies through which they ran and for spreading imperial influence in their domestic affairs, which often provoked anti-imperialist reactions and involved European interests in local crises.'[22] In the minds of European imperialists, railways were simultaneously tools of political consolidation, means of commercial development, and a justification to rule.[23] Railways represented not just mechanized mobility and technological advance; they were synonymous with nineteenth-century notions of progress, civilization, and development, as an emblem of the very notion of a modern, capitalist society.[24] Like the colonial railways, post-colonial railway development was a form of technocratic spectacle through which African political leaders imagined a prosperous future that mirrored the Western industrial development from which they had long been excluded.[25]

Third, railway is monumental: a visible promise of economic development and an image of political stewardship. Railway is a 'language of steel',[26] a discourse of modernization and technological development. Economic development increases the flows of goods and people, which leads to a growth in demand for new transport infrastructure.[27] Railway also expresses an 'expectation of modernity':[28] travellers craft new social, cultural, and economic identities and possibilities for themselves in an increasingly mobile society. A better rail transport system capable of transporting large volumes of goods over long distances at cheap prices can reduce transportation costs and increase the competitiveness of African countries in the global supply chain.[29] Moreover, visible mega-infrastructure like railways have the function of demonstrating the works of stewardship undertaken by incumbent elites to the people. It is

[21] Davis, Wilburn, and Robinson (1991).
[22] Ibid., p. 3.
[23] Headrick (1981).
[24] Hart (2016, p. 38).
[25] Ibid., p. 155.
[26] Following the 'language of asphalt' in Mrázek (2018).
[27] African Development Bank (2015).
[28] Ferguson (1991).
[29] African Development Bank (2015).

widely observable in Africa that prior to elections, the frequency of political leaders' ribbon-cutting on infrastructure projects intensifies.

Finally, constructing railways overseas is an essential component of China's Belt and Road Initiative (BRI). Chinese railway technology is one of its 'golden name cards', according to former Chinese Premier Li Keqiang,[30] and a crucial component of the BRI, Beijing's ambitious scheme to win diplomatic allies and open markets in Asia, Europe, and East Africa by funding and building infrastructure with a thematic emphasis on 'connectivity'. Especially considering the capital-intensive nature of railway development, traditional donors have shied away from engaging in railway projects. For many African countries, China Export and Import Bank (EximBank) is the only accessible source of funding for domestic railway development. Chinese railway projects overseas are frequently accompanied by port-upgrading projects and special economic zones, creating export-orientated infrastructure geared towards manufacturing. A majority of the Chinese-sponsored railways in Africa either run parallel to the existing colonial railways or rehabilitate existing lines, generating controversy where the memories and symbolic meanings of colonial railways still persist. Notably, the United States shares the concern of some countries in Asia that the BRI could be a Trojan horse for China-led regional development, military expansion, and Beijing-controlled institutions.[31] Chinese-sponsored railway projects overseas also involve multi-billion-dollar loans from Chinese policy banks that leads to speculations of 'debt trap diplomacy',[32] a point I will discuss in detail in the Conclusion.

In sum, mega-infrastructure can never be apolitical. Although railways are not always and everywhere 'state' projects, they do always need to be enabled by states. The narrow outcome of railway effectiveness involves a set of changes that railway implementation and operation engender. Railway effectiveness is embedded in broader economic, political, and external relations settings. Therefore, the relatively narrow definition of the dependent variable provides an entry point to deeper and wider analysis of African state effectiveness.

1.1.1 Measuring railway effectiveness

Railway effectiveness is measured by (1) *timely completion*: whether the railway was completed within or after the contracted and politically assigned

[30] Kynge, Peel, and Bland (17 July 2017).
[31] Council of Foreign Relations (2019).
[32] Chellaney (2017).

schedule and (2) *regular and safe operation*: whether the cargo and passenger services operate regularly and how many accidents occur. Railway operations are composed of freight and passenger services. While freight services generate higher operational revenues, passenger transport is important politically for the public and is a critical image-improvement opportunity for the African government.[33] Passenger services improve population mobility, while freight services reduce logistics costs, facilitate trade, and link markets to rural areas.[34] Completion and operation are the most fundamental elements of railway: they measure whether the railway is actually working, which is the basis for generating economic, social, and political impacts of the railway. Practically, the railway cases selected for this study were all concluded at least three years prior to the completion of this manuscript, providing enough time lag between railways' completion, operation, and my fieldwork for the measurement of railway effectiveness.

It is worth clarifying that by claiming the railways 'effective', I am not implying that the railways support development on a broader scale or can be termed 'successful'. The short-term measurement of project effectiveness does not directly speak to the long-term developmental outcomes, although this short-term success is the basis for longer-term development. In the empirical chapters, I touch on some developmental issues involved in railway projects, including land acquisition, environment, and project finance. Yet there are a large range of other issues, such as corruption, labour welfare, technology transfer, and so on, that are highly relevant to the development of host countries but covering all of them would be too ambitious and would dilute the focus of this book. The sheer emphasis on the 'speed' of delivery may come at an expense of projects' developmental impact due to the gloss-over of procedures such as socio-environmental impact assessment, community consultations, land compensation, and so on. Tentative findings from fieldwork show that the strength of the civil society and media determines whether these developmental issues can be satisfactorily addressed during project implementation, irrespective of the political emphasis on speed.

1.2 Structural and institutional explanations

Dominant explanations of state effectiveness emphasize either external determination or bureaucratic capacity. The relative role of African and external agency in determining development is a central question in literatures on

[33] African Development Bank (2015, p. 34).
[34] Muliba and Yepes (2017).

Sino-African relations and Africa's relationship with the external world more generally. Some scholars depict African states as passive and devoid of agency, and attribute dominant positions in African development to external actors. Another mainstream analysis of state capacity places emphasis on the highly effective bureaucracies in neo-patrimonial African states and neo-industrialized countries in East Asia. They find that Weberian bureaucracy in developmental states and 'pockets of effectiveness' in Africa are conducive to economic growth and industrialization. The two competing explanations for project effectiveness are derived from these two domains of literature; that is, the external agency theory and bureaucratic capacity theory. The external agency explanation is that the capabilities of the Chinese state-owned enterprises' (SOEs') determine the effectiveness of the railway. At the centre of this argument is the notion that the development of African countries is determined by external forces rather than domestic. In the case of Africa and China, it emphasizes Chinese agency over African agency. The bureaucratic capacity explanation believes that the bureaucratic capacity of railway corporations determines railway development.

This section contains two subsections, revisiting the structural and institutional explanations respectively and discussing their limitations in explaining African state effectiveness. Each subsection starts with a theoretical discussion of the alternative explanations and their limitations, followed by connecting these theoretical explanations to the examination of Chinese and African bureaucratic actors, their capabilities, and the mechanisms that lead to better project outcomes. Each subsection concludes with a summary of alternative explanations.

1.2.1 External agency

The first competing explanation for the divergent destinies of projects or policies is the external agency argument. The argument states that the variation of the commitment and capacity of the external actors, in this instance Chinese, determine project outcomes. Among the recent upsurge in the literature on China–Africa relations, many scholars reviewing China's engagement in Africa attribute a great deal of power to China at Africa's expense. The premise of this argument is that China is the dominant party and Africa is passive and lacks agency.[35] In this subsection, I briefly review the existing literature on Chinese agency in China–Africa relations and theoretical challenges to this

[35] See discussions in Mohan and Lampert (2013).

argument. Then, I present the external agency argument in detail through an investigation of various Chinese actors in Africa, especially SOEs. This subsection concludes with two testable hypotheses of external agency.

Chinese agency argument in Sino-African relations

Many researchers on the politics of China–Africa relations tend to attribute a great deal of power to China at Africa's expense.[36] They focus on the motivation, characteristics, and implications of Chinese engagement in the continent and globally, and argue that China's rapidly increasing engagement in Africa does not reflect a singular or specific policy towards the continent but is rather part and parcel of a wider policy thrust which manifests itself equally in China's relations towards other regions of the world.[37]

The drivers of China's more expansive global engagement are similar to those of the country's re-entry into Africa. China became a net oil importer in 1993, forcing it to search abroad for sufficient energy supplies to sustain domestic economic growth and so maintain social and political stability.[38] Moreover, facing a gradual overcapacity in domestic market and slowdown in economic growth, Beijing urges Chinese SOEs, the backbones of the national economy,[39] to explore overseas markets. The increasing presence of SOEs in Africa is part of Beijing's more active economic engagement globally. The SOEs are not only the drivers of China's overseas engagement but also the main providers of employment. In a populous country where a 4 per cent unemployment rate translates to 9 million people,[40] the growth of the SOEs which absorb such a large portion of the labour forces is crucial to maintaining the stability of the country.[41] Finally, China has taken up a more active foreign policy since 1989, seeking more diverse international partners. Especially since the tragedy at Tiananmen Square, developing countries were effectively elevated as the cornerstone of Chinese foreign policy in an effort to build coalitions to shield Beijing from Western criticism and sanctions. Given their numerical weight in international organizations, African states played an important role in the Chinese stratagem.[42]

The discussion of China's engagement in Africa mirrors the general discussion of Africa's external relations. Scholars of dependency theory depict

[36] Mohan and Lampert (2013).
[37] Tull (2006).
[38] Hensengerth (2011); Zweig and Bi (2005).
[39] Yu (2014).
[40] Hensengerth (2011).
[41] Pilling and Barber (2019).
[42] Tull (2006).

African states as weak and passive, and as having been subject to external determination since the colonial era. Africa has never ceased to exchange goods and ideas with Europe, Asia, and later America, and this relationship has been characterized by unevenness and asymmetry between Africa on the one hand, and Europe and Asia on the other. China–Africa economic relations resemble the continent's long history of relation with the external world characterized by structural asymmetry, where Africa has been situated in a marginal position within the global economic system, defined by its limited value as a provider of mineral resources.[43] The concept of a predatory or even 'neo-colonial' China is also widespread among African and Western intellectuals, media, and in the policy sphere.[44] Admittedly, the diversification of Africa's external economic ties potentially provides more choices and leverage for African states.[45] Yet many researchers find no significant difference between Chinese and Western approaches to Africa.[46] It is not evident that China–Africa trade differs significantly from Western–African trade patterns; nor is it clear that China's engagement will substantially improve Africa's prospects for development.[47] Some even fear that the expansion of China's economic interests may perpetuate this asymmetry and marginalization.[48] China's ambitious BRI, according to Taylor and Zajontz (2020), aims at integrating Africa into an ambitious Chinese-constructed infrastructure network: as China strategically displace its overcapacity and debt burden to Africa, these terms of this integration deepen Africa's dependent position and perpetuate its terms of (mal)integration into the global political economy.[49]

A group of Africanist scholars challenge the African passivity and argue that Africans have in fact been active agents in the *mise-en-dépendance* of their societies.[50] They argue that African elites have, since independence, conceived of their economic links with the outside world—whether in the form of either the export of their raw materials or foreign assistance—as an integral part of their calculus for power.[51] According to this approach, dependence and its possibilities have thus been one of the chief instruments that have enabled African rulers to obtain the means to continue to feed the patronage-based systems

[43] Clapham (1996); Bayart (2000); Tull (2006).
[44] Sanusi (11 March 2013).
[45] Zeitz (2019, 2021).
[46] Goldstein, Pinaud, Reisen, and Chen (2006); Tull (2006).
[47] Goldstein, Pinaud, Reisen, and Chen (2006).
[48] Tull (2006).
[49] Taylor and Zajontz (2020).
[50] Bayart (2000, p. 219).
[51] Chabal and Daloz (2004, p. 111).

on which their power has rested.[52] Far from seizing opportunities to reduce their countries' dependence, African rulers often maximize revenues from the export of existing resources at the expense of economic diversification.[53]

In the next subsection, I review the Chinese corporate and government actors involved in the railway cases of interest to this book, who are also the main agents in the infrastructure deals between China and African states.

Chinese agents and SOEs' capability

Chinese agencies directly involved in the Sino-African government-to-government agreements on mega-infrastructure projects include the SOEs, Ministry of Foreign Affairs (MoFA), Ministry of Commerce (MOFCOM), and policy banks, notably the China EximBank.[54] The large SOEs operating internationally have a symbiotic yet ambiguous relationship with the government, and there is conflicting evidence with regard to which party is in the driving seat.[55] As the three railway cases selected in this book are all financed by China EximBank, the Chinese government actors are the same for all three projects, and the different entities are the various Chinese SOEs. The external agency argument therefore posits that Chinese SOEs' capability determines the different effectiveness of Chinese-sponsored projects. This subsection reviews and compares the incentives and activities of these Chinese actors in the government-to-government projects, with a focus on the capacity of SOEs.

China's domestic development since the 1980s has generated one of the world's largest and most competitive construction industries, with particular expertise in the civil works critical for infrastructure development.[56] Even before Beijing's 'going global' initiative in 2000, these construction companies had started exploring overseas markets. Chinese SOEs quickly became able to outcompete market players from developed countries with their low supply-chain costs, high labour productivity, and low labour costs.[57] Notably, Chinese expats in Africa live in extremely basic conditions compared to their Western counterparts.[58] Another advantage of Chinese SOEs is their access to concessional loans from Chinese policy banks. The SOEs frequently identified projects themselves and proposed them to the host government, which would then 'request' that the Chinese government, especially the EximBank, fund

[52] Ibid., p. 115.
[53] Ibid., p. 113.
[54] Indirectly, the NDRC is also involved. See discussions in Bräutigam (2011) and Corkin (2016).
[55] Jakobson (2008).
[56] Xu (2014).
[57] Ibid., p. 837; Zhang, (2021).
[58] Bräutigam (2011).

them.[59] To apply for loans from EximBank, SOEs need to identify the project with the host government and initiate the concessional loan application. In practice, Chinese SOEs approach host governments with the engineering, procurement, and construction (EPC) contract, with the 'promise' that the project may be financed by loans from China EximBank. This 'EPC+Finance' model gives a financial competitive advantage to Chinese SOEs against contractors from the Organisation for Economic Co-operation and Development (OECD) and emerging donor countries. For the same reason, this model is welcomed with open arms by African elites. Cut-throat competition among the Chinese SOEs in the overseas construction market pushes them to consolidate their relationships with the EximBank to maximize their chances of receiving concessional loans and formulate close relationship with African elites (and brokers) to augment their access to governmental projects.

The Chinese bureaux directly involved are the Chinese Economic Councillor's office in the host country and the Department of Foreign Aid,[60] both under MOFCOM. Each year, the EximBank and MOFCOM's Department of Foreign Aid decide a list of recipient projects for concessional loans, limited by a maximum amount for each country. Projects that do not make this list will either be considered the following year or can apply for EximBank's commercial loans.[61] The MoFA, through its Department of Africa Affairs officially, is responsible for foreign policy implementation, and 'oversees and coordinates policies and cooperation and exchanges with relevant countries and regions'.[62] Within the Chinese government, MoFA faces competition for influence over foreign policy formulation from MOFCOM and several other government bodies that have expanded their international outreach in their respective fields, such as the People's Bank of China, the National Development and Reform Commission (NDRC), the Ministry of Finance, and the Ministry of State Security. This has resulted in intense rivalry between MoFA and other official foreign policy actors.[63] Whereas the Chinese embassy reports directly to MoFA, the Chinese economic councillor's office, nominally under the embassy's umbrella structure, is usually physically separate from the embassy and reports to MOFCOM instead. This can readily cause confusion, as it is apparent in some countries that the two offices do not exchange

[59] Ibid., p. 157.

[60] In 2018, the Department of Foreign Aid became the China International Development Cooperation Agency, a sub-ministry-level executive agency directly under the State Council.

[61] Interview with CH-8, China EximBank, 31 October 2018, by phone.

[62] Ministry of Foreign Affairs of the People's Republic of China (n.d.).

[63] Jakobson and Knox (2010).

information, as they work for separate ministries that may be competing for influence in Beijing.[64]

Through the 1993–2003 reform, Chinese SOEs had a stronger profit-seeking purpose, although they still maintained their identity as a policy arm of Beijing. The strength of China's SOEs is reflected in ninety-eight mega conglomerates—Central SOEs (*yangqi*) directly supervised and administered by Beijing via the State-Owned Assets Supervision and Administration Commission which was established in 2003.[65] The Central SOEs are regarded as the backbone of the national economy. The Central SOEs are usually composed of four layers of entities: (1) a parent company and (2) its controlled subsidiaries (the two required layers), along with two optional layers: (3) noncontrolled subsidiaries and (4) other firms that collaborate with the core company or its subsidiaries.[66] The analytical focus of this study is the second layer—that is, the controlled subsidiaries: the SOEs (*guoqi*). Existing research seldom differentiates Central SOEs and SOEs, and there has also been a tendency in practice to blur the distinction between the two.

Chinese construction SOEs demonstrate diverse capabilities for managing overseas projects. The SOEs' technical capability is composed of their overseas project management experience and market-specific experience. Unlike domestic projects, international projects generally involve stakeholders with different backgrounds and are delivered in relatively unfamiliar locations. Higher transaction costs may arise dealing with different regulative, normative, and cultural-cognitive institutions in host countries compared with those in domestic markets, which may lead to further delayed delivery and cost overrun.[67] Companies with extensive (long time and high volume) international management experience have accumulated the knowledge and expertise in managing projects and stakeholders in various host countries. The SOEs' extended history in the host country also means stronger market-specific knowledge and experience, as well as connections with host government. SOEs that were exposed to a specific market for a long time usually established linkages with the host government and hired more local employees, even at the management level, who allowed the company to make connections to local communities. This political and social capital accumulated with the SOEs' longer exposure to the market allows the SOEs to have their own judgement

[64] Gill and Reilly (2007).
[65] Yu (2014). The State-Owned Assets Supervision and Administration Commission website lists ninety-eight Central SOEs by June 2023.
[66] Lin and Milhaupt (2013).
[67] Javernick-Will and Scott (2010).

of the real situation in the country rather than over-rely on local bureaucrats; it allows SOEs to pre-emptively circumvent potential obstacles, and to have more established channels for problem resolution. SOEs that undertake initial market-entry projects have a high incentive to succeed and 'impress' the host government and society and are more reliant on the client for market-specific information, assuming the host government has and would provide precise data. However, the host government may either lack the data collection and preservation capacity or they can be overly ambitious in project proposals. Imprecise information from the host government therefore results in compromised project outcomes.

The project-specific technical skills are less relevant as a measure of Chinese SOEs' technical capacity. Over years of overseas operation, the fierce competition between Chinese construction companies forced them to expand beyond their core specialization.[68] The market share of a construction firm is, to a great extent, restricted by its technical specialism advantages: the more diversified technical specialties a firm possesses, the greater share of total business it may obtain.[69] SOEs rely for technical know-how upon subcontractors which are usually subsidiary SOEs from the same parent company, Chinese private companies, or provincial SOEs, who also have the incentive to expand into the global market, given the near-saturated domestic construction market. Therefore, it is not uncommon to find an SOE specialized in hydropower undertaking road and real estate projects, or dozens of different Chinese companies working on the same project, while their employees wear the safety hat of the general contractor.

Because of their intimacy with Beijing, the SOEs may lobby the central government to commit to the project, via their parent companies, the Central SOEs. The party secretary, board chair, and chief executive officer (CEO) (president) of a top Central SOE are of a rank equivalent to a vice-minister or even minister, whose appointment and dismissal need to go through the Political Bureau.[70] As the party appoints the state companies' CEOs, the latter naturally identify with the party-state, and assume the duty of protecting party-state interests in their Central SOEs. The Central SOEs' leaders therefore fulfil dual roles as high-ranking party cadres and commercial managers responsible for their company's business operations.[71] Other senior to middle

[68] Although recently Beijing has started to regulate such expansion of businesses outside of core expertise for Chinese SOEs overseas, according to an interview with a Chinese SOE manager in Beijing (24 March 2020).
[69] Low and Jiang (2003, p. 594).
[70] Li (2016).
[71] Yu (2014).

managers in Central SOEs are ranked as director-level (*juji*) to department-level (*tingji*); a number of them simultaneously occupy important positions in various quasi-official organizations affiliated with relevant ministries.[72] The Central SOE and SOE managers are trained in the party school system, which serves as a think tank and midcareer training centre for cadres.[73] Many top business leaders of the Central SOEs have been elected to the party's Central Committee and Central Disciplinary Committee.[74] This intimacy between the Central SOEs and the central government means that the leadership of the former has strong lobbying capacity, and it is also in the promotional interest of Central SOEs' leaders to deliver projects of political significance. For projects carried out by their subsidiaries overseas, the Central SOEs may leverage their connections in Beijing to promote the political significance of their subsidiary SOEs' projects. This may result in the projects being included in government initiatives and reports as flagship projects and increased Chinese official visits to the projects. The SOEs may also increase public awareness by engaging in media campaign on the projects to increase the project's political significance. If committed, the Chinese government may use diplomatic or financial leverage during bilateral meetings, at the Forum on China–Africa Cooperation, the Belt and Road Forum for International Cooperation, or other multilateral summits, to urge host governments to commit to the project and ensure its success.

In sum, the three railway cases examined in this book involve the same Chinese government actors but different SOEs. All projects involve the EximBank, MOFCOM (including the Chinese Economic Councillor's Offices in the host countries), and MoFA (including the Chinese embassies in the host countries). The only different Chinese actors of the three cases are the Chinese SOEs, who demonstrate differing capacities in terms of technical capabilities and degree of political leverage.

[72] Liou (2014). According to the *Provisional Regulations on State Civil Servants*, the ranks of Chinese civil servants are divided into fifteen levels: the first level is the premier of the State Council; the second to third levels are the vice premiers and state councilors of the State Council; the fourth level is the ministerial-level official position and the provincial-level official position; the fourth to fifth level is the ministerial-level deputy position and the provincial-level deputy position; the fifth to seventh level is the director-level official position, the department-level official position, and the inspector; these are also the levels of Central SOEs' senior to middle managers. The sixth to eighth level is the director-level deputy position and department-level position. Levels seven to ten are the principal position at the division level, principal position at the county level, investigator, the township-level principal, and the chief staff member; the ninth to thirteenth grades are the section-level deputy, the township-level deputy, and the deputy chief staff member; the ninth to fourteenth grades are staff members; the tenth to fifteenth grades are clerks.

[73] Lin and Milhaupt (2013).

[74] Li (2015).

The external agency argument

The 'Chinese agency' version of the structural explanation predicts that it is the agency of the Chinese SOEs, rather than African actors, that shapes the trajectories of projects. Chinese SOEs with higher technical strength and political connection could deliver railway projects more successfully in Africa. Chinese SOEs' capability can influence railway effectiveness through two mechanisms, which usually coexist. SOEs can work directly with African bureaucrats and citizens to solve the problems encountered during project implementation and operation. Alternatively, SOEs can work through Chinese government to generate stronger commitment by African state leaders. They can lobby the Chinese government to increase commitment to the project; the committed Chinese government uses diplomatic or financial leverage to encourage the host government's commitment to the project and ensure project success.

1.2.2 Bureaucratic capacity

Another alternative explanation for the variation of state effectiveness is *bureaucratic capacity*. This argues that the project or policy outcome is determined by the capacity of the implementing bureaucracy. High bureaucratic capacity, as measured by the strength of technical capability in solving obstacles within its domain, and political capability in eliciting elites' intervention to resolve issues outside its control (often inter-ministerial obstacles) enable high effectiveness. In this section, I first briefly review existing bureaucracy-centric literature on state capacity, especially the 'pockets of effectiveness' theory and the 'Weberian' bureaucracy discussion regarding the developmental state. Then I introduce the bureaucratic capacity theory by identifying and analysing the African government agents involved in the railway projects, particularly the railway corporations.

'Pockets of effectiveness' and 'Weberian' bureaucracy

There are two main streams of literature on bureaucratic capacity in developing countries: the Weberian bureaucracy literature in the analysis of developmental states in East Asia (and the application of this theory to Africa) and the study of 'pockets of effectiveness'. Drawing on the original insights of Weber,[75] researchers of the East Asian developmental states argue that replacement of a patronage system for state officials by a professional state

[75] Weber (1968).

bureaucracy is a necessary condition for strong state capacity.[76] Weberian bureaucracy is characterized by meritocratic recruitment, which is ideally based on education and examination, and predictable, long-term, tangible, and intangible career rewards that are more effective at facilitating capitalist growth than any other form of state organization.[77] The recent application of developmental state theory to Africa has been led by scholars including Kelsall (2013), Booth and Golooba-Mutebi (2012), and Mkandawire (2001), as well as other scholars from the African Power and Politics Programme at the Overseas Development Institute. They advocate 'developmental patrimonialism', arguing that the patrimonial nature of Africa is compatible with institutional features of developmental states, of which Ethiopia and Rwanda are models. African states are usually referred to in terms of neo-patrimonialism; that is, the elites are connected to the society through web-like patron-client networks, where politicians/bureaucrats exchange material or non-material favours for the support of their constituents or clients. This personal, clientelistic system endures within the impersonal, bureaucratic features of a modern state.[78] Corresponding to the developmental state literature, the 'developmental patrimonialism' scholars emphasize the maintenance of a competent and confident, vertically disciplined economic technocracy, free from the most damaging clientelist pressures, apart from centralized and long-term rent management, as conditions for achieving economic transformation and social development.[79]

In the study of bureaucratic capacity in developing countries, many scholars focus on a single effective bureaucratic agency in a generally ineffective state. These agencies are called 'islands of excellence' (PoEs)[80] or 'islands of excellence'.[81] Using Roll's (2014) definition, PoEs are 'public organisations that are relatively effective in providing public goods and services that the organisation is officially mandated to provide, despite operating in an environment in which effective public service delivery is not the norm'.[82] Existing literature has identified many characteristics of these PoEs. Frequently discussed characteristics include meritocratic recruitment to ensure high bureaucratic capability as well

[76] Evans (1995).
[77] Ibid.
[78] Mkandawire (2001); Booth and Golooba-Mutebi (2012).
[79] Kelsall (2013); Booth and Golooba-Mutebi (2012).
[80] Geddes (1990); Rauch and Evans (2000); Leonard (2010); Whitfield, Therkildsen, Buur, and Kjær (2015); Abdulai and Mohan (2019); Roll (2014).
[81] Therkildsen (2008). See studies on Ghana's Ministry of Finance (Abdulai and Mohan, 2019), Uganda's Ministry of Energy (Hickey and Izama, 2020), Rwanda's Ministry of Finance and Economic Planning (Chemouni, 2019), and Angola's Sonangol (Soares de Oliveira, 2007).
[82] Roll (2014, p. 24).

as a sense of corporate coherence between bureaucratic elites;[83] predictable, long-term career rewards to enhance coherence and reduce corruption;[84] stability of leadership;[85] and a 'technopol' leader, one who is technically capable and politically savvy and can navigate the wider political context, ensuring that they receive just enough of the right kind of political attention and occasionally fighting rearguard actions to avoid becoming vulnerable to political pressure.[86]

The PoE literature considers leadership, both organizational and political, as central to high bureaucratic performance. PoE scholars identify organizational leadership under a 'technopol leader' as a key causal mechanism connecting the political settlement to bureaucratic performance.[87] They are usually rewarded with the lengthy tenures required to build performance-based organizational culture and enjoy high political authority. They are also critical to stitching together reform-orientated coalitions of national and international actors that provided the relational basis for PoEs to emerge and flourish in the economic domain.[88]

The political support from ruling elites is an integral factor for the emergence and performance of PoEs. Roll (2014) and Whitfield et al. (2015) argue that bureaucrats 'must have political backing from ruling elites'.[89] For these scholars, one of the enabling conditions for PoEs is in policy areas reflecting elite commitment.[90] For ruling elites, building PoEs can be a strategic choice for the ruling elites to overcome 'systemic vulnerability' or patronage-based elite survival.[91] According to Slater (2010), ruling elites have an incentive to invest in bureaucratic capacity-building when they perceive themselves to be vulnerable to overthrow from below, a 'systemic vulnerability' that can incentivize them to devise means of distributing public goods to offset this risk.[92] PoEs are most likely to emerge within policy domains that are critical to fundamental state functioning and/or rulers' survival.[93] National oil companies in petrostates such as Sonangol in Angola are typical cases of PoEs.[94] They are

[83] Onis (1991); Evans (1992).
[84] Evans and Rauch (1999).
[85] Abdulai and Mohan (2019); Fyson (2009); Lawson (2012).
[86] Dominguez (1997); Joignant (2011); Roll (2014); Hickey (2019); Hickey and Mohan (2023).
[87] Roll (2014); Grindle (1997); Hickey and Mohan (2023); Hickey (2023).
[88] Hickey and Mohan (2023).
[89] Whitfield, Therkildsen, Buur, and Kjær (2015, p. 20).
[90] See Roll (2014). Other enabling conditions are: under the rule of strong political leaders facing low risks; and particularly during early/mid-term in office.
[91] Hickey and Mohan (2023).
[92] Slater (2010); Hickey and Mohan (2023).
[93] Hickey and Mohan (2023).
[94] Soares de Oliveira (2007).

associated with elite survival and resource accumulation, which is different from state-building but equally attracts rulers' commitment.[95]

In the meantime, scholars on PoE and state capacity emphasize the importance of bureaucratic autonomy from political pressures stemming from within the ruling coalition. Some scholars believe that 'effectiveness' is more likely if bureaucracy is depoliticized but responsive to political leadership.[96] Their argument is that if the bureaucrats are cut off from political exchange, their orientation turns inward towards the agency, its goals, and the values of colleagues within the agency. Most critically, the route to personal advancement becomes the successful performance of duties inside the agency. Using Rwanda's Ministry of Finance and Economic Planning (MINECOFIN) as a case study, Chemouni (2023) finds that MINECOFIN has enjoyed significant autonomy, protected from political interference, and that presidential elections do not translate into abnormal peaks of public expenditure, thus enabling MINECOFIN to deliver on its mandate.[97]

This emphasis on bureaucratic competence cannot effectively capture the short-term volatility during policy and project delivery, a factor associated with executive leadership. Bureaucratic effectiveness is a deterministic characteristic of state that cannot account for many non-linearities in project or policy delivery: project or policy implementation may have quite opposite outcomes even under the administration of the same bureaucracy. In emphasizing Weberian bureaucracy or PoE, the role of state leadership is frequently reduced to a background factor in existing scholarly work. Political championship is a theory emphasizing the role of human agency, particular the agency of political leaders in project delivery. Admittedly, project implementation is never a 'one-man show' and any political will on project implementation has to be achieved through line bureaucracies. Yet the bureaucratic capacity and the political championship theory is still mutually exclusive, as they emphasize either bureaucracy or political champions being the central factor for project success. I further discuss the relationship between competing explanations in subsection 1.4.1.

African bureaucracies in railway delivery

An alternative explanation for the variance in railway effectiveness is the variant capacity of African bureaucracies. The African bureaucracies directly involved in railway delivery are the railway corporations. The Ministry of Transport and other ministries and agencies in charge of land acquisition

[95] Hickey and Mohan (2023).
[96] Leonard (1991); Geddes (1994); Evans (1995); Grindle (1997, 2004).
[97] Chemouni (2019, pp. 31–2, 2023, pp. 155–6).

and compensation, national finance, water and electricity, telecommunications, security, environment, foreign affairs, and the judiciary also participate, to various degrees, in the negotiation, construction, and operation stages of the railways. In this subsection, I focus on the technical strength and political context of the railway corporations, which are the executing agencies and the epicentres of the projects.

The African railway corporations, usually parastatals under the management of the Ministry of Transport, are the owners of the railway projects. They are the very bureaucrats that engage with Chinese SOEs on a daily basis and implement the project, working with multiple levels of domestic politics, ranging from the executive to various ministries, subnational government, and the general public. The most prominent issues during railway implementation are land acquisition and compensation, electricity and water supply, labour conflicts, environmental protection, and community relations. Land, utilities, and environmental issues require cross-ministerial coordination, whereas labour and community relations are largely within the domain of the corporation.

The bureaucratic capacity argument

Divergent from the external agency theory but similar to the political championship argument, this bureaucratic capacity explanation argues African domestic agency in shaping project outcomes. Unlike the political championship argument that centres on the individual, especially the executive agency, this explanation, along with the PoE and developmental states literature, posits that successful project delivery is due largely to capable bureaucracy. A strong railway corporation leads to higher railway effectiveness through the following mechanisms. First, the railway corporation can solve obstacles within its domain effectively, thus achieving higher project effectiveness. Second, the railway corporation with strong political capability may elicit executive intervention to resolve deadlocks while solving cross-ministerial problems. The railway corporation may assert the significance of the project to lobby the executive to champion it. When the railway corporation encounters problems that involve various ministries and cannot be easily resolved, it may seek attention and assistance from the executive.

1.3 A theory of political championship

I introduce a theory of political championship to explain variance in railway effectiveness, and more broadly in African states' effectiveness to achieve infrastructural outcomes. The existing literature on state effectiveness has largely centred on structural and institutional explanations, and less emphasis has been placed on individual agency. The structural explanation focuses on the imbalanced relationship between Africa and the external powers, and the institutional explanation concentrates on the state characteristics, notably bureaucratic capability. Although by itself political championship is not sufficient to guarantee project effectiveness, it is an essential part of explaining state effectiveness that has been previously underexplored. The political championship theory focuses on domestic rather than external agency. By disaggregating African states and analysing the imbricated formal and informal powers of the presidency, the championship theory captures the varying characteristics of state effectiveness in project and policy delivery that cannot be explained by existing theories that focus on bureaucratic strength. This is an endeavour to bring the individual leader back to the study of the state without diminishing collective entities such as bureaucracies.

The rest of this section is organized as follows. I first review existing literature on political leadership in political science in general and in African politics. Then I introduce the two explaining variables: political commitment and leader's authority. Subsection 1.3.3 introduces the political championship argument. Finally, I remind readers of the normative implications of African agency.

1.3.1 Existing literature on political leadership

The study of political leadership amounts to a slim but persistent stream in the political science literature. The concept of leadership preponderates the literatures on leaders' memoirs and biographies as well as various self-improvement manuals for organizational leadership. Many scholarly works on political leadership explore the psychological aspects of leaders and followers, both in the external facet of public perception and in the internal drives to leadership and decision-making.[98] Another area of work is 'crisis' leadership, as many authors have recognized the particular salience of leadership in times of uncertainty.[99] Yet another burgeoning stream of literature studies whether leadership can be an explanatory factor for economic growth. Jones and Olken (2005) find that the exogenous shock of national leaders' death correlates with a dramatic reversal of growth, thus rejecting the structuralist view where leaders

[98] Bell (2014); Weinberg (2012).
[99] Weber (1968); Lodge and Wegrich (2012).

are incidental to the evolution of their national economies. Many papers have followed Jones and Olken in testing leadership effects on economic development, ranging from leaders' education[100] and education in economics[101] to leadership transitions.[102] Although persistent, the field of leadership study in political science has seen competition from the rise of structuralism, neo-institutionalism, and rational choice approaches.[103] Leaders in dictatorships have received more scholarly attention than their democratic counterparts. Many scholars believe that the phenomenon of leadership is antithetical to the practice of democracy,[104] and that governance systems thrive on variety, overlap, and competition among loci of initiative, voice, authority, and accountability, and such institutional pluralism produces smart, robust public policies as well as keeping the arrogance of power at bay.[105]

While the study of politics in advanced economies with highly institutionalized systems has tended to focus on formal institutions, individual personalities have retained the largest possible role in weakly institutionalized politics such as Africa's.[106] States are run not by an individual but by a wide range of institutions with diverse interests and capabilities: bureaucracy, judiciary, party, military, parliament, and so on. When these institutions are strong, the room left for individual leaders to shape the direction of particular projects and policies is weak. The more power is concentrated in the hands of the leader, the greater the influence of that leader.[107] Leaders matter the most in authoritarian states with weak institutions.[108] In many African states, power is heavily centralized in the hands of the executive; Ethiopia (before 2019), Rwanda, and Angola are cases in point. In many new democratic African states, although power-sharing institutions are established, the state is still top-heavy, with power concentration in the president's or prime minister's hands. The democratization of many African countries in the 1990s under the pressure of international aid introduced multiparty system and elections but did not go through a fundamental institutional change to reduce the power of the executive. For instance, despite undergoing two electoral turnovers, Kenya is still run by the same cohort of elites as it was during the one-party era.[109]

[100] Besley and Case (1995).
[101] Brown (2020).
[102] Meyersson (2016); Carbone and Pellegata (2020).
[103] Nye (2008); Carbone and Pellegata (2020); Ahlquist and Levi (2011).
[104] Musella and Webb (2015); Beerbohm (2015).
[105] Hart, Kane, and Patapan (2009); Rhodes and Hart (2014); Helms (2014a, 2014b).
[106] Carbone and Pellegata (2020); Rotberg (2012).
[107] Pollack (2001).
[108] Price (1974); Jackson and Rosberg (1982).
[109] Branch (2011).

The way in which Africa's core political dynamics have revolved closely around national presidents has been further articulated through the notion of 'personal rule'[110] and the somewhat more wide-ranging idea of 'big-man politics'.[111] This literature underlines that politics in Africa is less restrained and more personalized and informal, characterized by the prevalence of primary forms of reciprocity, where rulers continue to see their interests as tied to local communities rather than to systems of abstract rule.[112] The political leaders, or the 'big men', permitted patrimonialism to wield unregulated presidential control over state institutions, are thus able to exert a high degree of executive dominance that far exceeds a president's constitutional authority.[113] Not to mention that many African states have already installed hyper-presidents with strong constitutional power. The results are higher stakes and greater risks for those who engage in the political game and greater uncertainty for the general public.[114] However, the 'personal rule' and 'big-man politics' theories emphasize how leaders pursue personal enrichment and maintenance of the patronage system to remain in power, but less emphasis is placed, if any at all, on the leaders' role in achieving policy objectives. The 'big-man politics' and 'personal rule' literature also focuses almost entirely on the executive without discussion of the bureaucratic system. Political championship theory advances this literature by recognizing personal rule in policy and project implementation and emphasizing the efficacy of informal politics without understating the role of bureaucracy.

1.3.2 Commitment and authority

Political championship refers to the leader's endeavour to solve or circumvent obstacles that beleaguer the efforts of parties in processes of public goods delivery.[115] Political champions are usually the executives. In some occasions advisors to the executive or ministers also take the role of political champion.[116] It emphasizes the personalistic, idiosyncratic, and unpredictable characters of politics, an aspect that has yet to receive due academic emphasis.

[110] Jackson and Rosenberg (1982).
[111] Price (1974); Hyden (2012).
[112] Hyden (2012).
[113] Helmke and Levitsky (2004).
[114] Price (1974); Jackson and Rosberg (1982); Hyden (2012).
[115] This definition is derived from the definition of leadership in Young (1991).
[116] For instance, Arkebe Oqubay, an advisor to the Ethiopian prime minister, led the development of industrial parks, and the development of Nigeria's Abuja–Kaduna railway owed much to the close supervision of Chibuike Rotimi Amaechi, the transport minister.

This theory also highlights the informality in political decision-making and policy implementation.

Two essential elements of political championship are political commitment and leader's authority. Political commitment refers to political leaders' decision to prioritize a project. Many researchers have identified that rulers' interests have significant influence on policy choices.[117] In a world that judges governments as much by their economic performance as anything else, one might expect those African rulers who are seeking great power and international stature to take a keen interest in promoting economic development in their countries.[118] Mega-infrastructure projects like the railway may be a visible showcase of the ruler's stewardship to the people and a demonstration of economic achievement. In some African states, the sheer existence of 'prestige' projects like the railways matters more to the ruler than their effective operation.[119] In either case, a salient project that is crucial to the ruler's interests is likely to generate strong executive commitment. By making a conspicuous display of their concern for a particular project, the ruler is able to keep their subordinates alert to their wishes and desires, and bureaucrats, whose primary incentive is their career advancement, will think long and hard before sabotaging them.[120]

Rulers' choices and actions are largely responses to the prevailing incentives that are set by political institutions, the most essential of which is how they attain and relinquish power.[121] Institution is defined as the set of formal and informal rules which constrain and govern the interaction of agents subject to that institution.[122] Instead of minimizing the role of institutions, the approach proposed by this book focuses on how institutions shape the incentives of individuals in government, and how, in consequence, these individuals choose policies.[123] The political institution here particularly refers to the constitutional and informal rules of ruler selection. This argument starts from the premise that rulers prefer to remain in office, and the political rules of the game determine which strategies for staying in office are likely to work and, consequently, whether the project or policy is salient to rulers' legitimacy to remain in office.[124] All actions taken by political leaders are intended by them

[117] Whitfield, Therkildsen, Buur, and Kjær (2015); Geddes (1994); Doner, Ritchie, and Slater (2005); Moon and Prasad (1994).
[118] Jackson and Rosenberg (1982, p. 269).
[119] Strange (2022).
[120] Ibid., p. 268.
[121] Carbone and Pellegata (2020, p. 66).
[122] North (1990); Khan (2010).
[123] Geddes (1994); Helmke and Levitsky (2004).
[124] Geddes (1994, p. 8).

to be compatible with their desire to retain power.[125] The critical question is how political institutions shape the goal of some leaders to commit to certain projects or policies.

Competitive elections are a frequently discussed institutional variable that incentivize rulers' decisions. Nordhaus (1975) and later researchers on the 'political business cycles' rightly point out that competitive elections, as well as leaders' concern for favourable public opinion in non-competitive states, provide incentives for political leaders to commit to certain projects or policies: political commitment increases prior to elections when the incumbent seeks another term and decreases when the incumbent's priority shifts to power consolidation.[126] In competitive regimes, similar to the predictions of the 'political business cycle' literature, political commitment increases *prior* to elections when the incumbent seeks another term and decreases when the incumbent's priority shifts to power consolidation.[127] Prior to elections, the incumbent has the incentive to make sure that 'prestige' developmental projects demonstrate some success as a showcase of the administration's delivery effectiveness and stewardship to the people. The incumbent therefore increases their commitment to the project before the elections to guarantee the achievement of at least some demonstrable success. In less competitive states, contentious elections may lead to legitimacy threats to the incumbent, and thus the leader's commitment to developmental policies or projects increases *after* an election as the leader seeks to demonstrate their stewardship to the people. As the contentious elections could not provide credible legitimacy to the ruler, an alternative source of legitimacy, performance legitimacy in this case, provides a straw for the authoritarian ruler to cling onto.

Apart from elections, leadership commitment is also contingent on other factors such as crisis, natural resource, political patronage, and foreign leverage. In some countries, especially where the ruler's legitimacy largely rests on their ability to feed the patronage system in exchange for loyalty, projects may receive the ruler's exceptional commitment should they provide strong support to the patronage system. The success of the Kilamba Kiaxi social housing project in Angola is a typical example, where President José Eduardo dos Santos committed to the project's success as the selling of the subsidized apartments generates not only monetary returns but also the power of distribution in exchange for supporters' loyalty. This is a case I will return to in Chapter 4. In other words, my focus on electoral competition provides only one possible

125 Bueno de Mesquita, Smith, Siverson, and Morrow (2003, p. 8).
126 Nordhaus (1975); Dubois (2016); Guo (2009).
127 Ibid.

institutional incentive that leads to political commitment without denouncing others. This focus on electoral incentives does not imply that autocratic incumbents will never display commitment to mega-infrastructure projects. My point is simply that in competitive regimes, leaders have a heightened sense of urgency, leading them to push harder for project effectiveness than in non-competitive regimes.

A leader's authority refers to a leader's ability to build a coalition of key actors on the project or policy and push the delivery agenda forward. Coalition-building requires leaders to identify, mobilize, and motivate the right people.[128] Members of the coalition usually include key position-holders from line ministries, party members, legislation, and regional administration; it may also include organizations or companies not directly involved in project delivery, such as foreign companies, foreign government, and domestic 'political fixers'.

The leader's authority is derived from a combination of formal and informal institutions and personal charisma. The constitutional authority attached to the leadership position is crucial in generating compliance from subordinates. This authority is directly attached to the legal position and less influenced by whoever sits in the chair. This is similar to what Weber calls rational authority. In most developing countries, the leader's authority is broader than the constitutional power attached to the presidency or premiership. The authority in the political championship theory emphasizes the leader's ability to go beyond formal institutions and utilize informal ones to push the project agenda forward. Informal institutions refer to socially shared rules, usually unwritten, that are created, communicated, and enforced outside of officially sanctioned channels.[129] Ranging from bureaucratic and legislative norms to clientelism and patrimonialism, informal institutions shape political behaviour and outcomes, and in some contexts more strongly than formal political institutions.[130] Personal charisma is also frequently highlighted as a key source of leader's authority in generating obedience through trust, heroism, or exemplary qualities.[131] The informal and charismatic authority are both the personalistic aspects of leadership authority, in contrast to the impersonal rational or formal authority.

Leaders may use stratagems to inspire motivations and reduce antagonism from project or policy coalition members. The stratagems typically at the

[128] Khan (2018, p. 645); Bueno de Mesquita, Smith, Siverson, and Morrow (2003).
[129] Helmke and Levitsky (2004, p. 727). By contrast, formal institutions are defined as rules and procedures that are created, communicated, and enforced through channels widely accepted as official.
[130] Helmke and Levitsky (2004).
[131] Weber (1968, p. 342).

disposal of leaders for building coalitions via informal institutions are: (1) Co-option: the political champion may silence vocal opposition and reduce the level of resistance by providing material benefits or favours to individuals or a small group of opposition leaders.[132] The political champion may also replace people in key positions who obstruct their ideas to their loyalists to guarantee smooth project implementation. (2) Bypassing bureaucracies: the executive may issue directives to bypass bureaucratic obstacles, or create new bureaucracies or coordination mechanism to solve project or policy obstacles. (3) Reward and sanctions: the executive may increase monitoring and provide rewards and the threat of sanctions to induce higher effort in subordinates.[133] (4) Generating a shared expectation:[134] this creates a sense of mission for subordinates working on the project or policy by repeatedly emphasizing the importance of the project or policy through public discourse and presence at the project. This relates to Weber's classic discussion of charismatic authority, according to which the charismatic leader fulfils this role by virtue of personal trust in revelation, heroism, or exemplary qualities.[135] The political champion may achieve this by repeatedly emphasizing the importance of the project through public discourse. Ribbon-cutting for project launch and inauguration ceremonies is another ceremonial intervention frequently adopted by leaders. Leaders also demonstrate their endorsement of the project through frequent reference to and presence at the project.

A leader's authority is secondary to political commitment: authority matters only when the leader decides to commit to the project. Put another way, if the leader does not consider the project salient enough to champion it, the project will not achieve successful outcome despite the authority level of the leader. This is frequently the case in highly centralized authoritarian states.

1.3.3 The political championship theory

The political championship theory can be summarized as follows. Perceived threats from electoral competition generate strong political commitment from the ruler. A committed political champion with strong authority intervenes in project implementation by motivating bureaucracies and tempering resistance, leading to higher project effectiveness.

[132] Jackson and Rosenberg (1982, p. 25).
[133] Dixit (2002).
[134] See Hyden's (2012) description of affective economy and Helmke and Levitsky's (2004) discussion of informal institutions.
[135] Weber (1968, p. 342).

1.3.4 Normative implications of African agency

In this section, I discuss two potential risks of drawing African agency too far: the risks of ignoring the structural constraints and implying apologism for foreign actors. At the foundation of the political championship theory is the belief of African agency, which is real but not unlimited. This book's approach of comparing African agency in different countries allows for the investigation of specific structural and institutional conditions that give rise to agency. The assumption here is that agency and structure are co-constitutive, and that structure holds primacy over agency.[136] The African agency argument as early as those developed by Clapham (1996) and Bayart (2000) recognizes the structural dependency of the continent to international systems and global powers. The proposition of African agency in Sino-African relations is an argument against structural pessimism. Scholarly perception of Africa is liberated from victimization, poverty, and violence. It is also an argument that emphasizes interaction between African actors and China rather than one-way domination by the latter.[137] But drawing the African agency argument too far may risk denying that structure and agency are co-constitutive. This is captured by Lonsdale's 'agency in tight corners', by which he means that even in the tight structural corners of international relations, African individual and collective agency can still bear causal fruit.[138] Another helpful way of framing agency within structural constraints is distinguishing agency and power. Carmody and Kragelund (2016) argue that 'African agency' is not opposed to 'Chinese power', and that African states have been able to exercise agency at the margins in order to capture a greater share of national resource rents for themselves or their treasuries.[139]

African agency or the political championship theory should not be used as justifications for negative behaviours of international actors. Variations of Chinese (and other multinational) companies' behaviours in different African countries are attributable to the agency of actors from host countries, but other factors are also relevant. Requirements from home countries, financial institutions, the level of internationalization and localization of the companies, and so on can be defining factors for behaviours such as corruption, local spill-over effects, stakeholder engagement, and environmental footprint. Indeed, an emerging area of research has been the comparison between

[136] Emmenegger (2021).
[137] Brown and Harman (2013).
[138] Lonsdale (2000).
[139] Carmody and Kragelund (2016).

Chinese and OECD companies' behaviours[140] and firm-level differences,[141] as well as projects financed by Chinese policy banks and traditional creditors.[142]

1.4 Relationship between competing explanations

In this section, I compare the political championship theories and two competing theories and briefly discuss other potential alternative explanations. Subsection 1.4.1 discusses the mutually exclusive relationship between the three theories. Subsection 1.4.2 investigates the exercise of interventions: whether it is executive intervention, external intervention, or bureaucratic intervention that leads to superior project outcomes. Yet even if it is executive intervention that leads to better results, this executive commitment may be derived from within or from outside political influences. If the latter, then political championship only serves as an intermediary variable to external or bureaucratic agency. Therefore, it is important to determine the origin of political championship: whether it is endogenous (i.e. derived from a careful calculation of the ruling elites) or exogenous (i.e. generated by the political influence of external or bureaucratic actors). This is discussed in detail in subsection 1.4.3.[143] Finally, subsection 1.4.4 discusses four other alternative explanations for the variation in effective railway delivery.

1.4.1 Mutual exclusivity

The three competing theories, political championship, bureaucratic capacity, and external agency, are mutually exclusive. Process tracing assumes mutual exclusivity of alternative hypotheses. By mutual exclusivity, I mean only one theory is true. A potential challenge to the mutual exclusivity of the political championship theory, bureaucratic capacity theory, and external agency theory is that in project implementation, leaders do not implement projects by themselves but through bureaucracy and foreign contractors; it is therefore likely that all three theories contribute to the project's success. I argue that the three theories are mutually exclusive because different factors are central in

[140] Oya and Schaefer (2019).
[141] Morgan (2021).
[142] Zeitz (2021); Zhou (2022); Dye (2022).
[143] This chapter intentionally avoids using the language of hypothesis testing. For readers who are looking for rigorous causal inference from process tracing, I provide a summary of the seven hypotheses generated from three competing explanations, with their respective observable implications, in Appendix 1.

generating the outcome. Three theories each focus on a factor that is causal to the outcome of interest, and these factors—agency of the political leader, agency of the strong bureaucracy, and agency of Chinese actors—are mutually exclusive, and the key is to identify which factor is causal.

1.4.2 Executive, external, or bureaucratic intervention

In determining whether it is external agency, bureaucratic capacity, or executive intervention that drives project effectiveness, I design a series of process-tracing tests: hoop tests, which proposes that a given piece of evidence must be present for a hypothesis to be valid, and failing a hoop test eliminates a hypothesis.[144] If missing one intervention led to significant delay in problem resolution during project implementation, then I can confidently eliminate other interventions as potential causes. I also design a series of smoking gun tests, which propose that if a given piece of evidence is present, then the hypothesis must be valid,[145] to establish sufficiency of the hypothesis.

The political championship theory posits that executive intervention in the project leads to higher project effectiveness. If this is true, I should be able to observe top political leadership of the host country devoting superior commitment to and intervention in this project than other projects during their rulership. I should also be able to observe the effectiveness of executive intervention in shaping the project outcome: that the executive achieved project effectiveness through generating a sense of mission, bypassing bureaucracy, and/or co-opting opposition leaders. Moreover, I should observe that for the same project, when executive intervention declined from extensive to ceremonial, the efficiency of obstacle-solution also slowed down.

The external agency theory argues that the Chinese SOEs with higher technical capability are more likely to effectively solve obstacles during implementation, thus the project demonstrates higher effectiveness. If this explanation is true, I should observe that the SOEs stepped beyond their contractual obligations to help African counterparts solve problems during construction and operation. Such SOE interventions should have been sometimes risky and against commercial sense. Moreover, I should observe that even with less intensive executive intervention and no change in railway corporations' intervention, the project proceeded normally without delay.

[144] Mahoney (2012, p. 571).
[145] Ibid., pp. 571–2.

The bureaucratic capacity theory states that the effective railway corporation can solve obstacles within its domain effectively, thus achieving higher project effectiveness. For this argument to be true, first I need to show that obstacles within the domain of the railway corporation, including labour disputes and community relations, can be effectively solved. I should also observe that even with less intensive executive intervention and no change in Chinese SOEs' support, the project proceeded normally without delay.

1.4.3 Exogenous or endogenous political championship

Political championship can be generated endogenously or exogenously. Executive commitment enabled by the project or policy's salience to regime survival is endogenous championship, because this is a thought process of the political leaders themselves or within the intimate circle of the ruling elites, whereas African leadership commitment caused by the diplomatic leverage of foreign government or political lobbying of African bureaucracies is exogenous championship. Endogenous versus exogenous political championship is one of the essential differences between political championship theory and the two competing theories.

Empirically establishing endogeneity of the political championship is challenging. The thought process of the African leadership is largely unobservable. And even if I cannot observe evidence of Chinese or bureaucratic leverage, the missing data does not necessarily mean the data does not exist but may result from my limited access to high-level government officials in China and Africa.[146] To solve this problem, I trace the process of the origin of political championship and pay special attention to evidence of the timing of the emergence of political championship in relation to Chinese and bureaucratic lobbying. To establish that the origin of political championship is endogenous rather than imposed by China or the bureaucracy, I should observe that African political leaders showed strong ownership of the project prior to the Chinese government's and railway corporation's involvement. I should also find evidence that the political commitment to the railway was caused by the executive's perceived salience of the project rather than external influence. Moreover, negative cases contribute to the solution of this puzzle: if I can observe leverage exerted by China or a capable bureaucracy but still low project effectiveness, then I can confidently conclude that the Chinese agency

[146] Gonzalez-Ocantos and LaPorte (2021).

argument and bureaucratic efficiency argument cannot account for project effectiveness.

If Chinese SOEs are the driver of African political championship, I should be able to document SOEs inviting Chinese government officials to visit the project, lobbying the central government to attach political significance to the project, such as including the project as a flagship project of the BRI, and publicizing the project in the Chinese media to increase domestic public awareness of the project.[147] More crucially, I should also be able to observe that, during bilateral or multilateral meetings, the Chinese government clearly expresses expectations regarding the success of the projects to their African counterparts.[148] I should be able to collect evidence of the China EximBank using future financial opportunities or debt forgiveness as incentives to enhance commitment from African states.[149]

If the railway corporation is the driver of political championship, I should be able to document the railway corporation's early involvement in the project, prior to the establishment of political championship. I should also be able to collect evidence that the railway corporation successfully lobbied top political leaders to support the project, either through bureaucratic channels, or via Chinese counterparts, or through politically connected 'fixers'.[150]

1.4.4 Other potential explanations

In this subsection, I discuss four other alternative account of varied project development: single versus cross-country comparison, topology, popular agency, and financial sustainability. For popular agency and financial sustainability, I provide more empirically grounded discussion in Chapters 2 to 4.

Is it possible that the Kenyan railway develops better than its Ethiopian counterpart because the latter cuts across two countries and thus involves more complex coordination? Indeed, cross-national coordination takes time and may results in unpredictable delays for railway operations. But the design

[147] This is a series of straws in the wind tests, passing or failing of which does not necessarily validate or eliminate a hypothesis.

[148] This is a smoking gun test, the passing of which is sufficient for the hypothesis to be true but failing this test does not eliminate the hypothesis.

[149] This is another smoking gun test.

[150] The timing of a railway corporation's involvement is a hoop test, the passing of which is necessary but not sufficient for the hypothesis to be true; failing of this test eliminates the hypothesis. Bureaucratic leverage is a smoking gun test, the passing of which is sufficient for the hypothesis to be true but failing this test does not eliminate the hypothesis. See Goertz and Mahoney (2012); Mahoney (2012); Bennett (2010).

of this research rules out this alternative explanation by drawing causal inference from within-case analysis rather than cross-case comparison, with the latter playing a supporting role to show the political championship theory applies in different political contexts. In other words, I do not compare the Kenyan railway with Ethiopian and Angolan ones to show political championship matters; instead, I compare different phases of each railway to prove my theory.

The delivery of infrastructure projects, particularly railways, is significantly affected by the geographical characteristics. Delays in project delivery can frequently result from technical difficulties rather than political challenges. Could it be possible that delays in the Angolan railway were due to extensive land mines surrounding several sections of the railway? For the Kenyan railway, was the missed presidential deadline for Phase 2A due to this phase involving more tunnel and bridge construction than Phase 1? During fieldwork for each railway case, I asked those who directly participated in the railway construction to evaluate the main obstacles interrupting their work. Topography and other technical difficulties were sporadically mentioned, but the main causes of the delays were land acquisition in Kenya, financial shortage in Angola, and a myriad of factors in Ethiopia including cross-country negotiation as well as instability of electricity and water supplies. I further elaborate these points in the empirical chapters.

Another potential alternative explanation involves popular agency. Railway construction and operation directly affects host communities, whose support and rejection can, in turn, shape railway development. Readers of this book may find an exclusive concentration on elite politics that overlooks local population and civil society organizations. This predominant focus on elite and executive agency is not a claim that popular agency does not matter to state effectiveness. Among the three countries, only Kenya has a meaningful civil society, whereas the Angolan and Ethiopian regimes were relatively intolerant towards civil society and political opposition during the height of the railway construction and early operation. In Kenya, a country with a highly vibrant civil society and media environment, the multiparty elections every five years provide windows of opportunities for community voices to be politicized at the national and even international level.[151] Could it be possible that the Kenyan president's championship of the railway was incentivized by the heightened voices from civil society that were politicized by the

[151] Alden and Otele (2022).

opposition during election seasons? In Chapter 2, I show with empirical evidence that the Kenyan president's commitment to the railway project arose not from civil societies' or the opposition's push, but from his calculation of electoral survival. I also show that despite opposition voices from civil society and opposition political leaders to the Kenyan railway, the project still managed to complete and operate in a timely and regular manner because of the presidential championship.

How does financial sustainability affect railway project delivery? At the time of the Kenyan railway Phase 2A construction, the country had loan payments due and there were debates about restricting additional borrowing. In 2018, the new Ethiopian prime minister visited China to restructure the loans for the Addis Ababa–Djibouti railway. Two financial crises in 2008 and 2014 caused construction suspension of the Angolan railway. What is the role of financial crises in Angola's state effectiveness where government revenue mainly comes from oil export? Chapters 2, 3, and 4 provide empirically grounded discussions on project financial sustainability and African state effectiveness.

1.5 Conclusion

Why do Chinese-funded and -constructed railway projects developed starkly varied functionalities in different African states? And more profoundly, why do African states demonstrate varying capabilities in infrastructure development? Many scholars have strived to explain the varying state effectiveness through either the structural and institutional approaches outlined earlier. This book approaches these puzzles via three potential explanations. One existing explanation is that Chinese SOEs' capacity determines the effectiveness of the railway. This structural argument yields the determination of African development to external factors, in this case the Chinese SOEs. A second explanation posits that the bureaucratic capacity of the railway corporation determines the outcome of railway development. This institutional argument, however, fails to capture the volatility of project or policy implementation performance. I introduce a third explanation for state effectiveness: political championship. This theory invites the examination of political leadership and the role of individual agency within institutional constraints. It argues that projects or policies championed by top political elites are more likely to demonstrate higher effectiveness, and political championship is developed endogenously, from the political leaders' perception of project importance to elite survival, rather than exogenously; that is, influenced by bureaucratic or foreign lobbying.

In this chapter, I have introduced the three main competing theories in detail and designed empirical tests to evaluate the validity of the theories. I have also discussed in brief four other competing explanations of railway and state effectiveness. In the chapters that follow, I will evaluate each of the three theories against the empirical evidence from each of the three railway cases.

2

A Kenyan railway? A Kenyatta railway?

> A history that was first started 122 years ago when the British, who had colonized this nation, kicked off the train to nowhere ... it was then dubbed the 'Lunatic Express'. Today ... despite again a lot of criticism we now celebrate not the 'Lunatic Express' but the Madaraka Express [named after the day Kenya attained internal self-rule] that would begin to reshape the story of Kenya for the next 100 years.
>
> Uhuru Kenyatta, president of Kenya[1]

The Kenyan Standard Gauge Railway (SGR) was designed to relieve traffic congestion on East Africa's main transport corridor from Mombasa port to Nairobi and possibly as far as Kampala and Kigali. At the railway inauguration event on 31 May 2017, President Uhuru Kenyatta vaunted his development record as he sought a second term in the August elections, saying the railway line would herald a new chapter in Kenya's history.[2] This SGR Phase 1 (SGR-1) was financed through a loan from the Export and Import Bank of China (EximBank) and constructed by a Chinese state-owned enterprise (SOE), the China Road and Bridge Corporation (CRBC). From construction to inauguration, the 472-kilometre SGR-1 took only thirty months to complete.

On 16 October 2019, President Kenyatta launched the SGR Phase 2A (SGR-2A)[3] linking Nairobi to Naivasha. Passenger services started immediately, serving twelve adjoining stops and operating three times per day. Cargo services commenced two months later. The 120-kilometre line was completed in twenty-five months. SGR-2A was also financed by EximBank and constructed by the CRBC.

By June 2022, the Madaraka Express carried on average seventeen freight train trips per day and has transported 20.29 million tons of cargo.[4] The railway has transported 7.95 million passengers, running six passenger trains per

[1] BBC (31 May 2017).
[2] Ibid.
[3] The SGR Phase 2 is from Nairobi to Malaba; Phase 2A links Nairobi to Naivasha; Phase 2B Naivasha to Kisumu; and Phase 2C from Kisumu to Malaba.
[4] State Council Information Office (2022).

The Railpolitik. Yuan Wang, Oxford University Press. © Yuan Wang (2023). DOI: 10.1093/oso/9780198873037.003.0003

day, with an average daily seat occupancy rate of over 90 per cent. There have been no accidents since its operation and passenger trains strictly follow the schedule.[5] The Madaraka Express' operational figures humble the Ethiopian and Angolan railways.

Why was SGR-1 completed in a timelier fashion than SGR-2A, and why did it demonstrate higher effectiveness than the Ethiopian and Angolan railways? Regarding the two phases of the SGR, why was Phase 2A less efficiently constructed, which was majorly due to delays in land acquisition, than Phase 1 when the route of Phase 1 passes through mostly opposition majority counties, whereas more counties in Phase 2A support President Kenyatta's Jubilee Alliance? Having gained experience during the first phase, why did Kenyan bureaucracies and Chinese contractors demonstrate less efficiency during the second phase? Why were greater obstacles surmounted more effectively in Kenya? That land is privately owned in Kenya and publicly owned in Angola and Ethiopia, so we might expect land acquisition to be more time-consuming in Kenya; and moreover in Kenya land, labour, and environmental grievances were politicized, causing more obstacles to the SGR implementation, whereas in Angola and Ethiopia, resistance from elites and society to the railway project (and the larger state-led development agenda) was minimal. Nevertheless, the Kenyan SGR Phase 1 demonstrated higher effectiveness than Phase 2A, the Ethiopian, and Angolan railways. Perhaps even more puzzling is that political championship, an essentially personalistic and centralized approach to policy and project implementation, manifested itself more prominently within the multiparty Kenya than in highly centralized Ethiopia and Angola, where the executive has fewer institutional constraints.

This chapter examines the achievement of relatively higher effectiveness of SGR-1 than SGR-2A, the Ethiopian, and Angolan railways through process tracing the initiation and implementation of both phases of the Kenyan railway. I examine each piece of evidence against three possible explanations articulated in Chapter 1: political championship, external agency, and bureaucratic capacity. The two phases of the SGR were temporarily divided by the 2017 national elections, and executive commitment that was high before the election significantly reduced for Phase-2A. The political championship argument predicts that project effectiveness was achieved due to direct executive intervention into the SGR-1, before this intervention diminished in Phase 2A, and that the railways in Ethiopia and Angola did not receive consistent

[5] The only incident was on 18 November 2021, when a passenger train stopped midway and was delayed for three hours due to damage on the track. See Kurgat (22 November 2021).

political commitment. The external agency argument contends that the higher effectiveness of the Kenyan railway than the Ethiopian and Angolan railways resulted from the greater overseas management experience of the Chinese contractor for the Kenyan railway compared to its counterparts on the Ethiopian and Angolan railways. The bureaucratic capacity explanation argues that the high bureaucratic capacity of the Kenya Railway Corporation (KRC) led to the success of the SGR.

The rest of this chapter is organized as follows. In section 2.1, I discuss Kenya's institutional legacy of strong presidency and personalistic rulership through a review of the Jomo Kenyatta and Daniel arap Moi presidencies and how this legacy persisted within multiparty politics after 1992. Section 2.2 reviews the initiation of SGR-1, revealing the election-inspired championship of Uhuru Kenyatta. In sections 2.3 and 2.4, I explain in detail the strength of Kenyatta's commitment to and intervention in SGR-1, and its relative weakness during SGR-2A. I also discuss the role of Kenyan bureaucracy, especially KRC and Chinese actors during the project's lifespan, in section 2.5. Section 2.6 concludes.

2.1 Personalistic legacy in multiparty politics

Uhuru Kenyatta's political championship on the SGR has its institutional origins. Political championship is essentially a personalistic approach to project or policy implementation, and this personalism is an institutional legacy of the regimes of Jomo Kenyatta and Daniel arap Moi. Multiparty politics after 1992 did not alter the concentration of power in the presidency, personalistic power exercise by the executive, or the flouting of rational-legal authority in favour of highly personalistic presidential rule. Personalism refers, in line with Weber, to the reciprocal system in which political relationships are mediated through and maintained by personal connections between leaders and subjects, or patrons and clients. Authority and the social linkages through which it is exercised are vested in an individual, almost as their personal property, and within the context of this research, the executive, rather than in impersonal institutions or in a mandate conferred and withdrawn by citizens.[6] In this section, I discuss the institutional legacy of Uhuru Kenyatta's personalistic approach to the SGR by reviewing the rulership of his predecessors, Jomo Kenyatta, Daniel arap Moi, and briefly Mwai Kibaki.

[6] Pitcher, Moran, and Johnston (2009).

2.1.1 A legacy of personalism

Jomo Kenyatta, the first president of Kenya, established a *de facto* one-party state characterized by an all-powerful presidency and state patronage system. In the early months of 1960, prior to independence, two parties were formed, Kenya African National Union (KANU) under Kenyatta's leadership and Kenya African Democratic Union (KADU). Upon independence, Kenyatta rapidly consolidated his personal authority and created a government of national unity.[7] Kenyatta had little patience for dissidents and equated loyalty with obedience. He was reported to have said: 'I am sure for national affairs one party would be the best answer for the unity of Africa.'[8] In 1964, KADU merged into KANU, and Kenya became a *de facto* single-party state. The government also created registration hurdles for later-established opposition parties like the Kenya People's Union and tried to stymie it in its infancy through intimidation.

Kenyatta established a state patronage system to reward loyalty and co-opt potential opposition. The easy economic benefits of land consolidation, a cash crop boom in the mid-1970s, and the upsurge of tourism during this time provided the state with enough resources to distribute as patronage.[9] The state became a major employer of salaried labour and the chief and sometimes sole disperser of development funds, trade licences, and other amenities, and influenced the circulation of information through its control of the communications media. The increasing dependence of MPs and bureaucrats on executive patronage reduced the independent power of the legislature while centralizing political authority.[10] KANU remained a weak organization at the local level and lacked ideological coherence.[11] The party's ability to influence policy was further frustrated by the personal loyalty of the bureaucracy and a majority of the legislature to Kenyatta.[12] The price of recalcitrance could be felt at every level of society because of the state's country-wide monopoly over sanctions and resources.[13]

As Kenyatta's health deteriorated in the early 1970s and the strength of both parliament and the cabinet weakened, he preferred a highly personalized

[7] Throup and Hornsby (1998, p. 12).
[8] Branch (2011, p. 11), citing Musa Amalemba, 'Buluyia Political Union Visits Jomo Kenyatta at Maralal on Tuesday. 11 July 1961'. KNA MSS 12/21.
[9] Throup and Hornsby (1998).
[10] Branch and Cheeseman (2006).
[11] Throup and Hornsby (1998, p. 17).
[12] Branch and Cheeseman (2006).
[13] Mueller (2010, p. 85).

way of handling government issues.[14] In his residences across the country, the president received delegations from provinces and districts, listened to their grievances, and issued decrees in response. Although they started as ad hoc events, these delegation visits slowly became highly regulated modes of interaction between citizens and their head of state. These visits were organized by provincial commissioners, and whoever wished to meet Kenyatta to discuss specific matters could do so via prior agreement with the president's assistants.[15] Kenyatta's personalized form of governance was soon replicated by officers of the provincial administration. The president trusted provincial and district commissioners with 'responsibility for nothing less than the image and the impact of government',[16] granting considerable power to local administrators. Members of the provincial administration eagerly exploited the ill-defined powers granted to them by the president. This system of visiting delegations, via which a high degree of personalized power was centred on the president himself, had become institutionalized.[17]

By the time Moi acceded to the presidency in 1978, the economic situation was worsening. The cash crop boom of the mid-1970s was ending, tourism was in decline, and the easy economic benefits of land consolidation were nearly exhausted while the urban population was still expanding. Debt and inflation soared in the late 1970s and early 1980s. Severe droughts in 1979 and 1980, a fall in global commodity prices, and rapid population growth all adversely affected the economy, and inequality increased. As a result, resources for state patronage were in short supply, and Moi had to make difficult decisions about which groups to co-opt. Moreover, Moi lacked Kenyatta's political prestige and the legitimacy which Kenyatta had gained as the 'father of independence'.[18] Students took to the streets to demonstrate against Moi's rule. In 1982, the one-party state was codified in the Constitution, and Moi increasingly relied on oppressive measures against demonstrations and potential opposition.

Following the threatened *coup d'état* in 1982, Moi developed an increasingly exclusionary system of government and was further reliant on coercion. After an attempted *coup* against his government in 1982, Moi radically altered the composition of key cabinet positions in 1985 until they were largely held by members of his own Kalenjin community. Moi tended to have politicians and ministers centrally appointed, functioning to ensure that the will of

[14] Branch (2011).
[15] Ibid.
[16] Ibid., p. 73, citing Kenyatta's speech at the official opening of the Provincial Administration Seminar at the Kenya Institute of Administration in Kabete, 5 May 1969; KNA KA/4/17.
[17] Branch (2011).
[18] Throup and Hornsby (1998).

central government was enacted in the regions across the country.[19] Institutions intended to protect the political rights of the population, such as the judiciary, were weakened or simply bypassed.[20] Unable to maintain an inclusive one-party state via the extension of patronage, Moi increasingly resorted to authoritarian strategies with an increased willingness to harass opponents.[21]

2.1.2 Personalism in multiparty politics

In 1991, Kenya democratized, but Moi's rulership persisted. KANU's brutal repression of pro-democracy activists, including the detention and torture of opposition leader Kenneth Matiba, shocked the international community into belated condemnation of the Moi regime.[22] More significantly, the distribution of foreign aid and financial support was halted pending political and economic reforms.[23] In December 1991, Kenya passed legislation instigating multiparty politics and held elections the following year. Moi won the election due to the fragmentation of the opposition parties and rigging of elections. He continued to rule Kenya for another decade.

Amidst growing pressure towards political liberalization, Moi's regime engaged in spiralling corruption, which further encouraged the bypassing of formal institutions. Two factors contributed to this increasing corruption: first, the increasing likelihood of electoral defeat resulted in senior figures within the Moi government seeking to accumulate wealth at an accelerated rate in order to secure their 'retirement'.[24] Second, democracy itself proved expensive. The need to fund costly election campaigns provided an additional—and just as significant—motivation for spiralling corruption.[25] Kenyan elections have always seen a vast amount of official and unofficial expenditure. In 1992, it was estimated that, despite the economic difficulties facing the country, the ruling party spent over $100 million on the campaign.[26] Notably billions of dollars were looted from the state in the 'Goldenberg scandal'.[27] Rampant corruption

[19] Branch and Cheeseman (2009, p. 45).
[20] Ibid., p. 17.
[21] Ibid.
[22] Cheeseman (2010).
[23] Throup and Hornsby (1998).
[24] Branch and Cheeseman (2009, p. 12).
[25] Ibid.
[26] Ibid.
[27] In the 1990s, Kenyan government paid $600 million to Goldenberg International for non-existent gold and diamond exports, equivalent of more than 10 per cent of the country's annual GDP. Refer to Branch (2011, chapter 7) for a detailed description of the Goldenberg scandal.

created incentives for Moi to encourage a process of state informalization that continues to constrain anti-corruption efforts.[28]

When Mwai Kibaki superseded Moi in 2002, despite his declared intentions, no substantial reform was undertaken. Although Kibaki repeatedly promised reform, his agenda was vague and intangible, and little evidence is available to suggest fundamental overhaul of politics and governance took place under his rulership.[29] Kibaki did reshape the judiciary, citing corruption as a reason for sacking numerous judges and replacing them with his own candidates, turning the courts into instruments whose rulings advanced Kibaki's objectives. These included Kibaki's plans to stymie and then reconstruct a constitutional revision process that Kibaki feared would dilute his executive power.[30] Corruption persisted, human rights continued to be violated as part of the everyday business of government, and state-led theft of the wealth of certain regions endured.[31]

Although Kenya became a *de jure* multiparty state in 1991 and has experienced presidential turnover twice since then, the legacy of personalism has persisted. Kenya is yet to have a new generation of political leaders; rather, the country was and is still run by a government made up largely of individuals who learned their political craft in the pre-democratic period. Significantly, Raila Odinga, Uhuru Kenyatta, and William Ruto were handpicked by Moi as potential candidates to succeed him after his retirement in 2002. The three later joined Mwai Kibaki in dominating the political stage up to the present. As Daniel Branch commented: 'Along with Kibaki, Moi's men of the future helped keep Kenya stuck in its past.'[32] In the SGR case, Uhuru Kenyatta's personalistic approach of championing and intervening in the SGR to ensure project success was reminiscent of the political landscape and leadership style of Moi and his father, Jomo Kenyatta.

2.2 Standard Gauge Railway initiation: the rise of political championship

President Kenyatta's championship of the SGR was election-inspired. During the 2013 electoral campaign, Kenyatta made it a key campaign promise to develop a modern rail network in exchange for electoral sponsorship from

[28] Branch and Cheeseman (2009).
[29] Branch (2011, p. 284).
[30] Akech (2011).
[31] Branch (2011, pp. 285–6).
[32] Branch (2011).

Table 2.1 Facts on the Standard Gauge Railway

SGR Phase 1		**SGR Phase 2A**
USD 3.8 billion	**Contract amount**	USD 1.5 billion
The government of Kenya (15%) and the Export-Import Bank of China (85%, half commercial and half concessional loans)	**Funded by**	The government of Kenya (15%) and the Export-Import Bank of China (85%, half commercial and half concessional loans)
Kenya Railway Corporation	**Client**	Kenya Railway Corporation
China Road and Bridge Corporation	**Contractor**	China Road and Bridge Corporation
12 December 2014	**Construction commencement**	14 September 2017
60 months	**Duration of construction**	60 months
China Road and Bridge Corporation	**Operator**	China Road and Bridge Corporation
472-km single-track non-electric SGR from Mombasa to Nairobi; freight trains of up to 80 km/hr and passenger trains at up to 120 km/hr	**Characteristics**	120-km single-track non-electric SGR from Mombasa to Nairobi; freight trains of up to 80 km/hr hour and passenger trains at up to 120 km/hr

Source: China Road and Bridge Corporation Social Responsibility Report 2015 and 2017/2018 on Mombasa Nairobi SGR Project.

Jimmy Wanjigi, the initiator of the SGR. Kenyatta's commitment to the SGR also stemmed from his intention to use the Chinese-sponsored SGR in retaliation for Western denunciations of his actions prior to and during the 2013 elections, when Kenyatta and Ruto were prosecuted by the International Criminal Court (ICC) for organizing violence in the wake of the 2007 elections. In this section, I explain the initiation of the SGR project and how, inspired by the 2013 elections, the SGR evolved from a private sector initiative to a Kenyan national project, or, more precisely, a 'Kenyatta' project. Figure 2.1 shows the SGR development timeline and Table 2.1 displays basic facts of the SGR.

2.2.1 A private sector initiative

The SGR was originally a private sector initiative that was contracted and received government endorsement under Mwai Kibaki. In 2008, Jimmy

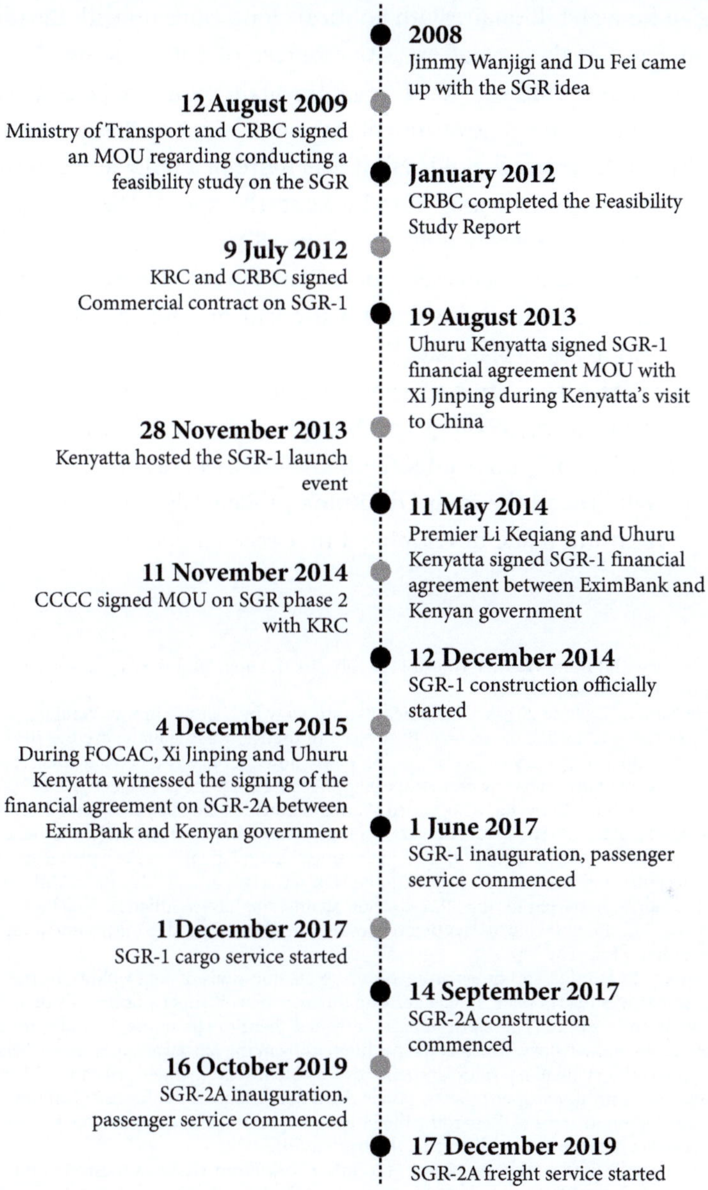

Figure 2.1 Kenyan Standard Gauge Railway timeline

Source: The author's composition based on China Road and Bridge Corporation Social Responsibility Report 2015 and 2017/2018 on Mombasa Nairobi SGR Project and media reports.

Wanjigi, a Kenyan billionaire with political clout, came up with the idea along with Du Fei, the then chief executive officer of CRBC Kenya,[33] to jointly deliver a modern railway for Kenya through public–private partnership (PPP).[34] 'We don't need government', Wanjigi said, 'the design was to spend KES50 billion to adjust the old rail. It was more of a renovation to straighten the existing railway line and thus increase the speed. We [Du Fei and I] calculated the investment would return in 18 years ... Kibaki got this idea, and Museveni liked it.'[35] This refers to a State House communiqué from 2008 by Kibaki and (Ugandan president) Museveni on joint construction of the SGR from Mombasa to Kampala.[36]

The SGR first drew Uhuru Kenyatta's attention during his 2013 electoral campaign. Since 2010, Wanjigi had brought together Uhuru Kenyatta from Kikuyu and William Ruto from Kalenji for the 2013 presidential election. The billionaire bankrolled the joint UhuRuto's Jubilee Alliance campaign, and in exchange Kenyatta made developing a modern rail network a key campaign

[33] Interview with Jimmy Wanjigi, Nairobi (26 July 2019). Later, Du Fei was promoted as the general manager of CRBC Headquarters.

[34] *Daily Nation* (26 June 2017). Confirmed by interview in Nairobi, Jimmy Wanjigi, 26 July 2019. This story of the SGR initiation was widely covered in the Kenyan media before the 2017 election. I wanted to triangulate this story with Wanjigi, but he is known for barely receiving interviewers. To my surprise, he accepted my interview request, perhaps because since the 2017 elections he had become a public enemy of Uhuru Kenyatta, who raided Wanjigi's house in October 2017 after Wanjigi exposed Kenyatta's electoral fraud. The media depicts Wanjigi as the initiator of the SGR, and believes that he received a good commission from it. But he maintained that he did not make a cent from the project. When he accepted my interview in July 2019, he was actively working with Raila Odinga and other opposition leaders preparing for the 2022 election against the Jubilee Alliance. Shocked by the handshake between Odinga and Uhuru days before our interview, he revealed to me his intention of running for the presidency himself.

Interviews with Wanjigi and other protagonists create questions of data validity, as the opposition has many grievances to articulate. Indeed, during the interview, Wanjigi emotionally described Kenyatta as 'greedy and egoistic'. These grievances motivated them to talk to me, an independent Oxford researcher, to share their story, which could be different from the official account, to the Western audience. But could the evidentiary value of their story be blemished by their grievances? I triangulated these interviews with newspaper reports, policy documents such as the Jubilee Coalition Manifesto, and non-opposition interviews. Regarding the interview quotes collected in this book, I assess the risk of the opposition interviewees of distorting the truth as low.

[35] Interview with Jimmy Wanjigi, Nairobi (26 July 2019). From Wanjigi's testimony, it is difficult to determine whether the SGR was initiated by himself or Du Fei. CRBC entered Kenya in 1984 and Du Fei's friendship with Wanjigi was long established. Regarding the brokerage culture of Chinese SOEs in Kenya, I interviewed a former Chinese manager who used to work in a different SOE, and whose former employer also worked with Wanjigi. He said: 'Project initiation is done by the client and the broker; for projects requiring strong technical expertise, such as selling aviation, Chinese SOEs usually proactively approach brokers to promote their products.' Railway construction is not an expertise CRBC possesses strongly—it is more known for road and bridge construction. Therefore, it is reasonable to believe that Wanjigi approached CRBC with the SGR idea. The SGR was a Kenyan initiative rather than a Chinese imposition.

[36] Ministry of Transport and Infrastructure (2013).

message, with an emphasis on PPP,[37] as clearly shown in the Jubilee Coalition Manifesto 2013:

> The Coalition Government will ... enact new Public Private Partnership legislation to encourage private investment in public projects, speeding up the delivery of infrastructure urgently needed to achieve Kenya Vision 2030.
>
> ... Improve the rail network to upgrade the links between major cities. This will include building a new Standard Gauge Railway from Mombasa to Malaba with a branch line to Kisumu in line with the [East African] Railway Masterplan.[38]

Wanjigi recalled: 'When the Jubilee Manifesto was being done, one thing we put in it was the railway. I still hoped for it to be PPP. In fact, a big emphasis in the Manifesto was on PPP, less government, and more private sector.'[39]

2.2.2 A Kenyatta railway

Kenyatta's ownership of the SGR was established as soon as he took office in 2013, and the SGR became a national project under the president's leadership. During Kibaki's presidency, the SGR was more of a commercial initiative than a government mega project. However, upon taking office, the Kenyatta administration elevated the priority of the SGR, including it as a key flagship project in Vision 2030, the long-term development blueprint for the country.

After Uhuru Kenyatta took office in 2013, Wanjigi suddenly found himself sidelined from the SGR. Wanjigi said: 'In 2013, Uhuru got into power, I don't know what happened, suddenly this [the SGR] is what the president wants. I told him I wanted to do the PPP, I further recommended a three-lane highway from Mombasa to Malaba with the use of those Chinese funds. The president told me: "You must let go".'[40] Wanjigi repeatedly clashed with Kenyatta over the cost and financial model of the project:

> The feasibility study was delivered by the CRBC. Even the bill of quantities was changing all the time. Imagine you build a house and the contractor does everything for you, and at the end of it they just hand you an invoice. What's

[37] Interview with Jimmy Wanjigi, Nairobi (26 July 2019).
[38] Jubilee Coalition (2013).
[39] Interview with Jimmy Wanjigi, Nairobi (26 July 2019).
[40] Interview with Jimmy Wanjigi, Nairobi (26 July 2019).

> going to happen? You are highly likely to be overcharged. Every time I mentioned this, Uhuru pushed back. It is his project! I told Uhuru: 'This is not viable. Only PPP will work'. Uhuru said: 'Let's not discuss this again.'[41]

It seemed that President Kenyatta was well aware of the high cost implication in this SGR deal with China, but this only reinforced his determination for the project to succeed: such an expensive project would be a disaster, and would damage the country's relationship with China, were it to fail.

Bearing the grievances of losing control of the SGR to Kenyatta, Wanjigi explained how the war between himself and Kenyatta was spread to the public sphere.

> I said I wanted a public divorce from this project. He [Kenyatta] told me to go ahead. So I commissioned a politician, Alfred Keter, to speak against it [the SGR]. The media was involved, lawyers involved, [Keter] attacked [the SGR] in Parliament and Transport Committee. Uhuru knew it was me. So he called me and asked me to stop.[42]

Alfred Keter, MP for Nandi Hills, went to the media as a whistleblower of the SGR financial arrangement on 4 January 2014. He revealed that the contract price of the SGR was three times what it should have been according to international standards, and the Kenyan government had undertaken an unlawful non-competitive tendering process to procure CRBC as the contractor on the SGR.[43] Keter framed the SGR as a scandal concerning a sum larger than Anglo Leasing Scandal and Goldenberg Scandal,[44] the two most notorious scandals in recent Kenyan history, combined.[45] On 15 and 22 January, Keter was summoned to present evidence at the Public Investment Committee's investigation into the procurement and financing of the SGR. Apart from the inflated price and flawed procurement process, he also challenged the integrity of CRBC: CRBC and its parent company China Communications Construction Company (CCCC) were debarred by the World Bank from participating in any of its projects for the period January 2009 to January 2017 due to fraud,

[41] Ibid.
[42] Ibid.
[43] Ronoh (4 January 2014).
[44] The Anglo Leasing scandal refers to eighteen contracts signed between the Kenyan government and several domestic and foreign phantom companies for security equipment and services totalling $770 million. Refer to Wrong (2009) for more information on both scandals.
[45] Ronoh (4 January 2014).

corruption, and flouting procurement regulations for a road project they undertook in the Philippines.[46]

The president's ownership of the SGR was also inspired by Western denunciation of Kenyatta and Ruto during the 2013 election. Uhuru Kenyatta and William Ruto were prosecuted by the ICC for organizing the 2007 post-election violence.[47] Before the 2013 Kenyan presidential election, Western leaders threatened to cut support if Uhuru was elected.[48] While the West was busy indicting Kenyatta and Ruto through the ICC, the Chinese government's olive branch was welcomed early. Kenyatta chose Beijing and Moscow as the first non-African capitals to visit after his inauguration in April 2013, highlighting his 'look East' policy.[49] During this visit, Kenyatta vowed to work closely with China following comments from the United States, the United Kingdom, and some European officials who said they would limit contacts with Kenyatta should he win owing to his indictment for crimes against humanity at the ICC.[50] Kenyatta and Chinese President Xi Jinping signed the Memorandum of Understanding (MOU) for China EximBank's financial support of the SGR. As one interviewee recalled, in the initial list of requests to EximBank, SGR was the largest funding ($3.8 billion) Kenya had ever requested, plus another $1.2 billion on power, road, dam projects, and so on.[51] The financial agreement was signed in May 2014 by China's premier Li Keqiang and President Uhuru Kenyatta during the premier's visit to Kenya.[52]

Receiving this large amount of financial and project support from China was a demonstration that Kenya did not depend on Western support. 'This was a big shock for the West—they were afraid of losing this friend', Wanjigi recalled. 'They reacted immediately. The Ambassador of the UK was at my house, but the president didn't want to meet with him, even as personal

[46] Public Investment Committee (2014).

[47] In the highly disputed and closely contested 2007 Kenyan presidential election, incumbent President Mwai Kibaki of the Party of National Unity (PNU) was declared the winner. Violence broke out in various parts of Kenya, and the Rift Valley was the epicentre of the violence. Retaliation violence by Kikuyus against Luo and other allies of Raila Odinga's Orange Democratic Movement (ODM) then followed in the Central Rift. This post-election violence caused thousands of deaths and the displacement of over half a million people, as well as hundreds of victims of sexual assault. The International Criminal Court prosecution alleged that Uhuru Kenyatta and William Ruto were among the six conspirators who orchestrated cooperation between the PNU and the Mungiki criminal organisation that carried out attacks on ODM supporters during the post-election violence.

[48] Interview with Jimmy Wanjigi, Nairobi (26 July 2019).

[49] Ng (19 August 2013).

[50] Reuters (19 August 2013).

[51] Interview with Jimmy Wanjigi, Nairobi (26 July 2019).

[52] Railway Technology (2016).

friend.'[53] Kenyatta's former friend and now enemy Wanjigi expressed the symbolic meaning of the SGR: 'The British had built a railway, now we were going to do it better. It was a battle between the West and East. And it is the East that he [Kenyatta] prefers.' The SGR project initiation and Chinese backing coincided with Kenyatta being denounced by the West. The new Chinese-sponsored SGR runs parallel to a century-old British-funded metre-gauge railway, symbolizing Kenya's shifting international relationship from Western states towards China.

Kenyatta was well aware of the debate within the Kenyan government about the flawed SGR procurement process and the dear price of this Chinese 'gift'. However, opposition to the project only increased Kenyatta's commitment to the SGR. The heated public debate on the SGR's price and procurement led some lawmakers and the Dockworkers Union to demand President Uhuru Kenyatta to postpone the ground-breaking ceremony.[54] But the ceremony went ahead as planned on 28 November 2013, when the president and the first lady tightened the first nut on the track.[55] Although SGR construction officially commenced on 12 December 2014, Kenyatta made a show of his determination on this project with the launch ceremony a year earlier to quiet opposition voices.[56]

2.2.3 Limited participation of the Kenyan Railway Corporation

The very limited involvement of the KRC during the project initiation phase from 2008 to 2012 demonstrates the relative weakness of KRC within the Kenyan bureaucratic system. In 2009, CRBC approached the Ministry of Transport and Infrastructure (MOT) and offered to conduct a feasibility study free of charge, on condition that the Kenyan government could not grant construction contracts to another company, but the government could freely use the study to inform their decisions regarding railway construction. An MOU was signed between the MOT and CRBC regarding the free feasibility study. Nduva Muli, the then managing director of the KRC, still insisted on doing an independent feasibility study, but the MOU bypassed the KRC.[57] The KRC's primary involvement in the railway was as late as April 2011, when the

[53] Interview with Jimmy Wanjigi, Nairobi (26 July 2019).
[54] Ronoh (4 January 2014); Public Investment Committee (2014).
[55] *The East African* (20 January 2014).
[56] Interview with Atanas Maina, former managing director of the KRC, by WhatsApp call, 15 November 2019.
[57] Interview with Jimmy Wanjigi, Nairobi (26 July 2019).

KRC was required to provide comments on CRBC's feasibility study. In the KRC's comment, Nduva Muli expressed grievance for not having been part of the MOU between MOT and CRBC and not having been included in the communication loop. Muli wrote:

> KR [Kenyan Railway] did not participate in developing the Terms of References for the study nor was it involved during the study. A study of this magnitude would require KR staff participating as counterpart personnel;
>
> KR had no access to the interim and progress reports and any comments and suggestions raised by the MOT and subsequently addressed by CRBC. Such reports and comments would be produced as a matter of routine and circulated for comments to enrich the final report.[58]

This shows the KRC was excluded during the initiation of the SGR even though development of the SGR should fall under the KRC's mandate, and Muli clearly wanted to be part of project initiation. The KRC was only called upon when technical comments were needed for the feasibility study. Had the KRC been a strong agency, the Ministry of Transport, CRBC, and Wanjigi could not have bypassed it. In fact, the SGR project improved the KRC's bureaucratic position. For the initiation of SGR-2A, instead of coordinating with MOT as it did in SGR-1, CRBC wrote to the KRC. This confirms the relatively weak position of the KRC in the Kenya bureaucratic system during SGR-1 and its increased significance during SGR-2A.

2.3 Construction and operation: exercising political championship

Railway construction and operation generates interactions with local communities, the environment, and administration which may present obstacles to project execution. The most common challenges during construction are land acquisition and compensation, labour disputes, availability of local materials and services, water and electricity provision, and security. During operation, the railway may face competition from road and truck unions, as well as the logistics sector's resistance to change. Successful navigation of these potential obstacles is crucial to the delivery and operation of the project. Kenya's election and multiparty politics not only inspired the president's commitment to the

[58] Letter from Nduva Muli, MD of KRC, to Cyrus Njiru, PS of MoT, re 'CRBC Feasibility Study MSA-NRB Railway project: Comments by Kenya Railways', on 4 April 2011.

SGR project, as explained in subsection 2.2.3, but also inspired Kenyatta to use the railway as campaign capital, and allowed grievances to be expressed politically throughout the project, and such politicization was heightened during election times. Although posing obstacles to project execution, this grievance politicization further strengthened Kenyatta's intervention in the SGR.

To guarantee the success of the project, Kenyatta took a personalistic approach and directly intervened in construction and operation of the SGR. In particular, the president effectively built a coalition of key actors to push for the effective overcoming of obstacles during construction and operation. Specifically, Kenyatta made the following strategies to build the SGR coalition via mobilisation, motivation, and co-option: (1) emphasizing the project's importance and generating a sense of mission; (2) bypassing formal institutions and seeking speedy solutions for SGR-related problems through informal networks; (3) co-opting opposition leaders and replacing uncooperative staffs. In the rest of this section I explain these strategies in detail.

2.3.1 Completion timeline and mission generation

During his first visit to the SGR construction site, Kenyatta set a new completion timeline for SGR-1, shortening the scheduled completion time by half. While Phase 1 of the SGR had been contracted to be completed within sixty months, Kenyatta now set a deadline to finish the project within thirty months. SGR construction commenced on 12 December 2014.[59] Kenyatta's primary site visit was on 23 January 2015 to sections 3 and 6. After this visit, he signed the KRC's visitor's book: 'Keep up the good work. Let's all ensure we complete the works on time by June 2017.' The president's photo with the quote and his signature was framed by the KRC outside the managing director's office (Figure 2.2).

Kenyatta's rationale for setting the completion date to June 2017 was election-driven. This completion date was scheduled two months before the August 2017 national elections when Kenyatta was seeking a second term. Kenyatta wanted to deliver the largest (and most expensive) infrastructure project the country had ever undertaken prior to the election. By launching the SGR during the peak of campaigning for the August election, Kenyatta's party, the Jubilee Alliance, openly used the railway as campaign capital. The railway project was presented as an example of the stewardship of the Jubilee

[59] China Road and Bridge Corporation (2016).

Figure 2.2 Kenyatta's instruction and signature on the Standard Gauge Railway completion time

Party, a railway that, according to the president, 'would begin to reshape the story of Kenya for the next 100 years', in contrast to the colonial 'Lunatic Express' that had been 'kicked off to nowhere'.[60] Kenyatta christened the new line the 'Madaraka Express', named after the 1 June holiday that marks the day in 1964 when Kenya attained self-governance from Britain, ahead of full independence.[61] One of the Jubilee's running slogans for the 2017 election—'We deliver!'—was printed on the skywalks of Mombasa Road. The opposition leader, Raila Odinga, who ran against Kenyatta in the August election, warned: 'Jubilee should not use the SGR as a campaign agenda ... This project is for Kenyans, and not just for the Jubilee Party.'[62] Odinga made these remarks after receiving a delegation of leaders who had decamped from Jubilee to his Orange Democratic Movement party.[63]

Kenyan bureaucrats and Chinese managers were proud to be part of this historical project. Atanas Maina recalled that when he took the managing director position of the KRC and created the SGR department in early 2014, most

[60] BBC (31 May 2017).
[61] Reuters (31 May 2017).
[62] Otieno (31 May 2017).
[63] Ibid.

employees wanted to be involved: 'The SGR itself became another organization [within the KRC]. Most people wanted to get involved, but there were not enough roles for them to play.'[64] Several Chinese managers at CRBC proudly said that only the best people in the company were selected for this Kenyan railway project.[65]

Time pressures were felt most keenly within the Kenyan government. It was the first time that various Kenyan bureaucracies had undertaken a project of this magnitude. Especially so for the KRC: the previous railway construction in Kenya was completed a century ago and the KRC, established in 1977, had no institutional memory of railway construction. For the National Land Commission (NLC), established in 2012, the SGR was among the first projects it undertook. County governor positions had been introduced in 2013 and governors did not have much experience hosting large national projects in their counties. The KRC and other Kenyan bureaucracies clearly would have had no incentive to influence the president to impose a shortened completion timeline, as would be predicted by the bureaucratic capacity explanation.

The most compromised was the environmental impact assessment (EIA). As a Kenyan supervisor of the SGR said frustratedly: 'The time pressure made the situation worse. The president wants a finished product, but he doesn't care what's happening on the ground. The contractors all focus on completing the project no matter what the collateral damage.'[66] One direct consequence of this was increased cost:

> For instance, for the RAP [Resettlement Action Plan] in Rongai area, the EIA and design just showed point A linked to point B, but no one had looked at what was in between. It turned out that this area was heavily inhabited, and it would have been cheaper to have the railway run somewhere else. The estimated cost of SGR at design stage was KES300bn, but when it was finished, it costs KES360bn. Not a small difference.

Despite the 'chaotic' process, the project was completed by 31 May 2017. On 1 June, passenger service commenced. A direct train linked Nairobi and Mombasa, taking only five hours and costing KES700 ($7). A ticket for the very uncomfortable, seven-hour bus journey was KES500 ($5), and the flight ticket

[64] Interview with Atanas Maina, Nairobi (13 August 2019).

[65] Interview with KE-1 (14 June 2017), KE-2 (16 June 2017), and KE-8 (9 July 2019), Chinese managers of the SGR from CRBC.

[66] Interview with KE-31, APEC supervisor of the SGR, Nairobi (8 August 2019).

was usually over $100. The SGR was so popular that in July 2017 when I visited Kenya, I had to book three days in advance to be sure of securing a train ticket.

2.3.2 Bypassing existing institutions

To meet the now halved completion timeline, Kenyatta bypassed existing institutions and created SGR-specific mechanisms to fast-track problem solving. Instead of relying on existing weekly cabinet meetings held at the State House, Kenyatta established a four-level escalation mechanism for the SGR, so that obstacles to project implementation were brought to the attention of the president. Kenyatta also intervened in a court case on land acquisition by ordering relevant political actors to solve the issue in parallel to the legal procedure. During railway operation, Kenyatta enforced three presidential directives to force usage of the SGR for freight, which is more expensive than transporting by trucks.

The Standard Gauge Railway coordination mechanism

Specifically for SGR-1, Kenyatta installed a coordination scheme that proved very effective. Atanas Maina, former managing director of the KRC, explained the four-level SGR coordination mechanism in detail: first, KRC SGR Team, CRBC, and CAED-APEC (the design review and construction supervision consultants, a consortium of a Chinese and a Kenyan firm) meet regularly to discuss. At every construction camp, they had offices. In the morning, they come to the KRC's MD office to report and seek approval. If within the authority of the MD, which was Atanas Maina back then, he gave the order to 'proceed.' If requiring higher approval, the MD escalates to KRC Strategy Projects Committee (SPC), which makes recommendations to the KRC Board at a formal Board Meeting. From 2011 to 2017, the board was chaired by General Kianga, appointed to this position by President Kibaki after retiring from forty-three years' service in the military. Kianga met with CRBC many times, sometimes in informal settings. Second, for policy intervention matters or inter-agencies matters, the issue was escalated to the Permanent Secretaries' Team chaired by Permanent Secretary of Transport. Third And the Cabinet Secretary of Transport James Macharia chaired a Cabinet Secretary's SGR Coordination Team Meeting of all seven ministries involved and gathered quarterly in Nairobi.

Finally and most importantly, the president himself chaired the Cabinet Sub-Committee on the SGR with seven ministries involved, most of which

were done during the quarterly site inspection visits. The president's site visits were not ceremonial. During each site visit, Kenyatta held working meetings with relevant ministers to listen to briefings regarding the construction progress and challenges.[67] The president would open each meeting by asking CRBC: 'Are we on time?', to which CRBC would reply: 'Yes, except ...' Land acquisition was a concern frequently raised during the meetings, as recalled by James Macharia, cabinet secretary for transportation: 'The president asked the minister for land to explain what had been done to clear the land ... If there were a problem, the president would give direct orders to the CEO of the National Land Commission regarding land acquisition and compensation.'[68] Through these on-site working meetings, issues including land acquisition, power supply, environmental protection, security, and so on were brought to the attention of the president. The chief economist in charge of the SGR in the Ministry of Transport commented on the president's site visit: 'You may not have to solve problems, just your presence would make everyone alert. No one wants to show that he is not doing a good job when in front of the president.'[69] Both Macharia and Maina, as well as many other people I interviewed in the Kenyan government and CRBC, found this SGR-specific coordination mechanism very effective. 'It took two and a half years [to complete the SGR] rather than five years as planned in the contract. The SGR is the only project in this country that has finished ahead of time!' Maina exclaimed proudly.

This four-level coordination mechanism is not a standard procedure for project implementation in Kenya. The standard procedure under the Uhuru Kenyatta administration is that cabinet secretaries make decisions which are then implemented. Cabinet meetings which discuss all kinds of issues are held every Thursday at the State House. Although the president receives daily briefs on all matters involving the cabinet, he only chairs full cabinet meetings when a major item is on the agenda.[70] For SGR-1, Kenyatta explicitly showed his commitment to the project, and was able to marshal relevant ministries and organizations and created innovative and effective mechanisms for SGR-specific coordination that bypassed existing bureaucratic arrangements.

Evidence does not support the KRC's exceptional convening power among other bureaucracies during SGR-1, as would be predicted by the bureaucratic capacity explanation. In fact, the importance of the KRC within the Kenyan

[67] Interview with KE-8 (9 July 2019), KE-4 (9 July 2017), Chinese managers of CRBC, and interview with KE-35, senior official of Kenya's Ministry of Transport, Nairobi (18 July 2017).

[68] Interview with KE-35, Nairobi (18 July 2017).

[69] Interview with KE-44, Chief Economist in charge of the SGR, Ministry of Transport, Nairobi (15 August 2019).

[70] Keter (17 July 2019).

bureaucratic system significantly increased due to the SGR. 'Since SGR, the KRC has been on the radar',[71] as a KRC interviewee revealed. Indeed, major media in Kenya never tired of reporting on the SGR, especially during the 2017 presidential campaign. Prior to this project, the KRC was not an exciting place to be. When Kibaki appointed Kianga as chairman of the KRC board, Kianga was a bit sceptical at first:

> When he [President Kibaki] asked me, I thought the railway was nothing exciting, it only had the century-old metre gauge line and I had heard it was dying. But the president said he had bigger ideas for the railways. He mentioned the idea of the SGR to modernize the railway system from Mombasa to Nairobi and beyond. This was the first time I heard about the SGR.[72]

It seemed that the KRC made full use of the SGR's escalation mechanisms to resolve inter-ministerial issues, including land acquisition and water, electricity, and network supply for stations, conflicting with the Kenyan Highway Authority when the proposed SGR route crossed a Japanese-funded road project. Even the operation of the SGR benefited from presidential directives to force usage of railway rather than road.

A court case: 'how can you stop a presidential project?'

One of the most famous court cases during SGR-1 implementation was related to land acquisition. Kenyatta directly intervened in this case before the ruling of the court, and set timelines for the solution of the land acquisition issue in parallel to the legal process. The construction of the SGR involved the acquisition of land, resettlement, and compensation for residents. The Kenyan government oversaw these issues, and 15 per cent of the $3.8 billion from the Kenyan government was allocated to resolving land acquisition.[73] In Kenya, land-related issues are historically very politically sensitive.[74] The NLC's land valuation process was where most disputes were generated: each property that the railway line passes through was given a price by the NLC, and when residents compared prices, complaints arose. Residents might appeal to the court, which took months or even years to resolve while railway construction continued during the appeal. One outstanding case that attracted nationwide attention was filed by an MP on behalf of his constituents to the High Court at

[71] Interview with KE-27, KRC, Nairobi (18 July 2019).
[72] Interview with Jeremiah Mutinda Kianga, chair of KRC board, Nairobi (19 August 2019).
[73] Railway Technology (2016).
[74] Boone (2011, 2012).

Nairobi in 2014 challenging the integrity of the SGR land acquisition process, environmental protection, and information disclosure.

Upon announcement of the SGR in 2013, the MP was newly elected, and he was frustrated with the lack of public participation in the SGR project in his constituency. He said: 'People all focus on getting the project through, but not the soft part of the project.'[75] Before going to court, he drafted letters to the NLC, Ministry of Land, Ministry of Transport, the County Governor, and the Office of the President. The NLC clearly expressed to the MP: 'We are under statutory clock. We cannot do things that are cosmetic in nature.'[76] It seemed that, according to the NLC, re-evaluating land acquisition and compensation and EIA, as well as increasing transparency of the SGR, are issues reduced to being 'cosmetic in nature'. The passive attitude of relevant bureaucrats motivated the MP to file a case in court with a senator of the same county. The senator and the MP raised the following three issues to the High Court: first, the compulsory acquisition of land for the SGR was not done in a manner that complied with statutory and constitutional provisions; second, the SGR was not being undertaken in compliance with environmental laws and principles; and third, there was a violation of the petitioners' right to access information relating to the SGR.[77]

The court ruled in favour of a two-week suspension of SGR construction in the contested area, which was perceived as a big success for the county that voted by 90.73 per cent in support of the opposition leader Odinga according to the results of the 2013 election.[78] This, however, infuriated the president. The Senator said to me: 'We managed to have the court stop the construction of SGR for two weeks. Two weeks!' He said triumphantly and repeated 'two weeks' twice, indicating that it was a big success to be able to suspend the SGR for this long. Indeed, although the SGR was involved in over 300 court cases,[79] this was the only case in which the court ruled a suspension of construction; almost all other cases went along while the construction was going on. But this suspension did not cause much disruption to the SGR project as a whole. The railway construction was divided into eleven sections and only the section passing this area was suspended. Because of the time sensitivity of this project,

[75] Interview with KE-38, MP, Nairobi (30 July 2019).

[76] Ibid.

[77] *Anonymous MP v National Land Commission & 4 others*, Petition No of 2014.

[78] The 2017 election results are not included because Kenya went through two presidential elections; the result of the first election was annulled and before the second election, Odinga withdrew and proposed that ODM supporters should boycott voting. Thus the 2017 election result shows predominant support for Kenyatta.

[79] A quick search at http://kenyalaw.org/caselaw on 24 November 2019 with input: 'standard gauge railway' and 'construction' showed 344 results.

the MP's case drew attention from the president. Before the court's final ruling, this case was brought to the attention of the president. The senator shared with me how Kenyatta directly intervened in this issue during his site visit:

> On 23 January 2015, Uhuru Kenyatta came to the launch of our county's section. When he got off the plane, I think someone had briefed him about the court case, and he was furious. People are afraid of Uhuru Kenyatta. ...The president said angrily: 'how can you stop a presidential project?' ... Then I explained the issues we were facing. The president said: 'This seems to be a simple issue.' He then called on the cabinet secretary for Land and said: 'These senators are not elected as furniture. I need this issue solved in seven days with a report.' ...
>
> We never had another meeting with the president. We had to follow up with CRBC through the KRC by ourselves which was very difficult. The railway was not yet handed over, so we could still get some repairs done. You cannot bother the president with the issue that the school in my county was not repaired. It was too small an issue. I have written thousands of letters to follow up, asking when it will be done, who will be in charge, etc. Even today, I was writing a letter regarding compensation for destroying a school.[80]

A senior official of KRC, reiterated Kenyatta's ownership of the SGR when I asked him about the MP's case: 'The president himself is the leader of this project. How can he [the MP] confront the president's project? This MP said he was fighting for the people, but also personal issues were involved.'[81] Later interviews revealed 'personal issues' that motivated the MP filing this case: his own land was trespassed by the railway (later he filed another case against the SGR for his own land). The MP intended to use this court case to impeach the governor for not speaking up for the people and advancing his own political career but the impeachment attempt failed.[82]

In 2016, the court ruled against the MP, stating that the SGR's land acquisition followed the law. The MP recalled the impact of this court case to his career:

> I was re-elected in 2017, with even higher margins than 2013. But it [the court case] hurt in the way that I was greeted coldly in national government ... there was a lot of political backlashes. I was not a popular guy in government.

[80] Interview with KE-40, senator, Nairobi (30 July 2019).
[81] Interview with KE-29, KRC, Nairobi (31 July 2019).
[82] Interview with KE-46, Nairobi (22 August 2019).

> People in my constituency were made to accept the railway and the compensation. The subtext was 'don't pursue this issue'. In fact, the [then] cabinet secretary of transport, Kamau, said that if he had had a gun, he would have shot me. Now the court has ruled, I did what I could ... My constituency was a bit numb on this. People were disappointed but they had to move on. Looking back, I was newly elected in 2013, so I took a more private sector approach. I look back and see those politicians raising voices for their individual interests rather than community interests.[83]

In this case, land grievances of the MP himself and his constituents were politicized to challenge the SGR. 'The president's project' was stopped by this young MP, which enraged Kenyatta. The president directly intervened and set a timeline for problem resolution during his site visit, in parallel to the legal procedure. The atmosphere in the Kenyan government was also against opposition to the SGR. The Kenyan SGR is more precisely a 'Kenyatta project', and opposition to the project is considered as opposition to the president himself.

Presidential directives

Introduction of the SGR led to a major shift in Kenyan logistics. The dominant mode of transport changed from road to rail, and logistics resources shifted from Mombasa to Nairobi. These changes were strongly resisted by the logistics industry and Hassan Joho, governor of Mombasa. To smoothen the operation of the SGR and to guarantee freight volume, Kenyatta issued three directives. First, all goods destined for Nairobi or further inland would be cleared at Nairobi Inland Container Depot instead of at the port of Mombasa. Second, the promotion tariff would be extended. The SGR freight service commenced on 1 January 2018. To promote its business, the KRC introduced a promotional tariff for container traffic. This discounted tariff was designed to be valid for three months, then extended to six months. In May 2018, following a presidential directive, the promotional tariff was further extended to 31 December 2018.[84] Repeated extension of the discount tariff shows that the SGR experienced difficulties in terms of attracting optimal amounts of cargo. Third, in early 2019, after the expiration of the promotional tariff, the president issued a directive that all containers coming to Nairobi from Mombasa should

[83] Interview with KE-38, Nairobi (30 July 2019).

[84] Kenya Railway Corporation (n.d.). SGR freighters pay a flat fee of Sh35,000 for a 20-foot container and Sh40,000 for a 40-foot container from Mombasa to Nairobi ICD. From ICD to Mombasa, KRC has also been charging Sh25,000 to transport a 20-foot container and Sh30,000 for a 40-foot container (Otieno, 15 May 2018).

go via the SGR except the ones that are not movable on the SGR (such as hazardous cargos, Out of Gauge Load cargo, and gas cylinders), which could be transported by road. The Kenyan government also monitors and restricts the weight of cargo moving by road at below 28 tons, so that all heavy containers must be transported by SGR.

Kenyatta's directives on the SGR also increased costs for logistics businesses and the cost of living in Kenya. Railway freight is more expensive than truck. A logistics business insider gave me a quick calculation of rail and truck options for a 20-foot container to illustrate this point.[85]

- **Truck option:** $900

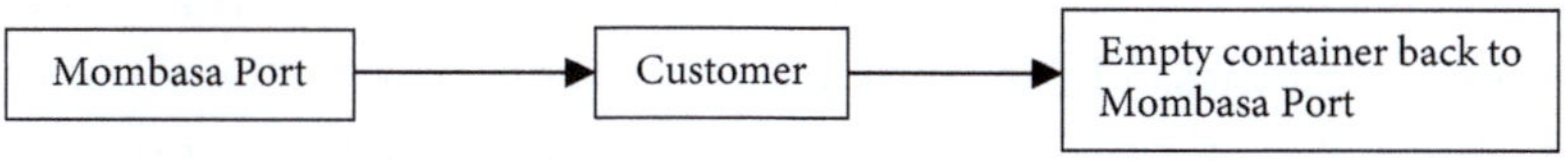

- **Rail option 1** – using SGR return: $1,230

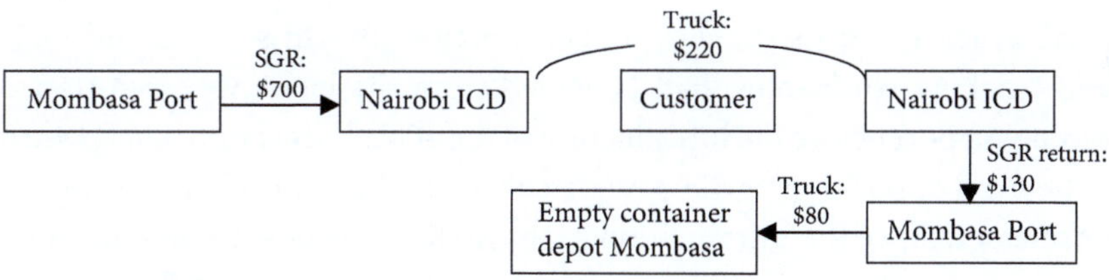

- **Rail option 2** – using truck return: $1,150

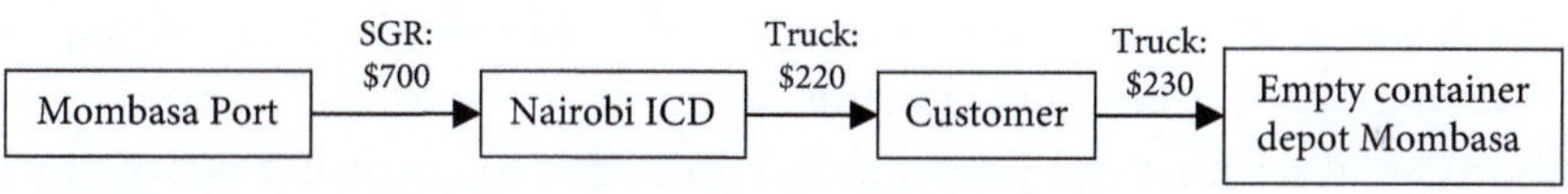

- **Rail option 3** – using truck return and through bill of landing (TBL): $1,200

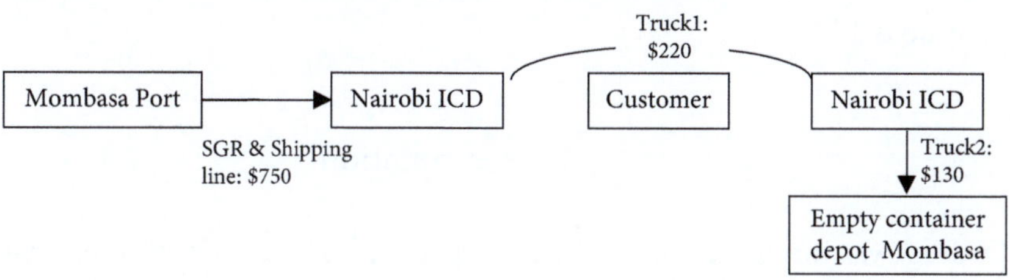

The increased logistics costs drove up the cost of doing business and ultimately increased the cost of living. The Kenyatta family, although active in the dairy and banking industries and the largest land-owner in Naivasha, has

[85] Graph based on interview with KE-56, East African Online Logistics, Nairobi (25 July 2019).

not entered the logistics sector, which is primarily controlled by actors in the coastal region, who are aligned with the opposition parties. The general public bears the brunt in the form of increased cost of living. A logistics business informant commented on this SGR directive:

> The railway makes no commercial sense. It is political. Railway is only efficient for distances over 900 kilometres. If the distance is less than that, it does not make sense. Now we are forced to use the train for a short distance. It is like if you want to go to five metres away and you are forced to drive a car.[86]

The introduction of the SGR and presidential directives shifted the landscape of the Kenyan logistics industry. Mombasa port, the gateway to East Africa, has been a source of legitimate but also illicit revenue for various networks.[87] Several national bureaucracies such as the Kenyan Port Authority (KPA) and the Kenya Revenue Service control incomes from the port and trade. However, local structures, in particular private container freight stations and logistics and trucking companies, had benefited from the lucrative cargo transiting Mombasa port before the introduction of the SGR. Local politicians (who tend to be from opposition parties) reportedly owned or controlled many of those businesses. Since the introduction of the SGR, those businesses have suffered tremendously.[88] The economy of Mombasa, the backbone of the power base of opposition politicians such as Governor Hassan Joho, has also suffered—with losses estimated at over US$300 million in 2018—as a consequence of the national government decision to promote the SGR.[89] Governor Joho has complained that the government's initiative to construct a large inland dry port and Special Economic Zone at Naivasha in the Rift Valley and to increase use of the Nairobi Inland Container Depot constitute attempts to 'kill Mombasa'.[90]

2.3.3 Co-optation

SGR-1 was instrumentalized by the president in his war with the coast over port revenues. Mombasa is an opposition stronghold and the town's population aligned itself with Raila Odinga's National Super Alliance rather than

[86] Interview with KE-56, East African Online Logistics, Nairobi (25 July 2019).
[87] Lamarque (2019).
[88] Mghenyi and Mudi (29 October 2018).
[89] Ibid.
[90] Lamarque (2019).

President Kenyatta's Jubilee Party in the election results of 8 August 2017.[91] At the heart of these disputes is the issue of port revenues. Many coastal residents are frustrated that considering its substantial contribution to the national budget, Mombasa port is managed by a national entity, the KPA, and its revenue is accumulated centrally in Nairobi and only redistributed to Mombasa on the basis of its standing as one of Kenya's forty-seven counties.[92] In mid-2014, Joho accentuated his demand by rallying other coastal and opposition leaders in a special session of the Mombasa County Assembly to pressure the national government to release control of the Port of Mombasa, on failure of which he would initiate a forcible takeover.[93] Publicly lobbying against the Kenyan government's control of the port and its ownership of land in Mombasa has been a consistent vote-winner for Governor Joho.[94]

Kenyatta effectively co-opted the most vocal opposition to the railway project, namely Joho. The governor of Mombasa was steadfast in opposition to the project from the very beginning. Initially over the land issue, he argued that resettlement and compensation should be viewed as a historical issue, and that 'ancestral interest' should be included in evaluations by the NLC and the KRC.[95] This dispute over who owns the land—the traditional local community without title deeds, or migrants from other parts of Kenya who were issued title deeds—was a long-standing political grievance along the coast. When SGR-1 cargo operation commenced, Joho vehemently opposed the railway project and especially the establishment of Naivasha Inland Container Depot. Arguing that it would kill transport businesses in Mombasa and destroy truck drivers' livelihoods,[96] he even threatened to take the state to court.[97] Joho's family business Autoport Freight Terminals Ltd was closed by Kenyatta to streamline operations at container freight stations.[98] However, Kenyatta successfully silenced this vocal opposition by offering shares in Nairobi and Naivasha Inland Container Depot to Joho's family business.[99] Later, news came that Autoport had reopened and was granted exclusive use of Nairobi Freight Terminal without any tendering process.[100] An interviewee from Mombasa wryly

[91] Ibid.
[92] Ibid., citing World Bank (2018).
[93] Chome (2015).
[94] Lamarque (2019).
[95] Wissenbach & Wang, (2017), citing the authors' interview with Hassan Joho, governor of Mombasa, Mombasa (July 2015).
[96] See news reports: Otieno (18 December 2018); Mghenyi and Mudi (29 October 2018).
[97] Atieno (1 February 2018).
[98] Kulundu (30 January 2016).
[99] *Daily Nation* (27 November 2018); Atieno (1 February 2018).
[100] Okoth (1 September 2019).

commented on the governor's behaviour: 'Now he is eating the goodies in silence. When you are busying eating, you don't talk.'[101]

Indirectly, the president changed the head of the KPA from an experienced technopole, from the coastal region to a proxy of Vice-President William Ruto (this is before conflict arose between Ruto and Kenyatta in 2019). In June 2018, the managing director of KPA, Catherine Mturi Wairi, was replaced by Daniel Manduku. Officially, Wairi's sacking was due to incompetence and failure to decongest the port's container depot.[102] But the more likely reason for sacking Wairi was to do with adjustments made to the port regulatory environment that put her at odds with other agencies. A KPA member of staff explained to me the tribal politics behind this recent replacement:

> The new managing director used to work in the Ministry of Construction, and had never been in the port industry. The previous one was from coastal—it is about tribal politics. In the KPA, we talk in Kiswahili with a Mombasa accent, they would notice if you were from upcountry. It is a war of upcountry against coast. In the KPA, coastal people think this organization is theirs.[103]

Although Kenyatta did not order the change of managing director himself, the KPA's managing director position is known to be close to the centre of Kenyan politics. The managing director answers to a six-person executive board made up of political appointees. Several interviewees commented to the effect that this board 'plays to the tune of the presidency', particularly in times of crisis.[104] We can confidently infer that Kenyatta was well aware of and approved this change of managing director, whether or not he directly ordered it to the KPA executive board.

2.3.4 Chinese agency during Standard Gauge Railway implementation

CRBC's intervention

Could the high effectiveness of SGR-1 be owed to the strong technical and management experience of the Chinese contractor, as predicted by the external

[101] Interview with KE-73, Haki Africa, Mombasa (12 July 2019).

[102] Oketch and Mwakio (14 July 2018). Change of managing director due to 'incompetence' happened two years ago, when the then managing director Gichini Ndua was removed under what was reported as a 'cloud of inefficiency'. See Lamarque (2019), citing Mutambo (8 August 2016).

[103] Interview KE-43, KPA, Nairobi (9 August 2019).

[104] Lamarque (2019), citing the author's interview with anon., political journalist, Nairobi (1 October 2017).

agency argument? CRBC had over thirty years' experience in Kenya before undertaking the SGR and were well connected to the Kenyan government. But the solutions to railway construction and operational obstacles were deeply embedded in Kenyan politics and CRBC had neither the intention of getting involved or the capacity to solve them.

The Chinese SOE had long overseas experience but limited railway expertise before the SGR. The company started exploring overseas markets as early as 1958[105] and the CRBC Kenya office was established in 1984. In the past three decades, the company has undertaken twenty-three road projects in Kenya, with a total mileage of 1,200 kilometres.[106] But CRBC and its parent company CCCC have only limited experience constructing railways. Domestically, CCCC participated in several highspeed railway constructions, including the Jinghu Highspeed Railway, linking Beijing and Shanghai. But it participated mostly as a subcontractor for a specific section or for roads and bridges connected to the rail. CCCC's branches specialize in road and port construction. When CRBC was awarded the SGR construction contract, both China Railway Construction Corporation and China Railway Group issued challenges to this decision to the Chinese economic councillor's office in Kenya, because they were the SOEs specialized in railway construction and operation.[107]

Evidence also shows that the solutions to railway construction and operational obstacles were usually deeply embedded within Kenyan politics, and that CRBC had neither the motivation nor the means of solving them. For this railway project, the KRC was the employer while CRBC was the contractor, so although CRBC is technically strong, it operated within the framework of the contract. During construction, local interests were reflected in the employer–contractor meetings, and CRBC accommodated KRC's requests to change designs (such as adding bridges or under-paths) to fit the local community and wildlife if the extra cost implications were reasonable. Moreover, controversies during construction were usually caused by Kenyan domestic politics and used by the opposition to criticize the Kenyatta administration. The Chinese contractor, CRBC, had no intention of meddling in ethnic conflicts, land disputes, or the politics of businesses in Kenya. Both the KRC and CRBC intended to limit the latter's role to the technical aspects of railway construction, while leaving the resolution of ethnic conflict and land disputes to the relevant bodies of Kenyan government.

[105] China Road and Bridge Corporation (2018).
[106] China Road and Bridge Corporation (2016).
[107] Interview KE-3, CRBC, Nairobi (9 July 2017).

Exogenous championship?

Could the success of the SGR Phase 1 have been a result of strong Chinese government commitment to the project, either via CRBC successfully leveraging strong Chinese governmental commitment to the project, or because Kenyatta's championship was exogenously inspired by Chinese government's diplomatic leverage? The Chinese government demonstrated strong commitment to the SGR by frequent official visits to the project. Yet inspection visits by Chinese officials aimed less at urging the CRBC to succeed in this project and more at claiming credit for its success. Moreover, I could not find evidence of the Chinese government diplomatically urging the Kenyan government to commit to the project.

The intervention of the Chinese government was minimal during SGR-1's construction. During interviews, officials from the Chinese economic councillor's office in Kenya repeatedly stressed that SGR-1 was a commercial project and that the role of their office was to support the company when needed but that ultimately the company was on the frontline.[108] In fact, SGR-1's success intensified the Chinese government's commitment to the project. From 2014 to 2019, Chinese political leadership visits to the SGR construction and operation are listed in Table 2.2. Chinese official inspections of the SGR started from the latter stage of construction and mostly concentrated after mid-2017, when construction was completed and operation had commenced; that is, when the SGR had demonstrated success. Inspections by Chinese officials were less to urge CRBC to succeed in the project and more to take credit for its success.

Although CRBC received political pressure and endorsement from the Chinese government regarding the SGR project, it was more likely because the SGR was enrolled in the large propaganda machine of the Belt and Road Initiative (BRI) and then the project became 'too big to fail'. The SGR was included in the list of Belt and Road flagship projects in 2016.[109] How the SGR became the flagship project was a mystery to my interviewees in CRBC's Kenyan office as well as at the Chinese economic councillor's office. When I asked what the process by which the SGR was included in the BRI was, the most common answer I received was that it was a 'natural' process and there isn't a clear boundary between Belt and Road and non-Belt and Road projects. The SGR fits the initiative's spirit of interconnectivity, and being both significant and successful, and finished at the time when the BRI was newly proposed, it naturally became a Belt and Road flagship project. The increasing political

[108] Interview KE-15, Nairobi (11 July 2017) and KE18, Nairobi (17 August 2019), anonymous officials from the Chinese economic councillor's office in Kenya.

[109] Interview KE-17, EXIM Bank Kenya, Nairobi (23 July 2019).

Table 2.2 Chinese political leadership visit to the Standard Gauge Railway

Leadership	Position	Date
Hao Peng	Chairman and Party Committee Secretary of the State-owned Assets Supervision and Administration Commission	5–6 August 2018
Wang Yang	Member of the Politburo Standing Committee, and Chairman of the Chinese People's Political Consultative Conference. China's No. 4 official	17 June 2018
Wang Jiarui	Special Envoy of President Xi Jinping and Vice Chairman of the Chinese People's Political Consultative Conference	30 November 2017
Zhong Shan (video inspection)	Minister of Commerce	22 September 2017
Wang Yong	Special Envoy of President Xi Jinping and State Councillor	31 May 2017
Wang Yi	Foreign Minister and State Councillor	10 August 2016
Zhang Dejiang	Chairman of the Standing Committee of the 12th National People's Congress (now retired)	27 May 2016

Source: CCCC website and interview.

significance of the SGR in China increased the pressure on CRBC. A Chinese manager from CRBC revealed: 'In the later stage, the influence of the project increased tremendously, we were also afraid of making mistakes.'[110] Another Chinese manager in the SGR operation team said: 'The SGR is the flagship project for the Belt and Road Initiative, even a tiny mistake would get high-level attention from China, thus we are under tremendous pressure.'[111] During inspections, Chinese officials often applauded CRBC for project quality, timely completion, and safe operation, and their expectations, including the expectations upon CRBC from the Chinese economic councillor's office in Kenya, were to guarantee safety and reduce negative news.[112]

Furthermore, EximBank did not use financial leverage to urge the Kenyan government to commit to the success of the SGR. An interviewee revealed that, when the Kenyan government wrote to EximBank regarding financial support for SGR-2B from Naivasha to Kisumu and 2C on to the Ugandan border, EximBank requested the Kenyan government to submit a feasibility

[110] Interview KE-8, CRBC, Nairobi (9 July 2019).
[111] Interview KE-9, CRBC, Nairobi (18 July 2019).
[112] Interview KE-9, CRBC, Nairobi (18 July 2019).

study, but the study was not submitted. Various other interviewees from Exim-Bank Kenya and Chinese economic councillor's office confirmed that it was the Kenyan government's decision not to pursue loans from China, rather than EximBank lacking willingness to issue the loans.

2.4 Standard Gauge Railway Phase 2A: diminished championship

After the 2017 election, Kenyatta's commitment to the SGR dwindled. No longer seeking re-election in 2022, Kenyatta's priority shifted to power consolidation. Politically, he shook hands in rapprochement with the veteran opposition leader, Raila Odinga, to address ethnic antagonism, corruption, and devolution.[113] Policy-wise, he proposed the Big Four Action Plan: enhancing manufacturing, food security, health coverage, and affordable housing. In the meantime, continuing the SGR to the Ugandan border as originally planned implied adding another US$3.68 billion to the already mounting debt to China.[114] Kenyatta returned from Beijing in April 2019 without securing new SGR financing; informants from EximBank shared that it was Kenya's decision not to take out new loans given existing debt levels and other policy priorities.[115]

SGR-1 and SGR-2A were managed and constructed by the same Kenyan bureaucracies and Chinese contractors, but Kenyatta's diminished commitment to the SGR-2A resulted in a ten-month delay to construction. The delay was due to prolonged land acquisition in Rongai, Ngong areas, and Nairobi National Park. As a CRBC interviewee revealed:

> Originally [SGR-2A was] expected to be completed in 2018, the completion time is now rescheduled to October 2019. This was mainly because there is a wealthy area outside Nairobi National Park, the land acquisition work was difficult. Coupled with the anti-corruption campaign in Kenya, the account of the National Land Commission [used for land compensation] was frozen by the Supreme Court, so the compensation funds were not in place.[116]

[113] BBC (2 December 2019).
[114] Olingo (27 April 2019).
[115] Interview KE-17, EximBank Kenya office, Nairobi (23 July 2019).
[116] Interview KE-8, CRBC, Nairobi (9 July 2019).

For Phase 2A, Kenyatta set a completion date of December 2018. 'The president wanted to launch Phase 2A at a Kenyan festival in December',[117] according to a CRBC informant. But the project was delayed until October 2019. Apart from the launch and inauguration ceremonies of SGR-2A, the president only visited the construction site once, at the Nairobi National Park, and the rest of the quarterly working meetings were held at State House. In contrast to Phase 1, land acquisition for SGR-2A was left up to the coordination of the KRC, the NLC, and the Ministry of Transport, without frequent on-site interventions from the president. Lacking a political champion, similar obstacles in SGR-2A were not solved as effectively as during SGR-1. When Kenyatta's attention to the project diminished, SGR-2A was delayed. If the bureaucratic capacity explanation were true, SGR-2A should not have experienced any delays because the relevant Kenyan bureaucracies and the Chinese contractor would have accumulated experience during Phase 1 and should have been more proficient in Phase 2A.

Moreover, the eight counties that the Phase 1 track passes through are opposition counties while most of the counties Phase 2A crosses support Jubilee. The 2013 presidential election results show that five out of eight counties are strong supporters of Odinga: Mombasa, Kilifi, Kwale, Taita-Taveta, and Makueni; Kajiado and Nairobi are more evenly divided between support for Kenyatta and Odinga; Machakos is the only county that strongly supported Kenyatta over Odinga (Table 2.3). In the 2013 governor election, six out of eight governors elected are Orange Democratic Movement (ODM), while Makueni county, although the governor is Muungano Party, had 99.73 per cent support for Odinga in the presidential election (Table 2.4).

SGR-2A passed through five counties. Kiambu and Nakuru are strong supporters of Kenyatta (Table 2.3). Nairobi and Kajiado was difficult for the SGR implementation before 2017 because the governor was from ODM. But the 2017 gubernatorial elections put two governors from Jubilee Alliance in Nairobi and Kajiado, so when the SGR-2A commenced construction, disagreement and grievance politicization from local administration of these two counties were not strong. Narok was the only county that was not held by Jubilee (Table 2.4).

SGR Phase 1 faced a higher level of grievance politicization and political obstacles than Phase 2A. It would be assumed that the implementation of Phase 2A should be less challenging than Phase 1, especially with regard to land

[117] Interview KE-6, CRBC, Nairobi (29 July 2019).

Table 2.3 SGR-1 and 2A passing county votes in the 2013 presidential election[118]

	County	Kenyatta	Odinga
SGR-1	Mombasa	23.79%	69.77%
	Kilifi	10.72%	83.74%
	Kwale	14.04%	80.74%
	Taita-Taveta	13.18%	81.56%
	Makueni	5.02%	90.73%
	Kajiado	52.36%	44.44%
	Machakos	55.41%	29.61%
	Nairobi	46.75%	49.00%
SGR-2A	Nairobi	46.75%	49.00%
	Kajiado	52.36%	44.44%
	Kiambu	90.12%	7.89%
	Nakuru	80.19%	17.14%
	Narok	46.38%	50.28%

Source: Independent Electoral and Boundaries Commission.

acquisition, the most frequently politicized issue. However, SGR-2A failed to meet the timeline set by the president and project completion was delayed until October 2019.

2.5 Discussion: societal capture versus state autonomy in democracy

The success of SGR-1 raises the question of societal capture and state autonomy in democracy: did Kenyatta use the SGR to fuel his patronage machines? And why, facing upcoming elections, did Kenyatta not use the SGR to favour his constituents, undermining project efficiency but boosting electoral fortunes? Precisely due to the intertwined nature of African democracy and the deeply rooted patron–client network that makes the state projects fallen prey to societal capture, scholars generally argue that centralized, long-term rent management provides a preferable incentive for development in Africa. Was the SGR an exceptional case where President Kenyatta preserved this state project from societal capture?

[118] 2017 election results are not included because Kenya went through two presidential elections: the result of the first election was annulled and before the second election Odinga withdrew and suggested that ODM supporters should boycott voting. Thus the 2017 election result shows predominant support for Kenyatta.

Table 2.4 SGR-1 and 2A passing county results in the 2013 and 2017 gubernatorial elections

	County	2013 Governor	2013 Party	2017 Governor	2017 Party
SGR-1	Mombasa	Hassan Ali Joho	Orange Democratic Movement	Hassan Ali Joho	Orange Democratic Movement
	Kilifi	Amason Jeffa Kingi	Orange Democratic Movement	Amason Jeffa Kingi	Orange Democratic Movement
	Kwale	Salim Mvurya Ngala	Orange Democratic Movement	Salim Mvurya Ngala	Orange Democratic Movement
	Taita-Taveta	John Mtuta Mruttu	Orange Democratic Movement	Joseph Jama Ole Lenku	Jubilee Alliance
	Makueni	Kivutha Kibwana	Muungano Party	Kivutha Kibwana	Muungano Party
	Kajiado	David K. Nkedianye	Orange Democratic Movement	Joseph Jama Ole Lenku	Jubilee Alliance
	Machakos	Alfred Nganga Mutua	Wiper Democratic Movement- Kenya	Alfred Nganga Mutua	Wiper Democratic Movement- Kenya
	Nairobi	Evans O. Kidero	Orange Democratic Movement	Mike Sonko	Jubilee Alliance
SGR-2A	Nairobi	Evans O. Kidero	Orange Democratic Movement	Mike Sonko	Jubilee Alliance
	Kajiado	David K. Nkedianye (Odm)	Orange Democratic Movement	Joseph Jama Ole Lenku	Jubilee Alliance
	Kiambu	William Kabogo Gitau	The National Alliance	Ferdinard Ndungu Waititu	Jubilee Alliance
	Nakuru	Kinuthia Mbugua	The National Alliance	Lee Kinyanjui	Jubilee Alliance
	Narok	Samuel Kuntai Tunai	United Republican Party	Samuel Kuntai Tunai	United Republican Party

Source: Independent Electoral and Boundaries Commission.

What makes SGR-1 exceptional was its route. SGR-1 passes through mostly opposition counties, and the president had no reservation to prioritize project implementation at the expense of the opposition and their constituents. The fact that his intervention in land acquisition might touch upon the interests of local politicians and residents did not bother the president as this was not his constituent in the first place. As we saw in section 2.3, local MPs and governors actively politicized SGR-related grievances for their votes and fortunes; the politicization only makes Kenyatta instrumentalizing the SGR-1 a way to weaken these opposition leaders. Similarly, Kenyatta's lack of intervention in SGR-2A is partly due to the fact that Phase 2A passes through mostly Jubilee supporters, and by intervening in the land acquisition issues, Kenyatta might damage some of his constituents' interests. The delay in SGR-2A was majorly caused by prolonged land acquisition in Rongai and Nairobi National Park. President Kenyatta visited the National Park to reiterate his determination to construct the SGR, knowing very well that the support of the National Park was local and Western civil society organizations. He wisely refrained from intervening in the land acquisition in Rongai, a residential area of the rich near Nairobi, not to risk standing at the frontline of trotting across the lands of the Nairobi rich.

The SGR was not fortunate enough to escape societal pressure in Kenya. Corruption is an area where mega-infrastructure projects are subject to societal pressure. Similar to the land acquisition, corruption is also a highly politicized issue during SGR implementation. Notably in 2018, eighteen officials related to the SGR were facing corruption charges, and two of them were managing directors of the KRC and NLC. On 20 June 2020, Kenya's Court of Appeal ruled that the tendering process of the SGR was illegal. Undoubtedly this expensive project was subject to multiple private gains, a fate shared by many other projects in Kenya. As a Kenyan journalist wittily commented: 'In Kenya, you know the price but not the value of a project.'[119] The controversy on SGR-related corruption started as early as 2014, prior to the SGR-1 construction, and Uhuru Kenyatta was well aware of the project's inflated price but chose to continue the project and quench opposition's challenges. The majority of the personal enrichment through the SGR went into the pockets of the incumbent bureaucrats. By keeping his eyes on speedy completion while ignoring corruption, Kenyatta allowed the SGR money to fuel his patronage machine inside the bureaucracy.

Another channel where the SGR fuelled Kenyatta's patronage network was through local procurement of materials and services. Transporting imported

[119] Interview with KE-77 (August 2016).

and locally manufactured materials to the SGR construction sites was a major source of CRBC's local procurement from 2014 to 2017. But as the majority of Kenyan logistics market share was taken by politically connected oligarchs, small, non-politically connected businesses access to the CRBC was very limited. A Kenyan logistics business owner explained:

> We couldn't go directly to CRBC because they had already granted bigger companies their logistics contracts, such as Landmark Logistics, which belongs to [vice-president] Ruto, and Mombasa Inland Container Terminal, which belongs to (former president) Moi's son ... Plus language barrier with the Chinese: we tried to contact CRBC, but no response. We tried to contact Kenya Railway, they said services had found contractors.[120]

In 2014, when the SGR financial framework was signed, President Kenyatta announced the project would have '40 per cent local input'. In the manufacturing industry, trade unions like Kenya Association of Manufacturers (KAM) and grassroots initiatives by manufacturers like Regional Mega Project Coordinating Council (RMPCC) lobbied for higher SGR local input and achieved progress, especially in the cement industry. Yet there was not much genuine support from Kenyatta on securing this 40 per cent due to his eagerness to finish the construction before the 2017 elections.[121]

In sum, the Kenyan railway demonstrated mixed evidence on this state project's autonomy from societal pressure. The president protected the project from falling prey to society pressure only when doing so did not risk harming interests of his constituents. Kenyatta's priority for the SGR-1 was to complete the project before the 2017 elections so that the 'Madaraka Express' can be used as his campaign capital. As many other projects in Kenya, the SGR was enmeshed in the spiralling web of corruption and benefited local corporations that were politically connected. Through these channels, Kenyatta was able to fuel his patronage machines with the SGR. On land acquisition, the very fact that the SGR-1 passes through mostly opposition counties dispelled Kenyatta's concern that the intervention in politicized land issues might damage the interests of his constituencies, as was the case in Phase 2A. As a result, Kenyatta actively intervened in the land acquisition during the SGR-1 and refrained from land conflicts during SGR-2A.

[120] Interview with KE-56, East African Online Logistics, Nairobi (25 July 2019). Also cited in Wang and Wissenbach (2019).

[121] For a more detailed analysis of the SGR's local sourcing, refer to Wang and Wissenbach (2019).

2.6 Conclusion

The Kenyan railway case shows that political championship was crucial to the project to achieving the high effectiveness of the SGR Phase 1, and that the absence of Kenyatta's championship resulted in delays in Phase 2A. President Kenyatta undertook a personalistic approach to SGR implementation, this personalism being a legacy inherited from his father, Jomo Kenyatta, and Daniel arap Moi, which persists in Kenya's multiparty politics today. Initially, the SGR was a private sector initiative, and Kenyatta took ownership of the project once he succeeded to the presidency in 2013. His championship of the SGR was election-inspired. During the 2013 electoral campaign, Kenyatta made it a key campaign promise to develop a modern rail network in exchange for the electoral sponsorship of Jimmy Wanjigi, the initiator of the SGR. Kenyatta's commitment to the SGR also stemmed from his intention to use the Chinese-sponsored SGR in retaliation to Western denunciation prior to and during the 2013 election. And in the 2017 elections, Kenyatta instrumentalized the SGR as his campaign capital. Kenyatta showed his commitment to the SGR-1 not only by frequently promoting and defending the project in his public discourse but also by his frequent visits to the project sites.

Kenyatta is a leader of high authority. People feared Kenyatta. And the president was also able to push for the project completion by intervening in the SGR construction and operation and setting timelines for completion and problem resolution; establishing escalation mechanisms whereby obstacles to construction could be channelled directly to the president's attention; issuing presidential directives to force cargo usage of the SGR; co-opting the opposition leader; and intervening in an ongoing court case. Kenyatta's championship was largely reduced during SGR Phase 2A, and delays in project construction arose even though Phase 2A passes through more favourable socio-political landscape than Phase 1.

The bureaucratic capacity argument and the external agency argument cannot explain the success of the SGR Phase 1 and construction delay during Phase 2A. Although the KRC's position in the Kenyan bureaucratic system considerably increased through the SGR project, at the initiation and early construction stages, the KRC was a weak agency in Kenyan government. The solution of cross-ministerial problems usually involved higher leadership involvement and could not be addressed by the KRC alone. Moreover, comparing SGR Phase 1 and Phase 2A, land acquisition for SGR-2A was left to the coordination of the KRC, NLC, and Ministry of Transport, without direct intervention from Kenyatta as in Phase 1. Despite the KRC's increased importance in the Kenyan bureaucratic system and strengthened capacity and experience in managing SGR construction, similar obstacles confronting SGR-2A were not solved as effectively. The intervention of the Chinese government, including the economic councillor's office and EximBank, was minimal during SGR construction, but the Chinese government's commitment to the SGR increased with the success of the SGR. The success of the SGR was used by the Chinese government primarily as a demonstration of the success of the BRI.

Technical difficulty, societal pressure, and financial sustainability arguments fall short of explaining the relative effectiveness of SGR-1. A CRBC manager revealed that SGR-2A indeed passes through uneven terrain and involves tunnel construction, but this was not the main reason of delay. The delay was mainly caused by difficulties in land acquisition in the residential area right outside of Nairobi.[122] Regarding popular agency, I have shown that Uhuru Kenyatta's championship of SGR-1 was election-inspired, playing the China card to retaliate against the West, and instrumentalizing the project as his campaign capital. Social and political opposition against the SGR came later than Kenyatta's championship and served to reinforce presidential commitment. Concerns about the massive loans SGR brought to Kenya (representing 12 per cent of Kenya's public external debt in 2021[123]) and the country's debt sustainability started gaining momentum since 2018 and became even more acute from May 2020, when the risk rating of debt distress was raised from moderate to high.[124] This concern has ultimately led to Kenyan government's decision of not pursuing another US$3.6 billion EximBank loans for SGR-2B and 2C but renovating the metre-gauge railway instead, at an estimated cost of US$400 million.[125] This concerns over SGR financial sustainability, however, cannot explain the delay in Phase 2A. In addition to the fact discussed earlier that Phase 2A's delay was mainly due to land acquisition, 85 per cent of the loans for Phase 1 and 2A were from EximBank, and the money was paid directly from EximBank to CRBC's bank account in Beijing, without passing through Kenyan government. Delay of disbursement in this case was unlikely.

[122] Interview with KE-7, CRBC-Nairobi, Nairobi (11 July 2017).
[123] Bräutigam et al. (2022).
[124] IDA and IMF (2020).
[125] Anyanzwa (19 June 2019).

3

Revolutionary democracy, developmental state, and capitalism

> The capital Addis Ababa needs to be connected to the port, because all of our throats will be strangled if [our connection to] the port is strangled. Thus, let us first connect to the port so that we can open our throat.
>
> This is an historic moment. [The Addis Ababa–Djibouti railway] will significantly expand development and enhance our competitiveness in international markets.
>
> Hailemariam Desalegn, former Ethiopian prime minister[1]

On 16 October 2016, Prime Minister Hailemariam Desalegn launched the Addis Ababa–Djibouti railway (ADR) in the capital city of Ethiopia. This railway project was initiated by Hailemariam's predecessor, Meles Zenawi, as the infrastructural foundation for the landlocked country's industrialization. The railway stretches 780 kilometres, connecting the capital city of Addis Ababa and the port of Djibouti, with fifteen major stations in between. The project was financed by Export-Import Bank of China (EximBank) commercial loans and contracted to China Railway Engineering Corporation 2nd Bureau (CREC) and China Civil Engineering Construction Corporation (CCECC) for construction and operation. The initiation of the ADR went smoothly, but soon the project was challenged by growing obstacles to land acquisition during construction. There was also a fourteen-month delay between the completion of construction and operation due to prolonged negotiations between Ethiopia and Djibouti regarding passengers' border-crossing and revenue split, as well as stable electricity and water supply. The ADR finally commenced operation in January 2018, running one passenger and four freight trains daily, operating at a loss.[2] As the loan repayment was due,

[1] Aglionby (16 January 2017).
[2] Figures obtained during fieldwork in May 2019.

The Railpolitik. Yuan Wang, Oxford University Press. © Yuan Wang (2023). DOI: 10.1093/oso/9780198873037.003.0004

the new prime minister Abiy Ahmed visited China and received an extension of the loan.

Why did the ADR go smoothly during initiation and preparation for construction but increasingly suffered from obstacles in the construction and operation stages? The Ethiopian state provides a more enabling environment for mega-infrastructure development compared to Kenya as Ethiopia was run by a dominant party with a centralized developmental agenda, a focus on infrastructure development, and limited tolerance for dissidents. Still, why did the ADR demonstrate less effectiveness than its Kenyan counterpart?

In this chapter, I address these questions by tracing the process of the rise and fall of the political championship for the ADR project. I divide the ADR project into three phases: (1) the ADR-Meles (initiation) phase, (2) the ADR-Hailemariam prior to the 2016 (construction) phase, and (3) the ADR-Hailemariam post-2016 and Abiy Ahmed phase. First, I explain the endogenous championship: after its near-defeat in the 2005 election, the Ethiopian People's Revolutionary Democratic Front (EPRDF) desperately needed to regain its legitimacy. Meles sought to build a 'developmental state'. Visible and developmental mega-infrastructure projects such as the ADR demonstrated the party's legitimacy to rule. Meles initiated and championed the ADR, making his time the 'golden era of railway development'. I also illustrate that exogenous leverage from bureaucratic and Chinese actors did not constitute the source of Meles' championship. During 2012–16, under Hailemariam, the ADR was still the government's priority, but he lacked the charisma and political acuity to exercise effective control within the ruling EPRDF as Meles did, and the development of the ADR gradually slowed down. Starting from late 2015, with growing pressure from the political crisis and deteriorating stability of the country, the EPRDF gradually shifted its priorities towards maintaining security. The new prime minister Abiy Ahmed's dazzling political reform distanced himself from his predecessors' doctrines of developmental state, and he eventually declared a civil war. The ADR was no longer among these priorities. Even the extraordinary efforts by Chinese contractors and the Chinese government were not enough to save the railway from operational delay and struggles. Projects like the railway lost the political championship but industrial parks gained the leader's commitment. I briefly investigate the relative success of the Hawassa Industrial Park under the championship of Arkebe Oqubay in 2015–16. This industrial park promised 20,000 employment positions and aligned well with the survival incentive of the government to maintain stability shortly prior to and during the political crisis.

3.1 From revolutionary democracy to developmental state

Since claiming power by overthrowing the military Derg regime in 1991, the EPRDF has gradually introduced what it termed 'revolutionary democracy'. Together with the international community's influence, this ideology sought to liberalize the political space and introduced multiparty elections as a key source of legitimacy. The near-loss of the 2005 elections was a wake-up call for the EPRDF. The party responded with an increasing political stranglehold and introduced what it called the 'developmental state', transforming the source of legitimacy from political participation to sustain economic growth. In this section, I review the EPRDF's base of legitimacy transition from 'revolutionary democracy' to 'developmental state', where the ADR served as a visible showcase and infrastructural foundation for developmentalism. I also review how Meles Zenawi rose from the Tigray People's Liberation Front's (TPLF's) internal power rift in 2001 to absolute political supremacy. Meles was the architect of the Ethiopian developmental state and the initiator of the ADR.

3.1.1 Revolutionary democracy

The dominant party of Ethiopia, the EPRDF, came to power in 1991 after defeating the military regime led by Mengistu Haile Mariam. The EPRDF had been led by the TPLF until 2018 when Abiy Ahmed Ali claimed the premiership. The TPLF grew out of the Ethiopian Student Movement in Addis Ababa University and Tigray University Student Association in the 1960s and 1970s, and later became a group of guerrilla fighters against the Derg regime in the northern region of Tigray. The TPLF followed the Marxist-Leninist ideology and exercised coherent leadership within the Tigray region. While fighting against the Derg, the TPLF was joined by three other regional parties: Amhara Democratic Party, Oromo Democratic Party, and Southern Ethiopian People's Democratic Movement (SEPDM), and formulated the EPRDF. In 1991, the EPRDF defeated the Derg and claimed power in Addis Ababa. In addition to the four member parties, the EPRDF has affiliated parties in five other regions. Formally, these regional parties are independent of the EPRDF but should not be perceived as opposition parties.[3] These parties are Afar People's Democratic Organization, the Somali People's Democratic Front,

[3] Aalen (2002, p. 83).

the Harari National League, the Gambella People's Democratic Front, and the Benishangul-Gumuz People's Democratic Unity Front. The EPRDF was instrumental in creating these regional parties and works closely with them (Figure 3.1).

After their rise to power in 1991, the EPRDF ideologists maintained revolutionary democracy as their core doctrine. This revolutionary democracy was a way to frame the change of power in an ideological way and therefore add legitimacy to the EPRDF's rule.[4] This was also a way to create a clear break with the Derg regime's legacies and demarcate a new role for itself.[5] The programmes of the revolutionary democracy ideology include the introduction of ethno-based federalism, liberalization of the economy, and a multiparty system with regular elections.[6] These liberalization programmes satisfied the interests of the international donor community, and thus secured Ethiopia's position as an important ally of the West in the fragile Horn of Africa. Yet, the democratization programmes followed the Marxist-Leninist organization and were to be led by an enlightened elite, the vanguard party of the EPRDF. Observers of Ethiopian politics pointed out this apparent contradiction in this ideology and concluded that the revolutionary democracy had appropriated the liberal tools of elections to ensure the legitimate survival of the EPRDF leadership.[7] As Aalen and Tronvoll put it, 'Ethiopia is not an incomplete democracy; it is

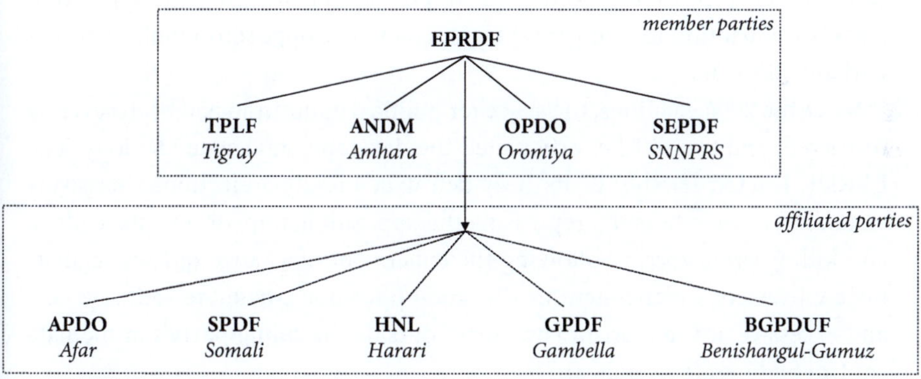

Figure 3.1 Ethiopian People's Revolutionary Democratic Front's composition and its affiliated parties.

[4] Aalen (2020).
[5] Ibid.
[6] Ibid.
[7] Bach (2011).

rather an authoritarian state draped in democratic window-dressing in which manipulated multi-party elections are [a] means to sustain power.'[8]

Introducing ethnic federalism was 'the best possible model' for a country that had recently survived the ravages of the relentless civil war and almost two decades of rule by a regime characterized by centralist government suppression of ethno-regional interests.[9] This was a model dictated partly by the necessity of ruling over a large and ethnically diverse country by an ethno-regional minority from Tigray (only 7 per cent of the population) and partly by an ideological programme aimed at reversing ethnic hierarchies and ousting the perceived Amharic elites in place under the Derg's rule.[10] Yet in practice, the regional states are dependent on the federal government because the tax bases assigned to the regional governments are weak, while the most lucrative sources, particularly foreign trade taxes, are given to the central government.[11]

Although researchers have questioned the genuineness of this liberalization under the vanguard party EPRDF, Ethiopia's political space for the opposition opened incrementally before the 2005 elections. During the May 2005 election campaign, the EPRDF permitted its first and only real democratic opening.[12] The party felt strong enough to accept 'free and fair' competition, mainly to improve its image and gain broader foreign support.[13] A special issue by the *Ethiopian Herald* was titled 'May 28, 2005: Historic crown of democracy in Ethiopia'. This led to unprecedented support for a pan-Ethiopian opposition party, the Coalition for Unity and Democracy. The opposition took a third of Parliament's seats.

Since the 2005 elections, the space for political opposition had been severely restricted, and the EPRDF articulated the developmental state ideology. The EPRDF reacted harshly to its near-defeat in the 2005 elections, massively extending its membership, repressing the opposition, imprisoning its leaders, and killing protestors.[14] Following the enactment of a range of laws regulating civil society, independent media, and opposition parties, as well as a new and excessive anti-terrorism law, voices outside the ruling party's immediate control had hardly been heard.[15]

[8] Aalen and Tronvoll (2009).
[9] Abbink (2011, p. 599).
[10] Ibid., p. 597.
[11] Aalen (2002, p. 75).
[12] Lefort (2007).
[13] Lefort (2007).
[14] Markakis (2011, ch. 11).
[15] Tronvoll and Hagmann (2012).

3.1.2 Developmental state

The 2005 electoral shock stimulated the EPRDF government to seek a new basis for legitimacy as the previous discourse of political legitimacy based on 'democratization' sank into further discredit.[16] The previous emphasis on democratic legitimacy was gradually replaced by a focus on national economic delivery or performance legitimacy.[17] In 2008, Meles expressed the new economic priority, 'The effort to promote democratization in Africa without the transformation of political economy from one pervasive and rent-seeking to one value creation has simply provided democratic to pre-reform zero sum politics all over the continent. It hasn't so far succeeded in establishing stable democracy.'[18] Hereafter, democracy became a secondary objective, even though it was presented as a tool to reach development, rather than as a goal in itself. As stated in the EPRDF's 2006 Congress Report, 'Democracy is a key instrument in promoting the struggle of putting in place the developmental political economy, and removing the rent collection political economy.'[19]

The single-minded pursuit of economic growth became the source of legitimacy of the EPRDF regime.[20] As Meles articulated in 2008, 'I am convinced that we will cease to exist as a nation unless we grow fast and share our growth.'[21] The EPRDF government favoured a strategy of industrial transformation through state investment in physical infrastructure, with an emphasis on improving agricultural productivity and attracting foreign investment in light manufactures.[22] Since the adoption of the Growth and Transformation Plan I (GTP-I) in 2010, infrastructure served as the foundation of the government's ambitious industrialization strategy. The GTP sought to maintain an 11 per cent growth rate per annum for Ethiopia to become a middle-income country by 2025. Manufacture should be the primary driver of growth, the realization of which depended on heavy state investment in infrastructure. Investment projects in major hydroelectric dams, such as Gibe III and the Great Renaissance Dam, the Addis Ababa Light Rail Transit, the railway system, and express roads were meant to foster the country's transformation

[16] LeFort (2015).
[17] Aalen (2020).
[18] Meles (2006), cited in Bach (2011).
[19] EPRDF (2006, p. 66), cited in Bach (2011).
[20] Meles (2012, p. 169).
[21] De Waal's discussion with Meles on 17 October 2008, cited in de Waal (2013).
[22] Weis (2015).

under the GTP. These highly visible projects were also tools for EPRDF's development discourse.[23] As the party fervently promoted the developmental state ideologies throughout the country, posters were put up with images of the ADR and other mega-infrastructure projects as symbols of modernity and better life.[24] In the total planned outlay of US$11.4 billion to be invested under GTP-I, 66 per cent was allocated for infrastructure development.[25] This also marked the highest rate of infrastructure expenditure in Africa. EPRDF's economic strategy proved to be successful. Ethiopia had been frequently referred to as Africa's economic miracle, maintaining close to double-digit growth rate since 2004 before the political turmoil in 2018. It was the fastest-growing non-resource endowed economy in Africa.

3.1.3 Meles' personalistic rule

Over the years, as party and state leader, Meles gradually manoeuvred among different factions of the EPRDF to strengthen his power base and rose to absolute political supremacy from the internal rift of the TPLF in 2001. Meles Zenawi became the leader of the TPLF in 1989, was the interim president of Ethiopia from 1991 to 1995, and served as prime minister for twelve years until his unexpected death in 2012. The Eritrea–Ethiopia war in 1998–2000 saw a dispute over military strategy that triggered the disintegration of TPLF leadership that nearly meant the removal of Meles. The relations between the two factions within the TPLF politburo deteriorated as the war proceeded. Meles was criticized for being too soft on Eritrea and was not trusted. As Milkias (2003) noted, 'As time passed, Meles could not even depend on support from the Tigray regional state, because delegates to the TPLF congress are normally picked by conferences held in its four zones—and most of his political opponents in the politburo and central committee spend far more time there, in close contact with the party's rank and file members, than he does.'[26] After the war, ideological disagreement emerged between the two groups on economic direction, Western influence, and party performance. These diverse areas of disagreement reflected the breakdown of trust among a previously coherent group of TPLF leaders.[27]

[23] Terrefe (2018).
[24] Ibid.
[25] Ministry of Finance and Economic Development (2010).
[26] Milkias (2003).
[27] Weis (2015).

Meles reacted by mobilizing the state apparatus to marginalize and expel his dissidents from the party. Several senior party officials were subsequently brought to court on allegations of corruption. These empty government positions were later filled with Meles' loyalists in the TPLF. Thereafter, frequent reshuffles in the cabinet and party organization allowed power concentration in Meles' hands. Therefore, the collegiate form of decision-making that characterized the EPRDF's first ten years in power was replaced with a more personalized style of leadership and Meles' ascension to a position of uncontested authority. Meles also emancipated himself from the collective leadership and party organization and was 'increasingly running [the] party and government as a one-man show'.[28] This also posed a main weakness of Meles' regime, leadership isolation, ruling as a secluded medieval emperor who communicated with their subjects through a curtain.[29] This made it impossible for his successor to reproduce the same conditions and take full control of the power apparatus.

After the electoral shock in 2005, the EPRDF expanded the party apparatus and became increasingly intolerant of dissidents. With 300,000 members before 2005, the EPRDF soon developed into a mass party with 5 million members. As numbers grew, the party's infrastructure withered.[30] A direct result of EPRDF's expansion was the party apparatus' growing detachment from the top of the power structure, the Prime Minister's Office.[31] Power concentration strengthened. Meles' office became the engine room of leadership.[32] According to de Waal (2015):

> [In the Prime Minister's Office,] Meles' own theoretical papers were debated with a close circle, including foreign intellectuals, seeking frank critique. Members of the EPRDF leadership attended, but largely as listeners. Once a conclusion was reached, it was promulgated as doctrine for the rest.[33]

There was also a blurred boundary between the party and the government, which made Ethiopian bureaucrats at all levels highly politicized.[34] Their performance as agents of the EPRDF overshadowed their role as civil servants.

[28] De Waal (2015, p. 249).
[29] Clapham (2009).
[30] De Waal (2015).
[31] Lefort (2013).
[32] De Waal (2015).
[33] De Waal (2015, p. 254).
[34] Aalen (2014).

3.2 Initiation: political championship under Meles

Two historical events fuelled the initiation of the ADR: Eritrea's separation from Ethiopia and the EPRDF's near-loss in the 2005 election. Ethiopia's war with Eritrea and the latter's separation resulted in Ethiopia losing its only connection to the sea. Developing a transport corridor connecting the landlocked country and the port of Djibouti was, therefore, a necessary component of Ethiopia's industrialization agenda. After the 2005 electoral shock, the EPRDF's basis for legitimacy changed to the single-minded pursuit of economic growth. The EPRDF government favoured a strategy of industrial transformation through state investment in physical infrastructure, and projects such as the ADR were instrumentalized to showcase the party's developmental achievement.

3.2.1 Meles' championship

The ADR, connecting the capital city to the port of Djibouti, was conceived as creating an economic and logistical channel, a crucial step for integrating the country into the global economy as a producer of export goods. Since Eritrea's separation in 1993, Ethiopia became a landlocked country with a growing reliance on the port of Djibouti. Ninety per cent of Ethiopia's imports arrive from the Djibouti port. Before the ADR, containers were transported by trucks, which took two and a half to three days and was costly. High logistics costs had been a bottleneck for Ethiopia's industrialization, making export products uncompetitive in the global market. There was a dilapidated French-constructed railway line connecting Addis Ababa to the port of Djibouti that was only used for passenger service along limited routes. The ADR was built to lay the foundation of industrialization, increase exports, and reduce fuel import and consumption as the ADR was electrified. The railway was thus a priority project in the GTP-I, together with the Great Renaissance Dam. To promote a green economy and reduce fuel consumption, which requires import with foreign currency, the ADR was designed to be an electrified railway. The rationale was that once the GERD was completed, the dam could generate enough electricity for the stable operation of the ADR.

Meles Zenawi initiated the ADR and closely managed it from the Prime Minister's Office. A former senior employee of the Ministry of Transport (MOT) referred to the ADR as 'Meles started this. This is a political railway line'. The initiation of the ADR did not receive unanimous support from the Ethiopian government, yet Meles championed the project and dissuaded dissidents. During a macroeconomic team meeting, a monthly meeting initiated and chaired by Meles to follow up on mega projects, the chief executive officer (CEO) of Ethiopian Road Authority objected, 'We don't need a railway because the volume of commodities for logistics is low, and trucks can do the work. It is better to upgrade roads.' Meles responded, 'We are not thinking railway for one or two years. We are thinking of 10 to 20 years and linking the global [market]. If we don't prepare the infrastructure before economic development, then we might get trapped.'[35]

In 2007, the Prime Minister's Office commissioned the establishment of the Ethiopian Railway Corporation (ERC) with a mandate to develop and manage Ethiopia's railway projects. The ERC's first chief executive, Getachew Betru, was handpicked by Meles and directly reported to and receive orders from the prime minister.[36] The ERC is independent from existing railway-related establishments, such as the MOT and Chemins de Fer Ethio-Djibouti (CFE), which manages the colonial railway. Most of the ERC's initial employees were selected from the Ethiopian Road Authority, rather than the CFE, even though CFE staff have railway management experience. At its establishment in 2007, the ERC was equipped with only a handful of people initially. Still, this nascent office was at the centre of the ADR: it was in charge of following up commercial loan applications with the China EximBank, selecting, and managing two Chinese contractors.[37]

Decision-making regarding the ADR bypassed the MOT, and the newly established ERC directly received orders from Meles. A senior staff member at the MOT repeatedly expressed his grievances, '[ADR-related] decisions were made at the head of state level. The Ministry of Transport was not involved. Very strange, no consultation with the Ministry of Transport.'[38] The MOT did not even participate in the ADR negotiation with China. On the Ethiopian side, only the Ministry of Finance and Economic Cooperation (MOFEC), ERC, and Meles himself participated.[39]

In 2011, Meles visited China and asked the then chairman Hu Jintao to support Ethiopian railway development. The Chinese government agreed

[35] Interview with ET-75, Ministry of Transport, Addis Ababa (30 April 2019).

[36] Rode, Terrefe, and da Cruz (2020).

[37] Since MOFEC can only borrow concessional loans, it recommended the ERC to directly apply to China EximBank for the loans to build the ADR, which is purely commercial. So as a very young office, the ERC signed the contract ofloan with EximBank, with MOFEC being the guarantee. Interview with ET-73, Ministry of Finance and Economic Cooperation, Addis Ababa (23 April 2019).

[38] Interview with ET-73, Ministry of Finance and Economic Cooperation, Addis Ababa (23 April 2019).

[39] Interview with ET-75, Ministry of Transport, Addis Ababa (30 April 2019).

to support the ADR and nominated some Chinese state-owned enterprises (SOEs) as contractors. Later that year, an engineering, procurement, and construction (EPC) contract was awarded to the CREC and CCECC.[40] The EximBank announced financing for the ADR in a Memorandum of Understanding (MOU) with the Ethiopian government in June 2012. Meles directly intervened in the ADR planning and negotiation. He participated in some of the negotiations with China and set the project's cost ceiling. A former employee of ERC recalled:

> It seems that Prime Minister Meles learned from somewhere that the cost of railway should be US$3.5mn/km, thus he informed us to stick to this price. Chinese railway company said, US$3.5mn/km was for a different project. During negotiation, we couldn't ask something that might incur cost. For instance, if we ask for more stations, the Chinese would say, it needed more money, but the upper limit was US$3.5mn/km.[41]

Meles effectively acted as a project manager for the ADR. Gitachu Betru, the former CEO of ERC, recalled, 'Meles was literally monitoring the progress every fifteen days. We have to report to him.' He further explained, 'the ADR was not only a transport project. You need to bring the political system towards you. Need support from the top, the executive level, and then trickle down to all layers including local authorities.'[42] Several Chinese interviewees who have worked on the ADR project since its initiation recalled that Meles acted as the project manager of the railway.

To closely monitor mega-infrastructure projects such as the ADR, Meles started the microeconomic team meeting. The participants who attended the meeting included half a dozen ministries plus several parastatals relevant to these projects. Relevant regional governments were also summoned to Addis

[40] Details of the contracts signed between Chinese state-owned enterprises (SOEs) and Ethiopian/Djibouti governments include: (1) The Ethiopian Railway Corporation signed the EPC contract with CREC in October 2011 for the Sebeta-Adama-Mieso section of the ADR, with a contract value of US$1.84 billion. (2) The Ethiopian Railway Corporation granted the EPC contract to CCECC on 16 December 2011 for the Mieso-Dire Dawa-Dewanle section of the ADR, with a contract amount of US$1.2 billion, later revised to US$1.4 billion. (3) The ERC signed the rolling stock supply contract with NORINCO on March 2013, with a contract value of US$259 million. According to the contract, NORINCO would provide forty-one electric locomotives, thirty passenger trains and 1,100 freight trains of various types. (4) China International Engineering Consulting Corporation and China Third Railway Survey and Design Institute jointly signed a supervision contract for the entire line of the ADR with the ERC, with a total contract value of US$46.5 million. (5) In 30 January 2012, CCECC signed an EPC contract with Djibouti's Ministry of Finance with a contract amount of US$505 million, later revised to US$579 million. Information from Yuan, Li, and Wang (2019).

[41] Interview with ET-47, Ethiopia–Djibouti Railway, Addis Ababa (27 April 2019).

[42] Gitachu Betru's speech at the Oxford University China–Africa Network, Oxford (1 December 2017).

Ababa to join the meeting. The macroeconomic team met monthly to check the performance of these projects, provide directions, and solve problems. If there was an urgent problem, the prime minister would also call for a meeting. Land acquisition was the most frequently raised issue during macroeconomic team meetings, a point that I will come back to in section 3.3. The macroeconomic team meeting was stopped under Hailemariam's rulership in 2016–17 when major projects were completed, and projects were allocated to the management of due ministries.[43]

As a relatively nascent agency, the ERC was less likely to leverage the commitment from the prime minister for its project, as would be predicted by the bureaucratic capacity argument. The ERC was established in 2007, and the ADR was the first mega-infrastructure project it undertook. At the time, the corporation was understaffed and heavily reliant on foreign consultants for technical work. The more likely scenario was that Meles was committed to the project and bypassed the MOT, which may have raised objections to the project, and directly instructed the ERC.

3.2.2 Chinese intervention during initiation

Chinese SOEs' involvement in the initiation of the ADR was minimal. Unlike in Kenya, where the China Road and Bridge Corporation (CRBC) was a joint initiator, Chinese SOEs were largely absent in the initiation of the Ethiopian railway, and their intensive participation only began in 2012, when construction commenced. Chinese SOEs became involved with the project after Meles and Hu's meeting in Beijing when the Chinese government proposed a list of SOEs for the Ethiopian government to choose from. Before Meles and Hu's meeting, the Ethiopian government invited an Indian consulting company who made a study. At that time it was confidential. Only few Ministers was sit to look that study. That study showed how railway is advantageous for the country of Ethiopia for long distance from one place to another. The Indians were expected at that time to come with resource, to implement the project but it was not possible at that time. China became the choice after Meles' meeting with Hu, and the MOFEC was instructed to start a negotiation.[44] Yet, the two Chinese SOEs' intervention in the ADR significantly increased only after construction had started in 2012, months before Meles' death. Tables 3.1 and 3.2 show the ADR timeline and characteristics, respectively.

[43] Interview with ET-70, Ethiopian Development Research Institute and Ministry of Industrialization, Addis Ababa (16 April 2019).

[44] Interview with ET-54, Ethio-China Development Cooperation Directorate in the Ministry of Finance and Economic Cooperation, Addis Ababa (29 June 2017).

Table 3.1 Addis Ababa–Djibouti railway project timeline

Time	Event
April 2010	CREC signs strategic partnership MOU on national railway network with ERC
August 2010	CREC signs design contract with ERC for the Sebeta–Adama–Mieso section
2011	Meles approaches Hu to support Ethiopian railway development
October 2011	CREC signs commercial contract with ERC for the Sebeta–Adama–Mieso section
December 2011	CCECC signs commercial contract with ERC for the Mieso–Dire Dawa–Dewanle section
January 2012	CCECC signs commercial contract with the government of Djibouti
June 2012	EximBank and the government of Ethiopia sign MOU regarding commercial loan for the ADR
January 2013	Construction commences in Ethiopia
September 2013	Construction commences in Djibouti
May 2014	First funding release from EximBank to Ethiopia
June 2014	First funding release from EximBank to Djibouti
July 2016	CCECC and CREC sign operation contract
October 2016	Launch in Addis
January 2018	Operation of passenger and freight services

Source: the author's composition based on CCECC internal presentation and interviews.

Table 3.2 Facts on the Addis Ababa–Djibouti railway

ADR	
Contract amount	USD$3.4 billion
Funded by	The government of the Republic of Ethiopia (30%) and the Export-Import Bank of China (70%, commercial loan)
Client	ERC
EPC contractor	CREC and CCECC The 320-kilometre stretch from Addis Ababa to Mieso was built by the CREC, while the CCECC built the 339-kilometre section from Mieso to the Djibouti border. The railway within Djibouti was contracted to the CCECC
Date of commencement	12 February 2012
Duration of construction	60 months
Operator	CREC and CCECC
Characteristics	780-kilometre electrified railway, freight trains of up to 80 kilometre/hour, and passenger trains of up to 120 kilometre/hour

Source: the author's composition based on interviews.

3.3 Construction: diminishing political championship under Hailemariam Desalegn

As with the Kenyan railway, the most significant challenge during ADR construction was land acquisition and compensation. In Ethiopia, even though land belongs to the government, land acquisition has been the most common cause of construction work delays. Like in Kenya, land is historically sensitive in Ethiopia, with many conflicts between regions and between the centre and regions revolving around land issues.[45]

3.3.1 'Legacy maintainer' to 'Mengist yelem!' ('There is no government!')

Meles' unexpected death[46] in August 2012 led to Hailemariam Desalegn assuming the premiership. After the 2010 elections, the EPRDF promoted a new generation of young leaders and retired several party veterans. This new breed of leaders represented a balance among the various ethnic blocs. Hailemariam was a Protestant from the traditionally marginalized South and was promoted as the deputy prime minister, giving hints about the political direction after Meles.[47] Following Meles' death, Hailemariam was appointed as the acting premier. A month later, on 21 September 2012, he became the prime minister. While Hailemariam represented the SEPDM, the three deputy prime ministers represented each of the coalition's remaining parties; that is, the TPLA, ANDM, and OPDO.[48] The political transition was smooth and peaceful, and many EPRDF cadres viewed the new prime minister as a 'legacy maintainer'.[49] Party leaders did not use the transition as an opportunity to change direction. Instead, their main priority after Meles' death was to maintain the status quo. In fact, a common perception during Hailemariam's first year as prime minister was that he mentioned Meles' legacy in nearly every public speech.[50]

Even though Hailemariam continued his predecessor's work, he lacked Meles' capability to navigate through various factions. He was less rhetorically gifted than Meles and lacked his predecessor's experience and political legacy

[45] Interview with ET-77, Ethiopian Road Authority, Addis Ababa (15 May 2019).
[46] Due to health reasons.
[47] Aalen (2014).
[48] Ibid.
[49] Lefort (2016); Fisher and Gebrewahd (2019).
[50] Aalen (2014, p. 193).

as a guerrilla leader that defeated the Derg and ended the civil war.[51] Most of Hailemariam's authority came not from his own resources, as was the case of Meles, but had been handed down to him through a constellation of powers characterized by diversity and rivalry, or even conflict, between them.[52] That he represented two historically marginalized groups—evangelical Christians and the southern peripheral people—made him a good compromise candidate who did not threaten any of the factions within the party and sought to govern more collectively.[53]

Hailemariam took over a Prime Minister's Office that had been an apparatus for feeding information to Meles for his assessment and decision-making. Thus, the office had become a highly isolated and powerful ruling machinery that was difficult to control for his successor. The military command and security and intelligence services were subservient to Meles not because of his position as prime minister, but because he served as the supreme intelligence, security, and military analyst, and because he was a member of the political-military inner circle that had defeated the Derg and run the country thereafter.[54] Hailemariam did not have these attributes. A senior official who served both prime ministers explained the difference between the decision-making styles of Meles and Hailemariam:

> Meles knew everything. Before a decision was made, he would first get information from line ministries. Then, get experience from other countries all over the world through Ethiopian diplomats, he would write and email to them to collect information from host country on this matter and reply by this time. Third, consult legal, economic, and social advisors. And finally, ask informal spies to obtain information for him on how that could be done in Ethiopia, who supported this decision, who oppose. Then, a guy working for him gathered all these sources of information to two to three pages for Meles, who then called on all his advisors. In the cabinet meeting or macroeconomic team meeting, if it was an issue with a specific ministry, the minister would come to the meeting with his advisors, they would report to everyone, then Meles would ask: 'Is there anything you would add or elaborate?' If not, then other ministers would raise questions, those are really challenging questions followed by intensive debates.

[51] Aalen (2014).
[52] Lefort (2016).
[53] Aalen (2014); Fisher and Gebrewahd (2019).
[54] De Waal (2015).

> With Hailemariam, there wasn't such process. For cabinet meetings, they just meet, and he seemed to be new for everything. Once he mentioned the merging of wildlife and forest ministries, and he raised the Kenya and Uganda example, saying that in those countries, these two ministries were merged as one. The then minister of environment said Uganda and Kenya did not have such merging experience. Hailemariam was shocked, and then he dropped this proposal.[55]

The weakening of central authority released regional forces that had been stifled during Meles' iron grip. Both in central and regional government, Hailemariam's authority was ignored: officials turned their backs on and even mocked the new government, right up to the highest levels. Men in the street concluded, 'Mengist yelem!'—'There is no government!'[56]

3.3.2 Strong commitment with diminished leadership authority

Under both Meles' and Hailemariam's rulership, the ADR was always a priority for the government, yet the leadership authority diminished. The ADR and many other projects and policies started during Meles' era were continued with Hailemariam. A senior staff member from the MOT observed that from Meles to Hailemariam, the railway project remained a priority of the government, 'Hailemariam kept doing the same thing, to keep Meles' legacy.'[57] In his speech in Tigray in 2017, Hailemariam referred to the ADR as serving a crucial function:

> First, the capital Addis Ababa needs to be connected to the port, because all of our throats will be strangled if [our connection to] the port is strangled. Thus, let us first connect to the port so that we can open our throat.[58]

However, Hailemariam lacked Meles' leadership capability to mobilize and motivate a coalition for ADR implementation. Hailemariam lacked the political skills to sideline other problems, such as the demands for political participation that Meles could put aside to focus on the development of the country's infrastructure and industrialization.[59]

[55] Interview with ET-75, Ministry of Transport, Addis Ababa (30 April 2019).
[56] Lefort (2016).
[57] Interview with ET-62, Ministry of Transport, Addis Ababa (22 April 2019).
[58] Fetsum (26 April 2017), cited in Terrefe (2018).
[59] Interview with ET-87, a consulting firm, Addis Ababa (16 April 2019).

As a result of this change of leadership, land acquisition, or 'Right of Way', was done very quickly under Meles but stagnated under Hailemariam's tenure. Right of Way was the leading cause of delays for construction works in Ethiopia. According to the Ethiopian Road Authority, land acquisition delays were accountable for over 70 per cent of performance delays.[60] Land in Ethiopia is government-owned and managed by the regional government, but this does not mean that land acquisition for government projects is a less painstaking task than in countries like Kenya featuring private ownership of land. For the construction of the ADR, the ERC requested the regional administration to coordinate for the Right of Way. Thus, the strength of federal control over regional administration was especially relevant for the Right of Way's effectiveness. For the ADR, the Right of Way started under Meles, with the bulk of the work being completed during Hailemariam's leadership. A senior manager of the ERC compared the effectiveness of land acquisition under Meles and Hailemariam, with slight contempt in his tone when discussing Hailemariam:

> Under Meles, it [Right of Way] was very quick for us. He gave instructions to regional government, like Oromia government, they listened to him, then they instructed local community to focus on the work. And whenever we went to local administration, we were well received, and the work was done smoothly.
>
> With Hailemariam, there is support, but not as much as from Meles. Hailemariam was the chair of the board of ERC during Meles' times. When he became the prime minister, he had many other issues to deal with. We met him, sometimes under his request and sometimes we wrote to him. But not under the macroeconomic team setting, we don't follow up after the meeting. There are legal procedures, and we just follow the legal procedure.[61]

Strictly procedure-following is frequently a measure for bureaucrats to subvert political decisions. Alex de Waal's (2015) observation of Ethiopian government performance under Meles reveals, 'Governmental institutions are hidebound and bureaucrats are skilled at subverting political decisions through procrastination, sabotage or—the most effective of bureaucratic measures—strict working to rule.'[62] A senior employee of the MOT made similar comments, 'On Right of Way, if Meles ordered, "clear within one month", like from Addis to

[60] Interview with ET-77, Ethiopian Road Authority, Addis Ababa (15 May 2019).
[61] Interview with ET-44, Ethiopian Railway Corporation, Addis Ababa (22 April 2019).
[62] De Waal (2015, p. 254).

Adama, then it got cleared. In Metehara, Hailemariam ordered, "clear within one month", nothing happened.'[63] Admittedly, the success of land acquisition in Adama and failure in Metehara is attributable to multiple factors.[64] Still, this quote points to the local administration's reactions towards central commands: the central control over regions was much more robust under Meles.[65]

Although Hailemariam's rule was a continuation of Meles', the Ethiopian and Chinese interviewees who participated in the ADR were nostalgic about Meles' administration. A senior manager of the ERC clearly stated, 'When Meles was the prime minister, it was the golden era for railway development in Ethiopia. Should Meles still be here, the Addis–Djibouti Railway would be in a different shape.'[66]

3.4 Political crisis and Abiy: a forgotten railway

3.4.1 Political crisis, democratic reform, and the Tigray war

Following the uprisings in Oromia and Amhara, Ethiopia declared a state of emergency, and the government's priority shifted away from economic growth to stability maintenance. In November 2015, Oromia, Ethiopia's most populous state with 35 per cent of the country's population, saw increasing unrest. The unrest was sparked by a government proposal to expand the borders of Addis Ababa into Oromia territory.[67] The Oromia uprising soon spread to Amhara, a region with the second-largest population (27 per cent). Amhara protests were partly based on solidarity with the Oromo and partly fuelled by the arrest of Demeke Zewdu, a leader against the contested incorporation of Wolkayit Tegede *wereda*, previously part of Gondar, into Tigray. Hailemariam declared a state of emergency in October 2016, followed by a massive crackdown on protestors: federal police fired on protestors, causing hundreds to be killed and tens of thousands to be detained. This political crisis ended with

[63] Interview with ET-45, Ministry of Transport, Addis Ababa (30 April 2019).

[64] For instance, the small town of Metehara is situated at the crossing of the boarders of Oromia, Amhara, and Somali regions and had ethnic conflicts in the early 2000s. Thus, it could be ethnically more difficult to claim the Right of Way.

[65] Terrefe's (2018) quote of a former senior official from the Ethiopian Ministry of Foreign Affairs also speaks to this point: 'Nowadays [under Hailemariam], you are beginning to see contradictions, frictions between the regional states and the federal government ... Things at Meles' time, visibly you could see, were more in line. More things were more in harmony. If you asked me, during his period, at the height of when he was in power, comparing at that time and now, definitely you see a difference.'

[66] Interview with ET-44, Ethiopian Railway Corporation, Addis Ababa (22 April 2019).

[67] Lavers (2018).

the resignation of Hailemariam in February 2018 and the claiming of power by Abiy Ahmed, the then deputy president of the Oromia region, two months later.

The declaration of a state of emergency was an indication that the government was 'overwhelmed'.[68] Although territorial grievances and high unemployment rates triggered the protests in Oromia and Amhara, they were able to generate such unprecedented support because of a broader range of issues, including political and economic marginalization and the domination of the TPLF within the EPRDF, human rights abuse, absence of democracy, and federal encroachment of regional affairs.[69] The protestors demanded more governance reform and political pluralism, and more and better jobs.[70] Occupied with the widespread protests, the government shifted its focus to maintaining stability and order, and centralized state-directed development became less of a priority.

Responding to these requests, Abiy Ahmed has, since his April 2018 inauguration, presided over a dramatic set of policy shifts. Abiy has sought to distance himself from the past twenty-seven years of EPRDF rule and announced a range of plans to alter longstanding EPRDF positions on the state's role in the economy and multiparty politics.[71] Instead of focusing on providing economic growth as regime legitimacy, Abiy's ambition was to transform Ethiopia into a multiparty democracy. As he stated in a meeting with political parties, 'Given our current politics, there is no option except pursuing a multiparty democracy supported by strong institutions that respect human rights and rule of law. This will allow us to mediate our differences peacefully and to ensure lasting progress.'[72] Abiy's economic reform agenda distanced him from the previous regime's emphasis on centralized, infrastructure-driven economic transformation and focused instead on economic liberation. In an interview with the *Financial Times*, he described himself as a 'capitalist'.[73] The reformist prime minister relied on his economic management team—some of the members are highly experienced returning diaspora representatives—and sought to privatize the economy starting with liberating the telecommunication industry. His foreign exchange reforms sought to ease financial repression accompanied by an increase in taxation.[74]

[68] Lefort (2016, p. 12).
[69] Fisher and Gebrewahd (2019); Lavers (2018).
[70] Cheru, Cramer, and Oqubay (2019).
[71] Fisher and Gebrewahd (2019).
[72] Gebre (23 July 2018).
[73] Pilling and Barber (21 February 2019).
[74] Collier (16 October 2019).

Abiy soon won applause for his political reforms and foreign policy settlements. Internationally, he made peace with Eritrea and proposed regional economic integration in the Horn of Africa.[75] The revived relationship with Eritrea has reduced Ethiopia's reliance on the port of Djibouti: a road project was later announced to connect the Ethiopian border to the port of Eritrea funded by the European Union.[76] Domestically, he addressed many issues at the centre of the protests, including releasing thousands of political prisoners, journalists, and activists, inviting Ethiopian diaspora communities and previously outlawed opposition groups based abroad to return, and easing restrictions on civil society and media. He also overhauled the cabinet and other top posts and committed himself to economic liberalization and democratic elections. In November 2019, Abiy pushed through the merging of four ruling coalition parties and five allied parties into a single, unified party, the Ethiopian Prosperity Party. The new party was intended to centralize decision-making, rebalancing authority executive organs and regional branches, and arguably a step away from ethnic power-sharing.[77] The TPLF leaders rejected it outright and formally exited the coalition in early 2020. Abiy ordered a military offensive against the government of Tigray in a national address on 4 November 2020, in response to a contested election in the region.[78] Originally planned to be a quick operation, the war lasted over a year and brought humanitarian atrocity, famine, and economic crisis in its wake.

Ethiopia's repeated entry into states of emergency and Abiy's unilateral ruling style arguably boosted the leader's authority. States of emergency, following Zwitter (2012, p. 97), refer to a *de facto* situation which 'prompts the state to temporarily change some structures so that it can more effectively and efficiently address the situation at hand'. From 2016 to 2022, Ethiopia entered four national states of emergency. The first was a ten-month, full-fledged state of emergency announced by Hailemariam in October 2016, following the Oromia and Amhara protests; the second one started immediately after Hailemariam's resignation in February 2018 and closed when Abiy assumed premiership in June 2018; the third, declared by Abiy in April 2020 in the wake of the pandemic, as the only non-political state of emergency; and the fourth announced by Abiy in November 2021 in the wake of the armed conflict in Tigray. States of emergencies in Ethiopia are perceived to be primarily

[75] Temin and Badwaza (2019); Nigatu and Abbink (2019).
[76] African Review of Business and Technology (25 February 2019).
[77] ICG (16 December 2019); Mosley (2020).
[78] BBC (29 June 2021).

serving the purpose of keeping the incumbent regime in power by using military forces and opportunistically using the court system to enforce laws and orders.[79] With extraordinary power resources at hand under states of emergency, the authority of the political leader is elevated. Despite his publicly declared pursuit of democracy, Abiy also demonstrates the tendency to formulate policy within the Prime Minister's Office rather than through existing institutional mechanisms.[80] Mosley (2020) lists examples of the new prime minister's unilateral decisions, including overriding TPLF concerns regarding normalizing relations with Eritrea, decriminalizing some political parties, and inviting opposition politicians back to Ethiopia, as well as bypassing the Ministry of Foreign Affairs to mediate intervention in the Sudanese political crisis in mid-2019.[81]

This elevated authority, however, was not directed towards the ADR, or any other infrastructure development. The ADR was gradually subject to the diminishing leadership after the start of the state of emergency. Although Hailemariam's official discourse still emphasized the importance of the ADR and the Renaissance Dam during my field visits to Addis in 2017, the ADR was *de facto* deprioritized. Railway construction was capital- and technology-intensive and could not absorb unemployed youths, who comprised the majority of insurgents. Under Abiy's economic liberation, the ADR was left to survive on its own and was not a popular topic to discuss with the prime minister. Although the Tigray war did not disrupt the ADR operation, the railway was unlikely to gain the leader's attention with widespread domestic and international attention on the war and its impact.

3.4.2 Declined commitment to the Addis Ababa–Djibouti railway

Since the October 2016 state of emergency, a lack of political commitment to the ADR was generally felt. The political attention was geared towards the industrial park projects instead. Unlike his counterpart in Kenya, who frequented the Standard Gauge Railway construction site, Hailemariam only paid a handful of visits to the ADR—all of them for ceremonial purposes (Table 3.3). During interviews, Chinese managers of the ADR spoke enviously of the neighbouring Kenyan railway. They believed the Ethiopian government's political support for the ADR was not as strong as the Kenyatta government's

[79] Abbink (2022).
[80] Mosley (2020).
[81] Mosley (2020, p. 5).

Table 3.3 Hailemariam's visits to the Addis Ababa–Djibouti railway

Time	Event
July 2013	Construction commencement event in Djibouti
8 April 2014	Ceremony for laying rail-tracks (construction commencement) in Addis Ababa
5 October 2016	Railway inauguration in Addis Ababa
10 January 2017	Railway inauguration in Djibouti
13 July 2017	Launch of the Dire Dawa Industrial Park, with a short railway experience trip

Source: the author's composition based on interviews and media reports.

towards the SGR. Even though the ADR was government priority and the political support was at the discourse level, the Chinese contractors' requirements addressed to the Ethiopian government were not truly implemented.[82]

Ethnic protests in various regions made it even more difficult for the ERC to cooperate with local administrations, especially regarding land acquisition. The Right of Way process started by obtaining the bill of quantity, and the local administration (*woreda* and city government) took the measurement of land. The ERC then claimed compensation based on the bill of quantities. Upon receiving compensation, the people were supposed to move to clear the land for construction. However, the local administrations feared the people. Because of the state of emergency, the local administration needed to appease the local population and thus preferred avoiding conflict.[83] As a result, it took a long time for the local administration to implement the necessary measurements, especially once the locals started asking for inflated prices. If the ERC disagreed with the price, there were prolonged negotiations, causing delays. After compensation, local residents were supposed to move by the proclamation on land expropriation,[84] yet several people refused to move, some even constructing illegally on the cleared land to seek more compensation. Local administration was hesitant to take action for fear that this would incite further insurgents.[85] 'Things moved very slow', a senior officer of the ERC explained. 'Local administrations, they make our lives miserable. Local administration is supposed to balance between local people and the national project, but now, they purely support local people.'[86]

[82] Interview with ET-14, CCECC, Addis Ababa (3 April 2019).
[83] Interview with ET-77, Ethiopian Road Authority, Addis Ababa (15 May 2019).
[84] Proclamation No. 455/2005, a proclamation to provide for the expropriation of land holdings for public purposes and payment of compensation.
[85] Interview with ET-77, Ethiopian Road Authority, Addis Ababa (15 May 2019).
[86] Interview with ET-44, Ethiopian Railway Corporation, Addis Ababa (22 April 2019).

Federal control over regional states further declined after the 2016–17 state of emergency. For national projects like the ADR, city and regional administrations had very little control over decisions affecting their region's infrastructure. Local administration's role in the ADR was limited to assisting with the Right of Way and protecting the railway from sabotage.[87] The ERC, in close coordination with the Prime Minister's Office and Chinese ex-pats, were the key decision-makers.[88] The political crisis made it more challenging to advance the ADR project. As Chinese managers observed, 'It seems that the ERC lacked authority in regional government.'[89] The fierce gunfire conflicts in several regions crossed by the ADR also frightened railway workers, who refused to go to work, thus causing construction delays.[90]

The ADR was launched in Addis Ababa in October 2016, and trial operations for ADR's passenger and cargo services commenced in January 2018, fourteen months after the Addis inauguration. This postponement of operation was because of the delayed arrangement of stable electricity and water supply and the prolonged negotiation with Djibouti regarding issues pending for cross-country coordination.[91] The ADR operation management was handled by a newly established joint venture, the Ethio-Djibouti Standard Gauge Railway Share Company (EDR). The EDR had an initial endowment of $500 million, with 75 per cent shares owed to Ethiopia (the ERC has 72 per cent; the MOT, MOFEC, and the Public Enterprise Authority each have 1 per cent) and 25 per cent to Djibouti. The EDR contracted the operation and maintenance to the two Chinese constructors of the railway for the first six years, with an element of staff training.[92]

The ADR runs four freight trains and one passenger train daily, operating at a loss.[93] Its freight service generated merely $36 million in 2018, realizing only a quarter of the predicted revenue in the feasibility study.[94] A primary reason for the limited freight service was its competition with road transport. Similar to the Kenyan railway, the ADR's main operational challenge was the

[87] Interview with ET-76, Dire Dawa Mayor's Office, Dire Dawa (14 May 2019).

[88] Rode, Terrefe, and da Cruz (2020).

[89] ET-4, CREC, Addis Ababa (19 June 2017).

[90] Interview with ET-29, CCECC, Dire Dawa (9 May 2019); ET-46, Ethiopian Railway Corporation, Addis Ababa (26 April 2019); ET-3, CREC, Addis Ababa (19 June 2017); and ET-5, CREC, Addis Ababa (20 June 2017).

[91] Ibid.

[92] Interview with ET-43, Ethiopian Railway Corporation, Addis Ababa (5 July 2017); and ET-44, Ethiopian Railway Corporation, Addis Ababa (22 April 2019).

[93] Data updated to the time I completed the fieldwork in April 2019. As I return to Addis in 2023, CCECC shared that starting from 2022, ADR's operational revenue can cover the costs. This was mainly because road transport was blocked in domestic conflicts.

[94] Interview with ET-35, EximBank Ethiopia office, Addis Ababa (7 April 2019).

rail–road competition. Road logistics, a traditionally highly lucrative sector, is controlled by a parastatal, the Ethiopian Shipping and Logistics Service Enterprise (ESLSE). Established in 1956, the parastatal acquired a truck-operating company and has since monopolized the Ethiopian logistics industry. The EDR reached an agreement with the ESLSE to handle cargo services, and the latter provides two cargo trains daily for the ADR, while the remaining goods are transported by trucks.[95] At the beginning of the operation, it was only one cargo, and upon negotiation, ESLSE increased the frequency to two cargo transportations daily. The newly established railway corporations were in a disadvantaged position for these negotiations.

Another difficulty for running the freight service was the ADR's uncompetitive tariff compared to road transport. The EDR did not have the right to set the tariff. The price was given by the ESLSE at a similar rate as truck transportation. A logistics insider provided a quick overview of logistics costs to transport cargos from Hawassa Industrial Park via Djibouti's port to a port in Europe by road and by rail, respectively. The road option from Hawassa Industrial Park to Europe (Rotterdam) via the port of Djibouti costs $4,071 and takes seventeen to eighteen days, while the railway option (plus the last mile of road) of the same route costs $4,433 and takes 15.3 days. Although railway transport is faster by two days, it costs $400 more than only using trucks, mostly driven by the last mile cost from Mojo railway station to Hawassa.

The ADR has been operating under tremendous financial stress. The management contract costs US$357 million for six years; the costs are higher than the revenue generated from the railway operation.[96] The railway also suffered from power fluctuation, which requires additional equipment, but the EDR was short of finance. Replacing outdated parts required further spending. Paying back the loan was especially difficult: Ethiopia's government had a difficult time even paying back the interest.[97] In 2018, Abiy went to Beijing for the Forum on China-Africa Cooperation (FOCAC) and asked the Chinese government to forgive the loans. He returned saying that the Chinese government has pledged to extend the debt repayment period for a loan it has acquired to construct the ADR from ten to thirty years.[98]

[95] Interview with ET-47, Ethio-Djibouti Standard Gauge Railway Share Company, Addis Ababa (27 April 2019).
[96] Ibid.
[97] Interview with ET-35, EximBank Ethiopia office, Addis Ababa (7 April 2019).
[98] Embassy of Ethiopia in Brussels (10 September 2018).

Political commitment to the ADR further declined under Abiy. As a senior officer of the operating company, EDR, stated, 'It seems that the Abiy government have forgotten the railway.' He explained, 'Railways require lifetime investment, linkage to the ports, additional equipment, training for staffs, etc. But now the government has said, it is not our priority to put money into the railway ... the prime minister does not want to hear about this project always consuming.'[99] Without political intervention, the operation's challenges were handled at the working level between the railway corporations and the Chinese contractors. Unlike Kenyatta's iconoclastic issuing of presidential directives to force the usage of the SGR despite the road logistics industry's grievances, Abiy has been reluctant to intervene in the road–rail competition. Soon after taking office, Abiy's corruption campaign has swept several parastatals, including the Metals and Engineering Corporation, the manufacturing conglomerate, and was dominated by the Tigray. But the ESLSE was kept intact under this corruption campaign as most of the company's senior leaders were from Oromia.[100] Although repeated states of emergency and Abiy's leadership style enhanced his authority, with the leader's attention directed elsewhere, this enhanced authority did not translate to ADR development.

The ADR operation continued during the Tigray war, with some interruptions. The operating revenue of the ADR in 2021 reached US$86.13 million, an increase of 37.5 per cent over 2020. A total of 449 passenger trains, 1,469 freight trains, and 77,357 Twenty-foot Equivalent Units (TEUs) of containers were sent along the line throughout the year.[101] The railway was closed for several days by Somali youth protestors, who blocked the railway to retaliate against Afar regional militia crossed borders to Somali and carried out deadly attacks in late July 2021.[102]

3.5 Chinese intervention

Chinese contractors played much more pronounced roles in the construction and operation of the ADR than their counterparts in the Kenyan railway. Still, contrary to the predictions of the external agency argument, strong Chinese intervention was not enough to address the obstacles facing the railway project. Although Chinese SOEs did not participate in the ADR initiation phase, which

[99] Interview with ET-47, Ethio-Djibouti Standard Gauge Railway Share Company, Addis Ababa (27 April 2019).
[100] Interview with ET-17, CCECC, Addis Ababa (11 April 2019).
[101] MOFCOM (16 January 2022).
[102] Tesfa-Alem (4 August 2021).

was in the hands of Meles, the CCECC's and CREC's support for the ADR outside their contractual liabilities significantly increased as the construction started in 2013. Chinese contractors' prominent intervention in the ADR was primarily motivated by financial calculations during construction, and during operation by political pressure in China. Chinese SOEs facilitated Ethiopia's and Djibouti's application to EximBank's loans by putting reverse pressure on the Chinese government for loan approval. As the ADR became a Belt and Road flagship project in 2017, it was 'too important to fail'. Operating under financial stress, Chinese contractors complained that they were 'politically kidnapped'[103] by the ADR.

3.5.1 Chinese intervention during construction

Financial support and 'reverse pressure'

Similar to their counterparts in Kenya, the CREC and CCECC provided financial support for the ERC during construction outside of their contractual obligations. When the ERC was temporarily short on funds for land compensation, the Chinese contractors paid out of their own pockets instead of waiting for daily cost accumulation. Frequently during construction, the ERC could not issue prompt payment to the contractors. Yet, the CREC and CCECC continued the construction work and seldom claimed compensation. Particularly at the beginning of construction, before the EximBank agreed to finance this project, it was Ethiopia's government that fully funded the construction of the ADR, and soon the ERC could no longer pay the Chinese contractors. Instead of suspending the work and resorting to legal action, the Chinese contractors continued the construction.[104] Chinese SOEs, therefore, bore increasing financial risks in this project. This was a stark distinction from local and Western contractors but a characteristic welcomed by the client. In an internal meeting of CREC that I was permitted to attend, the SOE presented a quote from a project completion report from a Western consultant to their Ethiopian government client describing Chinese contractors:

> Chinese contractors bring a fresh air to Ethiopian construction industry: they only care about the project itself, and lack legal knowledge on contract and engineering; they retain an indifferent attitude towards the contract, which may generate huge extra costs, but they do not make strong claims; yet at

[103] Interview with multiple Chinese managers of CREC and CCECC in Addis Ababa (2019).
[104] Interview with ET-9, CREC, Addis Ababa (21 June 2017).

> the same time they have the financial and technical strength to carry out any project. Thus they are indeed the best choices for clients.[105]

The newly established ERC did not have much experience regarding contract negotiation and project management. Thus, they preferred contractors that were willing to 'work with' them. The ADR was the first electrified railway in Ethiopia and Africa, so there was a technology imbalance between the ERC and the Chinese contractors. During negotiations, the ERC could have agreed to a term, but problems arose during implementation which were not predicted during contract negotiation. The ERC, therefore, frequently found itself stuck in the dilemma of doing the work due to its necessity, while the work was beyond the contract. For the ERC, it was less likely to persuade local and European contractors to complete the additional work, but when working with Chinese contractors, the ERC was able to persuade them.[106] An ERC staff member shared his discussion over a beer with colleagues regarding the difference in flexibility between Chinese and Turkish contractors:

> The difference is that for European [contractors], there is a rule, the contract is the bible. The Turkish will never try to step out of the rule. And at the same time, they will never let the ERC step out of the rule. If the ERC step out, they warn us: 'Don't ever try.' There is no flexibility in the level of the content of the contract.
>
> The Chinese, on the contrary, are flexible, which is a good part from our perspective. By flexible, I mean when the employer goes beyond the contractual right, they don't defend or push back. They say: 'Let's make a deal.' We tell them: 'You have to do this work!' The Chinese reply: 'No, no, this is not in the contract.' But we are the boss, so we insisted: 'Do this work.' And they calculate the loss or benefit they can get or lose by doing that work. If there is less harm, compared to what they are gaining, they can do it for free. But for the Turkish, if there is no loss even, they don't do it, the rule is the rule.[107]

Strikingly, an informant revealed that the Chinese contractors bore the risk to cover the Ethiopian government's US$90 million Sinosure credit premium on the ADR project:

[105] Presentation from CREC internal meeting.
[106] Interview with ET-42, Ethiopian Railway Corporation, Addis Ababa (24 June 2017).
[107] Ibid.

> The Ethiopian government ... did not have enough US dollars to cover the advanced credit premium for Sinosure, so we assisted them in paying the premium. The total amount we covered for them was $90 million ... Till now [July 2017], there were still $38 million outstanding from the ERC. It was a big risk for us.
>
> But without the credit premium, the project would be stopped. There will be international influence, and the cost of stopping the work was very high for us: there were 2,000–3,000 [Chinese] employees during the peak of construction, just their social security was $50–60 million per month, plus their salary and round-trip flight ticket to China. So even though we have the full right to stop according to the contract, we have to help them [Ethiopian government] solve their difficulties.[108]

Similarly, in Djibouti, the CCECC also invested financially in the railway to start the project before EximBank's confirmation of loans. The CCECC started construction of the 89-kilometre ADR in September 2013 when the government of Djibouti made only a 5 per cent prepayment to the contractor, while according to the construction contract, prepayment should reach 20 per cent for construction to start. Instead of waiting for Djibouti's government to make the full prepayment, the CCECC invested 10 per cent of the contract value as prepayment. This was a year ahead of EximBank's release of the loan, which arrived by June 2015.[109] The CCECC was confident about EximBank financing the project and took a considerable risk; or, more precisely, decided to pressure the Chinese government and EximBank to agree to this loan by bearing the risk to invest in this project.

The very fact that these projects have a high chance of receiving EximBank loans makes these SOEs' financial support to clients seem less risky. CREC's and CCECC's support to the ERC came mostly before the release of the loans from EximBank but after the MOU on loan agreement had been signed. The possibility still exists that even after the MOU, EximBank could decide not to fund the project. In the case of the ADR, the railway construction had carried on for two years before the first batch of loans was released in June 2014, and Chinese SOEs had made a growing investment in this project. The SOEs, therefore, pressured the Chinese government to approve the loan. This is called 'reverse pressure', or *daobi*. For EximBank to grant a commercial loan, the creditor has to insure through Sinosure and receive loan approval

[108] Interview with ET-5, Addis Ababa (20 June 2017).
[109] Interview with ET-24, CCECC, Djibouti (5 May 2019).

from the Ministry of Finance, the Ministry of Commerce, and the Ministry of Foreign Affairs. Some Chinese companies, in order to get overseas projects, promised resource mobilization from China. A former employee at the Chinese economic councillor's office in Djibouti explained how the office resisted multiple sources of pressure to grant approval for the EximBank funding:

> The embassy and economic councillor's office in Ethiopia were more positive about the ADR while we [in Djibouti] are more negative. During the first year of construction, the government of Ethiopia provided funding, but soon the project lacked funding. Chinese SOEs could not continue the work, so they came to us.
>
> On the Djibouti side, the economic councillor's office dragged for a year without providing the endorsement letter, while the railway construction continues. Senior leadership in MOFCOM, EximBank, the Chinese consulting company CIECC, even the president of Djibouti all tried to persuade us. We explained our opinion to all these agencies and received no reply. This project was not financially sustainable. We sustained this pressure for a year, and finally gave in.
>
> The endorsement letter was written by myself. I wrote: 'This project needs to be sustainable, considering reasonable and long-term development'. My opinion was, the ADR can drive railway infrastructure construction and achieve mutual connectivity, which fits the requirement of the Belt and Road Initiative. Yet in Ethiopia and East Africa there is not a railway network and the ADR is not a special line for commodity like coal or mining products. I feel the ADR cannot meet the initial expectation.[110]

Political leverage

Chinese SOEs also leveraged their political connections in Beijing to have the Chinese government diplomatically urge Ethiopian leadership to provide a greater commitment to the ADR. According to CREC's observation, Hailemariam's commitment increased shortly after attending the Belt and Road Forum in May 2017 in Beijing.[111] Hailemariam was seeking new project opportunities in China while attending the Forum. Prior to the Forum, the two Chinese contractors had repeatedly reported to the Chinese embassy and economic councillor's office regarding the railway operation delay. The Chinese ambassador and economic councillor in Ethiopia were very concerned and reported to political leaders in Beijing prior to the Belt and Road Forum

[110] Interview with ET-36, Djibouti (4 May 2019).
[111] Interview with ET-13, CREC, Addis Ababa (1 July 2017).

regarding the ADR.[112] During meetings with Hailemariam, China's Ministry of Finance expressed concerns about the delay of the ADR operation. While Hailemariam was preparing for his Beijing trip, Getachew Betru, the former CEO of ERC, promised to start the railway operation, under media scrutiny, by 10 May, three days before the Belt and Road Forum. On 9 May, CCECC received messages from Beijing inquiring about the status of the operation. In response, on the night of 9 May, a briefing was drafted by all the relevant parties—the Chinese contractors, ERC, and the supervisor—explaining that the electricity provision was not strong and stable enough to sustain the operation and sent back to Beijing.[113] Hailemariam provided this joint statement, stating that the Ethiopian government sought to address the railway operation's challenges.[114] Getachew resigned the next morning. Beyond this joint statement, however, the obstacles of the railway projects endured. This commitment generated by diplomatic pressure was not strong enough to resolve the challenges facing the ADR's timely completion, contrary to the expectations of the external agency argument.

Chinese government officials visited the ADR three times, once in 2015 and twice in 2018 (Table 3.4). By 2018, the railway had already started operation and had received Chinese domestic attention through the effective domestic media campaign by the CCECC. Interviews with other Chinese managers also revealed that the ADR, like the neighbouring SGR, is a Belt and Road flagship project and is widely covered in the Chinese media. Similar to their visits to the Kenyan SGR, the Chinese government's official visits aimed more for claiming the success of the railway.

3.5.2 'Political kidnap'?

During interviews in Ethiopia, I found that Chinese contractors were more eager to demonstrate the railway's operational success than their clients in the Ethiopian Railway Corporations. The CREC and CCECC entered a six-year service contract with the EDR for railway operation, maintenance, and technology transfer. This US$3,500 million operational contract started in January 2018, and payment was due every quarter. By April 2019, when I conducted the interviews in Ethiopia, the EDR had only cleared the full amount of the first quarter, the second-quarter payment was still short of US$8 million, and the

[112] Interview with ET-26, CCECC, Dire Dawa (9 May 2019).
[113] Interview with ET-11, CREC, Addis Ababa (26 June 2017).
[114] Ibid.

Table 3.4 Chinese official visits to the Addis Ababa–Djibouti railway

Name and position	Time	Projects visited
Qian Keming, vice-minister, Ministry of Commerce Liu Yandong, 18th Communist party of China (CPC), Central Committee, Politburo member; vice-premier, State Council; deputy director, CPC, Central Committee, Leading Group for Culture System Reform and Development	25 November 2015	ADR AU Headquarters, Eastern Industrial Park
Li Zhanshu, 19th CPC Central Committee member; Politburo, Standing Committee member; chairman of the 13th Standing Committee of the National People's Congress	11 May 2018	ADR, Addis Ababa Light Rail Transit, Ministry of Technology Data Centre
Xiao Yaqing, 19th CPC Central Committee member; director of State-Owned Assets Supervision and Administration Commission	7 November 2018	ADR

Source: the author's composition based on CCECC and CREC website and interviews.

remaining three payments had not been cleared.[115] The Chinese contractors had been operating out of their own pockets. I asked a senior Chinese operator why they continued the operation. He replied: 'This is a political question. The ADR is a Belt and Road project. The political meaning of the ADR is more significant than its economic meaning.' I further inquired what he meant by 'political meaning', and he explained, 'The ADR is China's first overseas electrified cross-border railway, and thus has strong demonstration effect. We should push it to succeed.'[116] As the ADR is a Belt and Road flagship project, it has to be a story of success: Belt and Road projects cannot fail. The Chinese contractors have repeatedly received verbal commands from both their headquarters and the Chinese embassy in Ethiopia that the operation 'should not stop!'[117] It seems that the EDR also realized the political significance of the railway to China. The Chinese manager said, 'During a meeting, the EDR told us: "if this railway stops, it would cause more negative influence to you than to us". So when there's a problem, they are not in a hurry but wait for us to solve it.

[115] Interview with ET-18, CCECC, Lebu (24 April 2019).
[116] Interview with ET-19, CCECC, Lebu (24 April 2019).
[117] Interview with ET-26, CCECC, Dire Dawa (9 May 2019).

They know very well that even if they don't pay us, we wouldn't suspend the operation. We felt as if we were politically kidnapped.'[118] A Chinese manager even expressed his confusion: 'It felt as if the ADR is a "Chinese railway", not an "Ethiopian railway".'[119]

This perception of the ADR as a Chinese rather than Ethiopian railway was particularly strong among residents living near the railway. Before the ADR, there was a century-old French railway along the same route. The French railway was very slow and had many stops, and the train would stop at every station. The old railway was part of the daily lives of local people: train stations were located in the city centre and served as convention centres for local traders. Many cities, such as Dire Dawa, developed as railway cities, and local people benefited from the railway and willingly carried the responsibility for the security of the train stations. This shiny electrified railway has no relation to the people: railway stations were miles away from the city centre, and there were fifteen stations in between, and the train only stopped at five stations at the time of my fieldwork. Locals referred to the ADR as a 'flying railway',[120] in the sense that the railway travelled at a flying speed and did not benefit the local people: it was a Chinese and federal government railway that would 'fly' through their community but did not have any connection to the people. The railway was more of an intruder into residents' lives, and residents along the ADR could not spare a sense of ownership towards the railway.

Without support from local residents, while the railway corporations were busy enough with their own difficulties, the Chinese operators found themselves working against various innovative disruptions to the railway operation created by the locals. If domestic animals passed the rail-tracks and were killed by the train, the railway operator should compensate the owners. As there was no legal document proclaiming the compensation amount, the compensation level had multiplied in the past year. At the beginning of the operation in 2018, owners of the killed livestock asked for hundreds of Birrs as compensation; now the price for a goat had inflated to thousands of Birrs, much higher than the market price.[121] A Chinese manager explained how residents smartly improved their negotiation skills for compensation:

> If a male camel was hit by the train, local residents would come and explain that there was a female camel at home and now because of the loss of the

[118] Interview with ET-19, CCECC, Lebu (24 April 2019).
[119] Interview with ET-26, CCECC, Dire Dawa (9 May 2019).
[120] Terrefe (2018).
[121] Interview with ET-18, ET-19, ET-20, CCECC, Lebu (24 April 2019).

> male, the female camel lost its value. So the compensation should cover two camels' price. If a female goat was hit by the train, local residents would say that this one was pregnant, and there was still a baby goat at home, without milk it would die. So we should pay for the price of three goats.[122]

The ADR passes through the borders of the Afar, Amhara, Oromia, and Somali regions, historically inflicted by ethnic conflicts, and locals' loss of livestock from the train became an easy trigger of conflicts and their anger towards the federal government. Once the train hit livestock, residents nearby came to stop the train; if they could not stop this train or if there were no local people nearby, they would stop the next train, putting big stones on the rail track and several dozens of villagers with guns, insisting that the train stop to discuss the compensation matter. To protect operational security, each train was equipped with four federal police officers. However, in Afar particularly, local people and the federal government were not on good terms. Seeing dozens of villagers holding guns, the federal police officers dared not step out of the train. Chinese operators often had to discuss the compensation issue with the villagers. A short resolution might take two hours, while the longest resolution took thirty-three hours, during which time the railway operation was suspended.[123] Most interceptions took place between Metehala and Mieso, where two-thirds of the trains would be stopped.[124]

Another disruption to railway operation was vandalism. Local residents cut and sold the electric wires, screws, and other removable parts on the rail track. Some kids even developed a competition to throw stones at the porcelain battery on top of each electric pole. Stolen or broken parts had to be replaced with new ones, yet the EDR did not have extra funding to make the purchase. To protect the railway from vandalism, the EDR hired 1,200 federal police officers to patrol along the rail line. Yet federal police had limited power in regional states even if they caught the suspects. Once caught, the suspects were sent to local police bureaus. Federal police did not have the power to conduct further investigations to collect evidence in the region. If the EDR could not provide clear evidence of vandalism, the conviction would not be established. Even if the EDR and Chinese contractors reported losing assets to local police stations, it was very rare for the local police station to send out an investigation team—many of the police stations were short of staff and did not even have cars, while the railway was far away from the villages. Thus, frequently, the

[122] Ibid.
[123] Ibid.
[124] Ibid.

suspects were released without punishment.[125] Moreover, as the EDR delayed the salary of the security officers hired to patrol the railway lines by several months, most of them were not at their posts. On record, there were over 800 vandalism cases in 2018, causing a loss of hundreds of thousands of dollars for the EDR. And there were many more cases off-record.

Unlike in Kenya, where President Kenyatta personally warned against the SGR's vandalism, the EDR did not receive political support from Abiy or even the MOT regarding railway vandalism. The EDR hosted two security conferences with the regional government, both ineffective. In both conferences, when the EDR said that the ADR was of national interest and a national asset, local administration started complaining that the railway corporations did not deliver their promised interest to the regional states.[126] Political support to the EDR was also minimal for compensation resolution: if the operators and residents could not resolve the compensation on the spot, the issue was then escalated to the headquarters of the EDR and federal police in Addis, as well as the Chinese operators' headquarters in Lebu. Should the problem persist, it would be escalated to the Chinese embassy.[127] Interestingly, it was the Chinese embassy rather than the Ethiopia MOT or the Prime Minister's Office that was involved in livestock compensation. This is starkly different from the SGR, where President Kenyatta openly dictated that vandalism would not be tolerated and even mentioned the death sentence at the SGR launch event in Mombasa: 'May God forgive me, I will approve death sentences for convicts of crimes as destruction of the rail track, capital offense, and economic sabotage.'[128] The Chinese operation managers of the ADR admire the presidential commitment to their Kenyan counterparts, which was reminiscent of the old days of Meles.

3.6 Hawassa Industrial Park: political championship during the political crisis

The Ethiopian government put industrialization as a key priority, with a focus on attracting manufacturing investment and the development of industrial parks as the key strategy, which required a political commitment at the highest level. Arkebe Oqubay, minister and advisor to Hailemariam, championed the

[125] Ibid.
[126] Ibid.
[127] Ibid.
[128] Sosi, (2017)

design of the new policy and its execution that included a pilot development of Hawassa Industrial Park. The comparison between the relatively effective industrial park and the railway project in this section demonstrates that the unsatisfactory development of the railways was largely due to the lack of political commitment. Arkebe repeatedly emphasized the importance of commitment when reviewing the development of Ethiopia's industrial policy: 'a country building industrialization from scratch. So the political commitment is important.'[129]

Ethiopia's government gave special attention to manufacturing development in particular and industrialization in general. The initial articulation of Ethiopia's industrial policy in the early 2000s concentrated on promoting manufacturing in a few sectors that are strategic for job creation and export promotion, and did not feature industrial park development. In September 2014, after examining extensive literature on varieties of industrial parks and completing a grand tour of industrial parks to six countries in Africa and Asia, Arkebe Oqubay and his team prepared a 100-page white paper based on consultation reports and Arkebe's field trip on park development lessons from China, Singapore, South Korea, Vietnam, Nigeria, and Mauritius and had a twelve-hour discussion with over one hundred policy-makers in the presence of Hailemariam.[130] This meeting set forth the institutional framework for Ethiopia's industrial park development, which included an Industrial Park Proclamation passed by Parliament in April 2015, set-up of the Industrial Park Development Corporation, and restructuring of the Ethiopian Investment Board and Ethiopian Investment Commission, chaired by Arkebe or Hailemariam.[131] Upon setting up the institutional framework, the government selected Hawassa, Hailemariam's hometown with a large population but few jobs, to establish a pilot park. One notable programme of the country's second five-year plan (GTP-II) was the establishment of industrial parks in Hawassa, Kombolcha, and Makelle.[132] The first phase of industrial park development quickly expanded to fifteen government-owned parks covering all regions. Industrial park site selection became political, as regional leaders claimed a 'right to have an industrial park.'[133]

Hawassa Industrial Park was built in 2015–16, when the ADR construction was finalizing and experiencing operation delays. The timely completion and successful operation of the Hawassa Industrial Park were largely due to

[129] Interview with Arkebe, Kunshan (7 April 2023) via Zoom.
[130] Arkebe and Kefale (2020).
[131] Arkebe and Kefale (2020).
[132] Interview with ET-65, Ethiopian Development Research Institute, Addis Ababa (10 April 2019).
[133] Interview with ET-67, Ethiopian Development Research Institute, Addis Ababa (12 April 2019).

the championship of the highly capable Arkebe Oqubay. Although Arkebe used to serve as the chairman of the ERC board, his ADR visits were only to accompany Hailemariam. Arkebe never visited the ADR by himself.[134]

Hawassa Industrial Park was a 'flagship' project for the Ethiopian government, and Arkebe championed the development of this park. The construction contract of five parks, including Hawassa, Kombolcha, Dire Dawa, Adama, and Bahir Dar, was awarded to the CCECC, which had experience in building industrial parks and infrastructure projects, including the same Chinese company that constructed the Mieso–Djibouti section of the railway. Ethiopian government used various financing mechanism including from treasury, concessional loans, and a significant US$1 billion Eurobond to finance park construction, and once the constructor was selected, the funding decision was made the same day.[135] The construction of Hawassa Park was completed within nine months. Arkebe was at the Hawassa Industrial Park construction site every weekend and worked closely with the Chinese contractor. As Arkebe himself revealed the government's 'extraordinary commitment', coordination among government agencies, and a close partnership with the firms investing in the park[136] required to complete the park construction:

> During the construction phase, I was travelling from Addis every weekend to Hawassa, to inspect and to understand the challenges. Every single week. I drove on Friday [from Addis to Hawassa], then returned on Sunday. That was the only way we could achieve because there are always, always unexpected problems happening every day, every week. It was through steep learning process that better ways of building the new generation of industrial parks was possible—sustainable, specialized, and bringing all government services. And that was how we managed to complete such a complex project in nine months and then operationalize it in ten to twelve months, having over 10,000 or 12,000 workers.[137]

A senior manager of CCECC also recalled the dedication of Arkebe:

> The industrial park was like Arkebe's child. He was very senior in government but catered to details on the industrial park project, acting like a project manager ... Back then Arkebe and I worked together every day. There was a week that I flew with Arkebe eight times.[138]

[134] Interview with CH-2, CCECC, Beijing (18 October 2018).
[135] Interview with Arkebe, Kunshan (7 April 2023) via Zoom.
[136] Ibid.
[137] Ibid.
[138] Interview with CH-2, CCECC, Beijing (18 October 2018).

Besides frequenting construction sites, Arkebe did not hesitate to replace staff that could not satisfy his demand for effectiveness. Like the ADR, Hawassa Industrial Park experienced difficulties in electricity supply. Arkebe held meetings with the leadership of Ethiopia Telecom and fired the manager responsible for signalling at the meeting.[139] 'He even fired a CCECC project manager!' the Chinese manager exclaimed, 'Hawassa Industrial Park was under tremendous time constraint. According to the contract, we were scheduled to finish the construction in May [2015]. When we [Arkebe and I] visited the construction site, it was a mess, Arkebe was furious, so he fired the CCECC manager in charge.'[140]

The extraordinary commitment of the political leadership can be illustrated through this pilot park. It was driven not only by the special attention needed for a pilot project to succeed but also by his promise to major investors. Arkebe explained:

> I had to spend time to ensure this project doesn't fail. Because [Hawassa Industrial Park] is a pilot, an experiment, and if it fails, then we will never be able to build another park again. Once it became successful, it is going to be a benchmark.

Before the start of construction, the government had already secured over twenty investors to invest in Hawassa Industrial Park, including PVH, the American apparel giant. When PVH and forty-eight other textile and apparel manufacturers met with Ethiopian government during their relocation tour in East Africa in 2014, the Ethiopian government clearly assured them that the government would 'make the park ready in nine months, 270 days.'[141] This promise was fulfilled, building the confidence of the investors. In 2020, Hawassa Industrial Park was the largest industrial park in Africa, specialising in the apparel and textile sector, employing close to 35,000 workers, one of the pioneer eco-industrial parks using a centralised zero-liquid technology.

Construction started in July 2015 and Hawassa Industrial Park opened in July 2017. During the inauguration ceremony, Hailemariam said, 'Our goal is to create millions of new jobs in labour-intensive and export-oriented light manufacturing ... the full operation of the Hawassa Industrial Park is the most evident and concrete example yet towards achieving our national vision

[139] Ibid.
[140] Ibid.
[141] Interview with Arkebe, Kunshan (7 April 2023) via Zoom.

and marks a milestone in our quest for industrialization.'[142] African heads of state were invited to Hawassa as a proud demonstration of Ethiopia's modern industrial parks.

3.7 Conclusion

In this chapter, I have examined the ADR trajectory to show the causal importance of political championship to project implementation. Meles initiated and championed the ADR as an essential demonstration of his developmental state programme. The prime minister dissuaded dissidents, established the ERC, handpicked its CEO, and made this parastatal the focal point of railway development in Ethiopia, operating in parallel to the MOT. During Meles' time, the federal government also kept firm control over regional states. Meles closely monitored the progress of the ADR and even participated in the negotiations with the Chinese contractors and EximBank. High political commitment from the head of state and Meles' strong capability to build an effective coalition for the implementation of the ADR guaranteed its initial success.

Meles' sudden death in 2012 and the accession of Hailemariam marked a continuation of political commitment to the ADR but a decline in the leader's capability. In the early years of Hailemariam's tenure (2012–16), he maintained Meles' legacy, and the ADR continued to be a political priority. Yet Hailemariam lacked Meles' astuteness to navigate various factional interests and effectively lead the coalition of actors for the ADR implementation established by Meles. The microeconomic team meetings that continued from Meles to Hailemariam were not a channel for problem resolution. Central control over regional states gradually weakened, causing increasing difficulties for the ADR's land acquisition. Despite his commitment to the ADR, Hailemariam lacked the leadership capability to either utilize the implementation coalition left by Meles or mobilize his own support for the ADR. Therefore, obstacles could not be resolved in a timely manner, as was the case during Meles' tenure.

Since the beginning of the uprisings in late 2016 and the repeated declaration of a state of emergency, the country's priority shifted from economic growth to stability maintenance. Political commitment further faded away for infrastructure projects like the ADR that could not provide massive employment opportunities. The final stage of the construction and operation was left

[142] Ethiopia Embassy in London (22 July 2017).

to the coordination of the ERC and the Chinese contractors. The ADR had been operating at a loss until 2022: the revenue from the operation could not cover the costs, not to mention the repayment of EximBank's loan. Without political commitment, the project development deteriorated.

The bureaucratic capacity theory could not account for the initial success and subsequent unsatisfactory development of the ADR. Contrary to the predictions of the bureaucratic capacity argument that political championship was generated by bureaucratic leverage, Meles was not only the initiator of the railway project but also created the railway corporation, while the MOT was sidelined from ADR's initiation to its operation. During project implementation, the newly established ERC had accrued experience in railway construction and managing Chinese contractors. However, the ADR trajectory was on a downward slope where issues during Meles' tenure were resolved much more effectively than under Hailemariam and Abiy. The bureaucratic capacity explanation emphasizes the success and failure of the project were due to bureaucratic capability and, therefore, cannot explain the development trajectory of the ADR.

The external agency argument also falls short in explaining the ADR's development track. Chinese intervention before late 2012 was almost invisible, but the ADR initiation progressed smoothly. Chinese SOEs bore a high risk of providing financial support to the ERC before the arrival of EximBank funding and put reverse pressure on the Chinese government to grant the ADR's commercial loan. To hasten the operation, Chinese contractors also leveraged their political connections in Beijing to pressure Hailemariam during his visit to the Belt and Road Forum. This improved the Ethiopian government's effective resolution of obstacles in the short run, but it was still another six months before the operation started. Under a political commitment from China that this Belt and Road flagship project 'could not stop', the Chinese contractors continued the operation despite ERC's significant payment delay and struggled between federal-regional politics and the politics between parastatals, complaining that they were 'politically kidnapped' by the railway project. Even with strong Chinese commitment, the ADR operation was still struggling.

4

Struggle to reconstruct

A railway of neglect

> After 33 years of dormancy, the first passenger and cargo railroad train whistled again in the city of Kuíto, capital of the province of Bié. Thousands of people gathered at the local station to see with their own eyes that the MPLA Executive wants to and is reducing their suffering.
>
> Movimento Popular de Libertação de Angola (MPLA, n.d.)

On 14 February 2015, in the border city of Luau, Angola's then president José Eduardo dos Santos hosted the opening ceremony of the Luau station of the Benguela railway (Caminho de Ferro de Benguela, or CFB). Dos Santos invited Joseph Kabila and Edgar Chagwa Lungu, the then heads of state of the Democratic Republic of Congo (DRC) and Zambia, respectively, to join this celebration. The 1,344-kilometre Benguela railway historically connected the three countries for exporting inland mineral products to the port of Lobito for the colonial European market. The Benguela railway project had the most favourable conditions among the three railway cases under study. The renovation work did not involve new acquisition of land and faced no competition from road transport, which had been the biggest obstacles for railway construction and operation in Kenya and Ethiopia. It was a rehabilitation of the existing metre-gauge railway instead of building new railway lines involving new standards and technology, as was the case in Kenya and Ethiopia. Historically, the Benguela railway was close to the hearts of local residents, and its reopening was long expected by the people domestically and Zambian and DRC miners as alternative routes were more time-consuming and expensive. The CFB expected almost no competition from road transport as many of the areas the railway passes through were not connected by road. Angola was a highly centralized state with a focus on post-war infrastructure reconstruction fuelled by oil revenues, and the railway was among the priorities of the government. The CFB Railway Corporation (CFB-EP) also had the institutional memory of operating a successful line, as the colonial CFB was one of the few lines that were popular and profitable on the continent.

The Railpolitik. Yuan Wang, Oxford University Press. © Yuan Wang (2023). DOI: 10.1093/oso/9780198873037.003.0005

Despite these practical favourable conditions, the Benguela railway is the least likely case for the political championship, bureaucratic capacity, and external agency theories, and the project demonstrated low effectiveness. The CFB was originally managed by the Office of National Reconstruction (GRN) and was transferred to the Ministry of Transport in 2010, yet this change of administration did not increase the speed of rehabilitation work. After the Ministry took over the railway, the rehabilitation work took another six years to complete. The initial contract to rehabilitate the CFB estimated completion within twenty months, but in the end the project took eleven years in total. The operational figure in 2019 shows that the railway only operated at one-tenth of its capacity, and the operation heavily relied on state support to cover the gap between costs and operational revenues. Even more troubling were the frequent accidents which, in some cases, led to fatalities.

In comparison, the Kilamba Kiaxi housing project, which also represents a least likely case for the bureaucratic capacity and external agency theories, demonstrates relatively higher effectiveness. The construction was completed within three years and after price adjustment the housing units were nearly fully occupied by residents. Similar to the CFB rehabilitation project, the Kilamba Kiaxi housing project was initially managed and financed by GRN and China International Fund (CIF), contracted to Chinese state-owned enterprises (SOEs), and later included in the Industrial and Commercial Bank of China financial scheme.[1] Both projects were also at one point referred to by the media as a 'ghost line' and 'ghost town'. Why did the Kilamba Kiaxi housing project exhibit higher effectiveness than the Benguela railway project?

In this chapter, I start by reviewing Angola's political system, with a focus on the 'parallel state', where decision-making lay outside formal institutions but was strongly concentrated under the presidency. This is followed by an introduction to Angola's post-war reconstruction programme and China's private and state roles in supporting Angolan reconstruction through the 'oil-for-infrastructure' model. The Benguela railway and Kilamba Kiaxi housing project were prioritized in this reconstruction programme. I will show that the fates of the two projects were shaped by the political championship of President Dos Santos for the Kilamba housing project and his essentially

[1] The financier of the Kilamba housing project is difficult to confirm. Various sources indicate the project was financed by the China Industrial and Commercial Bank, but whether the China Export and Import Bank (EximBank) and other Chinese financiers also jointly provided loans for this project was uncertain. But this confusion does not affect my analysis here.

ceremonial attention to the Benguela railway. I also show that Dos Santos' commitment to the Kilamba project was driven by the 2008 and 2012 elections, which, although not competitive, were moments for the MPLA to show deliveries of the reconstruction programme. I also review two alternative explanations; that is, the Chinese agency argument and bureaucratic capacity argument. I show that the lack of Chinese extra-contractual intervention and bureaucratic capacity was consequential to the low effectiveness of the Benguela railway, but strong championship by the president could have compensated for other conditions, as shown by the Kilamba case. Despite the lack of Chinese agency and bureaucratic capacity, the Kilamba project still achieved relatively high effectiveness.

4.1 Hyper-presidentialism and the 'parallel state'

Angola had reached the upper-middle-income status by 2005 according to the World Bank standards,[2] yet over half of its population still lived under the US$1.90 poverty line by 2018. The country is endowed with fertile land, a mild climate for agriculture, and an abundance of natural resources, particularly petroleum, diamonds, and gemstones. According to data from the World Bank, before the commodity price collapse, Angolan oil rent in 2014 amounted to US$33.6 billion, but by 2018, revenue from oil exports had gone down to US$25.4 billion. Little of this oil revenue trickled down to the wider population. In 2018, 51.8 per cent of the population were living in poverty on US$1.90 per day,[3] among the highest levels of poverty worldwide. The four decades of vicious war between 1961 and 2002 killed more than 500,000 people and internally displaced one-third of Angola's 13 million people; another 435,000 Angolans fled the country altogether and became refugees abroad.[4] Angola seems to represent a typical case of the resource curse: the contest for natural resource wealth was central to the prolonged civil war,[5] and from the war arose both a rich authoritarian state fuelled by resource revenues and an extremely poor population who are deprived of resource benefits.[6] At the centre of this

[2] The World Bank define upper-middle-income economies as those with a gross national income per capita between US$4,046 and US$12,535. In 2005, Angolan gross national income per capita (PPP) was US$4,310, which continued to rise to US$7,680 in 2014 under the oil boom.

[3] 2011 PPP adjusted (World Bank, n.d.).

[4] Human Rights Watch (2002).

[5] Addison (2001); Le Billon (1999).

[6] Karl (1997).

oil state is an all-powerful presidency operating through a parallel system of formal state institutions and a personalized power structure.

In this section, I first discuss the emergence of the MPLA party-state from the war and the gradual establishment of the hyper-presidency started by President António Agostinho Neto and continued by Dos Santos. I also note that this party-state, characterized by a hyper-presidentialism, adopted a democratic façade for domestic and international legitimacy after the end of the Cold War, and especially after the end of the civil war in 2002. I then review the 'parallel state'; that is, the Futungo–Sonangol nexus featuring an ultimate privatization of power within a small coterie of trusted advisors and expatriate advisors around the Futungo presidential palace and fuelled by the revenue flows from Sonangol, the national oil company.

4.1.1 The party-state with hyper-presidentialism

Following independence in 1975 from five centuries of Portuguese colonial rule, Angola soon entered a destructive twenty-seven-year civil war, itself preceded by an anti-colonial war that had started in 1961. The civil war was led by three liberation movements vying for supremacy: the Movimento Popular de Libertação de Angola (MPLA), the Frente Nacional de Libertação de Angola (FNLA), and the União Nacional para a Independeência Total de Angola (UNITA). The MPLA was established in the capital city Luanda and made up of urban elites from the capital, mixed-race Angolans (*Mestiços*), educated Angolans that had received the colonial *assimilado* status, intellectuals, and whites, though its wider ethnic base was the Mbundu ethnicity from Luanda. UNITA split from the FNLA and found its base in the countryside among the Ovimbundu people of the populous central high plateau in the provinces of Huambo, Bié, Benguela, and Moxico.[7] There was a short period of peace in 1991–2 before Jonas Savimbi, UNITA leader, took the country back into war as he was unsatisfied with his party's slim loss to the MPLA in the 1992 elections. The death of the rebel leader Savimbi in 2002 marked the long-expected peace and the consolidation of the dominance of the MPLA.

Angola is a party-state under the dominance of the MPLA, with blurred boundaries between the party and the state. In a country of 31 million people, the party's membership is currently 4 million, meaning that one in eight

[7] Benguela, Huambo, Bié, and Moxico are also the provinces that the Benguela railway travels through.

Angolans is an MPLA party member. The MPLA monopolized all aspects of the post-independence state apparatus, from the ministerial to the provincial administration, including the military and intelligence service, thereby blurring the distinction between the party and the state.[8] As Soares de Oliveira (2015) notes: 'No one of consequence in government can do without party membership, presidential proteges without a robust MPLA background will be fast-tracked up the party ranks to bring their party status into line with their influence at the presidential palace.'[9] Simply put, the relationship between the state and the party is 'so deep, multilevel, and enduring that no one knows where one ends and the other begins.'[10]

Starting with President Agostinho Neto and heightened by José Eduardo dos Santos, there had been a trend of power centralization at the presidency, producing hyper-presidentialism. The fact that Agostinho Neto had acquired prestige during his long years of exile and had led the liberation struggle gave him great influence in the MPLA.[11] Upon taking power in 1979, the external threats from UNITA and its South African ally provided an opportunity for Dos Santos to introduce institutional changes that greatly strengthened the presidency at the expense of the party leadership bodies. The constitutional changes in 1991–2 not only introduced multiparty elections but also confirmed the concentration of power at the presidency. At times there have been figurehead prime ministers to deal with issues that the president considered not essential but still required attention, and at others the president has dispensed with the office of prime minister altogether. Throughout, Dos Santos chaired the meetings of the Council of Ministers and acted as the effective head of the government. There was a high degree of presidential intervention in the day-to-day management of state affairs. Presidential advisors often had greater influence than ministers, leading to a situation where ministers were unable to assert their authority.[12] Messiant notes that, by the second half of the 1980s, 'power has progressively concentrated round the presidency, and the president has been able, despite lacking any other social base than the party-state, to impose himself by playing between the various party-state factions.'[13]

This party-state, in which the presidency held supreme power, maintained a multiparty façade; or, more precisely, as Messiant commented, 'multiparty

[8] Pearce (2015).
[9] Soares de Oliveira (2015, p. 93).
[10] Soares de Oliveira (2015, p. 93).
[11] Hodges (2004).
[12] Hodges (2004).
[13] Messiant (1992, p. 21).

politics without democracy'.[14] With the end of the Cold War, Soviet and Cuban support for the MPLA came to an end and the ruling party needed to quickly embrace political and economic reform. Multiparty elections were introduced in Angola in 1991, and the first elections were held the following year. In May 1991, a constitutional revision law (law 12/91) defined Angola as a 'democratic state based on the rule of law' and introduced a multiparty system. The 1992 presidential elections were the only set of elections that were close to 'free and fair'; Dos Santos won 49.6 per cent of the votes while Savimbi won 40.1 per cent. Savimbi rejected the election results as rigged, and took the country back into war. Post-war elections were installed more for gaining domestic and international legitimacy than facilitating the possibility of a meaningful change of government. The international pressure for democratization in other African states struggled for traction in Angola, where the regime's 'oil-clout' allowed it to implement political reform suggested by international imperatives at its own leisurely pace.[15] The introduction of elections was accompanied by limited political space for civil society, controlled media, and increasing intimidation of opposition parties and voters.[16] Post-war multiparty elections were held in 2008, 2012, 2017, and most recently 2022,[17] and the 2017 elections saw a transfer of political leadership to João Lourenço, Dos Santos' hand-picked successor.

The MPLA proved to be instrumental in electoral (and any other) campaigns and mobilizing voters. With a blurred line between the party and the state, the MPLA could essentially mobilize all necessary state resources for its campaign and to convince voters that they are better off sticking with the incumbent.[18] Official figures published in 2009 show that the MPLA spent US$8.7 million on its campaign, more than seven times the amount spent by the thirteen opposition parties combined.[19] In a context where the MPLA, winner of a long civil war, has the political, military, and financial means to dictate the rules of the electoral game, it is difficult to imagine how the elections could escape Dos Santos and the MPLA. In 2010, Angola enacted a new constitution that further fortified the power of the presidency and cancelled direct

[14] Messiant (2007).
[15] Chabal (2007).
[16] Roque (2009).
[17] The 2022 parliamentary elections concluded with the MPLA winning a 51.17 per cent majority, and UNITA received 43.95 per cent. International observers expressed concerns about potential fraud. See Demony and Cocks (30 August 2022).
[18] Chabal (2007).
[19] Vines and Weimer (2009).

presidential elections, allowing the president to be indirectly elected by the National Assembly.

4.1.2 The 'parallel state'

The concentration and individualization of power reached its zenith when Dos Santos ran the country through a parallel, informal power structure beyond the formal state institutions, including the ministries and party organs. The locus of power in the country lay in Futungo de Belas, the residential complex of the president by the sea on the outskirts of Luanda. The Futungo group, named after the presidential residence at the time, was the decision-making centre running parallel to the Cabinet and the MPLA since the 1980s. The group consisted of twenty or so unelected officials, businessmen, and former generals and centred on the president.[20] International brokers were also granted an increasingly central role, from arms sales and diamond concessions during the war to loan concessions for post-war reconstruction. For this small cast of foreign individuals, 'friendship' with the president and the Futungo group could transform into considerable business partnerships.[21]

Sonangol, the national oil company, was at the centre of the parallel system and generated continuous revenue flows for the Futungo group. The nation's oil bonanza, harvested through Sonangol, effectively provided the necessary financial resources to implement Futungo's decisions and maintained a wider patronage network in exchange for loyalty. Since its establishment in 1976, Sonangol had been under the political control of the presidency as a loyal instrument of the president's interest,[22] and thus was largely outside the purview of governmental and party scrutiny.[23] In 2016, Dos Santos even appointed his daughter Isabel, at the time Africa's richest woman, as the chairwoman of Sonangol. The oil company proved itself to be a 'pocket of effectiveness' in the largely ineffective state bureaucracies of Angola.[24] Sonangol possessed at its disposal financial means and human resources beyond the rivalry of any other branches in the bureaucracy.[25] The company was highly

[20] Hodges (2004); Soares de Oliveira (2007).
[21] Soares de Oliveira (2015).
[22] Soares de Oliveira (2007).
[23] Chabal (2007).
[24] Soares de Oliveira (2007).
[25] Ibid.

respected among international banks and oil companies, who referred to it as 'the Angolan miracle'.[26]

Sonangol not only managed the Futungo's phantom revenue flows but also enabled elite rentierism across the domestic economy.[27] Sonangol created business entrepreneurial opportunities for well-connected but less-competent individuals, a strategy which essentially aimed to ensure continuing support for the presidency by sharing rentier opportunities across the elite.[28] The system of patronage operated through diamond concessions, land titles, state contracts, business licences, and other economic favours but primarily relied on the distribution of oil wealth. This scheme provided Dos Santos with enormous resources he could use to buy off opponents and build alliances. In this way, Angola's economy was strongly controlled by a president who wielded power through personalized networks through the allocation of money and favours to clients in exchange for political support of their patrons.[29]

The Futungo–Sonangol nexus formulated a 'parallel state' that marginalized formal institutions in Angola.[30] Political decision-making under this parallel state became increasingly de-institutionalized. As an Angolan journalist revealed: 'This was no longer a matter of the Finance ministry or the party not knowing exactly what was going on. At this stage, only a handful of individuals had any clue about matters of life or death.'[31] They were also much more efficient than Angola's bureaucratic system. Dos Santos repeatedly created ad hoc commissions directly answerable to himself to operate tasks that the bureaucracy 'cannot cope with'.[32] These tasks included resolving urgent problems, managing prestigious projects and high-profile events, and managing foreign credit lines (GRN in this case). Dos Santos granted these commissions total financial independence from the Ministry of Finance and Central Bank and they could invoke presidential power at any time.[33] In 1996, Dos Santos even created the Eduardo dos Santos Foundation (FESA), which was perceived by some members of the MPLA as an attempt by the Futungo to further marginalize the party.[34] The Futungo–Sonangol nexus was further strengthened by an intelligence service and coercive apparatus

[26] Soares de Oliveira (2007, p. 605), citing the author's interview with an oil executive of a major European firm.
[27] Soares de Oliveira (2007).
[28] Ibid.
[29] Hodges (2004).
[30] Soares de Oliveira (2007).
[31] Soares de Oliveira (2015, p. 38), citing the author's interview with a journalist.
[32] Soares de Oliveira (2015, p. 44).
[33] Ibid.
[34] Messiant (2001).

directly answerable to the president. Dos Santos established a special task force within the intelligence services, which selected, distributed, and oversaw business opportunities for certain political and social figures, rewarded loyalists, co-opted dissenters, and enriched certain families. All of this worked to ensure tight, vertical control of the patronage system in order to maintain the status quo.[35]

This is not to declare the irrelevance of the MPLA and formal state institutions, however. The party remained a political 'machine' for legitimating the rulership of Dos Santos through mobilization of support.[36] The MPLA provided the president with a connection to the liberation movement, an aura of legitimacy through bringing peace, a national apparatus, and a reliable mechanism of regulating elite conflict, distributing patronage, and voter mobilization.[37] The party deeply penetrated Angolan government and society. An MPLA membership was needed to access bank loans, university places, medical services, job promotions, and so on. An MPLA membership was, and is still, the basic requirement for the career advancement of civil servants.[38] By allowing senior personnel in the MPLA to grow extremely rich, Dos Santos was able to stabilize the relations between the presidency and party, and enhance elite cohesion.[39] Although there is a genuine lack of competence in the Angolan bureaucracy (except Sonangol), the ministries were still responsible for tasks that kept the country operational.

Although the 1991 constitutional reform formally institutionalized multiparty democracy in Angola and the country has gone through five elections since then, the politics of Angola was characterized by a hyper-presidentialism and a parallel system of political decision-making. João Lourenço dismissed the Futungo group, but the hyper-presidentialism remains. The survival and prosperity of post-war Angolan elites was built on a strong presidency, efficient armed forces and urban coercive apparatus, and a capable national oil company. They were additionally supported by a coterie of advisors, who, together with the president, privatized state resources for their private benefit and established a parallel decision-making and implementation system that had sidelined formal ministries. Since the discovery of oil in the 1960s and the massive foreign investment in the oil sector this has always entailed, there had also been complex international networks of support. During the

[35] Marques de Morais (2012).
[36] Soares de Oliveira (2015); Chabal (2007).
[37] Soares de Oliveira (2015, ch. 3, pp. 91–130).
[38] Ibid., p. 100.
[39] Ibid., p. 101.

war, they laundered the wealth of insiders while contributing the government's war effort through the sale of weaponry. In peacetime since 2002, they helped sustain the concentration of power in the presidency and the parallel system through resource patronage and 'oil-for-infrastructure' arrangements.

4.2 National reconstruction and railway initiation

Upon gaining peace, the Dos Santos government prioritized the reconstruction of infrastructure that was largely destroyed during the four decades of war, and the CFB was high on the list of reconstruction projects. Unlike many African countries that are dependent on international aid, the abundance of oil gave Angolan elites a decisive trump card in their dealings with the international community. In seeking international partnerships for reconstruction, Angola first reached out to Western donors but, unsatisfied with the political conditions attached to the Western credit lines, primarily partnered instead with China. The readily available Export and Import Bank of China (EximBank) credit lines with no political conditionalities[40] were much welcomed by Dos Santos from 2004. In parallel to this state-to-state partnership, a Chinese businessman, Sam Pa, also capitalized on his war-time connections with Angolan elites and established a group of Hong Kong-based companies including the CIF. This section develops in two parts. It starts by reviewing Angola's post-war national reconstruction project and the 'parallel system' of Sino-Angolan relations; that is, the state-to-state relationship based on EximBank credit lines, and the private-to-state relationship led by Sam Pa's CIF and the GRN. Subsection 4.2.2 reviews the initiation of the Benguela railway project exclusively managed by the CIF and GRN.

4.2.1 National reconstruction and the 'parallel system' of China in Angola

Four decades of war disrupted the institutional continuity in Angolan bureaucracies. All industries, apart from the oil sector, perished. After winning the war, the MPLA found itself managing a country twice the size of France but with an acute shortage of qualified personnel in the public administration. Over 340,000 (5 per cent of the population then) Portuguese settlers departed around the time of independence in 1975, and because of the failure of the

[40] Except the recognition of the 'one China' policy.

colonial regime to invest in educating Africans, this exodus meant the loss of the majority of the country's technically qualified personnel.[41] Basic infrastructure, such as electricity systems, bridges, and railway lines, was destroyed or severely damaged in many places, and roads were mined, disrupting communications and raising the costs of production. There was a steep decline and subsequent stagnation of production in the non-oil sectors of the economy, accompanied by chronic macroeconomic instability. The war also fragmented the national market into a patchwork of isolated enclave markets, connected in some cases by occasional road convoys and in many others only by costly air transport.[42]

After securing peace, President Dos Santos' next project was the national reconstruction, with the main component being the rebuilding of infrastructure.[43] To ensure that certain strategic goods and investments were delivered effectively, as well as to expand his already considerable discretionary power, Dos Santos created several new special state agencies outside the regular state bureaucracy, given the latter's low capacity. In October 2004, President Dos Santos decided to create a specialized office, the Office of the National Reconstruction,[44] to 'systemically and permanently managing the most fundamental national reconstruction projects'.[45] It was established as a parallel system to the ministries based on the assumption that the ministries would not have the organizational and technical capacity to manage large inflows of money directed to the national reconstruction programme.[46] Dos Santos entrusted the chief of the Presidential Guard, General Hélder Vieira Dias 'Kopelipa', to head the GRN. This office, or Kopelipa more precisely, monitored the reconstruction programme, including the rehabilitation of the three railway lines, the reconstruction of the Port of Luanda, the reconstruction and construction of twenty-five airports nationwide, the construction of the Kilamba Kiaxi social housing project and other satellite towns, and the construction of new

[41] Hodges (2004). Sommerville (1986) described how technical positions were occupied by the Portuguese in Angola: the Portuguese 'monopolized all managerial and technical jobs and most skilled occupations right down to the level of truck and taxi drivers and street vendors' (Sommerville, 1986, p. 131).

[42] UNSA (2002).

[43] Apart from infrastructure, the reconstruction programme also included other aspects such as the privatization of national companies and diversification of non-oil sectors. See Soares de Oliveira (2015) for a detailed description of 'all other aspects' of the reconstruction programme.

[44] The Gabinete de Reconstrução Nacional (GRN) in Portuguese.

[45] Diário da República (22 October 2004).

[46] According to Corkin (2016), the GRN started as a monitoring entity over the Eximbank loan, following allegations that Angolan officials were skimming off massive commissions from the fund via questionable economic entities. The main culprit identified was António Van Dunem, secretary of the Council of Ministers, and the direct link between the president and the Cabinet was sacked shortly after his exposure.

roads.[47] The GRN was an instrument of Dos Santos. It directly reported to the president, and these projects were carried out independently from the Ministry of Transport and Ministry of Public Work. It also became the office that managed funds from China.[48]

To fund the ambitious reconstruction programme, Dos Santos started mobilizing international financing on the eve of the peace. Dos Santos wrote to the International Monetary Fund (IMF) in June 2001 requesting additional assistance after the IMF's Staff Monitoring Programme and in early 2002, called for a donor's conference to mobilize resources for the reconstruction project. The IMF raised concerns on the transparency of the oil sector and requested more transparency.[49] Western donors adopted a cautious approach to Angola's long-term development programme because of the primacy of the humanitarian crisis, security constraints, the perceived weakness of government commitment, and the (in)capacity to pursue pro-poor policies.[50] The political conditions attached to the loans were unacceptable to Angola and the donor's conference never materialized.[51] China emerged as a much preferred alternative as Angola's reconstruction partner. The Chinese loans came in large amounts, quickly, at a cheap price, and, most importantly, with none of the political conditions attached.

This Sino-Angolan state-to-state partnership started at the dawn of peace in May 2000; the Angolan defence minister visited China, and Angola's oil exports to China surged from 40,000 barrels per day in 1999 to 174,000 barrels per day in 2000.[52] In 2002, Dos Santos appealed to China, and later that year China Construction Bank and EximBank provided US$145 million for infrastructure development in Angola constructed by Chinese companies. The Angolan Ministry of Finance had little input in these arrangements as the funding was directly issued to Chinese companies.[53] On 26 November 2003, Angola's and China's Ministries of Commerce signed a 'Framework Agreement', providing the legal basis for the credit contracting process between the two states. According to the Agreement, Angola invites Chinese companies to

[47] CR20 (2020).

[48] Before the Cabinet reshuffle on 8 February 2010 when Kopelipa was voted 'non-confident' by Dos Santos, the GRN had managed US$6.5 billion Chinese loans, from CIF and EximBank (*Africa Confidential*, 1 March 2010).

[49] IMF (2003).

[50] UNSA (2002).

[51] As described in Corkin (2016, pp. 75–6), the IMF agreed to provide finance to Angola on two conditions: first, increased transparency and a macroeconomic stabilization policy, aimed at reducing inflation by cutting public expenditure and reducing borrowing; second, any large-scale infrastructure reconstruction programme would have to wait until Angola had achieved a healthier fiscal situation.

[52] Executive Research Associates (2009).

[53] Campos and Vines (2008).

bid and contract for the construction projects in Angola, while Chinese financial institutions provide credit lines for Angola. These loans are repaid by natural resource revenues,[54] thereby institutionalizing the 'oil-for-infrastructure' model.[55] From 2002 to 2018, Chinese loans to Angola reached US$43 billion, representing 30 per cent of China's total loans to the whole African continent in the past two decades.[56] The majority of the loans were issued by China EximBank. Angola has come to occupy an increasingly important position within Beijing's economic and foreign policy strategies, overtaking Saudi Arabia as the largest supplier of oil to China in 2006 and again in early 2010. Aguinaldo Jaime, head of Angola Central Bank at the time, confided to several interlocutors that apart from no political conditions attached, China's banks had enough liquidity to immediately disburse money, and saw loans as a continuous process, until the necessities of the borrower would end.[57]

China's deal with Angola was billed as a pact between two states, but in the shadows a parallel deal had taken shape, melding private interests with state power. The CIF, a private equity firm registered at 88 Queensway in Hong Kong, together with a network of companies known as the '88 Queensway Group',[58] and China's private engagement with Angola were the creation of a man known as Sam Pa, or Xu Jinghua. He was said to have worked for the external branch of Chinese intelligence in the 1980s and was a big player in weapons, oil, and diamond deals in Africa.[59] In 2004, when he travelled to Angola, he met with President José Eduardo dos Santos together with Hélder José Bataglia dos Santos, an Angolan-Portuguese businessman and broker, and Pierre Falcone, a French Algerian who had long enjoyed close links with the Angolan elites and particularly the president. A joint venture, China Sonangol International Holding Limited, came out of this meeting, to channel Angola's fast-expanding oil exports to China. China Sonangol was also registered at 88 Queensway in Hong Kong, together with over thirty companies. Manuel Vicente, the then chief executive officer (CEO) of Angola's national oil corporation Sonangol, became the chairman of the China Sonangol, and Sonangol held a 30 per cent stake in China Sonangol. In return for Angolan oil, Sam

[54] MOFCOM (28 November 2003).

[55] This China-Angola 'oil-for-infrastructure' arrangement is not a new creation of the two states but a continuation of the way the West had already been working with Angola. See Soares de Oliveira (2008).

[56] Annual loan data; see Bräutigam, Hwang, Link, and Acker (2019). Many researchers have documented specific loans and projects for each loans. See also Campos and Vines (2008); Executive Research Associates (2009); Corkin (2016).

[57] Executive Research Associates (2009).

[58] In 2008, the US government requested research into the '88 Queensway Group'. For the report, see Levkowitz, Ross, and Warner (2009).

[59] Burgis and Sevastopulo (2014).

Pa promised to build infrastructure, including low-cost housing, public water mains, hydroelectric plants, cross-country roads, and railways, according to the government. The construction contracts were awarded to the CIF. In 2005, the CIF was expected to disbursed an initial amount of US$2.9 billion to reconstruct over thirty projects, including the rehabilitation of the CFB (US$300 million), renovating the current Luanda airport, and constructing a new Luanda International Airport (US$450 million), a new sewage system for the capital, and so on.[60] These oil-collateralized loans, formulated between international partners like Sam Pa and members of the Futungo group, were not properly accounted for in the state budget.[61] The CIF was trusted with the reconstruction of over thirty projects managed by the GRN, and these projects were then subcontracted to Chinese construction companies, many of which were state-owned.

Using its connections, the CIF seems to have successfully positioned itself between the Chinese and Angolan governments (as well as between Sonangol and Sinopec) with its projects mostly being awarded to Chinese companies selected by the Queensway group, including many SOEs. When asked to clarify the relationship between the US$4.5 billion EximBank loan and Angola's relationship with the CIF in 2009, the then Chinese ambassador Bolum Zhang was unable or unwilling to go too far into specifics, especially concerning the value of the relationship, which some independent press sources place at near US$10 billion since 2002.[62] Zhang said that as the CIF was a 'private company', the Chinese embassy did not actively participate in or monitor its relationship with Angola.[63] He added that the CIF continued to benefit from the Hong Kong-based owner's 'close relationship' with President Dos Santos.[64] Although officially the Chinese government did not recognize its connection with the CIF, the Sino-Angolan state and private relationships were much more intertwined than officially recognized. It was Sam Pa's China Sonangol that purchased the Block 18 from Shell, a Block that was later acquired by Sinopec, one of China's state oil firms,[65] and Sam Pa was arrested in China in 2015 as part of an anti-corruption sweep affecting the leadership of Sinopec.[66]

Through a parallel system, China deeply engaged in Angola's post-war reconstruction. Chinese partnership allowed the exponential expansion,

[60] Executive Research Associates (2009).
[61] Chabal (2007).
[62] Wikileaks (09LUANDA51_a, 2009); also cited in Levkowitz, Ross, and Warner (2009).
[63] Ibid.
[64] Ibid.
[65] Burgis and Sevastopulo (2014).
[66] Burgis, Anderlini, and Hornby (14 October 2015).

diversification, and further internationalization of the parallel state.[67] China's private and official engagement with Angola in the form of China providing oil-backed loans for Angola's infrastructure construction has been known as the 'Angola model'. President Dos Santos summed this up in November 2007 when he stated that 'China needs natural resources and Angola wants development'.[68]

4.2.2 Initiation of the Benguela railway rehabilitation

Angola has three strategic railroads linking the Atlantic ports to the hinterland, from north to south. They are the Caminho de Ferro de Luanda (CFL), the CFB, and the Caminho de Ferro de Moçâmedes (CFM). The CFB was the most famous and only cross-border one as it connects the Atlantic port of Lobito to Luau on the border with the DRC, stretching 1,344 kilometres. Before the Angolan civil war halted the export of copper, it was the world's most profitable railway line from 1965 to 1974, by providing the shortest route to link Zaire's (today's DRC) Katanga mines and Zambian Copperbelt to Europe through the port of Lobito.[69] Its profit in the last full year of business in 1973 was equivalent to more than US$6 million dollars.[70] The economic and strategic importance of the Benguela railway made it a major target during the war. In particular, during the period of March to May 1976, UNITA guerrillas made a number of attacks on the railway, and Savimbi said that the line would be regarded as a major target for his fighters.[71]

Upon gaining peace, Dos Santos listed rehabilitating the CFB as a priority of the national reconstruction programme. In 2004, the GRN awarded the CIF a contract to restore all three railways, in addition to a list of other reconstruction projects in Angola. The idea was that once projects were selected and prioritized by the Angolan government, Sam Pa's corporate web would not only provide the credit lines to facilitate their execution but also broker deals with contractors and suppliers for their prompt implementation.[72] The contract negotiation was conducted exclusively between the GRN and CIF; one is former Angolan military and the other is a newly established company with no track record in construction, particularly the highly technical construction

[67] Soares de Oliveira (2015).
[68] Cited in Campos and Vines (2008).
[69] Relógio, Tavares, and Pacheco (2017).
[70] Macauhub (9 January 2015).
[71] Duarte, Pacheco, Santos, and Tjønneland (2015).
[72] Cardoso (2015).

of railways. The CIF approached several construction companies in China and selected China Railways 20th Bureau (CR20), an SOE, as its subcontractor. These were the first overseas projects for the CR20, who viewed this as an opportunity to enter the international market. The CIF and CR20 started negotiations in May 2004 and signed the Agreement on the Rehabilitation of the CFL on 28 October 2004 in a hotel meeting room in Beijing. They soon signed contracts on the rehabilitation of the Luanda and Benguela railways, and the new Luanda International Airport, with a contract value of US$2.5 billion for the three projects combined.[73] According to the contract, the work on CFB, including laying the rails, building new stations, and installing all signalling, was originally to have been completed by August 2007.[74]

The funding for the project was part of the US$2.9 billion expected loans from the CIF to Angola, managed by the GRN, or Kopelipa, who directly reports to the presidency independent of ministries. For the Benguela railway, and many other reconstruction projects under the GRN's management, major decision-making was concentrated in Luanda and China by the Angolan military officers in the GRN and Chinese engineers. Unequal information prevailed in these negotiations. A former employee of the railway institute explained:

> The norms used for the railroads were in Chinese, and the Chinese contractors skipped many protocols, then said they were following Chinese protocols. The GRN was military, they knew nothing about railway protocols.[75]

In addition to its lack of technical expertise, the GRN was operating under a strict timeline for the reconstruction projects. This even led to the omission of necessary procedures such as the feasibility study.[76] Many Angolan interviewees suspected that Chinese contractors simply copy-and-pasted a ready-made project design in China to Angola without adapting to local situations. As a GRN official explained: 'We went ahead with projects pressured by strict deadlines and did not take into account the forward planning that is required in a country like ours ... We overlooked crucial elements such as the fact that our ports would not be able to cope with the increased amount

[73] CR20 (2020). The CFM was originally subcontracted to CR20, but later CFM was completed by China HyWay, a private company established by Liu Daiwen, the deputy CEO of CR20, who directed the company's Angolan projects. The Luanda New International Airport was later subcontracted AVIC International, another Chinese SOE.

[74] Wikileaks (07LUANDA1015_a, 2007).

[75] Interview with AG-33, National Institute of Railway (INCFA), Luanda (30 March 2019).

[76] Corkin (2016).

of material being imported for these projects.'[77] When visiting the railway station in Lobito, I found even the sockets were Chinese standard, rather than adjusted to the European standard in Angola. The 1,344-kilometre CFB was scheduled to complete within twenty months according to the contract, but CR20 soon realized it was impossible. When implementing the project, the Chinese contractor found that the area was heavily mined. The prolonged demining process was one of the many reasons that led to the significant delay of the CFB rehabilitation.

A direct consequence of the GRN's grip on the projects was that Angolan bureaucrats with technical expertise were sidelined during the negotiation and contract formation. Line ministries in Angola, including the Ministry of Transport and Ministry of Finance, were excluded from the negotiation and the initial implementation of the project. As a former employee of the Transport Ministry explained:

> For a long time, national reconstruction projects under GRN operated under shadows, we in the Ministry of Transport did not know much about projects under GRN. Even for the security of infrastructure projects, GRN hired their own special security services, not known to the outside. Although the CFB was owned by Ministry of Transport, the Ministry did not know much about CFB.[78]

Similarly, the railway corporation CFB-EP were called upon only for follow-up and implementation. As a senior employee of CFB-EP recalled:

> During the negotiation, technical process, especially engineering infrastructure, the terms of reference [TOR] was pre-determined by central government and China. The TOR included a lot of specific issues, such as the physical characteristics of the rail, communication and signal system, cable for communication, and automatic systems of the railway. All these were dictated in the TOR, and CFB-EP just implemented them, with not much room for discussion. The TOR followed international standards, and then was adapted for the Angolan situation. CFB-EP's role was to follow up and implement.[79]

The CFB initiation process shows that the president fully entrusted the projects to the GRN and sidelined relevant bureaucratic agencies. Understanding the low bureaucratic capacity, Dos Santos chose to circumvent line

[77] Campos and Vines (2008). Interview by the authors conducted in Luanda (3 October 2007).
[78] Interview with AG-26, Ministry of Transport, Luanda (14 March 2019).
[79] Interview with AG-16, CFB-EP, Lobito (13 February 2019).

Table 4.1 Timeline of the Caminho de Ferro de Benguela

Date	Events
28 October 2004	CIF signed contract with CR20 to subcontract the rehabilitation work of the CFB
6 January 2006	**Launch of the CFB, construction started**
August 2007	Contracted completion date for the CFB
15 August 2007	CR20 directly signed contract with GRN
April 2010	Dissolution of GRN, the CFB transferred to Ministry of Transport
30 August 2011	**Opening of Huambo Station**
20 September 2011	**Opening of Benguela Station**
17 August 2012	**Opening of Luena Station**
27 August 2012	**Opening of Lobito Station**
2013	First EximBank loan arrived at CR20
14 February 2015	**Opening of Luau Station**
27 July 2017	Completion and handover
3 October 2020	Reception ceremony; CFB-EP officially received the Benguela railway from CR20

Source: the author's composition based on media reports and CR20 (2020).

ministries altogether rather than enhance their capacity, contrary to what President Kenyatta did with the Kenyan Railway Corporation. The president created the GRN, which was mostly composed of former generals without technical expertise, to implement the national reconstruction projects and negotiate with China. Bureaucrats with engineering expertise were excluded in negotiations with China, resulting in the Chinese engineers and Angolan military making decisions about technical details. Table 4.1 shows the timeline of the CFB.

4.3 Construction: Dos Santos' ceremonial attention

During the CFB's implementation, President Dos Santos only showed ceremonial attention to the project. The constant lack of political championship from the president resulted in the astonishing inefficiency of the rehabilitation process. The change of the CFB from the administration of GRN (2006–10) to the Ministry of Transport (2011–17) did not improve the implementation efficiency. Both Chinese SOEs and the embassy considered the project as commercial, and the Chinese contractor was hesitant to undertake extra-contractual liabilities. In this section, I show that the lack of political championship is essential to the low effectiveness of CFB. This low commitment from the president was coupled with bureaucratic impotence and minimal Chinese agency. The three factors jointly contributed to the prolonged delay in Benguela railway construction.

4.3.1 Ceremonial presidential commitment

The president and the MPLA lacked genuine interest in providing high-quality rail transport. The president and the party cared more about the statistics of reconstruction than the quality of service: it was more important for the president to be able to announce the statistics of how many kilometres of railways and roads his administration had reconstructed by the 2012 elections than to genuinely care about improving people's mobility. Passengers travelling on the railway were mostly the lower class of society rather than the elites, and it was far from the ruling elites' genuine interest to improve mobility for the poor. More importantly, this capital- and technology-intensive railway had little room for patronage distribution to elites, especially as over 95 per cent of the materials, from cement and steel to rice and wheat, were imported from China.[80]

However, knowing that the Benguela railway was very close to the heart of local residents, Dos Santos showed ceremonial commitment to the rehabilitation of the CFB. The CFB was historically popular for local residents, particularly those from the lower class. Train stations, located at the centres of towns, were busy gathering points for local traders, and working for the railway corporation was considered a job that could bring honour to the entire family. In 2011, when the first train whistled in the dusk, people woke up, singing and waving colourful cloth to celebrate the revitalization of the CFB. In its 2009/12 Government Program, prepared for the 2008 electoral campaign, the MPLA set out to complete the rehabilitation of the entire Luanda, Moçâmedes, and Benguela railway networks. The MPLA website also stated that with the rehabilitation of the CFB, there would be socio-economic recovery in the regions covered, namely the provinces of Benguela, Huambo, Bié,

[80] Interview with CH-15, CR20 Headquarters, Xi'an (28 October 2018).

and Moxico.[81] Several interviewees recalled that Dos Santos' 2012 electoral campaign incorporated substantial claims about the railway reconstruction.[82]

President Dos Santos visited the CFB four times between 2011 and 2015 (Table 4.2). Three of the four visits were directly targeted at opening stations in Huambo, Luena, and Luau, and one visit to Luena station was a side-trip from the president's visit to the province. These were ribbon-cutting, ceremonial visits rather than the Kenyatta-style 'onsite working meetings'. In fact, these visits were so ceremonial that, as disclosed by the CR20, they were mostly selected to be in late August so as to celebrate Dos Santos' birthday (on 28 August).[83]

The main obstacles for the CFB implementation were the demining process and the frequent delay of payments.[84] These obstacles were resolved at the ministerial level and did not reach the presidency. As a senior manager of CR20 explained:

> Technical issues, we refer to different ministries. The payment issue was under the infrastructure or planning department under the Ministry of Transport. For railway design and technical solutions, we coordinated with

Table 4.2 Dos Santos' visits to the Caminho de Ferro de Benguela

Date	Venue	Notes
30 August 2011	Huambo	CFB phased inauguration from Lobito to Huambo
April 2012	Luena, Moxico	Visited Luena and committed to the people that CFB will be inaugurated in Luena in August 2012
17 August 2012	Luena, Moxico	CFB phased inauguration from Kuito to Luena
14 February 2015	Luau, Moxico	CFB inauguration from Luena to Luau, with president of DRC and Zambia. The three presidents signed an agreement to increase products from Zambia and DRC to Lobito and increase goods transported from Angola to these countries

Source: the author's composition based on CR20 (2020) and media reports.

[81] MPLA (n.d.).
[82] Interview with AG-46, José Eduardo dos Santos University, Luanda (3 December 2018).
[83] CR20 (2020).
[84] Unlike in Kenya and Ethiopia, where land acquisition and compensation were the major obstacles for their respective railway implementation, land was not a main problem for the CFB in Angola. This is because this was a rehabilitation of the colonial railway, without new acquisition of land. The war displaced many villagers, and when they came back, they settled too close to the railway. People had not historically lived there and thus did not have ancestral rights to the land.

> CFB-EP. For demining, there was a bureau specifically in charge of demining. The high-level support we needed, such as security, they [the military] would dispatch soldiers to protect our assets and people.[85]

When asked about Dos Santos' intervention in the CFB project, the senior manager continued:

> The president visited for phased launch ceremonies. I didn't see him intervening in the railway project. He probably had many other issues to take care of. President Dos Santos was not involved much in this project. Even if we wrote to the president, he would assign the issue to different ministries.[86]

Instead of bringing technical obstacles encountered during implementation to the president's attention as in the Kenyan case, the CFB-EP and CR20 were keener on concealing the obstacles and presenting a successful picture of railway rehabilitation to the president. The Luena station, for instance, which was inaugurated by the president on the eve of the 2012 elections, was shut immediately afterwards as the stretch between Kuito and Luena was not actually ready to risk having people travelling with the train.[87]

4.3.2 A relatively weak bureaucracy

Apart from Sonangol and some parts of the security sector, it is difficult to claim strong bureaucratic capacity in any other Angolan agencies. The GRN was particularly corrupt and lacking technical expertise. Transferring the project to the Ministry of Transport did not significantly improve the implementation efficiency as the Ministry's decision-making is political and similarly corrupt. Without presidential commitment, the CFB was enmeshed in Angola's inefficient bureaucracies, a factor that was consequential to the low effectiveness of the CFB.

CFB–GRN (2006–10)

The Office of National Reconstruction managed the CFB reconstruction from 2006 to 2010. During the four years under the GRN, the Benguela railway project experienced two major suspensions: the first was due to the CIF's

[85] Interview with AG-1, CR20, Luanda (11 November 2018).
[86] Ibid.
[87] Soares de Oliveira (2015, p. 59).

financial mismanagement in 2007 and the second was caused by the 2009–10 financial crisis. Both suspensions were triggered by first the CIF's then the Angolan government's difficulties in issuing payment to the Chinese contractor CR20. And unlike the Chinese contractors of the Kenyan and Ethiopian railways, who were both willing to pay out of their own pockets to continue the project, CR20, also a state-owned company, chose to suspend the project when financial difficulties arose.

In 2007, many of the CIF's infrastructure projects ran short of funds and were suspended. Based on a report to China's Ministry of Commerce by a private Chinese company under contract with the CIF to renovate the CFM, the CIF repeatedly breached the contract and did not issue project payment on time.[88] This confirms rumours among the Chinese in Luanda that the GRN's loose management of oil credits and its opaque relationship with the CIF may be key factors in the delayed roll-out of politically important social and economic development projects. According to Western diplomats and Chinese businessmen, the CIF stopped paying bills for more than eight months in 2007. All work stopped, 2,000 Angolan day labourers were laid off on the Benguela railway project, and only a Chinese cook remained on duty.[89] On 15 August 2007, CR20 directly signed a contract with the GRN to rehabilitate the Luanda and Benguela railway, which circumvented the CIF.[90]

The feverish pace of Chinese engagement in Angola cooled markedly in 2009 as the global financial crisis gutted Angola's oil and diamond revenues, precipitating sharp reductions in GRN's expenditures. In 2008–9, Angola experienced a 32.4 per cent slump in oil revenues, which led to a 75.1 per cent drop in public investment, a sharp decline in hard currency reserves, and serious payment delays to contractors, especially in the construction sector. According to the Chinese Ambassador in Luanda, China had to recall more than 25,000 workers in 2009 due to the suspension of projects under the GRN's management. In August 2008, the Angolan government delayed US$460 million payment to the CR20.[91] The Benguela railway was suspended for a second time in 2009 and CR20 started laying off local employees and recalled over 3,200 Chinese employees back home. When the payment finally arrived in October 2010, the CFB had been suspended for almost two years.[92]

[88] 中国网 (5 April 2007).
[89] *The Economist* (13 August 2011).
[90] CR20 also signed the Luanda railway rehabilitation contract with the GRN on 24 July 2007. However, the CFM and New Luanda International Airport were not contracted to CR20.
[91] CR20 (2020).
[92] Ibid.

CFB–MOT (2010–17)

In 2010, Dos Santos reshuffled the Cabinet and voted 'no confidence' in Kopelipa, the head of GRN. Reconstruction projects that were originally managed by the GRN were then transferred to different ministries. Some in Luanda suspect that the president considered Kopelipa too ambitious and wanted to curb his patronage power, which mainly derived from siphoning off project finance under GRN's management.[93] In April, the president issued a presidential decree, stating that the management of CFB and two other railway projects together with the New Luanda International Airport and the Port of Lobito would move from under the GRN to the Ministry of Transport.[94] This was followed by another presidential decree in September to restructure the Ministry. This decree established the Instituto Nacional Dos Caminhos de Ferro Angola (National Institute of Railways, or INCFA) under the Ministry of Transport to supervise all three railway corporations.[95] The Ministry of Finance was forced to raise US$3.5 billion in domestic funding by issuing treasury bonds in 2007 to cover the payment to Chinese contractors; later these projects were included in the funding scheme of the second EximBank loan.[96]

Upon receiving ownership of these projects, the Ministry of Transport found that they had many technical and financial issues. 'Everything was political, not economical', exclaimed a former employee of the Transport Ministry who handled the transfer of projects from the GRN during an interview. The Ministry found the work was poorly done and the financing situation was confusing.

> We find that the executive project, which is a fully detailed planning of the projects, is not carried out. The exact terms were not done. These projects were under construction despite the fact that no proper feasibility study was done regarding the region, the soil, etc.[97]

The Ministry debated on whether to start the projects over or continue the half-completed work, finally deciding to continue the work and fix the

[93] *Africa Confidential* (1 March 2010).

[94] CR20 (2020).

[95] Presidential decree no. 195/10 of 2.9.2010. The INCFA was created in parallel with four other institutions under the Transport Ministry: INPA (Porto), (Road), ISHMA (maritime), and INAVIC (aviation).

[96] Campos and Vines (2008). As recorded by the CR20, in September 2007 the company received US$445 million prepayment of the CFL and CFB. By October 2010, the CR20 received another US$460 million payment from the government of Angola.

[97] Interview with AG-26, Ministry of Transport, Luanda (14 March 2019).

technical problems. However, the railway had so many problems that 'while fixing one problem in Bié, another problem came up in Moxico'.[98]

> For instance, [there was a] problem with CFB's communication lines. Trains running on CFB should be continuous rather than stopping everywhere. Yet due to problems with telecommunications, operators could not communicate with each other, so they use walkie-talkies, and if the person in charge fell asleep or the battery ran out, there would be a collision.[99]

When checking the financing arrangement of the projects, the Ministry of Transport found the project had been overcharged and that even the source of finance was unclear:

> We found that Angola paid US$13 million/km for CFB, which is much higher than [railways in] neighbouring Zambia, South Africa, and Mozambique, given the quality ... And when we received the project in 2010–11, we found that nothing has been paid by China's credit line. Instead, the money came from Sonangol![100]

Whether the funding for the CFB came from Sonangol, the Angolan national oil company, or from China Sonangol, the private company that was part of the '88 Queensway group', my informant from the Transport Ministry could not confirm. But this shows the opaque and confusing financial arrangement of GRN's projects. In October 2020, both Kopelipa and Leopoldino Fragoso do Nascimento, known as 'Dino', were accused of benefiting from the Angolan state's business with the CIF by the attorney general's office as part of President João Lourenço's fight against corruption.[101]

This transfer of ownership from the corrupt GRN to the Ministry of Transport did not significantly increase implementation efficiency. The Ministry was equally corrupt and lacking in bureaucratic capacity. In fact, the then minister of transport, Augusto da Silva Tomás, was jailed for fourteen years for corruption, embezzlement, money laundering, and abuse of power, making him the first high-profile official to be convicted since President João Lourenço took office in 2017.[102] Admittedly, the Ministry of Transport hosted technical experts that were excluded from the railway project when it was under

[98] Ibid.
[99] Ibid.
[100] Ibid.
[101] Cotterill (11 November 2020).
[102] Todayng (15 August 2019).

the GRN who could now participate in the project management. But even within the Ministry, major decisions were made politically. As a senior interviewee in the Ministry told me when I asked how the decision was made regarding whether to start over on the former GRN projects or to continue the half-completed work: 'it was all political', and they did not want to explain further.[103] The CFB under the Ministry took another six years before it was fully completed in 2017.

The railway corporation CFB-EP was poorly staffed and short of finance. The railway company had 13,000 workers before the civil war and the CFB was one of the very few lines in Africa that was profitable. In 2001, following the peace, the railway corporation had 1,600 employees, yet by the time of my fieldwork in 2019, the railway corporation only had 1,357 employees.[104] Although part of the reduced staff was due to the availability of diesel locomotives, which require less operators than steam locomotives, the main reason for this stark reduction in employees was due to the displacement of people during the war, and the suspension of the CFB service which led to the dispatch of many staff. The railway company was working on increasing its employees up to at least 2,500 according to a top leadership of the railway corporation,[105] but this could be difficult to achieve given the financial difficulty of the CFB-EP. By 2019, the railway operational revenue was far from covering the operational and maintenance cost. Indeed, the CFB-EP was low in administrative capacity, but the majority of the obstacles encountered during the rehabilitation of the Benguela railway were beyond the control of this public enterprise. The CFB-EP was largely excluded from negotiations and major decision-making, and major obstacles during the reconstruction, including delayed payment to the contractor, demining, and security, were beyond the CFB-EP's control.

The implementation of the CFB was characterized by low bureaucratic capacity. The transition from the GRN to the Ministry did not significantly improve implementation efficiency. The Ministry of Transport was also excluded by the GRN and CIF during the initiation of the CFB, and the Ministry's role only significantly increased after 2010, when the GRN was dissolved and the railway was transferred to the Ministry. Yet even after the Ministry and the railway corporation took over the railway project, the CFB rehabilitation still took another six years, indicating the weak implementation capacities of the railway administrations.

[103] Interview with AG-26, Ministry of Transport, Luanda (14 March 2019).
[104] Interview with AG-14, CFB-EP, Lobito (11 February 2019).
[105] Ibid.

4.3.3 Minimal Chinese agency

Extra-contractual interventions from the Chinese contractor were minimal in the CFB project; this is another consequential factor for the project's low effectiveness. Unlike the Kenyan and Ethiopian railways, the CFB was not a flagship project of the Belt and Road Initiative, and the payback of the EximBank loan was through oil revenue, not directly linked to the performance of the railway. The Chinese contractor, CR20, considered the CFB rehabilitation as a commercial project. A senior manager from CR20 told me, immediately after I closed my notebook and officially finished our interview: 'We are a profit-driven company; with money, we build, without money, we stop.'[106] This attitude was starkly different from the Chinese SOEs undertaking the Kenyan and Ethiopian railways, which bore considerable risk and paid out of their own pockets to keep the railways running. While the Chinese SOEs for the Kenyan and Ethiopian railways were actively publicizing their projects in China to show their contribution to promoting China's railway diplomacy[107] and African development, the CR20 barely promoted the Angolan CFB beyond its parent company. The CR20, originally a subcontractor of the CIF, was subject to investigations in China when the CIF's CEO Sam Pa was indicted and imprisoned in 2015. It was therefore understandable for the CR20 to not extol the virtues of the Benguela railway project in China in case of any further investigation from the Communist Party of China.[108]

One possible explanation is that CR20, compared to the two Chinese contractors for the Ethiopian and Kenyan railways, China Civil Engineering Construction Corporation (CCECC) and China Road and Bridge Corporation (CRBC), was less strong politically and financially, with less overseas experience.[109] The headquarters of the CR20 are in Xi'an, while the headquarters of both CCECC and CRBC were both in Beijing, so it can be inferred that the CR20 had fewer political connections than the other two SOEs. CR20 was also much weaker financially compared to CCECC and CRBC. The 2015 net profits of CRBC and CCECC were much more than CR20. In 2015 CRBC

[106] Interview with AG-1, CR20, Luanda (11 November 2018).

[107] Kynge et al. (17 July 2017).

[108] During interviews with the three Chinese contractors, I found both the CR20 and CRBC had a stricter corporate policy in terms of receiving interviews. The CRBC in Kenya had been bombarded by media scrutiny because of the Standard Gauge Railway, so they are more careful when receiving researchers.

[109] The Ethiopian railway was contracted to both CCECC and CREC. CREC is also politically and financially weak. Its headquarters are in Chengdu, and the 2015 net profit was US$34 million (中国中铁, 2015). Yet its partner CCECC could use its political leverage, financial strength, and international market experience to intervene in the Addis Ababa–Djibouti railway project.

and CCECC had net profits of US$452 million and US$166 million, respectively, whereas CR20 had much less net profit of only US$97 million.[110] Both CRBC and CCECC had started their overseas operation in the 1950s, while for CR20, Angola was their first attempt to explore the overseas market. It is safe to assume that CR20 was less adept at manipulating and elevating the political commitment from Beijing to increase Dos Santos' commitment through Beijing's diplomatic leverage.

Indeed, the commitment from the Chinese government to the CFB was also much less compared to the Kenyan and Ethiopian railways. Although Chinese government officials visited Angola multiple times, there were not many visits by the Chinese government to the CFB, according to CR20.[111] When I asked about the participation of the Chinese embassy in the CFB reconstruction project, a senior official at the Chinese embassy in Angola stated:

> The Chinese embassy should not intervene in a commercial project. If there are political factors that affect the projects, then the embassy can help reduce political obstacles. For instance, when a new president called off Chinese companies' projects that were signed with the previous president, then the embassy would require the new government to respect the contract. Chinese embassy is more neutral than embassies of Western countries—they would push for the commercial projects from their own countries.[112]

The transfer of CFB's financing source from the CIF, a private Hong Kong-based company, to China EximBank did not significantly increase the CR20 or Chinese government's commitment to this project. Admittedly, the EximBank money was directly issued to the bank account of the CR20, rather than going through the Angolan government. This arrangement effectively resolved the suspension issues resulting from delay of payment by the CIF and Angolan Ministry of Finance. However, this change of funding source did not significantly change the effectiveness of construction. After the CR20 received the initial funding from EximBank directly in 2013, the CFB construction still struggled for another four years before its final completion in 2017.

There was one exception. The Luau airport, with a contract value of US$80 million, was constructed to welcome Dos Santos and the presidents from DRC

[110] 中国交建 (2015);中国铁建 (2015). I used the USD–CNY exchange rate of 6.2 as of 31 December 2014. I select the year 2015 for net profit comparison because all three companies were engaged in their respective railway construction in this year, and it is also a year for which the data on all three companies is available.

[111] Interview with AG-1, CR20, Luanda (11 November 2018).

[112] Interview with AG-7, Chinese Embassy in Angola, Luanda (24 March 2019).

and Zambia to the launch ceremony of the CFB in Luau. Commercially it did not make sense to construct this airport as Luau is not a town that attracts visitors. Well aware of this, the CR20 still paid out of its own pocket to construct the airport and the financial difficulties of the Angolan government had since delayed the repayment of CR20. The Chinese SOE only received reimbursement in 2015, when the Luau airport project was included in the EximBank credit line.[113] The very fact that the CR20 was able to construct this project out of its own pocket shows that, although weaker than its Kenyan and Ethiopian counterparts, it was financially capable enough to bear some risks for the CFB-EP had the CR20 aimed to prioritize the fast completion of the project, but the leadership of the CR20 chose not to. Instead of playing the politics card in China, the CR20 used this project to directly cater to the presidents of Angola and neighbouring countries to further open up the Angolan market and expand to neighbouring DRC and Zambia.

The quality of Chinese construction was a frequently raised concern during my interviews in Angola. The CFB suffered from flawed design, for example the railway was operating at 30 kilometres/hour by the time of my fieldwork in 2019, despite being designed to run at 80 kilometres/hour. The CFB-EP blamed this on the low quality of the Chinese construction work.[114] The newly constructed railway stations have no elevators but only stairs; travellers with large luggage have to climb up and down. The railway's telecommunication system frequently malfunctions and was not translated into Portuguese. Quality issues exist beyond the CFB project. Lagoons appeared in the middle of the roads constructed by Chinese and Portuguese companies. Notably in 2010, a hospital in Luanda constructed by China Overseas Engineering Group Company, an SOE, threatened to collapse with deep cracks in the walls after being in use for only five years. Even the Chinese embassy recognized the widespread quality concerns of Chinese constructions in Angola. A senior official in the embassy explained: 'Infrastructure work in China constructed by the same company had no quality issues. But when Chinese companies come here, they exported hard infrastructure but the service was lacking. Nowadays the [Chinese] government emphasizes not only good construction but also good maintenance and operation as well.'[115]

In sum, the significant delay of the CFB construction was a joint product of the ceremonial presidential commitment, the gap in bureaucratic

[113] Interview with AG-5, CR20, Benguela (26 February 2019).

[114] Interview with AG-37, Centro de Estudos e Investigação Científica (CEIC), Luanda (16 November 2018).

[115] Interview with AG-7, Chinese embassy in Angola, Luanda (24 March 2019).

capacity, and minimal agency from the Chinese contractor and government. President Dos Santos lacked genuine interest in providing high-quality rail transport for the Ovimbundu people; he cared more about the statistics of reconstruction than the quality of service. The CFB project provided little room for patronage distribution to elites, especially as the majority of the materials were imported from China. The transition of the management from the corrupt GRN to the Ministry of Transport did not significantly improve the resolution of obstacles during CFB implementation. The Ministry and the railway corporation were poorly staffed, lacked resources, and were equally enmeshed in Angola's patronage machine. For China, the CFB was not a Belt and Road flagship project and the repayment of the loans was oil-backed, not directly linked to the project operation. The Chinese contractor and embassy considered this project as purely commercial, and were hesitant to step outside of their contractual liabilities to ensure prompt delivery. Moreover, Chinese construction quality even within the contractual framework was frequently questioned. The CFB presented a least likely case for the political championship, bureaucratic capacity, and external agency theories.

4.4 Struggling to operate

The reopening of the Benguela railway was highly anticipated and faced no competition from road transport. Despite these favourable conditions, the Benguela railway had been struggling to keep regular and safe operation. Its revenue was far from covering its operational and maintenance costs and heavily relied on state finance, and the Benguela railway had the highest number of accidents among all three railways under study. In this section, I first review the two favourable conditions for the Benguela railway operation, and then present the dire reality of its operation and the high frequencies of accidents.

The revival of the CFB was widely anticipated by residents living along the railway and miners in DRC and Zambia. The 168 stations of the Benguela railway were not only transport stations but also trading centres for the locals. Small farmers bought tickets and entered the railway stations to trade their goods. The Benguela railway has mostly benefited people from lower classes, rather than the middle or upper classes. Local people went to Lobito to buy fish and then sold it in Luena. The train had been very close to the heart of the people. In Lubango, for instance, people even celebrated holidays on the train, a tradition since colonial times. Before the CFB stopped operation in the 1970s, working for the railway system was a noble and prestigious job.[116]

Before the Benguela freight service reopened, most exports from the mining regions of Katanga in DRC and the copper belt of Zambia (which contains some of the world's largest deposits of copper, cobalt, and other minerals) were transported by truck and rail to Tanzania or (more often) to South Africa, which is 8,000 kilometres away. Shipping to these ports is slow and costly. By comparison, the distance from the Katanga region to Lobito is just 2,000 kilometres and—assuming a well-managed port and railway—much cheaper and quicker.[117] Mine operators in the DRC and Zambia were eager to have an alternative route to export minerals. When the CFB was not in operation, their ore took three weeks to reach Durban port by rail. When they tried sending the ore by truck with armed escorts, the convoys were attacked by bandits or sometimes the drivers and cargo vanished, with the trucks or their trailers identified months later in Mozambique or Tanzania.[118]

Another factor also worked to the advantage of the CFB operation; that is, the lack of road–rail competition. Different from the railways in Kenya and Ethiopia that face competition from road logistics, in Angola, the Benguela railway has been the only way for some areas to be connected to the outer world. From Kuito (Bié) to Luena (Moxico), there is no road connection, only railway. If a person were to go via road transport, they would have to go north from Kuito to Malanje, then down to Luena or directly to Luau, which is over 1,000 kilometres. Domestic mobility was so desperately needed that the Angolan government pushed the Chinese contractor to start phased operation as soon as a section was completed.

Despite the high expectations and low competition, the Benguela railway had been struggling to keep regular and safe operation. Upon completion of the CFB, based on a presidential order, the Angolan Transportation Ministry signed a US$55 million contract with the CR20 to take charge of maintenance for the line operated by CFB-EP.[119] By 2019, the CFB passenger service operated only four times per week. The speed was 70 kilometres/hour according to a government source,[120] but researchers of the railway observed a speed

[116] Information obtained via observations at the Benguela railway stations and casual chats with passengers waiting at the stations. Duarte, Pacheco, Santos, and Tjønneland (2015) and particularly Duarte (2010) provide very detailed description of the Benguela railway operation.

[117] Duarte, Pacheco, Santos, and Tjønneland (2015).

[118] Wikileaks (07LUANDA1015_a, 2007)—the author's interview with Vaz de Carvalho.

[119] Macauhub (30 August 2017).

[120] Interview with AG-19, Department of Transport, Huambo Province, Huambo (3 December 2018).

of 30 kilometres/hour.[121] On average, the railway transports between 1.2 million and 1.5 million people per year. In 2019, the CFB carried 400,000 tons of cargo per year, which is only one-tenth of its capacity.[122] This figure is even smaller than the cargo transported by the colonial CFB in 1973, which carried 3.2 million tons of goods, of which 1.6 million tons were international.[123] Domestically, the CFB carries drinks (beer), construction material, and food from Benguela province to the hinterland, and returns bringing agriculture products from the hinterland to Benguela. Internationally, starting from 2018, the CFB transports mineral products from DRC to Angola, and transports oil and construction materials, particularly cement, from Angola to DRC.[124] The connection between CFB in Angola and in DRC has not yet been completed by the time of writing this book. In Luau, passengers and cargos and transferred from one locomotive to another when passing the border. The product composition transported on the CFB is quite similar compared to colonial times, when Belgian Congo imported food and construction materials from Angola and received minerals in return.

The contemporary CFB's passenger service is popular. Before the CFB was rehabilitated, people were isolated. Roads in Angola were not good, and residents in Moxico, the province at the east end of the country, were not connected to even its neighbouring provinces. The operation of the CFB allows people to buy and sell products. My visit to the Huambo train station saw many people from Moxico who came to Huambo to purchase stuff and to then trade back in Moxico where they are more expensive. There were also local traders selling bread, peanuts, and drinks at the train station. Most of these traders were female. When I visited, a train was scheduled to leave on Monday morning and the train station was half-packed the preceding afternoon. My local guide said people started gathering at the station even two days ahead, and slept in the station so as to get on the train. The operation of the train relieved the lack of food products in places like Luena, where agricultural production and transport connections were interrupted by the forty years of war. As an interviewee from the CFB-EP recalled: 'In Luena, 3 kg of tomato costs 13,000 kz, and the cost of life was too high before the railway went there. So people were impressed by and appreciative of the revival of CFB.'[125]

[121] Duarte, Pacheco, Santos, and Tjønneland (2015).
[122] Interview with AG-1, CR20, Luanda (11 November 2018).
[123] Universidade Catolica de Angola (2018).
[124] Interview with AG-16, CFB-EP, Lobito (13 February 2019).
[125] Ibid.

The total number of accidents on the Benguela railway was unidentifiable—both CR20 and the CFB-EP were reluctant to disclose the figures. However, a quick review of the CFB Facebook page shows that there were two suspensions of phased services, one on 27 January 2019 due to the derailment of a freight train in Bié province and another on 14 February 2019 due to a collision of two trains in Moxico. Both had no fatalities—only the slight injury of a train driver in the latter accident. A quick internet search reveals that since its operation, in Bié province alone, apart from the aforementioned derailment in January 2019, Benguela railway had another two major collisions, on 17 February 2013 and 16 September 2020. Both were collisions of freight and maintenance trains, and the 2013 incident caused twenty injuries.[126]

The operational revenue of the Benguela railway was far from covering the cost of operation and maintenance when I visited the CFB in 2019. The main difficulty of operation, according to CFB-EP, was the lack of finance.[127] The CFB operation heavily relied on state finance, but the state's difficulties during the drop in commodity price from 2017 to 2019 made it even more hesitant and less capable of continuing to finance the CFB operation.[128] The CFB-EP was exploring possibilities for privatization,[129] but progress here was also slow. The Angolan government had announced, as early as 2012, 'plans to sell off commercial and operational aspects of the railroads to private companies, whilst keeping a controlling stake'.[130]

4.5 Kilamba Kiaxi social housing project: Dos Santos' political championship

Initially also managed by the CIF and GRN and later included in the Chinese policy bank's financing scheme, why did the Kilamba Kiaxi social housing project demonstrate much higher effectiveness than the CFB? In this section, I introduce the Kilamba Kiaxi social housing project. Through comparing the Kilamba project to the CFB, I intend to show that the championship by the president could have compensated for the bureaucratic and Chinese factors in the CFB project, as Dos Santos' championship saved the Kilamba housing project from complete failure.

[126] Angop (22 September 2020).
[127] Interview with AG-14, CFB-EP, Lobito (11 February 2019).
[128] Universidade Catolica de Angola (2018).
[129] Interview with AG-14, CFB-EP, Lobito (11 February 2019).
[130] Macauhub (26 March 2012).

Similar to the CFB rehabilitation project, the Kilamba Kiaxi housing project was managed by incompetent bureaucracies and lacking Chinese agency, but with Dos Santos' championship, the Kilamba project demonstrated relative success. The housing project was initially managed and financed by the GRN and CIF and later included in the Industrial and Commercial Bank of China financial scheme, and both projects were at one point referred to by the media as a 'ghost line' and 'ghost town'. But the first phase of the Kilamba project grew to accommodate over 95,000 residents after the initial market prices were significantly reduced.[131] The difference was that the Kilamba housing project was an effective instrument for Dos Santos' rent distribution.[132] The houses themselves became a tangible good that could be strategically distributed to members of the state administration and MPLA loyalists. The Kilamba project received a presidential commitment to achieve relatively higher effectiveness. The capital- and technology-intensive nature of railway projects made it hard for the Benguela railway to feed into the patronage system of the president. The railway also primarily benefits the poor of the UNITA stronghold—that is, Benguela, Huambo, Bié, and Moxico—which is geographically distant from Luanda.

The Kilamba Kiaxi city on the outskirts of Luanda began as a reconstruction project initially under the management of the GRN and contracted to the CIF. It, together with the rehabilitation of three railways, was on GRN's initial list of reconstruction projects. The CIF, like in the case of the Benguela railway, subcontracted the project to China International Trust Investment Corporation (CITIC), a Chinese SOE. After the dissolution of the GRN in 2010, the Kilamba Kiaxi project was transferred to Sonangol Imobiliária e Propriedades (SONIP), a subsidiary of the state oil company.[133] The Kilamba Kiaxi housing project, despite previously being described as a 'ghost city', has been nearly fully occupied since 2014.[134]

Among the many promises, the president said during the 2008 legislative elections that he would deliver 1 million houses in four years. The slogan was 'My Dream, My Home' (*Mew Sonho, Minha Casa*), and this plan was adopted in 2009 as the National Urbanism and Housing Programme.[135] In 2006, the official formal housing deficit was estimated at 878,068 housing units, or 60

[131] Buire (2017); Cardoso (2015).

[132] Croese (2016).

[133] In August 2014, the president further transferred the responsibilities of SONIP to Imogestin; see RedeAngola (23 August 2014).

[134] China–Africa Research Initiative (2 April 2014).

[135] Diário da República (22 March 2009); also cited in Croese (2016). This target was not met by 2012, and the government announced a five-year extension of the programme until 2017.

per cent of the existing housing stock, while figures from a national survey conducted in 2008–9 indicated that 90.9 per cent of the urban population lived in inadequate conditions.[136] Therefore, affordable housing was much needed in Luanda at this time. The Kilamba Kiaxi social housing project became the symbol of this promise to the people. It was the first of the projected thirty-six satellite cities to be built nationwide. The project initially involved the construction of 20,000 apartments, with support infrastructure, at a value of US$3.5 billion. Phase two of the project included an additional 5,000 units that were completed in 2015, in addition to the construction of service-related infrastructure. A third phase of the project foresees the construction of a total of 70,000 apartments.

Originally managed under the GRN, on 27 September 2010 following a presidential decree, the Kilamba project was transferred to SONIP, a subsidiary of the state oil company Sonangol. SONIP then subcontracted the management to Delta Imobiliária, whose partners are Manuel Vicente, the CEO of Sonangol from 1999 to 2012, Kopelipa, and Dino, the president's head of telecommunications. These three elite figures represent 'the triumvirate that dominates Angola's political economy'.[137] Although the presidential decree changed the ownership of the Kilamba project officially from the GRN to SONIP, in reality it was in the hands of the same 'triumvirate', simply with a different hat. Instead of delivering the housing project to a line ministry, President Dos Santos decided to keep Kilamba close to himself through his most trusted men. This was mostly because the selling of apartments generated monetary commissions and, more importantly, provided the power to decide who could enjoy the bright new apartment and who stayed in the slum.[138] These continued monetary and political rewards after construction completion were not enjoyed by the Benguela railway project, where illicit personal gain was mostly harvested upfront.

The CITIC delivered the first batch of 115 buildings, corresponding to 3,118 apartments, on 11 July 2011 in an inauguration ceremony chaired by Dos Santos. In his speech, Dos Santos considered it 'the largest housing project ever built in Angola, [constituting] a profound example of the social policy carried out in the country to solve the housing deficit'.[139] Delta Imobiliária announced

[136] Instituto Nacional de Estatística (2010); also cited in Croese (2016).
[137] Marques de Morais (2012).
[138] Interview with AG-48, Angolan journalist, Luanda, 15 December 2018. Also see Pitcher (2017); Soreide (2011).
[139] Marques de Morais (26 September 2011).

for-profit prices ranging from US$120,000 to US$300,000. For a country where over half of the population live on under two dollars per day, the price was so out of reach for 95 per cent of Angolans that by mid-2012, only about 300 flats had been sold out of the initial offering of 3,118. Faced with the September 2012 elections, the government decided to 'save this prestigious project'.[140] The government assigned forty-three apartments to every ministry and party loyalists with orders that they be distributed internally to senior civil servants on acquisition terms unavailable to other Angolans.[141] Later SONIP introduced a heavily subsidized rent-to-buy scheme by SONIP, which offered 3 per cent on mortgages, and the cost of the cheapest units was cut from US$120,000 to US$84,200, which brought apartment ownership within the reach of middle-level civil servants.[142] Two weeks after introducing this subsidized scheme, SONIP announced that it had sold 72 per cent of its stock and created a waiting list.[143] To get on the list, one must, first and foremost, be an MPLA loyalist. There was also evidence of preferential access to the Kilamba housing for MPLA supporters in the aftermath of the 2012 elections;[144] many of these loyalists that moved in were too poor to afford the flat themselves.[145] In February 2016, Joaquim Israel, administrator of Kilamba city, announced that the city had 95,000 inhabitants.[146]

The Kilamba Kiaxi project, apart from serving as an instrument of patronage allowing Dos Santos to reward supporters, was also a prominent case for Dos Santos to demonstrate his reconstruction success internationally. The Kilamba city became a popular site for distinguished international figures to visit. These included Liberia's president Ellen-Johnson Sirleaf, Mozambique's president Armando Guebuza, King Mswati II of Swaziland, the president of East Timor Ramos Horta, and Xi Jinping, who inspected the project on 20 November 2010, three years before he claimed China's chairmanship.[147]

Compared with the Benguela railway rehabilitation, Dos Santos was much more committed to delivering a high degree of effectiveness in the Kilamba housing project. Admittedly, it is difficult to claim the Kilamba project was a success because of the frequent complaints from Kilamba residents concerning

[140] Cain (2014).
[141] Soares de Oliveira (2015, p. 67).
[142] Cain (2014).
[143] Angonotícias (26 February 2013); also cited in Buire (2017).
[144] Croese (2016).
[145] Interview with AG-48, Angolan journalist, Luanda (15 December 2018).
[146] Angonoticas (15 February 2016); also cited in Buire (2017).
[147] Marques de Morais (2011), 26 September (2011).

construction quality and basic property service. Additionally, it failed in its purpose to be a social housing project as originally intended, instead largely benefiting bureaucrats and the politically connected middle class. By comparing the Kilamba project and the Benguela railway, I only claim that the housing project is *relatively* more effective than the railway. In fact, given very few post-war reconstruction projects can claim to be an absolute success, the fact that the Kilamba project still achieved some level of effectiveness and transformed from a 'ghost city' to nearly fully occupied deserves some credit when compared with the railways and other projects. The president announced the building of 1 million houses as his campaign promise and the Kilamba project was expected to be a profound example of state-led housing development nationally and internationally. He kept this project close to himself and in the hands of his most trusted men. What converted a 'ghost city' to an internationally recognized 'wonder'[148] was the state-subsidized housing purchase scheme and the allocation of apartments to bureaucrats and MPLA supporters. The decision to reduce the housing price in Kilamba and the introduction of the state-subsidized rent-to-buy scheme was not officially announced by Dos Santos himself, but came from SONIP/Delta. However, the three people in charge of SONIP/Delta (Kopelipa, Dino, and Vicente) were so close to the presidency, and the Kilamba project so high profile, that we can safely assume that these strategies were discussed with Dos Santos and obtained his informal consent.

4.6 Conclusion

Despite the favourable practical conditions for the CFB reconstruction project, it demonstrated low effectiveness. The multi-year delay of CFB construction and difficult and unsafe operation were caused by the lack of political championship from Dos Santos, bureaucratic weakness, and minimal Chinese agency. President Dos Santos and the MPLA lacked a genuine interest in providing high-quality rail transport. Although he mentioned the rehabilitation of the three railways in his 2008 campaign messages, the Dos Santos government cared more about announcing the statistics than the quality of service, particularly when the majority of the people travelling on the railway were the rural poor. The capital- and technology-intensive railway had little room for

[148] According to the Mozambican president, Armando Guebuza, when he visited the project. Cited in Marques de Morais (26 September 2011).

patronage distribution to elites, especially as over 95 per cent of the materials were imported from China. Dos Santos' four visits from 2011 to 2015 were ceremonial in nature, limited to cutting ribbons at the multiple launch ceremonies of the railway. Unlike his Kenyan and Ethiopian counterparts Uhuru Kenyatta and Meles Zenawi, the all-powerful Angolan president shied away from solving the implementation problems, many of which required cross-ministerial coordination. These obstacles were left to the ineffective coordination of Angolan bureaucrats and Chinese expats.

In addition to the lack of political championship, the Benguela railway was managed by weak bureaucracies and constructed by profit-driven Chinese contractors. The GRN was corrupt and lacked any of the necessary technical railway expertise, while the initial GRN–CIF nexus excluded Angolan technical experts from negotiations and key decision-making. The Ministry of Transport was not a strong bureaucracy either. The CFB-EP were understaffed with low administrative capacity. The Chinese contractor was hesitant to go beyond the contractual framework, in the manner of its Ethiopian and Kenyan counterparts, to bear financial risks to solve problems. The Chinese government was also hesitant to intervene in this 'commercial project'. The CR20 was not as financially capable or internationally experienced as its counterparts in the Kenyan and Ethiopian railways. The Chinese SOE CR20 operated within the frame of the construction contract while the Chinese embassy strictly considered this project 'commercial' rather than 'political', meaning that the Chinese government should only be involved if diplomatic efforts were needed.

In comparison, the Kilamba Kiaxi housing project represents the least likely case for the bureaucratic capacity and Chinese agency theories, but the project still demonstrated relatively higher effectiveness due to Dos Santos' championship. The CFB and Kilamba projects are typical cases of the Angolan post-war reconstruction programme, where very few projects can be claimed as an absolute success. In fact, Angolan state actions outside of Sonangol almost always demonstrate a low degree of effectiveness. The Kilamba Kiaxi housing project is an exception, which shows a higher degree of effectiveness thanks to the political championship of President Dos Santos. What makes the Kilamba Kiaxi project different from the CFB was that the housing project could provide continuous monetary gain and political power through the sale of the apartments. It was also used by President Dos Santos to demonstrate his ability to transform people's living conditions, by delivering 1 million houses as his 2008 electoral campaign promised.

Through the introduction of a state-subsidized rent-to-buy scheme and meticulously allocating Kilamba apartments to party loyalists during and after the 2012 elections, Dos Santos and his intimate circle were able to maintain the patronage system that underpinned his regime, as well as gaining personal enrichment.

5

Big brother and small boy?

African executive extraversion under Sino-African power asymmetry

> It looks like this project was imposed on us by the Chinese, it looks like a giant guy and a very weak and small guy who does not know what he is doing in the picture. But this is not the case.
>
> Atanas Maina, former director of the Kenyan Railway Corporation[1]

> China's role has been talked about too much ... I hear some describe the approach of Chinese loans as predatory. It is not like that. During loan negotiations, every clause was articulated and discussed, it was a commercial arrangement, not even a concessional loan.
>
> Gitachu Betru, former chief executive officer of the Ethiopian Railway Corporation[2]

> This is purely a commercial project. The client pays, we construct; the client does not pay, we stop.
>
> Chinese contractor for Angola's Benguela railway[3]

Since the turn of the century, China's engagement with Africa has significantly increased, a phenomenon that has generated extensive scholarly and policy debate. China's loans to the continent skyrocketed from US$130 million in 2000 to US$7 billion in 2019, reaching a peak in 2016 with US$28 billion.[4] Through aid and financing support, China has helped build or is building more than 6,200 kilometres of railroads in Africa.[5] In addition to infrastructure cooperation, Chinese engagement with Africa in trade, investment, and aid has

[1] Interview with Atanas Maina, Kenyan Railway Corporation, Nairobi (13 August 2019).
[2] Speech in Oxford by Gitachu Betru, Ethiopian Railway Corporation, Oxford (1 December 2017).
[3] Interview with AG-1, CR20, Luanda (11 November 2018).
[4] Bräutigam, Hwang, Link, and Acker (2019).
[5] Xinhua News (28 December 2017).

The Railpolitik. Yuan Wang, Oxford University Press. © Yuan Wang (2023). DOI: 10.1093/oso/9780198873037.003.0006

significantly expanded in the past two decades. China's emergence as a major player in Africa has generated an increasing number of scholarly debates. On the positive side, researchers find that the filling of the African infrastructure gap, boost to growth, increased foreign investment and technology transfer, and availability of new sources of loans give African countries more agency through increased choice.[6] On the negative side, some researchers interpret China's interest in resource extraction, infrastructure construction, and economic exchange as a continuation of the long-established patterns of asymmetrical economic relations that Africa has with the external world, deepening the continent's dependence vis-à-vis external economies.[7] This argument has even led to media speculation about China's 'neo-colonialism' in Africa.

In the three preceding empirical chapters, I primarily focused on how African domestic politics, particularly political leaders, shaped the trajectories of Chinese-sponsored railway projects. I proposed a two-step answer to the overarching puzzle of why Chinese-financed and -constructed projects that are similar in nature develop different trajectories in different African states. First, it is the primacy of African domestic politics, rather than the 'Chineseness', that determines the trajectories of Chinese-sponsored projects. Second, it is the agency of African political leaders' commitment to and intervention in the project, rather than institutional factors such as bureaucratic capacity, that define the effectiveness of infrastructure delivery (i.e. the political championship theory).

In this chapter, I engage with the broader Sino-African relations and the dependency–extraversion debate. I explore *how* and *why* African actors, particularly political leaders, were able to effectively exercise their agency and shape the project trajectory despite the China–Africa power asymmetry. I argue that Chinese-financed and -constructed projects in Africa coincided with rulers' strategies for political survival in the host countries. Instead of reducing their dependence on external economies, African rulers tend to utilize their dependent positions through foreign trade and financial support. Internationally, they strategically assess their available choices to ensure that the state receives the largest amount of foreign funding and on the most favourable terms. Domestically, they instrumentalize the Chinese-sponsored projects and Chinese loans to demonstrate their performance legitimacy and feed the patronage machines. Instead of dealing with a homogenous China,

[6] Greenhill, Prizzon, and Rogerson (2013); Bräutigam and Zhang (2013); Morgan and Zheng (2019).

[7] Taylor and Zajontz (2020).

African actors work with a plethora of Chinese actors that sometimes disagree with each other. The fragmented nature of Chinese actors in Africa helps to balance the asymmetric relationship by diluting China's power and enhancing African agency.

The four sections in this chapter are organized as follows. Section 5.1 expands on the theoretical debate between dependency theory and extraversion theory that was briefly mentioned in Chapter 2. I argue that in the dependency–extraversion debate, African extraversion theory provides the right direction of African agency but does not locate the specific dynamics of agency. In section 5.2, I advance the extraversion theory by arguing that it is presidential agency that largely shapes projects and bilateral relations. In section 5.3, I present the comparative empirical evidence drawn from case studies in Kenya, Ethiopia, and Angola to show that African leaders were well aware of their structural asymmetry with China and that they were active agents in this dependent relationship. I show how Chinese-sponsored railways were instrumentalized by African rulers for their domestic political survival. This African agency is further enabled by the fragmented nature of Chinese actors. Section 5.4 concludes.

5.1 Sino-African structural asymmetry

The structural asymmetry between Africa and the external world is captured by dependency theory, and the recent scholarly debate on China's engagement in Africa and developing countries in general has marked a revival of dependency theory.[8] Some media and policy debates even refer to China's approach as 'neo-colonialism', a stronger term that embodies many of the same characteristics as dependency theory. In this section, I first summarize the classical dependency theory and review the neo-dependency argument in Sino-African debates. This is followed by three theoretical critiques of dependency theory. I then discuss the African extraversion theory and explain how this thesis advances that theory by emphasizing the agency of African political leaders—what I call the political champions. This executive version of African extraversion theory provides the theoretical grounding for the comparative empirical evidence in section 5.2.

[8] Taylor and Zajontz (2020); Zajontz (2022a, b).

5.1.1 Dependency theory and neo-dependency in Sino-African debates

The assumed dependence of post-colonial Africa has been one of the most-discussed features of African countries' relationships with the rest of the world. Originally developed to explain the underdevelopment of Latin America in the 1960s, dependency theory was applied to Africa after the Arusha Declaration of 1967 in Tanzania.[9] Dependency theory can be summarized as follows. First, African countries are comparatively disadvantaged regarding their positions and functions in global production.[10] The overall trend of international trade is characterized by African countries exporting primary materials to more advanced economies while importing value-added, manufactured products. Second, African countries are dependent on foreign capital, personnel, and know-how for domestic development. A direct result of this is that the transformation of primary material is controlled by foreign capitalists, with little profits accruing to the dependent countries. In the long run, this form of development enables a balance of capital transfer favourable to advanced economies and detrimental to developing economies.[11] Third, the economic development of the dependent countries has benefited a small group of African elites at the expense of the economy and population of the country as a whole. The result is insufficient capital accumulation to sustain self-generating capitalist development in the dependent countries, and so the level of dependence strengthens over time.[12] The core of this theory is to consider the external determinants of African development as primary and almost wholly negative.[13]

The recent debates on China's growing presence in Africa return to dependency theory and argue that China's economic and political engagement with Africa has deepened the continent's dependence. This deepening of dependency was purportedly achieved through China's interest in natural resources and African countries' debt sustainability, and a large portion of these debts was accumulated through Chinese loans for infrastructure construction. China's thirst for African natural resources and 'oil-for-infrastructure' (the 'Angolan model') echoes the dependency argument. We can see exploitation of mineral resources and raw materials of the peripheral countries for the purpose of developing the core of the global economy, as well as the

[9] Leys (1996, p. 112).
[10] Cardoso and Faletto (1979, p. 18).
[11] Ibid.
[12] Ibid.; Leys (1996).
[13] Leys (1996, p. 112).

development of capitalist enclaves managed by local (dependent) capitalists. Most African countries are dependent on multilateral and bilateral donors as a crucial source of their financial revenues, and therefore excessive debt is not uncommon on the continent. In other words, international borrowing has become the primary concern of the contemporary version of African dependence.[14] Even in non-resource-rich countries, China's Belt and Road Initiative (BRI), which emphasizes inter-connectivity through infrastructure and trade, is sometimes presented as a reproduction of dependency by further indebting African countries.[15] Some researchers go so far as to argue that China's BRI aims at integrating Africa into an ambitious Chinese-constructed infrastructure network, which will deepen Africa's dependent position and perpetuate its terms of (mal)integration into the global political economy.[16]

5.1.2 Critique of dependency theory

Three main intellectual critiques of dependency theory are summarized as follows. The first criticism is its global scope and lack of specificity, with confusion embedded in the concept and mechanisms of dependency.[17] The fuzziness of the concept of 'dependency' is compounded with the overloaded definition of 'development', which may refer to a wide range of indicators such as GDP growth, political democratization, or even freedom. Added to this is the lack of methodology to study it, as the theory does not generate testable hypotheses and therefore cannot be scientifically tested. Even Cardoso himself stated: 'I do not agree with the idea that to improve the quality of analysis, the theory of dependency should be formalized so that, after testing hypotheses derived from this formalization, one could venture out into the world waving the banner of the percentage of variation explained by each factor.'[18]

The second criticism is that dependency theory does not offer an explanation for the large divergence in development trajectories among developing countries given their similar external conditions. In particular, the success of East Asian countries raises an additional criticism of dependency analysis: that external flows could have a positive impact on development.[19] In Africa, there

[14] Chabal and Daloz (2004, p. 112).
[15] Taylor and Zajontz (2020).
[16] Ibid.
[17] Stallings (2020).
[18] Cardoso (1977, p. 21), cited in Stallings (2020).
[19] Evans (1995).

is some evidence that ethnic Chinese served as catalysts for industrialization in Mauritius and Nigeria,[20] and that African states can achieve industrial development through the 'flying-geese' model of foreign investment in manufacturing, particularly through knowledge and skill transfer.[21]

The third criticism, which is also the main focus of this chapter, is its neglect of domestic forces. Dependency theory or the neo-dependency argument in China–Africa relations correctly identifies the imbalanced economic and political relationship between Africa and the global powers, but it fails to recognize the political ambitions and leeway of African agents.[22] It implies an immobility of the periphery and fails to give the post-colonial state the centrality it holds as mediator between the internal and external realms or recognize the empowerment this brings.[23] Similar to the dependency school, the neo-dependency argument in Sino-African relations posits that the self-perpetuating underdevelopment of the periphery is due to its structural inferiority in the global economy. It therefore sees escaping from poverty and technological backwardness as impossible under the existing global trade system and the monopoly of multinational corporations. As a solution, Taylor and Zajontz (2020) promote 'autonomous and continuous development' and argue that African resources should be returned to the hands of Africans.[24]

5.1.3 A strategy of extraversion

Admitting dependence as an unfavourable structural condition facing African countries historically as well as today, the African extraversion school argues that 'subjection can constitute a form of action'.[25] This position is well captured by Bayart (2000): the asymmetry between sub-Saharan Africa and the international economy is real but Africans have been active agents in the dependence of their societies.[26] Since independence, African elites have conceived of their economic links with the outside world—in the form of either the export of their raw materials or foreign assistance—as an integral part of their calculus

[20] Bräutigam (2003).
[21] Bräutigam (2008); Bräutigam, Tang, and Xia (2018). The 'flying-geese model' shows that countries tend to be leaders or followers in particular parts of global value chains depending on their level of costs and skills (Akamatsu, 1962).
[22] Bayart (2000, p. 217); Soares de Oliveira (2007, pp. 307–8).
[23] Soares de Oliveira (2007, p. 308).
[24] Taylor and Zajontz (2020, p. 15).
[25] Ibid., p. 219.
[26] Ibid.

for power.[27] Dependence and its possibilities have thus been one of the chief instruments that have enabled African elites to continue feeding the patronage-based systems on which their power has rested.[28] In this way, dependency has allowed African elites to maintain the survival of the state and their personal rulership, despite the fact that advancing national betterment has not been foremost as a priority or outcome of post-colonial governance.[29]

Utilizing a state's dependent position through the strategy of extraversion is a preferred option for African ruling elites. The underlying logic is that the ruling elites tend to take a short-term economic view, seeking to maximize immediate returns rather than investing for future development.[30] Therefore, far from seizing opportunities to reduce dependence, African rulers tend to maximize revenues from the export of existing resources at the expense of economic diversification.[31] African incumbents today also prefer using international support as a means of extracting rents and maintaining both the state and their personal power.[32] Other strategies, such as the extraction of local resources through, for instance, levying taxes, would carry high political costs because they would generate societal demands for governmental accountability.[33] The readily available financial support from bilateral and multilateral donors allows African states to enjoy a much higher level of financial resources than they would otherwise have possessed.[34]

Both dependency theory and the extraversion argument acknowledge that the structural dependence of African countries exists. Their divergences, however, are twofold. First, dependency theory, by emphasizing that 'structure matters',[35] implies an immobility of the African states in their dependent relationship with the rest of the world, while the extraversion theory holds that subjection can formulate actions and emphasizes the role of African agents in managing and benefiting from the dependency.[36] Second, the two theories disagree on the possibility of development under dependency, especially capitalist development. Dependency theory holds a pessimistic view towards the underdevelopment of the periphery, and argues that capitalist development

[27] Chabal and Daloz (2004, p. 111).
[28] Ibid., p. 115.
[29] Clapham (1996, p. 17); Whitfield, Therkildsen, Buur, and Kjær (2015, p. 29).
[30] Kelsall (2013).
[31] Chabal and Daloz (2004, p. 113).
[32] Clapham (1996, p. 17).
[33] Tull and Blasiak (2011, p. 8).
[34] Chabal and Daloz (2004, p. 115).
[35] Frank (1998).
[36] Bayart (2000).

is unachievable under the dependency structure,[37] whereas the extraversion school maintains that capitalist development may be achieved if it coincides with the rulers' aspirations towards the elongation of their incumbency and/or self-enrichment.[38] This mutual interest is not impossible because rulers frequently seek personal survival and legitimacy through support from domestic capitalists and the strengthening of the economy.

5.2 African executive extraversion

The African extraversion theory correctly captures the direction and incentives of African agency but it does not answer the questions of *where* within the broad concept of elites the agency is located and *how* that agency is exercised. Instead of the broad reference to 'African elites' as the locus of African agency, I advance the extraversion theory by emphasizing the agency of African political leaders (i.e. the political champions) in instrumentalizing Sino-African railways. I argue that foreign projects like the railways coincide with the African ruler's strategy of political survival, and were effectively used by the ruler. Internationally, African rulers strategically manage their available choices to ensure that the state receives the largest amount of foreign funding on the most favourable terms. Incentivized by their domestic political survival, African leaders instrumentalize foreign funding and foreign-sponsored projects to demonstrate their performance legitimacy and feed the patronage machines.

Instead of reducing their dependence on external economies, African rulers tend to utilize their dependent positions through foreign trade and financial support. The reality of asymmetric power between Africa and the international system may reduce the range of actions available to African leaders when they interact with external actors, but it does not eliminate their options entirely.[39] Far from seizing opportunities to reduce dependence, African rulers tend to maximize revenues from the export of existing resources at the expense of economic diversification. When negotiating international financial support, African states almost always have a degree of choice over whether or not to accept aid from a particular source at a particular time.[40] On occasions where the donor-sponsored programmes may undermine the rulers' ability to distribute patronage to a political support base and thus to retain their position

[37] Leys (1996); Fieldhouse (1999).
[38] Clapham (1996, p. 5).
[39] Tull and Blasiak (2011, p. 7).
[40] Whitfield and Fraser (2009, p. 28).

in power, they may choose to resist those programmes.[41] The existence of a large variety of donors, and the emergence of new donors such as China who are not as keen on the principles of democracy and liberal economy as Western donors usually are,[42] have granted African rulers more options. This even allows them to leverage donors against each other to extract maximum revenues from external support.[43]

Domestically, African political leaders instrumentalize the foreign-sponsored projects for their domestic political survival. Advancing Bayart's classical extraversion theory, I argue that it is not African elites per se but political leaders that actively use foreign-sponsored projects to achieve domestic political survival. African rulers eloquently elaborate on their performance to domestic and international audiences through the delivery of the railway, although they may or may not genuinely be interested in the mobility of people and goods. The highly visible and costly nature of railways makes them an easy subject to instrumentalize for a ruler's survival. Chinese-financed and -constructed projects in Kenya, Ethiopia, and Angola were used as electoral campaign capital, a showcase of performance legitimacy, and to weaken the opposition and feed the patronage system in exchange for political support. The very fact that projects can be instrumentalized for political purposes further incentivizes leaders' commitment to project success.

Externally, the fragmented nature of Chinese activities in Africa helped balance the asymmetric relationship by diluting China's power and enhancing African agency. Many scholars in Sino-African relations have moved away from the concept of 'homogenous China' and acknowledge the heterogeneity of Chinese actors in Africa.[44] Multiple Chinese agents are involved in the financing and construction of any mega-infrastructure project in Africa. A state-owned enterprise (SOE) is usually the contractor and they will report to the State Assets Supervision and Administration Commission. Meanwhile, bilateral loans will be sourced from policy banks, which seek advice from the Ministry of Foreign Affairs and the Ministry of Commerce prior to approving any loans. On top of this, any projects by SOEs and the BRI in general are subject to the power of the National Development and Reform Committee. These fragmented actors generate complicated factions between the state and state capital, as well as interest groups across different state agencies and

[41] Ibid., p. 29.
[42] Chabal and Daloz (2004, p. 118).
[43] Zeitz (2019); Phillips (2018); Cabestan (2020).
[44] Corkin (2016); Mohan and Lampert (2013); Xu (2014).

across SOEs.[45] When operating abroad, Chinese SOEs and policy banks frequently find it difficult to secure the support they need from Chinese agencies that have conflicts of interest. Chinese SOEs frequently must deal with fierce competition from other SOEs. This fragmented nature of Chinese engagement in Africa has enabled African elites to influence the practices of Chinese SOEs and policy banks.

In sum, the reality of asymmetric power between Africa and the international system may reduce the range of actions available to Africa when they interact with external powers, but it does not eliminate their options entirely.[46] Acknowledging the dependence of African countries, African leaders that benefit from their dependent position with external powers actively participate in the process of inserting their societies as a dependent partner in the world economy to fulfil their political ambitions. In this process, the emergence of China affords African rulers the agency that comes with choice, allowing them to triangulate between traditional and emerging donors to extract the best deals or simply make previously unachievable developmental plans feasible. Domestically, foreign funding and foreign-sponsored projects are likely to be instrumentalized to achieve African leaders' domestic political survival.

5.3 Chinese-sponsored railways as instruments for executive extraversion

African leaders were well aware of their structural asymmetry with China and were active agents in this dependent relationship. By initiating mega-infrastructure projects and seeking Chinese financial and implementation support, African rulers used these symbolic infrastructure projects and their relationship with China to achieve political aspirations. These aspirations are relevant to the ruler's political survival, including domestic patronage, electoral capital, legitimacy to rule, establishing regional leadership, and triangulation between different sets of donors. This section starts with data on Sino-African trade and loans to show the structural asymmetry in this relationship. I then present the empirical evidence on African executive extraversion through railways. I show that the railways are African leaders' initiatives. While acknowledging the structural asymmetries, African leaders still actively sought to engage with China on the railway deals, which further deepened their

[45] Ye (2019, p. 698).
[46] Tull and Blasiak (2011, p. 7).

dependence. I then discuss the domestic incentives for African rulers' extraversion strategy. This is followed by the external enabling factor for executive extraversion; that is, the fragmentation of Chinese actors.

5.3.1 Structural asymmetry

African countries' economies have, since independence, been integrated into a global economy dominated by Western states and, more recently, Asian states including China, which is unfavourable to Africa and deepens dependence.[47] This structural dependence between African states and China is illustrated in the export of primary products such as agricultural products and hydrocarbons and minerals, on the one hand, and China's export of manufactured goods and loans on the other (Table 5.1). Kenya's exports to China were valued at US$110 million and imports from China were US$4 billion during 2018, according to the United Nations COMTRADE database on international trade. In 2017, Ethiopian exports to China were valued at US$289 million during 2017 and Ethiopia imported US$5 billion in return. Angolan imports from China were US$2 billion during 2018 and its exports to China were US$25 billion in the same year. Table 5.1 shows the top five exported and imported goods between the three African countries and China. The data clearly indicates that the three African countries exported primary products and imported manufactured goods, presenting classical cases for dependency theory. A key component of the Chinese-sponsored railway project is the import of Chinese machinery, locomotives, and rail-tracks. These imports further deepened the trade imbalance between China and our three African countries. Yet similar to the loan dependence, while African leaders were well aware of the railway deals' implication of trade dependence for China, they still continued with the railway deals.

The expensive Chinese-sponsored infrastructure projects and loans that come with them have raised serious questions about the debt sustainability of the recipient countries. Yet instead of seeking to reduce debt from China and other donors, African leaders still sought Chinese funding for the costly railway projects. Media and policy circles are frequently suspicious of so-called Chinese 'debt trap diplomacy' seeking to entrap countries into borrowing more than they can afford to finance infrastructure projects and then seizing strategic assets as loan collateral, citing the Chinese-sponsored Hambantota

[47] Taylor and Zajontz (2020); Carmody (2016).

Table 5.1 Kenya, Ethiopia, and Angola top five trading goods with China

Kenya exports to China (2018)		Kenya imports from China (2018)	
Ore, slag, and ash	$63mn	Electrical, electronic equipment	$617mn
Raw hides, skins, and leather	$12mn	Machinery, nuclear reactors, boilers	$540mn
Vegetable textile fibres not specified elsewhere, paper yarn, woven fabric	$6mn	Railway, tramway locomotives, rolling stock, equipment	$255mn
Coffee, tea, maté, and spices	$5mn	Articles of iron or steel	$255mn
Live trees, plants, bulbs, roots, cut flowers	$5mn	Vehicles other than railway, tramway	$163mn
Ethiopia exports to China (2017)		**Ethiopia imports from China (2017)**	
Oil seeds, oleaginous fruits, grain, seed, fruits	$198mn	Machinery, nuclear reactors, boilers	$1bn
Raw hides, skins, and leather	$43mn	Electrical, electronic equipment	$956mn
Coffee, tea, maté, and spices	$8mn	Vehicles other than railway, tramway	$427mn
Ore, slag, and ash	$8mn	Articles of iron or steel	$383mn
Footwear, gaiters, and the like	$8mn	Iron and steel	$268mn
Angola exports to China (2018)		**Angola imports from China (2018)**	
Mineral fuels, oils, distillation products	$24bn	Electrical, electronic equipment	$439mn
Wood and articles of wood, wood charcoal	$14mn	Machinery, nuclear reactors, boilers	$406mn
Salt, sulphur, earth, stone, plaster, lime and cement	$8mn	Articles of iron or steel	$157mn
Fish, crustaceans, molluscs, aquatics invertebrates	$5mn	Iron and steel	$147mn
Ore, slag, and ash	$2mn	Vehicles other than railway, tramway	$99mn

Source: Trading Economics (n.d.).

Port in Sri Lanka as an example.[48] Data shows that between 2000 and 2018, the Chinese government extended US$148 billion worth of loans to Africa, with Angola, Ethiopia, and Kenya comprising three of the top four borrowers from

[48] Chellaney (2017); Parker and Chefitz (2018).

China since 2000.[49] China's loans to Kenya skyrocketed from US$12 million in 2005 to US$9 billion in 2018, with the Standard Gauge Railway (SGR) Phase 1 and 2A responsible for US$3.7 billion and US$1.8 billion, respectively.[50] Chinese loans to Ethiopia totalled US$1 million in 2005 and reached US$14 billion in 2019.[51] Chinese loans to Angola are oil-backed, unlike loans to Kenya and Ethiopia, and totalled US$43 billion in 2019.[52] It can be argued that the elites of Kenya, Ethiopia, and Angola were well aware of their dependency on China prior to the three mega railway projects, but instead of seeking to escape from it, they initiated these expensive projects and sought to engage further with China.[53]

5.3.2 Executive extraversion through railways

Realizing their asymmetric relationship with China and incentivized by their domestic political survival, African leaders still actively reached out to China for support on the railway projects, incurring significant amounts of debt, in classic cases of extraversion through railways. In this section, I elaborate on the African executive extraversion strategy through railways. I first show that the three railways are African initiatives and that the heavy involvement of China does not change their identity as African railways. I then show that the debt and bilateral trade implied in the railway deals may have deepened the host countries' dependent position in the global economic system. African rulers were well aware of these implications but still reached railway deals with China. The next subsection discusses the domestic survival incentives of this executive extraversion strategy; that is, instrumentalizing the railways for legitimacy and/or patronage purposes. The second subsection explores how the fragmented Chinese actors enabled African actors to shape the behaviours of Chinese actors and the trajectories of the railways.

African initiatives

The three railways in this study are African initiatives rather than Chinese impositions. In fact, the initiation of these mega projects had no Chinese

[49] Bräutigam, Hwang, Link, and Acker (2019).

[50] Ibid., with updates on the 2019 figure. This is different from Kenya's debt to China, which also shows a similar trend. Kenya's debt to China stood at US$737 million in 2014, the first year of Kenyatta's presidency, before ballooning to US$6.4 billion in December, representing growth of 766 per cent. See Guguyu, 8 July 2020.

[51] Bräutigam, Hwang, Link, and Acker (2019), with updates on the 2019 figure.

[52] Ibid.

[53] Mwita (8 August 2020).

involvement. To implement the projects, Kenya, Ethiopia, and Angola all originally sought Western support, and China's participation in the three projects came relatively late. When seeking external support, the African leaders were well aware of the structural asymmetry between their respective countries and foreign powers. China's emergence as a capable donor allowed African countries to transform the railways from abstract ideas into shiny tracks on the ground.

The Kenyan SGR emerged initially as an East African Community (EAC) initiative. The very idea of the SGR started in 2004 following an EAC summit, which issued a directive to prepare the EAC Railway Masterplan for rejuvenating the region's existing rail system that was on the brink of collapse.[54] The Masterplan study was completed in January 2009.[55] The short-term goal of the Masterplan was to, 'through public-private-partnership, pull the railway back from the abyss by restoring reliable service on the track lines', including the metre-gauge railway from Mombasa to Kampala.[56] China did not play any role in the EAC's SGR initiative; instead it was a Canadian company, CPCS Transcom, that was contracted to conduct the Masterplan study. Kenya became the first among EAC member states to complete the SGR. The initiation of the SGR in Kenya took from the beginning of 2018 to the end of 2013. Initially, the SGR plan was more in line with the EAC Masterplan: renovation of the railway through public–private partnership (PPP) with a reasonable amount of KES 50 billion (~US$575 million). Jimmy Wanjigi and the chief executive officer (CEO) of China Road and Bridge Corporation (CRBC) Kenya developed the railway idea through PPP, and this was intended to be a private-sector initiative from which the Kenyan billionaire and Chinese SOE could profit. In 2013, when the newly inaugurated President Uhuru Kenyatta visited China, the railway project was included in China EximBank's financial scheme.

The Addis Ababa–Djibouti railway (ADR) was also an Ethiopian initiative; or, more precisely, Prime Minister Meles Zenawi's initiative. After the ruling party's near loss in the 2005 parliamentary elections, the Ethiopian People's Revolutionary Democratic Front (EPRDF) sought to change their base of legitimacy from democratization to economic development. In light of this political imperative, Meles championed the railway's initiation. In 2005, Ethiopia's Ministry of Transport created the 'Technical Advisory Group',

[54] East African Community (n.d.).
[55] Ibid.
[56] CPCS (2009).

which published the *Indicative Framework for Railway in Ethiopia* report.[57] Upon receiving this report, Meles established the Ethiopian Railway Corporation (ERC), centrally managing all of Ethiopia's rail projects. The CEO of the corporation directly reports to the prime minister. The first task of the ERC was to come up with a National Railway Plan, a 5,000-kilometre railway development including eight corridors, and the foreign consultants for the Plan were all European firms. Similar to the neighbouring SGR, Chinese companies did not play a role in formulating the idea of the Ethiopian railway, which was an Ethiopian initiative with advisory support from European partners.

The rehabilitation of the Caminho de Ferro de Benguela (CFB) was an initiative of the Angolan government responding to the national imperatives of the post-war reconstruction effort. The Benguela railway, which was the largest and most ambitious infrastructure project in colonial Angola, was a target of UNITA insurgents during the four decades of devastating war. This crucial line linking the Angolan port of Lobito with the hinterlands of Angola and with the neighbouring Democratic Republic of the Congo and Zambia was rendered inoperative. The initial discussion around rehabilitating Angola's rail network started in 2000 without China's participation, but the project was soon suspended as the country was still at war and had difficulty fund-raising. In 2000, the Angolan government announced a pre-study named the ANGOFERRO project, which was an ambitious investment of US$4.2 billion by the Angolan government and DAGAF, a consortium of German firms, to reconstruct the major railways in the country over the following eleven years. DAGAF was supposed to rehabilitate the rail-tracks, thirty-six bridges, and twenty-nine train stations on the Benguela railway.[58] Yet this initial attempt to rehabilitate Angolan railway systems was suspended. The Benguela railway was then included in the loans from the China International Fund, which was awarded a contract in 2004 to rehabilitate the railway, among other reconstruction projects in Angola.

Deepening of dependence

The three African-initiated railways, particularly their debt implications, arguably deepened the host countries' dependent position in the global economic system. The construction of the railways involved large imports of machinery from China, and, instead of benefiting the host countries, the three

[57] Rode, Terrefe, and da Cruz (2020).
[58] Inisterio do Planeamento (2005), cited in Duarte (2010).

railways link ports to the hinterland of the respective countries allowed China (and other foreign powers) to conveniently shape imports.[59] So far, the operation of the railways has not changed the imbalanced bilateral trade structure with China and they may further deepen African countries' trade imbalance with and dependence on China.

Kenya, Ethiopia, and Angola welcomed the mega railway projects funded through multi-billion-dollar Chinese loans, despite the fact that the projects deepened their dependent relationship with China. With a large amount of 'no-(political-)strings-attached' funding and infrastructure expertise, China EximBank and the SOEs present an ideal partnership choice for Africa to actualize their infrastructure development. The 485-kilometre SGR Phase 1 is priced at USD$3.8 billion, and China EximBank is providing Kenya with financing for roughly 85 per cent of the Nairobi–Mombasa project through a combination of commercial and concessional loans.[60] Phase 2A allowed Kenya to secure another US$1.5 billion in commercial loans from EximBank. The 750-kilometre Ethiopian railway costs US$3.4 billion, with 70 per cent financed by commercial loans from China EximBank and the remaining 30 per cent covered by the Ethiopian government.[61] The US$300 million Benguela railway was financed through the 'oil-for-infrastructure' scheme of EximBank. The three African states seemed to worry less about their soaring debt and their liability to pay back the loans in two decades and more about maximizing their immediate revenues. A majority of the three railways are financed by loans from China EximBank. The whole Ethiopian railway loan and more than 50 per cent of the Kenyan railway loan are under commercial rather than concessional terms. This debt increase at such an alarming rate not only creates a responsibility for payment for future generations but also increases the cost of living in the borrowing countries.[62]

Large imports accompanying Chinese-sponsored railways could have further depressed African capitalist development. Both Kenya and Angola negotiated a certain percentage of local sourcing of materials and services to create indigenous business opportunities. These initiatives, if implemented strictly, could be a significant step towards reducing the trade imbalance and benefiting local economies. However, the Kenyan presidential request of 40 per cent local content in SGR-1 was more for public discourse and was not strictly

[59] Okoth (5 May 2019).
[60] Pilling and Feng (4 April 2017).
[61] BBC (5 October 2016).
[62] Interview with KE-52, Centurion System, Nairobi (18 July 2017).

implemented, and the situation only improved in Phase 2A, when strict monitoring procedures were installed. The Kenyan railway contract includes a clause that 40 per cent of the inputs, including employees, materials, and subcontractors, should be locally procured. This clause was trumpeted as a major success for Kenya in the railway deal by Kenyatta, particularly because China EximBank required its projects overseas to have at least 70 per cent Chinese content. Kenya learned from the experience of SGR and sought to have the later phases of railway construction build the local manufacturing capacity. In the SGR Phase 2A contract from Nairobi to Naivasha, the Kenyan Railway Corporation (KRC) and CRBC agreed on 40 per cent local input and implemented a monitoring mechanism to retain receipt of local sourcing of materials and services, which was then added up to check whether the sum reached 40 per cent.[63]

The Angolan requirement of 30 per cent local content was not implemented at all and over 95 per cent of materials used during railway construction were imported. In 2015, the Angolan National Assembly passed a piece of legislation (LEI 14/15 de 11 de Agosto de 2015 DR I Serie nº 115) requesting foreign-sponsored projects to have 30 per cent local contents from Angola. However, interviews from both the Angolan and Chinese sides indicate that the Benguela railway construction sourced over 95 per cent of materials from China. The imports vary from cement and steel to rice and wheat. This was partly because post-war Angola could not provide the materials for CFB construction at the required quantity, standard, and speed. Administratively, there was no person in charge of overseeing the implementation of the 30 per cent rule.[64] In Ethiopia, there was no relevant arrangement in the railway contract regarding the proportion of local elements that should be guaranteed during construction.[65] The EPRDF government has historically been sceptical about the private sector and obscured the line between 'productive enterprises' and 'rent seekers'.[66] Without specific requirements on the inclusive development of the Addis Ababa–Djibouti line, the Chinese contractors' only concern was cost-effectiveness when considering local procurement, employment, and subcontracting. Based on a rough estimate by a Chinese manager at the China Railway Engineering Corporation (CREC), the company has locally sourced around 25–30 per cent of the total materials and employees.[67]

[63] Interview with KE-23, Kenyan Railway Corporation, Nairobi (18 July 2017).
[64] Interview with AG-26, Angola Ministry of Transport, Luanda (14 March 2019).
[65] Interview with ET-13, CREC, Addis Ababa (1 July 2017).
[66] Clapham (2017, p. 100).
[67] Interview with ET-13, CREC, Addis Ababa (1 July 2017).

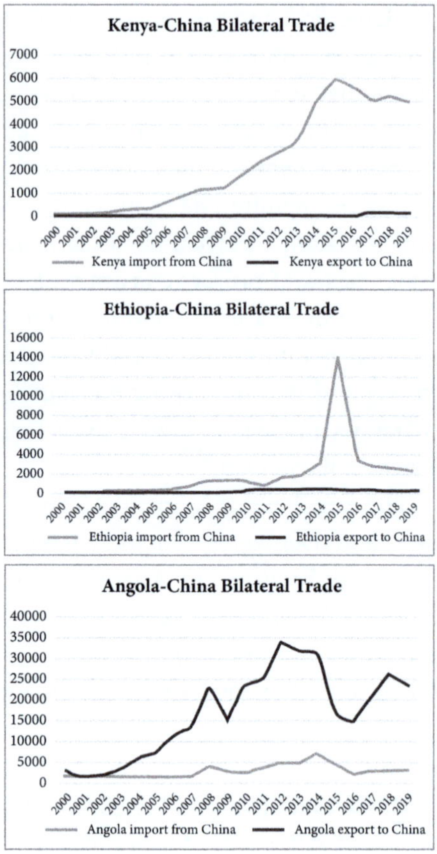

Figure 5.1 Bilateral trade (US$ million unadjusted)
Source: UNComtrade data.

The operation of railways has not significantly changed the import and export structure of the three African countries. Figure 5.1 shows that from 2000 to 2019, Kenya and Ethiopia were in increasing trade deficit with China. The trade categories in Table 5.1 indicate that Kenya and Ethiopia import manufactured products from China and export agricultural and mineral products to China. It is too soon to make any lasting macroeconomic judgement of the ADR and SGR at this point, as the freight operation for both railways only started in 2018. However, the two-year figures show that this imbalanced bilateral trade structure and deficit have not changed since the introduction of the railways. China's reliance on Angola's natural resources allowed Angola to export oil in large amounts to China, which is a typical dependence of countries with resource endowment. The SGR and CFB are minimally integrated with any export and industrial zones in Kenya and Angola, respectively. The Ethiopian ADR and industrial park projects were designed to boost the industrialization of the country, but in reality the industrial parks are spread across the country rather than designed strategically along the railway. The last-mile truck transportation costs for each container from Hawassa Industrial Park to Modjo dry port were as high as $375 in 2018.[68]

It seems that when seeking China's help for railway finance and construction, Kenya, Ethiopia, and Angola were well aware of their structural asymmetry with China and that the debt and trade implications of the railway deals could further deepen their dependence. Kenyatta and Dos Santos both sought to protect domestic capitalists by requiring 40 per cent and 30 per cent local content, respectively, in the railway projects; however, lacking an effective monitoring and implementation mechanism, these initiatives were implemented to varying degrees of success. The Kenyan railway only guaranteed 40 per cent of local input for SGR Phase 2A, and materials for the Angolan railway were almost entirely imported. It is too soon to draw any definitive conclusion regarding the macroeconomic implications of the railways, but it seems that railways do not change the bilateral trade imbalance with China. It will still take some years for rail transport to be effectively connected to domestic industrial and export zones to assist industrialization, as the railways were designed to achieve. Why did African leaders engage with China to complete the railways, an activity that arguably deepened their dependence? In the next subsection, I will turn to the domestic drivers of African leaders' extraversion through the railways.

Domestic incentives: political survival

Domestically, railway projects coincided with African leaders' strategies of political survival, and the projects were effectively instrumentalized by the leaders. Railways are visible and expensive. They are expressions of state power, visible promises of economic development, and images of political stewardship.[69] Railways therefore became ready tools for rulers to demonstrate their performance legitimacy and feed the patronage machines that are crucial to the rulers' power. This instrumentalization is most clearly seen in politically assigned project timelines. Coincidentally during the construction, Kenyatta, Meles (and his successor Hailemariam), and Dos Santos all emphasized fast completion for the railway, minimizing the social and environmental aspects of railway construction as 'cosmetic' in nature. The leaders' emphasis on fast delivery reflects their incentives to instrumentalize the railways for

[68] PVH 2018, 'Export by Rail in Ethiopia: A PVH Perspective', presentation (12 June 2018).
[69] Chapter 2 provides a more detailed discussion of the politics of mega-infrastructure and railways.

their respective domestic political survival, for performance legitimacy and/or patronage.

Kenyatta's legitimacy to rule relies on his winning the highly competitive presidential elections, and the SGR became his campaign capital in the 2017 elections. In the Kenyan elections held on 8 August 2017, there was fierce competition between the incumbent Jubilee Alliance under the leadership of Kenyatta and the National Super Alliance (NASA), led by the veteran opposition leader Raila Odinga. The provisional results released by Kenya's election commission showed a slight advantage for the incumbent president: Kenyatta received support from 54.2 per cent of votes counted, compared to 44 per cent for Odinga.[70] The SGR-1 was scheduled to complete construction in 2019 but the president requested that CRBC complete the SGR within two and a half years, by June 2017, two months before the presidential elections. To guarantee the project was delivered on time, Kenyatta visited the construction site on a quarterly basis, bringing half of his cabinet with him, and held on-site work meetings. The passenger service started the day after the inauguration, with government-subsidized promotional ticket prices, and the 'Madaraka Express' became highly popular among Nairobi residents. By launching the SGR, the largest (and most expensive) project Kenya has undertaken since independence, at the peak of his electoral campaign, Kenyatta openly used the SGR as his campaign capital. The railway project is presented as an example of the stewardship and delivery capacity of the Jubilee. The Jubilee made one of its running slogans 'We deliver!'

The ADR was initiated following the contentious 2005 election as a visible demonstration of the new-found performance legitimacy of Ethiopia's dominant party, the EPRDF. The 2005 parliamentary elections resulted in a slim and controversial win for the incumbent EPRDF government. The EPRDF reacted by clamping down on the opposition leaders and further reducing the freedom of opposition and expression. This pushed the EPRDF government to seek a new basis for legitimacy as the previous discourse of political legitimacy based on 'democratization' sank into further discredit.[71] Prime Minister Meles sought to portray Ethiopia as a developmental state, favouring state-led investment in infrastructure and industrialization. The ADR, connecting

[70] Burke (10 August 2017). This election result was nullified by the Supreme Court and the second presidential elections were held in November 2017. Odinga, still insisting that the elections were rigged, dropped out of the campaign before the second voting. As a result, Kenyatta had a landslide victory in the second elections.

[71] LeFort (2015).

the capital city to the port of Djibouti, was conceived to create an economical logistical channel, a crucial step for integrating the country into the global economy as a producer of export goods. Meles personally followed up on the railway project and acted effectively as a project manager to push the delivery agenda forward. The highly visible ADR was instrumentalized by the EPRDF government to formulate a developmental discourse symbolized by tangible mega-infrastructure projects.

In Angola, a resource-endowed state that at times holds elections that kept Dos Santos' presidency for three decades, the president sought to use the Caminho de Ferro de Benguela and Kilamba Kiaxi social housing project as campaign capital, demonstrating his performance legitimacy. In the 2008 elections, the first elections after gaining peace six years prior, Dos Santos made building 'one million houses' by 2012 his campaign promise.[72] Providing high-quality rail transport was also included in the Movimento Popular de Libertação de Angola's (MPLA's) 2009/2012 Government Program prepared for the 2008 electoral campaign. The Caminho de Ferro de Benguela was close to the heart of the Ovimbundu people living along the railways. They have also been steadfast supporters of the opposition UNITA. Dos Santos instrumentalized the CFB to demonstrate his service to the people. He attended the CFB's phased inauguration events four times among a dozen railway inauguration ceremonies. Dos Santos and the ruling MPLA party were more interested in announcing the number of railways successfully renovated under his rulership, a showcase of his performance legitimacy, than effectively increasing the mobility of people. Despite the railway's subsequent operational difficulties and the frequent internal complaints of Kilamba residents, the CFB and the Kilamba Kiaxi social housing project became popular visiting sites for distinguished international figures to tout the country's promising economic future and as a model for African social housing.

With rare exceptions, African states are connected to the wider society through patronage networks, extending to as high as the presidency. The president and his close associates seek to control access to state resources as a means of assuring their hold on power, with the resources used to reward their supporters in society. Highly visible and expensive foreign-sponsored mega-infrastructure projects are ready targets to feed the patronage machines

[72] This campaign promise was not fulfilled in 2012. In 2008 the country was still excited by the oil boom, and the plummet of oil prices subsequently made the Kilamba project a campaign embarrassment in the 2012 elections. A million houses were not completed in the country and even until 2014 the Kilamba Kiaxi was criticized as a 'ghost city' by international media.

that provide the basis of power for the president. African leaders' instrumentalization of Chinese-sponsored railways for domestic patronage constitutes a classical strategy of extraversion.

In Kenyatta's acquiescence, the SGR became the target of multiple bureaucrats receiving kickbacks from the project, which generated multiple corruption charges. These included the minister and permanent secretary of transport Michael Kamau and Nduva Muli. More recent news indicates that two Kenyan politicians heavily involved in the SGR case, Atanas Maina, director of KRC, and Muhammad Swazuri, head of the National Land Commission, have been taken to court on corruption charges related to land compensation.[73] For many observers, the cost of SGR-1 exceeds its value, and this exorbitant cost suggests that national elites may have benefited illicitly from the contracting process. Critics from within the ruling Jubilee Alliance and the Kenyan media suspected large-scale corruption. On 20 June 2020, Kenya's Court of Appeal ruled that the tendering process of the SGR was illegal. The SGR's tendering process has been widely challenged within the Kenyan government, in court, and in the media since 2014. Kenyatta turned his eyes away from his subordinates' plundering of the SGR; instead he focused on the in-time completion of the project prior to the 2017 elections.

The SGR operation was further instrumentalized by the president to weaken the financial basis of the coast, the opposition stronghold. Mombasa county has historically been an opposition stronghold, and Governor Joho of Mombasa county opposed the SGR from day one. The governor was even banned from attending the SGR inauguration ceremony in 2017. Mombasa's economy heavily relies on logistics services, where Joho's family has multiple investments. The introduction of the SGR has shifted transport logistics from road to rail, and the presidential directive to clear the goods in Nairobi instead of Mombasa has also shifted the Kenya Port Authority (KPA), the governmental cash-cow, from the coast to upcountry. As a KPA interviewee revealed: 'It is a war between the upcountry and the coast. In KPA, coastal people think it is theirs.'[74]

In Angola, President Dos Santos created a highly centralized patronage network fuelled by the oil revenues, and the availability of Chinese credit lines allowed the president to strengthen his hold on power and turn away from Western requests for transparency and democracy. Dos Santos effectively built a power structure with the Futungo–Sonangol nexus at the centre,

[73] Achuka (12 August 2018).
[74] Interview with KE-43, Kenya Port Authority, Nairobi (10 August 2019).

where decision-making authority was concentrated in a handful of trusted elites. This meant the revenue flows extracted by Sonangol from the country's oil resources contributed to the government budget and, more importantly, maintained a wide patronage network in exchange for loyalty. Key to this power structure is the availability of sufficient resource revenues. The International Monetary Fund and other Western donors questioned the opacity of the resource revenues and conditioned their loans on transparency and governance reform, which would shake the core of Dos Santos' power base. The condition-free loans from China fit neatly into this power structure and unavoidably enmeshed in the spiralling corruption that reached directly to Dos Santos' family. Public service provision became an opportunity for Dos Santos to give privileged access to elites[75] and to reward loyalists at election time, as in the Kilamba case. Admittedly, some reconstruction projects benefited Angolan citizens, but the loans and infrastructure projects mostly benefited political elites, who extracted monetary rents from domestic natural resources and maintained a clientelistic relationship with the outside world instead of serving the population.[76]

In sum, from their very initiation, the Chinese-sponsored railway projects were African initiatives focused on serving the rulers' domestic political survival. Recognizing their asymmetric relationship with China, African leaders still actively reached out to China for financial and technical support on the railway projects. The railway deals incurred significant amounts of debt and further imbalanced bilateral trade, therefore deepening the host countries' dependent position in the global economic system. In Kenya, Ethiopia, and Angola, the highly visible and costly Chinese-sponsored railways were instrumentalized by the political leaders for their domestic political survival through demonstrating performance legitimacy and/or feeding the patronage network. Therefore we can see that the political leaders of the three African countries demonstrated a classical strategy of extraversion through railways.

5.3.3 External enabler: a fragmented China

When negotiating and implementing infrastructure deals, the asymmetric relationship between China and Africa amounts to a form of 'dialogic' relationship.[77] Seen from afar, the Sino-African relationship is like 'a giant guy

[75] Ostheimer (2000), also cited in Corkin (2016).
[76] Clapham (1985, p. 183).
[77] Bayart (2000, p. 224).

and a very weak and small guy who does not know what he is doing'.[78] Yet a closer examination shows that instead of Africa passively receiving the deals offered by China, in reality African actors have actively shaped the behaviours of Chinese engineers, SOEs, EximBank, and even the Chinese government for African domestic benefits. Instead of dealing with a unitary China, African actors have been working with a plethora of Chinese actors with their respective interests and who sometimes disagree with each other. This fragmentation of Chinese actors lessens the asymmetry of bilateral relations. In other words, the fragmented nature of China serves to dilute Chinese power and enhance African agency.

African officials who have negotiated and worked with China EximBank and SOEs frequently find them more accommodating than other bilateral or multilateral donors and Western multinational corporations. Back in the early 2010s when negotiating the railway deals, EximBank was just about to commence infrastructure lending, and many SOEs had only recently opened up their international businesses, while African treasuries, national banks, and ministries of finance had been negotiating with traditional donors for quite a long time on this type of infrastructure loans. While negotiating with China, African bureaucrats were more familiar with the nature of the contract. For them, the only difference was the magnitude of the loans. African bureaucrats therefore found China EximBank very accommodating. As EximBank was financially strong but the Kenyan government was more familiar with infrastructure loans, this EximBank negotiation was therefore more 'dialogic' than negotiations with traditional donors like the World Bank. As a senior Kenyan official who participated in the SGR loans negotiation with EximBank revealed:

> If we say this does not work, EximBank would take the term out, and add things that fit Kenya. There was a lot of give and take and lots of feedback. The negotiation took only one year, the first disbursement was six months after the negotiation. We signed two agreements: the loan agreement and ESCROW agreement.
>
> Compared to our negotiation with the World Bank on financing the Rift Valley Railway, the negotiation started in 2004, and nothing came through until 2011, the negotiation itself took three years. We signed fifteen agreements and there was intensive involvement of lawyers, for merely 140 million

[78] Interview with Atanas Maina, former director of the Kenyan Railway Corporation, Nairobi (13 August 2019).

> dollars. The EximBank even allowed us to use a local bank as the ESCROW bank, which had never happened with World Bank and other donors.[79]

Similar to their experience with EximBank, African bureaucrats find Chinese SOEs more accommodating to their requirements than Western contractors. This 'dialogic' relationship between African railway corporations and Chinese SOEs is enabled by some Chinese SOEs' limited international experience and their preference to preserve client relationships. In contrast to Chinese SOEs' accommodating nature, Western multinationals are 'contract-binding'.[80]

What makes the China–Africa relationship in the above cases particularly 'dialogic'? In other words, why were China EximBank and SOEs more accommodating to African requests than Western financiers and multinational contractors? The implementation of the BRI and the Forum on China–Africa Cooperation involves a wide array of state agencies—Chinese SOEs, policy banks, the Ministry of Foreign Affairs (MoFA), the Ministry of Commerce (MOFCOM), and the National Development and Reform Committee (NDRC)—which all face diverse constraints and have respective interests. Their implementation is different and often deviates from the ambitious messages in the strategy. An overseas infrastructure project may trigger multiple interests between Chinese state agencies that are difficult to coordinate, and its implementation can be highly fragmented.[81] In the case of the ADR, for instance, a former ambassador of China's MoFA revealed the conflict of interests and difficulties of coordination between various Chinese agencies regarding whether to permit loans for this railway:

> If I say that the Addis–Djibouti railway [loans] should wait, the NDRC would question me: 'What do you know! The central government asked us to be aware of China's industrial overcapacity and reduce domestic production capacity, does MoFA understand this? And whether the railway makes economic sense is not a decision by the MoFA, but by the MOFCOM. The MOFCOM has already confirmed that Ethiopia will be able to pay back the loans, why is the MoFA arguing against something they do not understand?'[82]

Apart from their ability to facilitate loans from policy banks (usually after fierce competition with other SOEs), Chinese state firms were not receiving

[79] Interview with KE-23, Kenyan Railway Corporation, Nairobi (18 July 2017). See discussions in Chapter 3, section 3.5.1, under 'Financial support and reverse pressure'.

[80] Interview with ET-42, Ethiopian Railway Corporation, Addis Ababa (24 June 2017).

[81] Ye (2019); also see Mertha (2009) and Brødsgaard (2017) for discussion of Chinese politics and policy-making as 'fragmented authoritarianism'.

[82] Interview with CH-6, Ministry of Foreign Affairs, Beijing (19 October 2018).

governmental support. Rather, they frequently found themselves navigating the conflicting interests of different agencies. During the implementation of these overseas infrastructure projects, SOEs were frequently ineffective in gaining cross-agency support, particularly because the SOEs can pursue commercial profits abroad.[83] A senior manager of an SOE emphasized:

> State-owned enterprises are ultimately enterprises. An enterprise's risks are carried by the enterprise, not by the government. We need to apply for loans from banks, and the loans are repaid by the enterprise, not the government. The government does not unconditionally support SOEs. We are responsible for our own profits and losses. The [Chinese] embassy can at best help us evacuate in crisis. The policy banks such as the EximBank and China Development Bank, etc., approved our loan applications not because we are state-owned, but because we are more professional; if we could not pay back the loans, the banks could hold us to lifelong accountability.[84]

Contrary to the belief of a powerful and homogenous China and a holistic, Beijing-driven policy towards Africa, African elites have been dealing with a fragmented China in loan negotiations and project implementation.[85] Politically connected Chinese SOEs and policy banks encountered complicated factions between the state and state capitals at the central and provincial levels, as well as interest groups across different state agencies and across SOEs. Their overseas operation did not receive cross-agency support from Beijing. Many of the SOEs and policy banks were new to international negotiations and they were struggling to balance their political and business identities. As a result, African elites found Chinese actors more accommodating to their requirements than traditional donors and Western multinationals. In dealing with a fragmented China, African elites were therefore able to influence the practices of Chinese actors for African interests.

5.4 Conclusion

Despite their structural inferiority in dealing with the second-largest economy in the world, Kenya, Ethiopia, and Angola actively use this dependency relationship for their domestic political survival in their different ways. This

[83] Ye (2019).
[84] Interview with CH-11, China Minmetals, Beijing (11 October 2018).
[85] Ye (2019); Mertha (2009); Brødsgaard (2017).

strategy of executive extraversion through the railways has the following three elements. First, the ideas for the Kenyan, Ethiopian, and Angolan railway projects were African initiatives rather than impositions from China. The weighty involvement of Chinese actors in these projects does not change the fact that ownership of the three railways is African, not Chinese. Second, the significant amount of debt and the bilateral trade implications that came with the railway deals arguably further deepened the African countries' dependency within the global economic system, and with China in particular. In all cases, African rulers were well aware of their inferiority in the global economic system vis-à-vis China, yet instead of disengaging with China (and other global powers), they actively engaged with the external world to achieve their own political calculation. Third, the highly visible and expensive Chinese-sponsored railways, and the Chinese loans that came with them, gave African leaders exceptional space for their domestic political survival through demonstrating performance legitimacy and/or feeding the patronage network.

In Kenya, President Kenyatta instrumentalized the SGR as his electoral campaign capital to compete for the 2017 presidential elections, where the project was a visible demonstration of the Kenyatta administration's delivery effectiveness and stewardship. With Kenyatta's quiet acquiescence, his subordinates received kickbacks from this project, generating multiple corruption charges. The president also used the project as a tool to transfer the cash-cow Kenyan Port Authority from the opposition's stronghold to the capital. In Ethiopia, the ADR was initiated following the contentious 2005 election as a visible showcase of the EPRDF's newly established performance legitimacy. In Angola, President Dos Santos used the Chinese-sponsored projects as campaign capital in the window-dressing elections to demonstrate his performance legitimacy. The condition-free Chinese credit lines allowed Dos Santos to strengthen his power without increasing transparency and democracy, as Western donors had requested. The Kilamba Kiaxi social housing project also benefited bureaucrats and MPLA loyalists for their support in the elections.

The fragmented nature of China's involvement further enabled African elites to shape the practices of Chinese actors for African interests. The seemingly homogenous Sino-African cooperation and the BRI are fragmented in practice, characterized by conflicts of interest between various bureaux in Beijing. Chinese SOEs and policy banks have not been receiving cross-agency support from Beijing; rather, they have been parts of a fragmented China's conflicted interests. This has enabled African elites to achieve more African interests in negotiation and implementation, even more than with traditional donors and Western companies.

The executive extraversion argument of this chapter also challenges dependency theory and advances the classical extraversion theory. Dependency theory, by emphasizing the structural asymmetry between Africa and the external powers, assumes African immobility and holds a pessimistic view regarding development possibilities of the periphery. The extraversion theory argues that African elites, benefiting from their dependent position with external powers, actively participate in the process of inserting their societies as a dependent partner in the world economy. I argue that foreign projects like railways coincide with an African ruler's strategy of political survival and were effectively used by the rulers to demonstrate their performance legitimacy and feed their patronage machines. We could infer from the executive extraversion theory that in Sino-African relations, particularly in the case of infrastructure cooperation, it is the primacy of African domestic elite politics, rather than the 'Chinese-ness', that determines the trajectories of bilateral projects. Furthermore, as I argue in other chapters, it was the agency of African political leaders' commitment to and intervention in the projects, rather than external or bureaucratic factors, that defined the effectiveness of railway delivery.

Conclusion

In this concluding chapter, I synthesize the book's main findings and discuss the policy relevance of this research. I proposed a two-step answer to the overarching puzzle of why Chinese-financed and -constructed projects that are similar in nature develop different trajectories in different African states. First, it is the primacy of African domestic politics, rather than the 'Chineseness', that determines the trajectories of Chinese-sponsored projects. Second, it is the agency of African political leaders' commitment to and intervention in the project, rather than institutional factors such as bureaucratic capacity, that define the effectiveness of infrastructure delivery. I term this the political championship theory. This Conclusion has four sections. Section 1 revisits the political championship theory and competing explanations. This is followed by an outline of the case study findings in Section 2. Section 3 discusses the theoretical and empirical contribution this research makes. The final section concludes with the policy relevance of this research by discussing three policy questions.

1 Political championship: leaders' agency within structural and institutional constraints

This book asks why infrastructure projects that are similar in nature demonstrate sharply contrasting levels of effectiveness in different African states. The effectiveness of a project is a proxy for state effectiveness. I argue that perceived threats from electoral competition generate strong political commitment from the state's leadership; that is, a political champion. When a political champion has high authority, their intervention in the project implementation creates motivations for bureaucrats and tempers resistance, leading to higher project effectiveness. This is a theory seeking to 'bring the individual back in' to the study of the state. It accounts for the personalistic, idiosyncratic, and unpredictable character of public goods delivery, an aspect that has yet to receive due academic scrutiny.

The political championship theory starts from the premise that a ruler's actions are largely responses to the prevailing survival incentives created by existing political institutions, especially electoral institutions, and that a ruler's interests significantly affect policy choices. An institutional incentive

The Railpolitik. Yuan Wang, Oxford University Press. © Yuan Wang (2023). DOI: 10.1093/oso/9780198873037.003.0007

that generates political commitment is the ruler's perception of threats from electoral competition. In competitive regimes, it predicts that political commitment increases *prior* to elections when the incumbent seeks another term, and decreases when the incumbent's priority shifts to power consolidation. In less competitive states, contentious elections may lead to legitimacy threats to the incumbent, and thus the leader's commitment to developmental policies or projects increases *after* an election as the leader seeks to demonstrate their stewardship to the people. It is conceivable that leadership commitment is also contingent on other factors such as crisis, natural resource, political patronage, and foreign leverage.

If a committed leader has high authority—that is, the leader can effectively build a coalition of key actors on the project or policy and push the delivery agenda forward—then their intervention leads to higher project effectiveness. The source of a leader's authority is a combination of formal and informal institutions, as well as their personal charisma. As the political champion is usually the executive or a high-ranking politician, they already enjoy the constitutional power attached to their positions. In most developing countries, the leader's authority is broader than the constitutional power attached to the presidency or premiership. Here, authority is a concept that goes beyond the binary between formal and informal institutions, but emphasizes that power is continuous. The power behind leadership actions sometimes comes from the constitution and sometimes comes from informal institutions, including bureaucratic and legislative norms, clientelistic practices, informal institutions that shape political behaviours and outcomes, and personal charisma. The set of strategies that leaders may employ includes increased monitoring, provision of rewards and threat of sanctions to induce higher effort in subordinates, co-opting opposition leaders, and generating a sense of mission and ideology.

In this book, I also evaluate two competing theories drawn from the structural and institutional explanations of state effectiveness for development. The bureaucratic capacity theory argues that project outcomes are determined by the capacity of the implementing bureaucracy. High bureaucratic capacity, as measured by the technical capability of a bureaucracy to solve obstacles within its remit, and the political capability to leverage executive intervention for resolving inter-ministerial obstacles, leads to higher effectiveness. This competing theory is drawn from two streams of literature that explain state effectiveness in developing countries through institutional characteristics, particularly bureaucratic strength: the Weberian bureaucracy literature and the study on 'pockets of efficiency'. African railway corporations, usually under the management of the Ministry of Transport, are the owners of the railway projects. They are the bureaucrats that engage with Chinese state-owned enterprises (SOEs) on a daily basis and implement the project across multiple levels of domestic politics, ranging from the executive to the various ministries, the subnational government, and the general public. Projects under the management of a strong railway corporation are likely to demonstrate high effectiveness.

Another competing theory emphasizes that external agency, rather than African domestic agency, determines project outcomes. According to this argument, it is the variation in the commitment and capacity of the external actors, in this case Chinese contractors, that determines the different project outcomes. This theory is derived from the structural explanation of underdevelopment—that is, dependency theory—which makes predictions of state effectiveness. It argues that China–Africa economic relations also conform to the dependency paradigm, which is characterized by structural asymmetry, given Africa's marginal position within the global economic system defined by its limited value as a provider of mineral resources and deprived of agency to determine domestic development. The 'Chinese agency' version of the external agency theory argues that variation in capacity across Chinese SOEs determines the different outcomes of Chinese-sponsored projects. The Chinese SOEs are crucial actors in China's engagement overseas, alongside Chinese government actors such as the Ministry of Foreign Affairs, the Ministry of Commerce, and the Export and Import Bank of China (EximBank). The same Chinese government actors are involved in each of the railway projects, but the Chinese SOEs involved differ. Strong Chinese contractors, as measured by their overseas project management experience and political connections in Beijing, would generate higher project effectiveness according to this argument.

2 Railways and beyond

I provide evidence for this argument by process tracing three Chinese-sponsored railways in Kenya, Ethiopia, and Angola. The Kenyan Standard Gauge Railway Phase 1 (SGR-1) and the Ethiopian Addis Ababa–Djibouti railway (ADR)-Meles both demonstrate that political championship is crucial for resolving major obstacles during project implementation. This empirical analysis also allows for the identification of three main stratagems adopted by political leaders: bypassing the bureaucracy, co-opting the opposition, and generating a sense of mission attached to the project. The SGR Phase 2A, the

ADR construction and operation after the eruption of political crisis in 2015, and two phases of the Angolan Caminho de Ferro de Benguela (CFB) show that an absence of championship for a project results in less effectiveness, despite high bureaucratic capacity and strong Chinese intervention. The leadership transition from Meles to Hailemariam shows that leader authority is another factor that is important for successful project implementation. Despite his commitment to the ADR, Hailemariam lacked Meles' astuteness to navigate through various factional interests or effectively lead the coalition of actors for the ADR implementation that was established by Meles. Central control over regional states gradually weakened, and obstacles were not resolved in a timely manner as they were during Meles' tenure.

The Kenyan railway case demonstrates that the political championship of President Kenyatta was crucial to the SGR to achieving high effectiveness during Phase 1, and that the absence of Kenyatta's championship resulted in delays in Phase 2A. Kenyatta's commitment to the SGR was election-inspired. Facing the highly competitive presidential elections in 2017, the incumbent president Uhuru Kenyatta instrumentalized the SGR project, the largest and most expensive project Kenya had undertaken since independence, as his campaign capital, demonstrating his stewardship to the people and his administration's capacity to deliver. The president showed his commitment to the SGR-1 not only by frequently promoting and defending the project in his public discourse but also by his hands-on approach during quarterly site visits.

Kenyatta was a leader of high authority, and the president deployed several effective strategies to push for the project completion. He intervened in both the construction and operation of the SGR by setting timelines for completion and problem resolution; establishing escalation mechanisms that could channel obstacles faced during construction directly to the president's attention; issuing presidential directives to force cargo usage of the SGR; co-opting the opposition leader; and intervening in an ongoing court case.

Kenyatta's commitment to the project cooled off after the election (SGR Phase 2A), as he was not seeking another term in 2022 elections, and the president's priority shifted away from delivering the SGR towards consolidating his power. Apart from the launch and inauguration ceremonies, the president only visited the construction site once. As a result, SGR-2A suffered from a ten-month delay even though Phase 2A enjoyed a more favourable socio-political landscape than Phase 1.

The two competing theories, bureaucratic capacity and external agency, cannot account for the success of the SGR Phase 1 and construction delay during Phase 2A. Crucially, the construction of SGR-1 and -2A was managed by the same Kenyan bureaucracies and Chinese contractor, and we can reasonably assume that they accumulated valuable experience during the management of Phase 1. Yet despite the Kenyan Railway Corporation's increased importance in the Kenyan bureaucratic system and the improved capability of both the Kenyan bureaucracies and Chinese contractor in managing SGR construction, without Kenyatta's direct intervention, similar obstacles confronting SGR-2A were not solved as effectively as in SGR-1.

President Kenyatta's championship was not the result of bureaucratic and external leverages. Although the Kenyan Railway Corporation's status in the Kenyan bureaucratic system significantly increased with the implementation of the SGR, at the initiation and early construction stages, the Kenyan Railway Corporation was too weak an agency in the Kenyan government to leverage political commitment from the presidency. The intervention of the Chinese government, including the Economic Councillor's office and the EximBank, was minimal during SGR construction but significantly increased when the SGR demonstrated success. Instead of intervening to guarantee the success of the SGR, the Chinese government utilized the SGR's success as a demonstration of the success of the Belt and Road Initiative.

The Ethiopian ADR is divided into three subcases: ADR-Meles, ADR-Hailemariam, and ADR-post crisis. The ADR-Meles subcase shows that the political championship of Prime Minister Meles was crucial to pushing the project agenda forward. The 2005 parliamentary election was the most contested ever, where the ruling Ethiopian People's Revolutionary Democratic Front (EPRDF) lost the capital city of Addis Ababa and allocated ninety-two seats to the opposition, the Coalition for Unity and Democracy. The EPRDF government, led by Prime Minister Meles Zenawi, adopted the 'developmental state' as its new basis of legitimacy. State-led mega-infrastructure projects such as the ADR became visible expressions of the developmental state model. The ADR had always been a priority for the EPRDF regime, and both Prime Minister Meles and his successor Hailemariam Desalegn committed to the project. Meles not only strongly committed to the railway project but was also a highly capable leader. The prime minister closely monitored the progress of the ADR and effectively acted as a project manager. He dissuaded dissidents, established the Ethiopian Railway Corporation, handpicked its chief executive officer, and made this parastatal the focal point of railway development in Ethiopia, operating parallel to the Ministry of Transport. High political commitment from the head of the state and the strong capability of Meles to build an effective coalition for the implementation of the ADR guaranteed its initial success.

The ADR-Meles and ADR-Hailemariam subcases are divided by the leadership transition in 2012 due to Meles' sudden death. The ADR in the early years of Hailemariam's tenure (2012–15) exhibited a continuation of political commitment to the ADR but a decline in the leader's authority. Hailemariam maintained Meles' legacy and the ADR continued to be a political priority. Yet Hailemariam lacked Meles' astuteness to navigate through various factional interests and effectively lead the coalition of actors for the ADR implementation that was established by Meles. The Hailemariam administration still frequently referred to the ADR as a national priority, but Hailemariam lacked the leadership authority to either utilize the implementation coalition left by Meles or mobilize his own support for the ADR. Obstacles therefore could not be resolved in a timely manner as they were during Meles' tenure.

The eruption of the political crisis in November 2015 marked a third subcase for the ADR: the ADR-post crisis. Since the beginning of the uprisings and the declaration of the state of emergency, the country's priority shifted from economic growth to stability maintenance. The new prime minister Abiy Ahmed (2018–) further distanced his administration from the developmental state ideology of the previous administrations and Abiy even described himself as a 'capitalist'. Political commitment further faded away for infrastructure projects like the ADR that could not provide massive employment opportunities. Since Abiy's announcement of the Tigray war in November 2020, political commitment to the railway dwindled further. The final stage of the construction and operation was left to the coordination of the Ethiopian Railway Corporation, Ethiopia-Djibouti Railway, and the Chinese contractors. Without political commitment from Abiy, the project development has been challenging.

The bureaucratic capacity and external agency theories could not account for the initial success and later unsatisfactory development of the ADR. During project implementation, the newly established Ethiopian Railway Corporation accrued experience in railway construction and managing Chinese contractors. However, the trajectory of the ADR followed a downward slope where issues under Meles were resolved much more effectively than under Hailemariam and Abiy. Chinese intervention before late 2012 was almost invisible, but the ADR initiation progressed smoothly. Following a political commitment from China that the Belt and Road flagship project would not stop, the Chinese contractors continued the operation despite significantly delayed payments by the Ethiopian Railway Corporation, Ethiopia-Djibouti Railway, and struggled between federal-regional politics and the politics between parastatals, complaining that they were 'politically kidnapped' by the railway project. Even with strong Chinese intervention, the ADR operation had been struggling.

The commitment of Ethiopian prime ministers to the ADR was not due to bureaucratic or Chinese leverage. Meles not only initiated the railway project but also created the Ethiopian Railway Corporation, while the Ministry of Transport was sidelined from ADR's initiation to its operation. Line bureaucracies in Ethiopia therefore could not have inspired Meles' championship. After the eruption of the political crisis, to hasten the start of railway operation, Chinese contractors also leveraged their political connections in Beijing to put pressure on Hailemariam during his visit in China. This improved the Ethiopian government's effective resolution of obstacles to railway operation in the short run, but it was still another six months before operation started.

The two subcases of the Angolan CFB demonstrate that the lack of leadership commitment resulted in not only the significant delay of construction but also difficult and unsafe operation. Political championship, bureaucratic capacity, and Chinese (extra-contractual) intervention were all absent, leading to significantly delayed completion and problematic operation. Throughout the decade of railway construction, President José Eduardo dos Santos only paid ceremonial attention to the project, and for him the announcement of the number of railways renovated was more important than actually having people and goods moving on the railway. The National Reconstruction Office (GRN) was politically strong but highly corrupt and technically weak, while the Ministry of Transport was technically strong but politically irrelevant. The Chinese contractor hesitated to go beyond the contractual framework, as its Ethiopian and Kenyan railways counterparts did, to bear financial risks and assist problem resolution. As the Chinese loans were resource-guaranteed and not attached to the operation of the railway, the effectiveness of the railway was not as pressing a concern for the Chinese government as it was in Kenya and Ethiopia. The Chinese embassy in Angola considered the project to be 'commercial' and reduced its intervention to the minimum.

This is a book about and beyond Chinese-sponsored railway projects in Africa. The theory advanced by this book can be applied on a broader scale. The political championship theory applies to the understanding of the variations in state effectiveness amongst developing countries with relatively weak institutionalized politics, including most African and Latin American and some Asian states. It is in weak institutional settings that the personalism, characterized by volatility and idiosyncrasy of policy and project delivery, becomes prominent. Notably, Liu Zhijun, the former minister of railways in China, championed the high-speed railway system development in China. Researchers have identified that a 'lack of political will' explains many instances of insufficient progress in policies, projects, and reforms by international organizations like the World Bank.[1] In developed countries, researchers also acknowledge the very critical roles that can be played by political champions in building consensus and driving projects forward. Sustained political support and the patronage of a political champion were apparent in the cases of the Attiki Odos in Athens, the Meteor project in Paris, the Oedo Line in Tokyo, the Big Dig project in Boston, the Øresund Link in Sweden/Denmark, and the Perth–Mandurah railway in Australia.[2] However, in these strongly institutionalized countries, the supremacy of the political champion is more limited than in states with weak institutions.

3 What makes this book unique?

This book stands uniquely in the scholarship of African state and Sino-African relations on six fronts. First, by analysing executive leadership in the state's infrastructure delivery, this book advances a research agenda to 'bring the leaders back in' to the study of the state. Existing studies of state capacity and effectiveness frequently neglect the role of the leader's political will, and political leadership rarely receives scholarly attention in this literature. Instead, scholars tend to concentrate on structural and institutional factors such as state–society relations, Weberian bureaucracy, and the power of the state, while 'political will' and leadership are frequently overlooked or simply reduced to a background factor. This insufficient study of leaders' agency is, to some degree, a result of the access limitation of data on the microfoundations of contemporary political leaders. As a result, researchers of state effectiveness (as well as state capacity and state-building) find it difficult to capture the non-linear and idiosyncratic effects in policy implementation. The recent rise of individual leaders in major powers such as the USA and China makes it even more urgent to understand leaders' agency in domestic and international politics. By focusing on the agency of the political leaders, this book and the political championship theory capture the volatile, personalistic, and idiosyncratic characteristics of state effectiveness in project delivery and broader policy implementation that cannot be explained by either the structural or institutional explanations alone. The theory is illustrated by detailed

[1] Heaver (2005); FAO (2012).
[2] Dimitriou, Ward, and Wright (2012).

case studies decorated with quotes from those who have directly worked with the political champions.

Second, in the study of leadership in political science, the political championship theory differs from existing studies of political leadership, which centre either on the psychological aspects of leaders and followers or the effects of leadership on the economy. The agency of leaders is a factor that scholars intuitively know but analytically overlook in the mainstream political science literature of the past two decades. In addition to highlighting the agency of leaders, the theory advanced by this book contributes to the study of leadership by providing institutional incentives for political leadership, in particular how competitive elections may generate a leader's commitment to a specific project or policy.

Third, by differentiating the president from the presidency, the political championship theory highlights the de-institutionalization of power without undermining formal institutions. The role of leaders is more pronounced in African politics literature, where politics in Africa is often presented as less restrained and more personalized and informal. It is characterized by the prevalence of primary forms of reciprocity, where rulers continue to see their interests as tied to local communities rather than to systems of abstract rule. The political leaders, or the 'big men', permit clientelism to wield unregulated presidential control over state institutions, and are thus able to exert a high degree of executive dominance that far exceeds a president's constitutional authority. Yet Africanists tend not to distinguish the president and the presidency, and when speaking of presidential power they use the language of institutions—that is, the presidency is powerful—and equate it to the power of the individual president.[3] Or they tend to go to another extreme of emphasizing the personal aspect while ignoring formal institutions. For instance, in the study of 'personal rule' and 'big-man politics', scholars of African politics focus more on clientelism, where leaders pursue personal enrichment and maintenance of the clientelistic system to remain in power, but less, if at all, on formal institutions and the leader's role in achieving policy objectives.[4] The political championship theory brings back the individual in the analysis of African presidentialism by distinguishing an individual president from the presidency, thereby highlighting the de-institutionalization of power and politics without undermining formal institutions. The theory recognizes that sources of leadership authority derive from a combination of the leader's institutional

[3] See discussions in Chaisty, Cheeseman, and Power (2018); Carbone and Pellegata (2020).
[4] See, for instance, Jackson and Rosberg (1982); Clapham (1982).

positions, the traditional patronage system, and personalistic characteristics such as charisma.

Fourth, this study proposes a possibility that short-term electoral institutions can be effective in generating leadership commitment to and intervention in developmental projects, countering the argument of developmental state theory. Scholars of developmental states criticize the fact that, in developing countries, politicians in a democracy may be preoccupied with electoral success: they tend to rely on projects or policies to fuel their patronage machines or favour their constituencies, undermining project efficiency while boosting their electoral votes and personal enrichment. Developmentalists therefore conclude that electoral competition creates short-term survival incentives for the elites, which are not as effective for development as the incentives created by centralized, long-term rent management in developmental states. The comparison of railway implementation in Kenya, a democracy, and Ethiopia, a developmental state (before February 2018), shows that short-term electoral institutions in Kenya can be as effective as the long-term centralized ones in terms of generating leadership commitment to and intervention in developmental projects. The Kenyan president's incentives to garner support through the patron–client network coexisted with genuine incentives to demonstrate their administrative effectiveness and ability to deliver mega-infrastructure projects.

A fifth unique point of this book is the articulation of the African agency argument in the Sino-African relations literature. This research challenges the dependency theory and the neo-dependency argument in Sino-African relations. This theory argues that China's interest in natural resources and desire to displace its overcapacity and debt burden onto Africa have deepened Africa's dependent position and perpetuate inequitable integration into the global political economy. I show that despite the China–Africa structural imbalance, African elites were able to influence the practices of Chinese actors and shape the trajectories of the railway projects in their respective countries. It was therefore the primacy of African domestic politics, rather than their 'Chineseness', that determined the trajectories of Chinese-financed and -constructed projects. More precisely, it was African political leaders' agency in committing to and intervening in the projects that defined the effectiveness of infrastructure delivery. This argument follows the African extraversion theory that Chinese-sponsored infrastructure projects were used by African elites to achieve domestic purposes, such as winning electoral campaigns, weakening the opposition, and laying the infrastructural foundation for industrialization.

Finally, this book provides detailed and comprehensive documentation of three Chinese-sponsored railway projects in three African states. The empirical data was drawn from 250 interviews and multiple short episodes of participatory observation with Chinese contractors in Africa. I was resident in Kenya when the SGR was widely publicized in 2014 and visited the Kenyan railway almost on a yearly basis from 2015 to 2019. I visited the Ethiopian railway twice, in 2017 and 2019, and stayed in Angola for a consecutive five-month period from 2018 to 2019. The repeated visits allowed me to document project development over time, granting this book a unique cross-temporal perspective. The Kenyan and Ethiopian railways are Belt and Road flagship projects, so this book contributes to the burgeoning literature on China's Belt and Road projects by demystifying the interactions between Chinese state actors and host countries. This large amount of highly detailed and original information is supported by a wide body of multilingual documentary material, including policy and media reports, and non-traditional and restricted sources such as legal documents, Chinese companies' internal publications, corporate contracts, and communications between Chinese companies and African and Chinese government agencies acquired via investigative journalists. Navigating through multiple languages, the primary and secondary data of this book presents a balanced view that documents perspectives from both China and Africa instead of relying overly on one side. This empirical documentation is especially valuable for the scholarship on Sino-African relations and China's Belt and Road Initiative given the hard-to-access nature of Chinese state actors and their projects.

4 Three policy questions

In this final section, I engage with three policy questions that frequently appear in China–Africa media and policy debates and how this study could inform these debates.

How should we understand China's 'debt trap diplomacy'?

Concerns with debt from China are often framed as China's 'debt trap diplomacy (DTD)', suggesting that China deliberately seeks to entrap countries in a web of debt to secure strategic advantage or an asset of some kind.[5] The

[5] Chellaney (2017).

argument is that China is supporting infrastructure projects in strategically located developing countries, often by extending huge loans to their governments. As a result, countries are becoming ensnared in a 'debt trap' that leaves them vulnerable to China's influence. The projects that China is supporting, as the DTD argument claims, are often intended not to support the local economy but to facilitate Chinese access to natural resources, to secure geostrategic locations, or to open the market for China's low-cost (and local quality) export goods; in many cases, China even sends its own construction workers, minimizing the number of local jobs that are created. A most frequently cited example of China's DTD is the Hambantota port in Sri Lanka, where the government agreed to sell an 80 per cent stake of the Hambantota port to China for about $1.1 billion in order to help Sri Lanka 'solve its finance problems'.[6] In 2018, the claim that Mombasa port had been used as collateral to secure the Kenyan SGR loans first appeared in *The East African* and was later cited in multiple local and international newspapers, which generated debate on Kenya being entrapped by China's multi-billion-dollar debt.[7]

DTD has been debunked by several important papers.[8] Three key arguments stand out. First, China is not a major driver of African debt distress. For instance, Kenya's total external debt stock in 2020 was US$38 billion, while its bilateral debt only amounts to US$11 billion.[9] Although China is the largest bilateral creditor, Kenya's debt to China constitutes less than a third of Kenya's total debt, as the country has also borrowed from multilateral institutions such as the International Monetary Fund and World Bank, as well as private creditors. Second, examination of lending contracts reveals that China did not have the intention to secure assets from loan default. Bräutigam et al.'s (2022) investigation of the SGR contracts shows that, instead of a deliberate debt trap with Mombasa port as collateral, the SGR contracts were carefully and creatively designed to reduce the risks of a sovereign default and enhance the bankability of the project.

Finally, the DTD brings us back to the dependency theory where African countries' domestic development is dependent on external finance and technical assistance, independent of African countries' will and capacity (see Chapter 5). China's engagement with developing countries has marked a

[6] Ibid.

[7] Omondi (20 December 2018).

[8] See Rithmere and Li (2019) on the Hambantota port case and Bräutigam, Bhalaki, Deron, and Wang (2022) on the SGR case. For more general discussions of debt trap diplomacy, see Bräutigam (2020); Singh (2020); and Jones and Hameiri (2020), among many others.

[9] World Bank International Debt Statistics 2022, accessed on 29 September 2022 from https://datatopics.worldbank.org/debt/ids/creditorcomposition/KEN.

revival of scholarly debate around dependency theory. Deepening dependence has purportedly been enabled by China's purchase of natural resources and African countries' indebtment, with a large portion of debt from Chinese loans for infrastructure construction. Framing China–Africa relations in this way portrays African countries as situated at the periphery of the global economic system and as deprived of agency to foster domestic development.

The 'debt trap' argument fails to consider the agency of African countries in dealing with external creditors. When African countries face a variety of financiers, they could in theory have more bargain power in negotiation. China emerged as an alternative source of finance from the West, with no political conditions (except one-China policy) attached, readily available large sums of money, and willing to support the development model the African government chose. This is therefore welcomed with fanfare by African governments. In addition, when African governments have access to a more diverse array of external finance, their dependence on individual donor and creditor is reduced, and they ought to have greater influence over the outcomes of negotiations with these donors, aligning outcomes more closely with their preferences. Borrowing governments use their borrowing relationships to reduce their dependence on individual creditors, thereby giving them a stronger negotiating position than before. In other words, China provides African countries with 'agency of choice' vis-à-vis traditional donors.[10] The ultimate question is whether African elites and governments can wisely make use of development finance from China and other bilateral, multilateral, and private creditors to increase domestic productivity and people's welfare so as to reduce structural dependence in the long run. The fact that Chinese development finance has no political conditions attached makes it especially important to investigate host-country domestic politics when studying Chinese-sponsored projects and development finance.

To summarize, DTD argues that China is Africa's main creditor, and that the intention of Chinese development finance was to serve the strategic interest of China at the expense of Africa. In fact, China is only one of many creditors African states borrow from, and the surge of Chinese development finance over the past two decades should not conceal the fact that, in most African countries, Chinese development finance is not the main source of external debt distress. The 'debt trap' argument dangerously leads us back to the developmental pessimism depicted by dependency theory, where African countries are deprived of agency to determine their domestic development. It

[10] Greenhill, Prizzon, and Rogerson (2013).

is important to recognize the agency of African actors to strategize amongst their available choices of external finance to boost domestic development and people's welfare.

Does African civil society have agency?

There seems to be a perpetual impression that 'the African state is weak, its people are weaker',[11] particularly within the international system. The current discussions of African agency predominantly concentrate on the agency of African elites, bureaucrats, and the state most generally;[12] scholarly work on the agency of non-state actors from Africa is limited but emerging.

The extraversion of African civil society groups is not a new phenomenon, however. In the forms of extraversion, resistance, and politicization, African civil society has been actively engaged with external powers to advance their own agenda. Historically, researchers have captured the globalization of African trade unions. Unions across French Africa, with the support of the General Confederation of Labour (CGT) in Paris, were successful in pressing for the French Code de Travail for its African colonies in the early 1950s.[13] Mohan and Lampert (2013) discuss how African citizens and businesses have increasingly reached out to China as a source of useful resources for personal and business progression. And significant numbers of African traders, since the mid-1990s, have travelled to China, especially Guangzhou, to buy Chinese consumer goods for export to Africa, and these traders became strong competitors for African manufacturers and Chinese traders in Africa.[14] Resistance to Chinese projects was also frequently politicized by local politicians, the most evident case being the Zambian 2006 elections when only the Chinese miners were picked out as targets of the opposition leader Michael Santa's harsh criticism of mining practices in his attempt to cater to the local mining community and labour unions.[15] Similarly, as we see in Kenya, community grievances towards the SGR were politicized by opposition politicians as a way to criticize the incumbent government (Chapter 2).

This book's argument of African presidential agency is not a claim that popular agency does not matter. A holistic account of all aspects of African agency

[11] Clapham (1996).
[12] See works by Soulé-Kohndou (2019); Zhou (2022); and Oya & Schaefer (2019), for instance.
[13] Cooper (1996).
[14] Mohan and Lampert (2013).
[15] Lee (2017).

is not the purpose of this book, but I recognize that African popular and civil society agency is another area that has been less systematically analysed and is a promising area for future research.

Are Chinese-sponsored projects helping Africa's development?

The short answer is 'it depends'. The key factor is whether the host country can effectively use Chinese-sponsored projects for their domestic development. Among Chinese-sponsored infrastructure projects discussed in this book, China is not a donor. Chinese government financing in these cases should not be considered as Chinese foreign aid. It should be distinguished from OECD-DAC's definition of Official Development Assistance.[16] Framed officially as 'win-win' cooperation, China's state financing to Africa appears to be driven by bilateral trade ties and natural resource endowments in recipient countries.[17]

Positive and negative perceptions and evidence regarding Chinese-sponsored projects in Africa coexist in the media, policy, and academic debates. Commonly raised issues include that Chinese infrastructure projects drive economic development, corruption, environmental impact, job creation, local procurement and subcontracting, quality of construction, and so on. We also see the same issue exhibited differently in different countries. Corruption was a major issue in media's exposure of the Kenyan and Angolan railway deals and a commonly raised challenge when I interviewed people participating in these projects; in Ethiopia, however, corruption never appeared as a challenge during the development trajectory of the railway and industrial park projects. China EximBank's negotiation with the Kenyan and Angolan governments accepted their requirements of 40 per cent and 30 per cent local input, respectively, but no requirement was made of the government of Ethiopia during negotiations. The quality of work of Chinese infrastructure was a major concern in Angola, but in Kenya and Ethiopia, roads constructed by Chinese companies were termed 'China road' for their superior quality. Implementation of the negotiated fruits also matters. Some successful terms coming out of the negotiation rooms need to be guaranteed by strong implementation capacity. In the Kenyan and Angolan railway cases, a 40 per cent and 30 per cent local

[16] Bräutigam (2011); Strange, Dreher, Fuchs, Parks, and Tierney (2017); Dreher, Fuchs, Parks, Strange, and Tierney (2018).

[17] Dreher, Fuchs, Parks, Strange, and Tierney (2018).

content element was agreed during their respective negotiations with China but was not realized during implementation (at least during SGR Phase 1; see Chapters 2 and 4). If fully implemented, the railway construction could serve as a driving force for local business development.

This comparison shows that the state capacity of the host government matters. This includes whether the host country is able to come up with and effectively implement regulations regarding socio-environment impact of companies. The common perception that Chinese policy banks and contractors are strong in negotiation skills is not necessarily true (Chapter 5). Around many negotiation tables, African negotiators can be as skilled as and even more experienced than their Chinese counterparts. As Soulé-Kohndou (2019) correctly points out, skilful and experienced African bureaucrats are sometimes sidelined or had to accommodate political interventions from above. The Ethiopian and Angolan railway cases (Chapters 3 and 4) also share this point. Lacking transparency of these infrastructure deals make it difficult for African countries to learn from each other's experience in negotiating with China. An area for African policy-makers to accumulate experience and mutually learn is to share their experience of dealing with China.

In host countries with relatively weak state capacity, however, requirements from financier and Chinese government can also help regulate contractors' behaviours. Indeed, the Chinese government has issued a series of laws and regulations to guide the responsible business conduct of Chinese companies' overseas operations. Chinese government has put increasing emphasis on corporate overseas stakeholder management, reducing negative reputation, and mitigating negative environmental footprint. The White Paper on 'China's International Development Cooperation in the New Era' released in January 2021 emphasizes that 'adhering to the concept of justice and interests is the value orientation for China to carry out international development cooperation.'[18] In 2017, EximBank revised the due diligence procedures for its credit business, procedures for loan issuance, payment review, and so on to strengthen the monitoring and management requirements for environmental and social risks in all aspects of the business process. EximBank installed an 'environment veto system' where enterprises that do not comply with the national industrial policy and environmental protection policy and are listed in the environmental 'blacklist' shall not be considered for EximBank loans.[19]

[18] State Council (2021).
[19] China Export and Import Bank (2019).

In sum, whether Chinese- (and other foreign-)sponsored projects contribute to the development of host countries brings us back to the argument of African agency, where ultimately it is African states that determine which projects to pursue and how to connect foreign-sponsored projects to domestic development. This, however, should not be a justification for negative behaviours of international actors. Requirements from home countries' governments and financial institutions, as well as firm-level characteristics such as the levels of internationalization and localization of the companies and so on, can be defining factors for corporate behaviours such as corruption, local spill-over effects, stakeholder engagement, and environmental footprint. An area of future research is whether China's domestic requirements may extend to corporate practices in Africa.

APPENDIX 1

Hypothesis testing and data collection

This Appendix discusses the book's methodology in relation to the Introduction and theory chapters. Section 1 elaborates on the hypothesis testing by outlining testable hypotheses and observable implications for the three competing theories: political championship, external agency, and bureaucratic capacity. In section 2, I discuss my data collection methods in detail, which include elite interviews, participatory observation, and second-hand document triangulation.

1 Hypothesis testing

In explaining state effectiveness, this book engages with three competing explanations emphasizing structural, institutional, and individual agency factors, respectively. In this methodological Appendix, I derive testable hypotheses and outline observable implications for the benefit of readers with technical interest in causal inference. This section is a technical complementary to Chapter 1.

Political championship is the actions of individuals in top political positions (usually the executive) who endeavour to solve or circumvent the obstacles that beleaguer the efforts of less senior actors in processes of public goods delivery. The political championship theory emphasizes that political commitment and the leader's authority are independently necessary and jointly sufficient for the success project delivery and therefore that absence of one variable results in suboptimal project outcomes. The mechanism of the political championship theory is outlined in Figure A.1. This theory generates the following hypotheses:

- $H_{\text{POLITICAL CHAMPIONSHIP}}1$. Perceived threats from electoral competition generate strong political commitment from the ruler.
- $H_{\text{POLITICAL CHAMPIONSHIP}}2$. A committed political champion with strong authority intervenes in project implementation by motivating bureaucracies and tempering resistance, leading to higher project effectiveness.

The 'Chinese agency' version of the structural explanation predicts that it was the agency of the Chinese state-owned enterprises (SOEs), rather than African actors, that shaped the trajectories of the projects. Chinese SOEs with higher technical strength and political connection could deliver railway projects more successfully in Africa. Chinese SOEs' capability can influence railway effectiveness through two mechanisms, which usually coexist. Firstly, SOEs can work directly with African bureaucrats and citizens to solve the problems encountered during project implementation and operation, as outlined in $H_{\text{EXTERNAL AGENCY}}1$. Alternatively, SOEs can work through Chinese government to generate stronger commitment by African state leaders, as $H_{\text{EXTERNAL AGENCY}}$ 2 and 3 show. The external agency explanation consists of three hypotheses.

- $H_{\text{EXTERNAL AGENCY}}1$. SOEs with higher technical capability can effectively solve obstacles during implementation, thus the project demonstrates higher effectiveness.

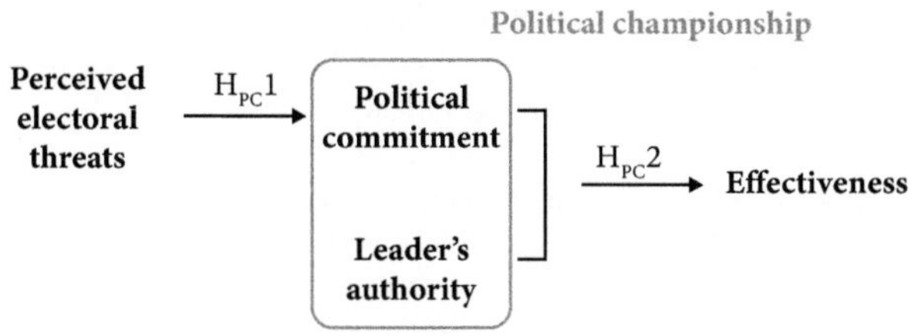

Figure A.1 Mechanism of political championship theory

- $H_{EXTERNAL\ AGENCY}2$. SOEs lobby the Chinese government to increase commitment to the project.
- $H_{EXTERNAL\ AGENCY}3$. Committed Chinese government uses diplomatic or financial leverage to encourage the host government's commitment to the project and ensure project success.

Divergent from the external agency theory but similar to the political championship argument, this bureaucratic capacity explanation argues African domestic agency in shaping project outcomes. However, unlike the political championship argument that centres on the individual, especially the executive agency, this explanation, along with the 'pockets of effectiveness' and developmental states literature, believes that successful project delivery is due largely to capable bureaucracy. The bureaucratic capacity theory generates the following two hypotheses:

- $H_{BUREAUCRATIC\ CAPACITY}1$. The railway corporation can solve obstacles within its domain effectively, thus achieving higher project effectiveness.
- $H_{BUREAUCRATIC\ CAPACITY}2$. The railway corporation with strong political capability may elicit executive intervention to resolve deadlocks while solving cross-ministerial problems.

Figure A.2 illustrates the two alternative arguments in relation to the political championship theory. Table A.1 demonstrates the hypotheses of three theories and their respective observable implications.

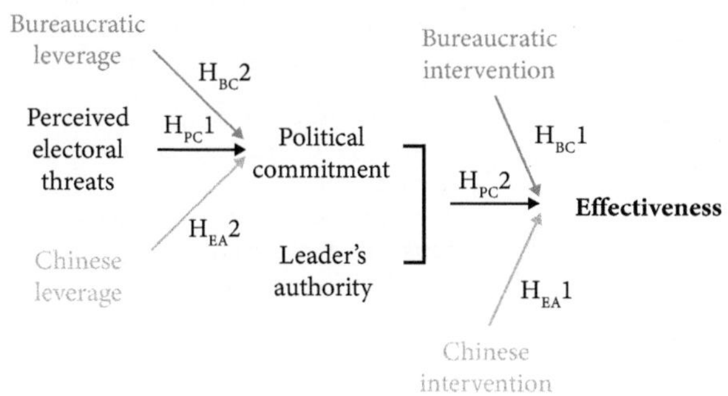

Figure A.2 Alternative arguments and hypotheses

Table A.1 Competing hypotheses and observable implications

Hypotheses	Observable implications
$H_{\text{POLITICAL CHAMPIONSHIP}}$1. Endogenous political championship	• African political leaders showed strong ownership of the project prior to the Chinese government's and railway corporation's involvement in the project. • The political commitment to the railway is generated from the executive's perceived salience of the project rather than exogenous influences. • Political commitment is not only at the discourse level but also shown as the leader's close engagement with the project and frequent follow-up on project progress. • Top political leadership of the host country devoted superior commitment to this project than to any other projects during their rulership.
$H_{\text{POLITICAL CHAMPIONSHIP}}$2. Executive intervention	• The effectiveness of executive intervention in shaping project outcome: the executive achieved effectiveness through generating mission, bypassing bureaucracy, and/or co-opting opposition leaders. • For the same project, when executive intervention reduced from extensive to ceremonial, the efficiency of obstacle resolution slowed down.
$H_{\text{EXTERNAL AGENCY}}$1. Chinese SOE's intervention	• The SOEs stepped beyond their contractual obligation to help African counterparts solve problems during construction and operation, sometimes even in a commercial sense. • Even with less intensive executive intervention and no change in the African railway corporation's intervention, the project proceeded normally without delay.
$H_{\text{EXTERNAL AGENCY}}$2 and 3. China-leveraged political championship	• SOEs engaged in public campaigns in China to raise Chinese public awareness on the project. • SOEs lobbied the Chinese government to heighten the political significance of the project in China. • Chinese government urged African leaders to commit to the project during bilateral meetings or multilateral platforms. After visiting China or receiving state visits from Chinese officials, the African leaders' commitment to the project notably increased.
$H_{\text{BUREAUCRATIC CAPACITY}}$1. Bureaucratic intervention	• Obstacles within the domain of the railway corporation, including labour disputes and community relations, were effectively solved. • Even with less intensive executive intervention and no change in Chinese SOEs' support, the project proceeded normally without delay.
$H_{\text{BUREAUCRATIC CAPACITY}}$2. Bureaucracy-leveraged political championship	• The railway corporation was involved in the project prior to the executive. • The railway corporation lobbied the executive to increase the political importance of this project. • The executive's intervention in resolving inter-ministerial deadlocks, especially in land acquisition, was due to lobbying from the railway corporation.

2 Data collection

Evidence for the process-tracing exercise was collected through a combination of in-depth interviews and participatory observation during fieldwork, as well as second-hand documents. The forty weeks of fieldwork stretching from 2017 to 2019 were spent in the following countries: Ethiopia (ten weeks, including one week in Djibouti), Kenya (ten weeks), Angola (thirteen weeks), and China (seven weeks). The total time, location, and length of the fieldwork are listed in Table A.2. My field research for this book greatly benefited from the networks and intuition developed during my previous working experience. I worked in Nairobi from July 2013 to December 2014 in a local non-governmental organization (NGO) conducting research on Chinese businesses in Kenya. In July 2015, I visited Kenya for two weeks and drove along the Standard Gauge Railway to observe and conduct interviews with Chinese managers and local politicians in Nairobi, Emali, Taita Taveta, and Mombasa.[1]

Elite interviews

The history of the railway projects is like a jigsaw puzzle and conducting interviews during fieldwork is like working with pieces of the puzzle, with each core interviewee's unique position and experience as an important piece of the whole picture. As I interviewed more people that worked on the case project from different organizations and levels, my mental image of the puzzle became more complete and clearer. Journalists, lawyers, scholars, NGO practitioners, and citizens whose livelihoods were affected by the case projects also held key complementary pieces of the puzzle.

The context-specific observations for the process-tracing exercise are primarily drawn from interviews during fieldwork. Elite interview is appropriate given my focus on the decision-making process as well as the behaviour of and interaction between African elites, Chinese SOEs, and Chinese government involved in the railway projects. Interview contents capture varying perspectives, discuss processes, unearth competing interpretations

Table A.2 Details on the times and venues of fieldwork

Time	Venue (city/country)	Length (weeks)
17 Jun to 8 Jul 2017	Addis Ababa/Ethiopia	3
8 Jul to 19 Jul 2017	Nairobi/Kenya	2
7 Oct to 8 Nov 2018	Beijing, Xi'an/China	4
9 Nov to 15 Dec 2018	Luanda, Huambo/Angola	6
16 Dec 2018 to 7 Feb 2019	Beijing, Xi'an/China	3
8 Feb to 31 Mar 2019	Benguela, Luanda/Angola	7
1 Apr to 22 May 2019	Addis Ababa, Dire Dawa/Ethiopia; Djibouti	7
2 Jul to 31 Aug 2019	Nairobi, Mombasa/Kenya	8
Total		**40**

[1] A working paper came out of this fieldwork. See Wissenbach and Wang (2017).

of events, identify the micro-foundations of macro-patterns, and frame hypotheses.[2] The meta-data on the interviewees' expression, tone, behaviour, and so on also allows me to make a more informed judgement of the evidentiary value of the data.

Researchers have also identified the disadvantage of interviews, particularly in terms of objectivity and generalizability.[3] Respondents sometimes offer self-serving and distorted accounts, and any one interview provides a narrow viewpoint on the phenomenon of interest. A researcher's identity may affect the objectivity of the research by affecting the access and content of the interviews. Increasing the transparency of the interview process is an effort towards reducing these disadvantages.

During the forty weeks of fieldwork, I conducted 250 interviews, excluding the casual talks with host-country citizens on the street or on the train. Appendix 3 is a list of interview themes and questions, and Appendix 4 includes a detailed list of interviewees. The length of interviews varied from 30 minutes to 5 hours, with an average of 1 hour for English and Chinese interviews, and 1.5 hours for Portuguese interviews via interpreter. While semi-structured interviews were used in most cases, some interviews were informal and unstructured. Saturation was reached in most categories, except for interviews in the category of 'other Chinese companies' during fieldwork in China, and for three categories in Angola.

Saturation for interviews in China ranges from low to medium, but this was compensated for by interviews within the same categories in Africa. The saturation for the 'other Chinese companies' category is low, but this does not affect the data analysis because this category is mainly designed to cultivate connections. The poor information environment largely explains this limited saturation in China and Angola. I compensate for this with secondary works on the railway published by the Chinese contractor and by scholarly work on the country.

I used a stratified-snowball sampling method to identify potential interviewees. Prior to fieldwork, I came up with a list of institutions that I planned to approach. Because of the narrow focus of my research on three railway projects, I was able to quickly and precisely sketch the most relevant institutions involved in various stages of the projects. These include Chinese contractors, the Chinese government, other Chinese companies operating in the host countries, African railway corporations, African governments, academia, media, businesses, and local and international NGOs. During fieldwork, my initial set of respondents provided referrals for additional contacts. My connections from previous experience working in Kenya and the United Nations Development Programme Beijing office allowed me to get into contact with some Chinese journalists, NGO practitioners, and Chinese SOE managers in Africa. My access strategy in Angola and Ethiopia was to connect with the respective Chinese SOE contractors for the railway projects first, then ask the Chinese SOE to introduce me to African railway corporations and the Ministry of Transport. I concluded each interview with this question: 'regarding my research interest, who else do you think I should speak to?' In most cases, informants were able to give me some names and even their phone or WhatsApp numbers or email addresses, and WeChat accounts for Chinese potential informants. On rare occasions, the informants were willing to make a quick introductory phone call in my presence to the next interviewee. This was especially the case with bureaucrats in the same institution and when introductions were made from higher to lower levels of a hierarchy.

[2] Weiss (1994); Kapiszewski, MacLean, and Read (2015).

[3] Ibid.

Most of my interviews were semi-structured. I entered each interview with a list of themes I wanted to explore with the interviewee. The themes are as follows: railway characteristics, railway politicization, local linkages, Chinese companies, railway impact, land acquisition and compensation, and social and environmental impact assessment. Under each theme, I prepared a list of open-ended questions (see Appendix 3 for the themes and questions). This list became handy when I was preparing for interviews with high-level officials who had only limited time. I came to the interview with a selected list of questions and tried to address as many of them as possible. For most of my interviewees who were mid-level bureaucrats participating in the case projects, the interviews were less structured. I started by asking about their specific roles in the project, and gradually led the topic to the themes of research interest but allowed the conversation to unfold in a relatively flexible fashion. Yet this inquiry sometimes made some interviewees uncomfortable: recalling the daily details of project management could be emotional and stressful for many of my informants. They preferred redirecting the discussion to the general perspectives on Sino-African relations, as well as the economic and diplomatic importance of these projects—they preferred talking about the fact that they were part of projects of significance.

While obtaining verbal informed consent, I asked the interviewees' preference of quotation and anonymity. This research topic is sensitive since it involves state-to-state deals and the projects I investigated penetrate deep into host-country politics, involving many corruption charges in Kenya and Angola, and the resignation of leading officials in Ethiopia. Most of my Chinese, Angolan, and Ethiopian interviewees and some Kenyan ones preferred to anonymize themselves. Some even insisted on obliterating their institutional affiliation. I respected all anonymity requests. Instead of using names, I designed an identification code for each interviewee. The full list of interviewees, their affiliations, interview formats, date, length, and location are provided in Appendix 4.

Because of the sensitive nature of this research, I did not audio-record any interview but asked for my informants' permission to take notes instead. For the interviews completed in 2017, I used my laptop to take notes during the interview. For the 2018–19 fieldwork, I took notes on notebooks and typed them into Evernote, with encryption if highly sensitive, as soon as possible after the interview. Often the transcription was completed in taxi backseats in traffic jams.[4] For both approaches to notetaking, I tried to preserve as much content of the conversation as possible and jotted down meta-data in parentheses or in the rim of the notebook during the interview and extended the broken sentences immediately after the interview. Inevitably some exact wording of the interviewees' sentences was lost during this process, but it was possible to paraphrase them without losing the interviewees' meaning. Quotations in this book are the best recollection of the precise phrases used, rather than word-for-word reproductions.

My fluency in English and Chinese allowed me to conduct interviews in Ethiopia, Kenya, and China without a language barrier. Yet in Angola, my beginner-level Portuguese only allowed me to get around and have a conversation in local markets, but it was not enough to engage in in-depth discussions on railway development. One-third of my informants were able to speak English, and I worked with five different translators to conduct Portuguese

[4] Looking back of these two types of notetaking methods, I find the notebook/transcription approach preferable. Directly taking notes from a laptop could still be threatening for some interviewees. A stand-up laptop screen between the interviewee and myself concealed the information I typed and could reduce trust. Admittedly, laptop notetaking allowed me to preserve more full sentences from the informants, yet transcribing the notes from notebook to laptop provided another opportunity to review and analyse the interview (which is not usually a pleasant mental process). Thus I found the transcribed notes were better organized and presented than when direct notetaking from laptop.

interviews for the two-thirds that spoke Portuguese and French only. Because of the change of fieldwork location and funding availability, I worked with five Portuguese–English interpreters and one Portuguese–Chinese interpreter; see Table A.3 for a list of these interpreters by ethnicity, age, and gender. Among them, one was a young male and four were female, and one of the female interpreters was senior and well established locally. I could certainly observe the change of power dynamics different interpreters brought to the interviews.

Interviewing via interpreters may affect trust-building with interviewees. Trust was especially difficult for interviewing in Angola because of the authoritarian nature of the state, and most government officials were not used to the culture of research. After João Lourenço was declared president in 2017, there was an increase in political freedom—people can now criticize the previous administration. But Lourenço's anti-corruption campaign alerted some government officials, who, during interviews, suspected me as an investigative journalist trying to expose the deals related to the railway. Under this context, trust-building might be either enhanced or damaged by the presence of interpreters. The presence of a local interpreter who can quickly connect with the informant and can introduce the foreign researcher as someone credible may increase the informant's willingness to share information.[5] In Angola, working with a limited budget, I asked for translation help from my local friends, who had experience studying abroad and their family members were usually political insiders. During one interview with a senior manager of the Caminho de Ferro de Luanda, a young Angolan lady who had recently received an engineering degree in the UK helped me with translation. After introducing herself, the informant, who was also an engineer, was very impressed with the interpreter's engineering background, and they started talking intensively in Portuguese. My limited Portuguese allowed me to detect when the informant asked her why she was translating for me: she said she was just helping out a friend. When I re-entered the conversation, I found the informant was more at ease with me. However, working with young, female Angolan interpreters had its own problems: one interpreter complained to me that the informant tried to set up a date with her after the interview.

Another challenge in working with interpreters is the lost information in translation. Working with a professional interpreter could reduce this risk of losing important conversational content. Still, some meta-data I observed could not be matched with the exact words. I emphasized word-by-word translation to all interpreters I worked with, but it might not be practical in most cases. Many interviewees preferred not to stop at each sentence and

Table A.3 List of Portuguese interpreters by ethnicity, age, and gender

	Ethnicity	Age (approx.)	Gender
Interpreter-1	Portuguese	42	Female
Interpreter-2	Angolan	25	Female
Interpreter-3	Angolan	30	Female
Interpreter-4	Angolan	25	Male
Interpreter-5	Chinese	30	Female

[5] Fuiji (2013) also discussed how her local interpreter served as a guide and a translator of interview contents as well as culture norms.

wait for translation. Usually what happened was that the interpreter listened to a whole paragraph of an answer from the interviewee while taking notes, then translated this whole paragraph to me. Inevitably some content of the interviewee's answer disappeared during this process. Moreover, interpreters might not be able to sense that even a slight change in the wording of the sentence might reveal important information for my research. In one interview, when I asked whether an environmental impact assessment was conducted prior to railway construction, my interviewee answered 'yes', and soon changed his answer to 'no'. My interpreter only translated this 'no' and omitted the initial 'yes'. This was easy to pick up with some basic knowledge of the language, but I can imagine some cases where my knowledge of language was not enough to identify the loss in translation. More devastating loss of information would appear if, due to limited accessibility and funding, the interpreter that was available was not familiar with some technical terms in the conversation.

A final difficulty I find working with an interpreter is the prolonged interview time. On average, my interviews in English lasted for 1 hour. Adding interpretation usually doubled the length. The longest Portuguese–English interview I did was 2.5 hours and it was very exhausting for everyone. The average Portuguese–English interviews were slightly over 1 hour, which was practically 30 minutes of information if conducted without interpreter.

Participatory observation

During fieldwork in Ethiopia and Angola, I conducted short episodes of participatory observation: three weeks in Addis Ababa (Ethiopia) in July 2017, three weeks in Benguela (Angola) in February 2019, and one week in Dire Dawa (Ethiopia) in May 2019. I was accommodated alongside the respective Chinese contractors of the railways under study. I followed the traditional ethnographic mindset to step outside of myself and give credibility to another's way of approaching a problem.[6] Through living in the same compound with the Chinese managers in the SOEs, I was able to live their lifestyle, having three meals daily with them, receiving visits from senior management from their headquarters, and participating in internal Chinese Communist Party meetings. The experience allowed me to view the railway projects, African governments, and host countries in general from the perspective of these Chinese managers. This proved to be particularly useful in developing intuition regarding the behaviours and incentives of Chinese SOEs. Staying with the Chinese contractors also allowed me to have many informal conversations with the managers about how the project was conducted, and many pieces of project-management information were shared at the lunch and dinner table, when Chinese project managers sat at a round table together. Most of these lunch and dinner discussions were about the projects and issues at hand such as railway operation obstacles, rather than the railway construction, which was already completed. But these discussions could still reflect the Chinese managers' perspective towards working with a host-country government. These informal discussions were not directly quoted in this book, partly due to ethical concerns, but the information collected informally contributed to forming my intuitions and contextual knowledge of the cases.

[6] Schatz (2013); Pachirat (2018).

Second-hand documents

This research also relies on a good number of second-hand documents. They include policy papers and news reports related to Sino-African relations in general and the case projects in particular. I also collected a wide range of NGO reports and scholarly research on various aspects of the projects; railway corporations and other African government websites that contain railway information; and corporate websites and the three corporate social responsibility reports of the China Road and Bridge Corporation (CRBC) on the Kenyan railway. Importantly, a recently published book in Chinese written by a manager of CR20 on the Angolan railway projects, *Guo Jia Rong Yu* (translated as *National Pride*), presents a detailed record of how CR20 undertook the railway projects in Angola over the past decade. Apart from these conventional sources of second-hand documents, I also relied on over 1,600 pages of documents regarding the Kenyan railway uncovered by investigative journalists and lawyers. Based on the trust established during the interviews with these journalists and lawyers, I was further entrusted with copies of these documents, with 300 pages in hard copy and 1,300 pages in soft copy. These are highly sensitive pieces of information on the contracts and the Kenyan government's internal debates, communications, and meeting minutes regarding this highly contentious railway. These documents completed my understanding of the history of the Standard Gauge Railway to a very large degree and served an essential purpose of triangulating with interview and media data, even though I made only very limited direct citations to these documents in the book.

APPENDIX 2

Doing fieldwork in Africa

My interest in studying Sino-Africa infrastructure development can be traced back to my residence in Kenya during 2013 to 2014. In May 2014, Chinese premier Li Keqiang visited Kenya and signed the financial agreement for the Mombasa–Nairobi Standard Gauge Railway with Kenyan president Uhuru Kenyatta. For months, the railway occupied the headlines of local and international media. When identifying my research question and formulating the research design for this book, it became clear to me that I wanted to explore this railway project and more broadly Chinese infrastructure engagement with Africa. Even with prior working and living experience in Kenya, doing fieldwork in Africa can be challenging. In this Appendix, I reflect on how my identity shapes my fieldwork access, data collected, and potential bias in analysis, in the hope that this transparency of process will permit readers to make a more informed analysis through which a case and the conclusions were reached, as well as avoiding pitfalls when conducting their fieldwork on similar topics.

When conducting fieldwork, I have both visible identities as a Chinese, female doctoral researcher in a UK-based institution and invisible identities that my research was funded by the Chinese government and that I used to work in Kenya.[1] My Chinese nationality and my funding from the China Scholarship Council (CSC) of the Ministry of Education granted me a higher level of trust from Chinese companies and embassies in Africa. When accessing these Chinese informants, I presented the scholarship award letter from the CSC to them prior to the interview. Accessing Chinese state-owned enterprises (SOEs) is increasingly difficult for non-Chinese scholars interested in Sino-African relations. In Kenya, Ethiopia, and Angola, I was able to quickly gain access to the railway contractors. In the Angolan case, the headquarters of the Chinese contractor, CR20, is located right next to my parents' home in Xi'an, and most of the employees in CR20 were from the same province as I am. This provincial fellowship proved to be especially helpful for the Chinese managers to accept me as an 'insider', inviting me to their compound in Luanda and Benguela and to enjoy the meals from their corporate cafeteria made by a cook from our province. Chinese managers in Africa welcomed me as a Chinese student who was interested in their work and was curious about their stories. Some Chinese informants expressed their appreciation of my listening to and being curious about their stories. Because of safety concerns, particularly in Angola and Ethiopia, they were not allowed to freely explore outside of the corporate compound, and their opportunities to meet people outside of their working circle were very limited. Most of them were thus willing to openly share their experience with me.

Trust could turn to suspicion, however, as I spent more time in the host country and gathered more information, especially sensitive information related to corruption and government dysfunction in each case. My first fieldwork trip to Ethiopia was in July 2017, and for two weeks I lived in the same compound as the Chinese managers of the SOE in Addis Ababa that constructed the railway, participated in their internal meetings, and had daily meals with them. During working hours, I asked for interviews with different managers of the company. The SOE's Addis office had around twenty-five Chinese managers at that time, and I had in-depth interviews with ten of them and many more casual conversations.

[1] The visible and invisible identity distinction: see Reyes (2018).

I started by interviewing working-level managers and planned to leave the chief executive officer (CEO) to the end. Midway through my three-week stay with them, I interviewed six or seven mid-level managers. I sensed that their trust in me as an innocent Chinese student who simply wanted to complete her thesis reduced and their suspicion of me as a data collector from a Western institution increased. Two of the Chinese managers that I had already interviewed approached me separately, at night, asking about my intention in conducting research with all these detailed questions, and the word 'spy' came up several times. I was inexperienced in handling this insecurity-generated suspicion from interviewees and had a three-day mental breakdown, with racing thoughts of powerless me standing against this gigantic SOE and my parents' safety in China. With my then supervisor's advice of 'playing the innocent card', I continued my daily routine with them, and readjusted my interview strategy to meet with the CEO first—the meeting with the head proved to be effective in dissolving suspicion-inflicted gossip among mid-level managers.

Although my Chinese identity helped me gain access to Chinese companies in Africa, this 'insider' position did not translate into better informant access in Beijing. Researchers have identified that insider status is not always superior, especially with elites.[2] I found it was more difficult for me to work my way up the bureaucratic hierarchy in Beijing than in Africa. Even though I had worked in the United Nations Development Programme (UNDP) Beijing office from 2015 to 2016, my past professional connections did not easily convert into interview access. A Chinese manager from an SOE, whom I had met through my previous connections from UNDP, told me blatantly that the leaders in her company were extremely busy and could not be bothered to accept my interview. It was especially difficult for me to obtain access to the Export and Import Bank (EximBank) in Beijing, but EximBank employees in Africa were much more open to interviews.

Some Chinese informants considered my research as a channel for propaganda, precisely because of my nationality and government funding. Several Chinese managers from different SOEs told me that they hoped I would help promote their companies by writing good stories. They believed that articles written by a researcher from a Western institute could be perceived as more 'objective' than their corporate reports, and thus could be more acceptable to an international audience.

While interviewing African bureaucrats, I could sense some mistrust and reservations about sharing opinions. My initial local contacts in Ethiopia and Angola were introduced by the Chinese companies. Some Chinese managers brought me along with them for a working meeting with their African counterpart and then introduced me to the African bureaucrats as their 'friend' who had a few questions. Although I insisted on the Chinese managers' absence while interviewing African informants, I suspected that the African informants might consider my interview as an extension of their meeting with the Chinese managers—they treated me with respect and caution, and their perspectives on China and Chinese contractors in the interviews were very positive. This chain of referral granted me quick access to the core African officials involved in the case projects. But the disadvantage was that this introduction from Chinese state companies and my Chinese identity may have given the impression to African bureaucrats that, rather than talking with an independent researcher, they were sharing information with a 'Chinese' researcher who was somehow connected to the state-owned corporation or even the state itself. This impression makes it especially difficult to establish trust with African interviewees, and several of them asked if I was a journalist, or even a spy. But my institutional affiliation with a Western university complicated this 'spy' identity even more.

[2] Herod (1999).

My identity as a researcher from a Western university opened my access to many African informants. Many African elites were impressed with the 'Oxford' brand, and an Oxford alumni network is also relatively established and helpful in countries like Kenya. In Kenya, I was able to meet with a billionaire with political clout, KE-57 in the interviewee list in Appendix 4. I was connected to him through an Oxford alumnus in Nairobi (KE-59) and had a marathon interview of 5 hours. Living a secretive life and known to shy away from the limelight, KE-57's acceptance of my interview was very surprising. The meeting was scheduled in a quiet Italian restaurant, and he knew the owner well. During our conversation when he went to the restroom, his two bodyguards separated; one escorted him to the restroom, the other stood by our table, looking at me, and they both disappeared when he came back. Our table was behind a wall that divided the room in half; all the other guests were advised to sit outside, while only two of us sat inside. He was in the shadow of the wall so that no-one from the outside could see him, while I sat next to him, in the shadow but exposed to the outside.

He decided to take me through everything, quite openly, over the 3-hour conversation. He was genuine in sharing this Kenyan's railway story, to cut clear his relationship with the project, which was a politically sensitive topic then. During the interview, he also openly criticized Uhuru Kenyatta, who had been a schoolmate and friend of his; later, as their friendship soured. The very fact that I was an Oxford researcher interested in the Standard Gauge Railway probably inspired him to accept the interview—a meeting with me provided him a potential opportunity to convey his viewpoint to Western and maybe Chinese audiences. Here, Oxford proved a good brand to have in the field. As a 'political hot potato' (in his own words), he was probably under surveillance and my meeting with him could be reported to some high-level officials, which could impose risk on my safety in Kenya. We did not have follow-up meetings; the later communications were all completed through WhatsApp.

Being a female also proved to have a gendered advantage in accessing informants in male-dominant societies, but my female identity was not necessarily helpful in rapport-building and personal safety. A great majority of my interviewees in all four countries were male. In Ethiopia and Angola, learning that I was conducting research by myself, several Chinese managers invited me to stay with their company, emphasizing that it was not safe to live and travel by myself. Indeed, safety was a major concern for Chinese companies in Africa, and most of the companies have a compound for all Chinese employees to live and work in. Chinese employees were not usually allowed to leave the compound unless for work or some group activities. I accepted some invitations, which became valuable opportunities for participatory observation. These short episodes of ethnographic research gave me the chance to live the same lifestyle as those Chinese contractors on the railway projects and think from their perspective. However, twice in Angola I was sexually harassed by managers in the same compound, so I had to move out at short notice. Although I was not physically hurt, the psychological damage took a long time to recover from. When interviewing male African elites, I found some informants appreciated a young female researcher being curious about and listening to their participation in the legacy projects and setting up a follow-up meeting was fairly easy. However, I felt that sometimes they were more interested in me than my interview questions. Some even suggested more meetings under more informal circumstances such as for a drink.

Research in authoritarian states with restricted freedom of speech and powerful state surveillance system can be challenging. During my fieldwork in July 2017 in Addis Ababa, I lived in the same compound with a Chinese SOE. The Ethiopian cleaning lady that came daily to clean my room was able to speak fluent English and French, knew the name of the sons of the then chief economic advisor to the Ethiopian prime minister and which cities in China the sons were working in, and was genuinely curious about my research. To protect my own and my interviewees' safety, I encrypted transcripts with the name of informants separated from their interview content, stored this information on my laptop via Evernote online, and tried my best not to let my laptop out of my sight. I was lucky not to have anything happen to me or my interviewees after this fieldwork, but navigating my research in a small authoritarian setting (the Chinese SOE) within a larger authoritarian environment (Ethiopia) was quite a mental challenge.

Fieldwork and interviews are crucial data collection methods in qualitative research. Yet researchers have also identified the stylistic aspects of fieldwork: respondents are influenced by their perceptions of the researcher: the same person interviewed about the same topic by two researchers may end up with very different stories.[3] Transparency of data collection process and careful triangulation of interview data are therefore of crucial importance to balance between unique and stylistic qualities of fieldwork and research objectivity. To improve transparency, I present a detailed recall of and reflection on my data collection process in this Appendix, in the hope of helping readers understand how I draw my conclusions, as well as informing other similar researchers of pitfalls and some solutions during fieldwork.

[3] Kapiszewski, MacLean, and Read (2015).

APPENDIX 3

List of interview questions

1 Groups of potential interviewees

1. Chinese railway contractors (in the questions in section 2, Chinese state-owned enterprise (SOE) means the railway contractor)
2. Chinese government (Chinese embassies and economic councillor's offices, Ministry of Foreign Affairs, Ministry of Commerce, China EximBank)
3. Host-country railway corporations
4. Host-country government (Ministry of Transportation, railway corporation, Ministry of Finance, Ministry of Trade)
5. Academic institutes, media (Chinese, local, international), civil society organizations, local residents using the railway, trade unions (truck and logistics construction-related industries), host-country businesses (particularly subcontractors and service providers of the railway projects)

2 Interview themes

During interviews, I did not hold this long list of questions and go through them one by one. This list of questions was for interview preparation only. I familiarized myself with all the questions and themes before entering an interview, and jotted down the major themes, in a couple of words at the top of my notebook, that I would like to explore with the informant. I usually started each interview by inquiring about the specific job description of the informant, and then led the questions onto railways as the conversation got underway. For interviews with senior officials under strict time pressure, I brought into the interview rooms a dozen carefully selected questions from this list, and the interviews were led by the questions.

Railway characteristics

- What was the completion time and operation starting time?
- How often does the railway operate for freight and passenger services? What's the ticket price? Could the operational revenue cover the operation and maintenance costs?
- Initiation of the railway: who initiated the project? How was it initiated? And under what context?
- What was the tendering process to select the contractors? How did the Chinese SOE obtain the construction contract? Was the SOE involved in the project initiation? What was the Chinese SOE's role in facilitating the financing from EximBank?
- What is the financial arrangement of the railway, in terms of percentage of commercial and concessional loans and African government's pair-funding, and when was the loan secured, before or after construction started?

- What is the railway loan repayment arrangement? Is the operation successfulness linked to the success of the loan payment? Or does the loan have nothing to do with the operation but is paid back by other commodities?
- Are there industrial parks or other development projects alongside the railway?

Railway politicization

- Was the railway a hot topic in the elections?
- How does the host government perceive the railway and Sino-Angolan cooperation in general? (Key question. Explore further based on the interlocutor response)
- How does the Chinese government in the host country perceive the railway and Sino-Angolan cooperation in general? (Key question. Explore further based on the interlocutor response)
- What is the domestic discourse on the railway to the general public? (From secondary source)
- How do people from different regions (capital city, cities along the railway line, cities without railways passing, passengers of the railways) perceive the railway?

Government commitment

- How many times have host-country ministers, president or prime minister, and other cabinet members visited the Chinese SOE and the railway construction site during the construction phase?
- Compared with other projects in the host countries, did the president or prime minister frequent the railway more often, or less, or no visible difference?
- What are the other projects that might be at the top of the president/prime minister's agenda in the past decade during the railway construction years?
- What are the major obstacles during railway construction? How are they solved? (Ask for specific cases)
- Do the Chinese SOEs feel the host-country government (which ministry? who specifically?) facilitated the solution of the construction-related obstacles? (Key question. Explore further based on the interlocutor response)
- Are the Chinese SOEs and Chinese government satisfied with the railway operation status? (If there was a time gap between completion and operation, how long was it? were the Chinese SOEs and/or Chinese government concerned about it? if so, what did they do to facilitate the operation? is the host-country government cooperative in precipitating commencing the operation?)

Spill-over effect to local industries

- Ask Chinese SOEs and host-country government: local subcontracting percentage? Which are the local companies hired? Subcontracting firms selecting criteria?
- Ask local companies: are local subcontractors and companies who work with the Chinese SOEs on the railway project satisfied with their experience working with the Chinese? Especially in terms of profit, Chinese business culture, and so on?

- Ask local companies: how were you selected to work on this project?
- (Maybe not ask this question, but try to figure out): are the local companies involved in the railway construction and operation with African government connections? Was this government connection explicitly used by the host-country side or the Chinese SOE to help them get the contract? anything the companies paid in return? (what do the owners of these companies think of host-country government and current politics?)

About the Chinese companies

- When did the SOE arrive in the host country? Explore the SOE's development history in the host country and in Africa. What are the other projects undertaken by the SOE in this country? What is the role of the railway project in the development history of this SOE in the host country (is this a market entry project)?
- How (tendering through host-country government or Chinese government? or no tendering at all?) and when did the SOE receive the railway construction contract?
- Chinese SOE's public relations and corporate social responsibility office: function, staffing, practices of social engagement and environmental protection activities during the railway construction, specific corporate social responsibility (CSR) budget? Published CSR report?
- Perceptions from host communities on the Chinese SOE and the railway: positive or negative? Did they benefit from the railway or CSR project of the Chinese SOE? Did they participate (such as labour worker) in the railway construction/operation? (Key question. Explore further based on the interlocutor response)
- How is the learning curve of the Chinese SOE in local government relations, international and local media, and local community relations perceived during the construction period?
- Who are the major local government offices the Chinese SOEs work with on the railway project?
- What is the role of the Chinese embassy and economic councillor's office in the railway project?
- How many times did the Chinese SOE's headquarters leadership visit the railway project? Did the Chinese government visit the railway project? If so, who are they?
- Chinese SOE and government perception towards the railway: do you perceive this as a political project or an economic project? Why? Has this perception changed over time?

Impact of the railway

- Has the railway improved the lives of residents in the capital city and other cities that the railway passes through?
- What are the main types of goods for cargo services? Is there an economic promoting effect? How did the railway change the logistics service of the country?
- Is there any symbolic meaning of the railway mentioned during the interview?
- Future railway construction plans?

Land acquisition and compensation

- Is land acquisition an easy process? If not, what were the problems?
- Which county or village generates the most contention in terms of land acquisition? (A question for me to plan the next visit)
- When contentions arise, how are they resolved? Illustrate with specific examples. What was the highest level of politicians in the host country and China ever involved?

Environmental impact assessment (EIA)

- Was the EIA completed before construction? Can you share it with me?
- Are there any environmental or wildlife preservation concerns during railway construction and operation? How were these concerns addressed?
- Any protection measures for railway trespassing preservation areas?

APPENDIX 4

List of interviewees

Table A.4 List of interviewees in China (total interviews: fourteen)

Name	Affiliation	Interview method	Date	Length	(Researcher's) Location	Note
Category 1. Chinese contractor Saturation: Low						
CH-1	CCECC-headquarters	Semi-structured face-to-face	15-Oct-18	60 min	Beijing	
CH-2	CCECC-headquarters	Semi-structured face-to-face	18-Oct-18	2 hrs	Beijing	Introduced by CH-1
CH-3	CRBC-Nairobi	Semi-structured, phone	20-Oct-18	90 min	Beijing	Introduced by CH-14
CH-4	CRBC-Nairobi	Non-structured casual talk	25-Oct-18	60 min	Beijing	Lunch meeting
CH-5	CRBC-headquarters	Semi-structured face-to-face	26-Dec-18	45 min	Beijing	Introduced by CH-11
CH-15	CR20-headquarters	Semi-structured face-to-face	28-Oct-18	60 min	Xi'an	
Category 2. Chinese government Saturation: Low						
CH-6	Ministry of Foreign Affairs	Semi-structured face-to-face	19-Oct-18	2 hrs	Beijing	Introduced by CH-14
CH-7	Ministry of Foreign Affairs	Semi-structured face-to-face	23-Oct-18	40 min	Beijing	
CH-8	China EximBank-Kenya	Semi-structured, phone	31-Oct-18	60 min	Beijing	
CH-9	Ministry of Commerce Department of Foreign Aid	Semi-structured face-to-face	21-Dec-18	60 min	Beijing	
CH-10	China EximBank-headquarters	Semi-structured face-to-face	26-Dec-18	30 min	Beijing	
Category 3. Other Chinese companies Saturation: Low						
CH-11	China Minmetals	Semi-structured face-to-face	11-Oct-18	60 min	Beijing	
Category 4. Academia Saturation: Medium						
CH-12	Michigan State University	Semi-structured, phone	19-Oct-18	45 min	Beijing	
CH-13	Peking University	Semi-structured face-to-face	19-Oct-18	30 min	Beijing	
CH-14	Peking University	Semi-structured face-to-face	19-Oct-18	45 min	Beijing	

Name	Affiliation	Interview method	Date	Length	(Researcher's) Location	Note
Category 1. Chinese contractor Saturation: High						
KE-1	CRBC-Nairobi	Semi-structured face-to-face	14-Jun-17	60 min	Oxford	
KE-2	CRBC-Nairobi	Semi-structured face-to-face	16-Jun-17	60 min	Oxford	
KE-3	CRBC-Nairobi	Semi-structured face-to-face	09-Jul-17	60 min	Nairobi	Introduced by 1
KE-4	CRBC-Nairobi	Semi-structured face-to-face	14-Jul-19	60 min	Nairobi	
KE-5	CRBC-Nairobi	Semi-structured face-to-face	11-Jul-17	60 min	Nairobi	
KE-6	CRBC-Nairobi	Semi-structured face-to-face	29-Jul-19	60 min	Nairobi	
KE-7	CRBC-Nairobi	Semi-structured face-to-face	14-Jul-17	60 min	Nairobi	Introduced by KE-1, Interview with KE-5's present
KE-8	CRBC-Nairobi	Semi-structured face-to-face	09-Jul-19	3 hrs	Nairobi	Introduced by CH-5
KE-9	CRBC-Nairobi	Semi-structured face-to-face	18-Jul-19	60 min	Nairobi	Introduced by KE-8
KE-10	CRBC-Nairobi	Semi-structured face-to-face	18-Jul-19	30 min	Nairobi	Introduced by KE-9
KE-11	CRBC-Nairobi	Semi-structured face-to-face	07-Aug-19	20 min	Nairobi	
KE-12	CRBC-Nairobi	Semi-structured face-to-face	07-Aug-19	60 min	Nairobi	
KE-13	CRBC-Nairobi	Semi-structured face-to-face	11-Aug-19	60 min	Nairobi	
KE-14	CRBC-Mombasa	Non-structured casual talk	12-Jul-19		Mombasa	
Category 2. Chinese government Saturation: High						
KE-15	Chinese economic councillor's office-Kenya	Semi-structured face-to-face	11-Jul-17	60 min	Nairobi	
KE-16	Chinese economic councillor's office-Kenya	Semi-structured, WeChat message	15-Jul-19		Nairobi	
KE-17	China EximBank-Kenya	Semi-structured face-to-face	23-Jul-19	60 min	Nairobi	
KE-18	Chinese economic councillor's office-Kenya	Semi-structured, phone	17-Aug-19	60 min	Nairobi	
KE-19	Chinese economic councillor's office-Kenya	Semi-structured face-to-face	20-Aug-19	50 min	Nairobi	

Continued

Table A.5 *Continued*

Name	Affiliation	Interview method	Date	Length	(Researcher's) Location	Note
Category 3. Other Chinese companies Saturation: Medium						
KE-20	AVIC-Nairobi	Semi-structured, phone	08-Jun-17	60 min	Oxford	
KE-21	Ruiji Corporation	Semi-structured face-to-face	29-Jul-19	45 min	Nairobi	
Category 4. Host-country railway corporation Saturation: High						
KE-22	Kenyan Railway Corporation (KRC)	Semi-structured face-to-face	12-Jul-17	40 min	Nairobi	Introduced by KE-3
KE-23	KRC	Semi-structured face-to-face	18-Jul-17	30 min	Nairobi	Introduced by KE-35
KE-24	KRC	Semi-structured face-to-face	07-Aug-19	60 min	Nairobi	
KE-25	KRC	Semi-structured face-to-face	13-Aug-19	90 min	Nairobi	
KE-26	KRC	Semi-structured, phone	12-Sep-19	30 min	Oxford	
KE-27	KRC	Semi-structured face-to-face	18-Jul-19	90 min	Nairobi	Introduced by KE-3
KE-28	KRC	Semi-structured face-to-face	12-Aug-19	45 min	Nairobi	
KE-29	KRC	Semi-structured face-to-face	31-Jul-19	60 min	Nairobi	
KE-30	KRC	Semi-structured face-to-face	31-Jul-19	45 min	Nairobi	Introduced by KE-29
KE-31	APEC Supervisor of the SGR	Semi-structured face-to-face	08-Aug-19	90 min	Nairobi	
KE-32	KRC	Semi-structured face-to-face	19-Aug-19	45 min	Nairobi	
KE-33	Nairobi Inland Container Terminal	Semi-structured face-to-face	19-Aug-19	60 min	Nairobi	
KE-34	KRC	Semi-structured face-to-face	19-Aug-19	60 min	Nairobi	

Category 5. Host-country government
Saturation: High

KE-35	Ministry of Transport	Semi-structured face-to-face	18-Jul-17	30 min	Nairobi	
KE-36	Kenyan Treasury	Semi-structured face-to-face	18-Jul-17	60 min	Nairobi	Phone number provided by KE-20
KE-37	Kenyan Wildlife Service	Semi-structured face-to-face	24-Jul-19	2 hrs	Nairobi	
KE-38	MP	Semi-structured face-to-face	30-Jul-19	45 min	Nairobi	
KE-39	National Land Commission	Semi-structured face-to-face	24-Jul-19	60 min	Nairobi	
KE-40	Senator	Semi-structured face-to-face	30-Jul-19	45 min	Nairobi	
KE-41	National Land Commission	Semi-structured face-to-face	05-Aug-19	45 min	Nairobi	
KE-42	National Land Commission	Semi-structured face-to-face	05-Aug-19	30 min	Nairobi	Introduced by KE-41
KE-43	Kenyan Port Authority	Semi-structured face-to-face	10-Aug-19	60 min	Nairobi	
KE-44	Ministry of Transport	Semi-structured face-to-face	15-Aug-19	60 min	Nairobi	
KE-45	Kenya Highway Authority	Semi-structured face-to-face	16-Aug-19	60 min	Nairobi	
KE-46	Governor's office of Makueni	Semi-structured face-to-face	22-Aug-19	60 min	Nairobi	
KE-47	Governor's office of Makueni	Semi-structured face-to-face	22-Aug-19	60 min	Nairobi	

Continued

Table A.5 *Continued*

Name	Affiliation	Interview method	Date	Length	(Researcher's) Location	Note
Category 6. Academia, business, and civil society and international organizations Saturation: High						
KE-48	Phoenix TV Nairobi Office	Semi-structured, phone	05-Jun-17	60 min	Oxford	
KE-49	Cambridge University	Semi-structured face-to-face	05-Oct-19	60 min	Oxford	
KE-50	IFC	Semi-structured face-to-face	14-Jul-17	60 min	Nairobi	
KE-51	Institute of Economic Affairs	Semi-structured face-to-face	18-Jul-17	40 min	Nairobi	
KE-52	Centurion System Ltd	Semi-structured face-to-face	18-Jul-17	60 min	Nairobi	
KE-53	Chinese University of Hong Kong	Semi-structured, phone	24-Oct-17	45 min	Oxford	
KE-54	Save the Children	Semi-structured face-to-face	08-Jul-19	60 min	Nairobi	
KE-55	Journalist	Semi-structured face-to-face	19-Jul-19	60 min	Nairobi	
KE-56	East Africa Online Logistics	Semi-structured face-to-face	25-Jul-19	2 hrs	Nairobi	Introduced by KE-55
KE-57	Private businessman	Semi-structured face-to-face	26-Jul-19	3 hrs	Nairobi	Introduced by KE-59
KE-58	HSF Foundation	Semi-structured face-to-face	25-Jul-19	60 min	Nairobi	
KE-59	Economist	Semi-structured face-to-face	22-Jul-19	5 hrs	Nairobi	
KE-60	Environmental advisor to the Standard Gauge Railway (SGR)	Semi-structured face-to-face	02-Aug-19	60 min	Nairobi	
KE-61	HSF Foundation	Semi-structured face-to-face	01-Aug-19	45 min	Nairobi	Introduced by KE-58
KE-62	Kenya International Freight and Warehousing Association (KIFWA)	Semi-structured face-to-face	02-Aug-19	2 hrs	Nairobi	
KE-63	Shipper's council	Semi-structured face-to-face	05-Aug-19	60 min	Nairobi	

KE-64	Kenyan Association of Manufacturer	Semi-structured face-to-face	07-Aug-19	45 min	Nairobi	
KE-65	Journalist	Semi-structured face-to-face	08-Aug-19	60 min	Nairobi	
KE-66	IFC	Semi-structured face-to-face	09-Aug-19	60 min	Nairobi	
KE-67	Environmental advisor to the SGR	Semi-structured face-to-face	10-Aug-19	60 min	Nairobi	
KE-68	Journalist and lawyer	Semi-structured face-to-face	13-Aug-19	30 min	Nairobi	
KE-69	University of Nairobi	Semi-structured face-to-face	14-Aug-19	60 min	Nairobi	
KE-70	Environmentalist	Semi-structured face-to-face	15-Aug-19	45 min	Nairobi	
KE-71	*Daily Nation*	Semi-structured face-to-face	23-Aug-19	45 min	Nairobi	
KE-72	JICA-Nairobi	Semi-structured face-to-face	23-Aug-19	30 min	Nairobi	
KE-73	Haki Africa	Semi-structured face-to-face	12-Jul-19	60 min	Mombasa	
KE-74	Muslim for Human Rights	Semi-structured face-to-face	13-Jul-19	60 min	Mombasa	
KE-75	Human Rights Agenda	Semi-structured face-to-face	13-Jul-19	60 min	Mombasa	
KE-76	Truck driver association	Semi-structured face-to-face, group interview of five participants	13-Jul-19	90 min	Mombasa	Introduced by KE-75
KE-77	Independent journalist	Semi-structured face-to-face	Aug-2016	60 min	Nairobi	

Table A.6 List of interviewees in Ethiopia (total interviews: ninety-two)

Name	Affiliation	Interview method	Date	Length	(Researcher's) Location	Note
Category 1. Chinese contractor						
Saturation: High						
ET-1	CREC-Addis	Semi-structured, phone	06-Jun-17	30 min	Oxford	
ET-2	CREC-Addis	Non-structured casual talk	17-Jun-17	30 min	Addis	
ET-3	CREC-Addis	Semi-structured face-to-face	19-Jun-17	90 min	Addis	
ET-4	CREC-Addis	Non-structured casual talk	19-Jun-17	2 hrs	Addis	
ET-5	CREC-Addis	Semi-structured face-to-face	20-Jun-17	60 min	Addis	
ET-6	Norinco-Addis	Semi-structured face-to-face	20-Jun-17	30 min	Addis	
ET-7	CREC-Addis	Semi-structured face-to-face	21-Jun-17	60 min	Addis	
ET-8	CREC-Addis	Semi-structured face-to-face	21-Jun-17	20 min	Addis	
ET-9	CREC-Addis	Semi-structured face-to-face	21-Jun-17	60 min	Addis	
ET-10	CREC-Addis	Semi-structured face-to-face	21-Jun-17	2 hrs	Addis	
ET-11	CREC-Addis	Semi-structured face-to-face	26-Jun-17	60 min	Addis	
ET-12	CREC-Addis	Semi-structured face-to-face	26-Jun-17	60 min	Addis	Introduced by ET-10
ET-13	CREC-Addis	Semi-structured face-to-face	01-Jul-17	90 min	Addis	
ET-14	CCECC-Addis	Semi-structured face-to-face	03-Apr-19	2 hrs	Addis	
ET-15	CCECC-Addis	Semi-structured face-to-face	04-Apr-19	60 min	Addis	
ET-16	CCECC-Addis	Semi-structured face-to-face	04-Apr-19	45 min	Addis	
ET-17	CCECC-Addis	Semi-structured face-to-face	11-Apr-19	60 min	Addis	
ET-18	CCECC-Labu	Semi-structured face-to-face	24-Apr-19	60 min	Addis	
ET-19	CCECC-Labu	Semi-structured face-to-face	24-Apr-19	45 min	Addis	
ET-20	CCECC-Labu	Semi-structured face-to-face	24-Apr-19	60 min	Addis	
ET-21	CREC-II	Semi-structured face-to-face	29-Apr-19	90 min	Addis	
ET-22	CCECC-Djibouti	Semi-structured face-to-face	02-May-19	60 min	Djibouti	
ET-23	CCECC-Djibouti	Semi-structured face-to-face	02-May-19	30 min	Djibouti	

ET-24	CCECC-Djibouti	Semi-structured face-to-face	05-May-19	60 min	Djibouti	
ET-25	CCECC-Dire Dawa	Semi-structured face-to-face	09-May-19	60 min	Dire Dawa	
ET-26	CCECC-Dire Dawa	Semi-structured face-to-face	09-May-19	60 min	Dire Dawa	
ET-27	China Railways 16th Bureau	Semi-structured face-to-face	09-May-19	45 min	Dire Dawa	
ET-28	China Railways 11th Bureau	Semi-structured face-to-face	09-May-19	60 min	Dire Dawa	
ET-29	CCECC-Dire Dawa	Semi-structured face-to-face	09-May-19	60 min	Dire Dawa	
ET-30	CCECC Northern Company	Semi-structured face-to-face	10-May-19	45 min	Dire Dawa	
ET-31	CCECC-Addis	Semi-structured face-to-face	17-May-19	45 min	Addis	
ET-32	CREC-II	Semi-structured face-to-face	17-May-19	60 min	Addis	
Category 2. Chinese government Saturation: High						
ET-33	China EximBank-Ethiopia	Semi-structured face-to-face	27-Jun-17	60 min	Addis	Introduced by KE-1
ET-34	Chinese embassy in Ethiopia	Semi-structured, phone	29-Jun-17	60 min	Addis	
ET-35	China EximBank-Ethiopia	Semi-structured face-to-face	07-Apr-19	60 min	Addis	
ET-36	Chinese economic councillor's office-Djibouti (former)	Semi-structured face-to-face	04-May-19	30 min	Djibouti	

Continued

Table A.6 *Continued*

Name	Affiliation	Interview method	Date	Length	(Researcher's) Location	Note
Category 3. Other Chinese companies Saturation: Medium						
ET-37	Huajian Industrial Park	Semi-structured face-to-face	07-Jul-17	30 min	Addis	
ET-38	Djibouti Port Corporation	Semi-structured face-to-face	04-May-19	60 min	Djibouti	
Category 4. Host-country railway corporation Saturation: High						
ET-39	Ethiopian Railway Corporation (ERC)	Semi-structured face-to-face	23-Jun-17	30 min	Addis	Introduced by ET-9
ET-40	ERC	Semi-structured face-to-face	16-May-19	30 min	Addis	
ET-41	ERC	Semi-structured face-to-face	23-Jun-17	30 min	Addis	Introduced by ET-9
ET-42	ERC	Semi-structured face-to-face	24-Jun-17	60 min	Addis	Introduced by ET-41
ET-43	ERC	Semi-structured face-to-face	05-Jul-17	30 min	Addis	
ET-44	ERC	Semi-structured face-to-face	22-Apr-19	60 min	Addis	
ET-45	ERC	Semi-structured face-to-face	25-Apr-19	60 min	Addis	
ET-46	ERC	Semi-structured face-to-face	26-Apr-19	45 min	Addis	
ET-47	Ethiopian-Djibouti Railway Corporation (EDR)	Semi-structured face-to-face	27-Apr-19	90 min	Addis	
ET-48	Chemin de Fer Djibouti-Ethiopien	Semi-structured face-to-face	01-May-19	60 min	Addis	
ET-49	EDR-Djibouti	Semi-structured face-to-face, with interpreter	05-May-19	45 min	Djibouti	Introduced by ET-22
ET-50	EDR-Dire Dawa	Semi-structured face-to-face	11-May-19	30 min	Dire Dawa	
ET-51	Chemin de Fer Djibouti-Ethiopien-Dire Dawa	Semi-structured face-to-face	11-May-19	60 min	Dire Dawa	Introduced by ET-48
ET-52	ERC	Semi-structured face-to-face	16-May-19	60 min	Addis	

Saturation: High

ET-53	Ministry of Finance and Economic Cooperation (MOFEC)	Semi-structured face-to-face	28-Jun-17	30 min	Addis	
ET-54	MOFEC	Semi-structured face-to-face	29-Jun-17	60 min	Addis	Introduced by ET-53
ET-55	MOFEC	Semi-structured face-to-face	30-Apr-19	60 min	Addis	
ET-56	MOFEC	Semi-structured face-to-face	29-Jun-17	30 min	Addis	
ET-57	Ethiopian Airlines	Semi-structured face-to-face	29-Jun-17	30 min	Addis	
ET-58	Ministry of Environment	Semi-structured face-to-face	03-Jul-17	30 min	Addis	
ET-59	Ministry of Environment	Semi-structured face-to-face	03-Jul-17	20 min	Addis	
ET-60	Ministry of Foreign Affairs	Semi-structured face-to-face	05-Jul-17	60 min	Addis	
ET-61	Ministry of Transport (MOT)	Semi-structured face-to-face	05-Jul-17	70 min	Addis	
ET-62	MOT	Semi-structured face-to-face	22-Apr-19	40 min	Addis	
ET-63	Ethiopian Investment Commission	Semi-structured face-to-face	05-Jul-17	60 min	Addis	
ET-64	Ethiopian Development Research Institute (EDRI)	Semi-structured, phone	09-Apr-19	45 min	Addis	
ET-65	EDRI	Semi-structured face-to-face	10-Apr-19	90 min	Addis	
ET-66	EDRI	Semi-structured, phone	18-May-19	30 min	Addis	
ET-67	EDRI	Semi-structured face-to-face	12-Apr-19	80 min	Addis	
ET-68	EDRI	Semi-structured face-to-face	12-Apr-19	30 min	Addis	
ET-69	EDRI	Semi-structured face-to-face	16-Apr-19	30 min	Addis	
ET-70	EDRI, Ministry of Industry	Semi-structured face-to-face	16-Apr-19	45 min	Addis	
ET-71	Ministry of Environment	Semi-structured face-to-face	18-Apr-19	30 min	Addis	
ET-72	MOFEC	Semi-structured face-to-face	18-Apr-19	45 min	Addis	
ET-73	MOFEC	Semi-structured face-to-face	23-Apr-19	60 min	Addis	
ET-74	EDRI	Semi-structured face-to-face	24-Apr-19	30 min	Addis	
ET-75	MOT	Semi-structured face-to-face	30-Apr-19	90 min	Addis	
ET-76	Dire Dawa Mayor's Office	Semi-structured face-to-face	14-May-19	30 min	Dire Dawa	Introduced by ET-50
ET-77	Ethiopian Road Authority	Semi-structured face-to-face	15-May-19	60 min	Addis	

Continued

Table A.6 *Continued*

Name	Affiliation	Interview method	Date	Length	(Researcher's) Location	Note
Category 6. Academia, business, and civil society and international organizations Saturation: High						
ET-78	Ethiopian private logistics company	Semi-structured face-to-face	23-Jun-17	60 min	Addis	Introduced by ET-9
ET-79	Ethiopian private logistics company	Semi-structured face-to-face	12-Apr-19	60 min	Addis	
ET-80	Private individual	Non-structured casual talk	24-Jun-17	60 min	Addis	
ET-81	Independent journalist	Semi-structured, phone	30-Jun-17	60 min	Addis	
ET-82	Addis Ababa University	Semi-structured face-to-face	03-Jul-17	30 min	Addis	
ET-83	United Nations Development Programme	Semi-structured face-to-face	03-Jul-17	30 min	Addis	
ET-84	Investment banker	Semi-structured face-to-face	06-Jul-17	70 min	Addis	
ET-85	Ethiopia Strategic Foreign Relations Research	Semi-structured face-to-face	06-Jul-17	90 min	Addis	
ET-86	Investment Fund in Addis	Semi-structured face-to-face	10-Apr-19	60 min	Addis	
ET-87	Global Thorton, consulting firm	Semi-structured face-to-face	16-Apr-19	60 min	Addis	
ET-88	Dalberg	Semi-structured face-to-face	17-Apr-19	60 min	Addis	
ET-89	Secretary to Arkebe, former economic advisor to the prime minister	Semi-structured face-to-face	17-Apr-19	90 min	Addis	
ET-90	Embassy of Angola in Ethiopia	Semi-structured face-to-face	18-Apr-19	50 min	Addis	
ET-91	Institute of Political and Strategic Studies	Semi-structured face-to-face	5-May-19	60 min	Djibouti	
ET-92	National Cement	Semi-structured face-to-face	14-May-19	45 min	Dire Dawa	Introduced by ET-16

Table A.7 List of interviewees in Angola (total interviews: sixty-four)

Name	Affiliation	Interview method	Date	Length	(Researcher's) Location	Note
Category 1. Chinese contractor Saturation: Medium						
AG-1	CR20-Luanda	Semi-structured face-to-face	11-Nov-18	60 min	Luanda	
AG-2	CR20-Huambo	Semi-structured face-to-face	01-Dec-18	60 min	Huambo	
AG-3	CR20-Huambo	Semi-structured face-to-face	01-Dec-18	60 min	Huambo	
AG-4	CR20-Benguela	Semi-structured face-to-face	24-Feb-19	45 min	Benguela	
AG-5	CR20-Benguela	Semi-structured face-to-face	26-Feb-19	60 min	Benguela	
AG-6	CR20-Luanda	Non-structured casual talk	24-Mar-19		Luanda	
Category 2. Chinese government Saturation: Low						
AG-7	Chinese embassy in Angola	Semi-structured face-to-face	24-Mar-19	45 min	Luanda	
Category 3. Other Chinese companies Saturation: Medium						
AG-8	Jiangzhou Farm	Non-structured casual talk	29-Nov-18		Huambo	
AG-9	CTCE-Luanda	Non-structured casual talk	08-Dec-18		Luanda	
AG-10	AVIC-Angola	Non-structured casual talk	15-Dec-18		Luanda	
AG-11	Haoyuan	Semi-structured face-to-face	29-Mar-19	60 min	Luanda	

Continued

Table A.7 *Continued*

Name	Affiliation	Interview method	Date	Length	(Researcher's) Location	Note
Category 4. Host-country railway corporation Saturation: Medium						
AG-12	Caminho de Ferro de Luanda (CFL)	Semi-structured face-to-face, with interpreter	21-Nov-18	60 min	Luanda	Introduced by AG-1
AG-13	CFL	Semi-structured face-to-face, with interpreter	23-Nov-18	30 min	Luanda	Introduced by AG-12
AG-14	Caminho de Ferro de Benguela (CFB)	Semi-structured face-to-face, with interpreter	11-Feb-19	60 min	Lobito	
AG-15	CFB	Semi-structured face-to-face, with interpreter	22-Feb-19	30 min	Lobito	
AG-16	CFB	Semi-structured face-to-face, with interpreter	13-Feb-19	70 min	Lobito	
AG-17	CFB	Semi-structured face-to-face, with interpreter	18-Feb-19	30 min	Lobito	
Category 5. Host-country government Saturation: High						
AG-18	Department of Agriculture, Huambo Province	Semi-structured face-to-face, with interpreter	30-Nov-18	60 min	Huambo	
AG-19	Department of Transport, Huambo province	Semi-structured face-to-face, with interpreter	03-Dec-18	40 min	Huambo	
AG-20	Municipal administration of Lobito	Semi-structured face-to-face, with interpreter	12-Feb-19	60 min	Lobito	
AG-21	Department of Culture, Benguela Province	Semi-structured face-to-face, with interpreter	19-Feb-19	90 min	Benguela	
AG-22	Governor's Office of Benguela	Semi-structured face-to-face, with interpreter	21-Feb-19	45 min	Benguela	
AG-23	Lobito Administration Office	Semi-structured face-to-face, with interpreter	22-Feb-19	90 min	Benguela	
AG-24	Porto du Lobito	Semi-structured face-to-face,	25-Feb-19	60 min	Lobito	

AG-25	Communication department, Ministry of Transport	Semi-structured face-to-face, with interpreter	13-Mar-19	60 min	Luanda
AG-26	office of study of planning and statistics in MOT	Semi-structured face-to-face, with interpreter	14-Mar-19	2 hrs	Luanda
AG-27	Instituto de Gestão de Activos e Participações do Estado (IGAPE)	Semi-structured face-to-face	19-Mar-19	30 min	Luanda
AG-28	Communications e Jurisdiction Departments, Ministry of Transport	Semi-structured face-to-face, with interpreter	20-Mar-19	2 hrs	Luanda
AG-29	MOT	Semi-structured face-to-face	21-Mar-19	40 min	Luanda
AG-30	Instituto Nacional Dos Caminhos de Ferro Angola (INCFA)	Semi-structured face-to-face, with interpreter	24-Mar-19	60 min	Luanda
AG-31	Project planning and Development, MOT	Semi-structured face-to-face	25-Mar-19	45 min	Luanda
AG-32	Ministry of Environment	Semi-structured face-to-face	29-Mar-19	20 min	Luanda
AG-33	INCFA	Semi-structured face-to-face, with interpreter	30-Mar-19	60 min	Luanda
AG-34	Gabinete do Corredor do Lobito, MOT	Semi-structured face-to-face	30-Mar-19	40 min	Luanda
AG-35	Ministry of Finance	Non-structured casual talk	31-Mar-19		Luanda
AG-36	MP of Benguela	Semi-structured face-to-face, with interpreter	01-Apr-19	45 min	Luanda

Continued

Table A.7 *Continued*

Name	Affiliation	Interview method	Date	Length	(Researcher's) Location	Note
Category 6. Academia, business, and civil society and international organizations Saturation: High						
AG-37	Centro de Estudos e Investigacao Cientifica at the Universidade Católica de Angola (CEIC)	Semi-structured face-to-face	16-Nov-18	60 min	Luanda	
AG-38	ADRA	Semi-structured face-to-face	20-Nov-18	60 min	Luanda	
AG-39	Norwegian Christian Aid	Semi-structured face-to-face	27-Nov-18	60 min	Luanda	
AG-40	CEIC	Semi-structured face-to-face	28-Nov-18	60 min	Luanda	
AG-41	Open society Angola	Semi-structured face-to-face	28-Nov-18	60 min	Luanda	
AG-42	Open society Angola	Semi-structured face-to-face	10-Dec-18	40 min	Luanda	
AG-43	Journalist	Semi-structured face-to-face	28-Nov-18	60 min	Luanda	
AG-44	Church-based organization	Semi-structured face-to-face	30-Nov-18	60 min	Huambo	
AG-45	ADRA-Huambo	Semi-structured face-to-face, with interpreter	02-Dec-18	60 min	Huambo	
AG-46	José Eduardo dos Santos University	Semi-structured face-to-face, with interpreter	03-Dec-18	60 min	Huambo	
AG-47	Journalist	Semi-structured face-to-face	11-Dec-18	45 min	Luanda	
AG-48	Journalist	Semi-structured face-to-face	15-Dec-18	90 min	Luanda	
AG-49	JICA-Luanda	Semi-structured face-to-face	11-Dec-18	60 min	Luanda	
AG-50	Câmara de Comércio Angola-China	Semi-structured face-to-face	12-Dec-18	30 min	Luanda	
AG-51	Development works-Luanda	Semi-structured face-to-face	12-Dec-18	90 min	Luanda	
AG-52	China International Fund (CIF)	Semi-structured face-to-face	13-Dec-18	75 min	Luanda	

AG-53	CIF	Non-structured casual talk	22-Mar-18		Luanda
AG-54	Secil cement Lobito	Semi-structured face-to-face	15-Feb-19	60 min	Lobito
AG-55	Researcher	Semi-structured, phone	15-Feb-19	60 min	Lobito
AG-56	Journalist	Semi-structured face-to-face, with interpreter	18-Feb-19	90 min	Lobito
AG-57	ADRA-Benguela	Semi-structured face-to-face, with interpreter	19-Feb-19	90 min	Benguela
AG-58	Omunga	Semi-structured face-to-face, with interpreter	26-Feb-19	90 min	Benguela
AG-59	CEIC	Semi-structured face-to-face	11-Mar-19	30 min	Luanda
AG-60	Strategic studies centre	Semi-structured face-to-face	14-Mar-19	45 min	Luanda
AG-61	Academia (didn't capture university name)	Semi-structured face-to-face	18-Mar-19	60 min	Luanda
AG-62	Academia (didn't capture university name)	Semi-structured face-to-face, with interpreter	22-Mar-19	40 min	Luanda
AG-63	University of Winsor	Semi-structured, phone	25-Mar-19	45 min	Luanda
AG-64	University of Augusto Neto	Semi-structured face-to-face	26-Mar-19	60 min	Luanda

Bibliography

Aalen, L. (2002). *'Ethnic Federalism in a Dominant Party State: The Ethiopian Experience 1991–2000'*. Chr. Michelsen Institute.

Aalen, L. (2014). 'Ethiopia after Meles: Stability for How Long?' *Current History*, 113(763), 192–6.

Aalen, L. (2020). 'The Revolutionary Democracy of Ethiopia: A Wartime Ideology Both Shaping and Shaped by Peacetime Policy Needs'. *Government and Opposition*, 55(4), 653–68.

Aalen, L., & Tronvoll, K. (2009). 'The End of Democracy? Curtailing Political and Civil Rights in Ethiopia'. *Review of African Political Economy*, 36(120), 193–207.

Abbink, J. (2011). 'Ethnic-Based Federalism and Ethnicity in Ethiopia: Reassessing the Experiment after 20 Years'. *Journal of Eastern African Studies*, 5(4), 596–618.

Abbink, J. (2022). 'The Looming Spectre: A History of the "State of Emergency" in Ethiopia, 1970s–2021'. In J. Nicolas Bach (ed.), *Routledge Handbook of the Horn of Africa* (pp. 302–16). Routledge.

Abdulai, A.-G., & Mohan, G. (2019). *'The Politics of Bureaucratic "Pockets of Effectiveness": Insights from Ghana's Ministry of Finance'*. Manchester: Effective States and Inclusive Development Research Centre.

Achuka, V. (12 August 2018). 'Swazuri, Railways Boss Arrested over SGR Land Compensation'. The *Standard*. Retrieved from www.standardmedia.co.ke/business/article/2001291560/sgr-billions-sink-swazuri-atanas.

Addison, T. (2001). *From Conflict to Reconstruction*. UNU/WIDER.

Africa Confidential. (1 March 2010). 'Reshuffling Luanda's Beijing Connections'. Africa Confidential. Retrieved from www.africa-confidential.com/article-preview/id/10372/Reshuffling_Luanda%27s_Beijing_connection.

African Development Bank. (2015). *'Rail Infrastructure in Africa: Financing Policy Options'*. African Development Bank.

African Review of Business and Technology. (25 February 2019). 'EU Launches Road Project in Eritrea'. *African Review of Business and Technology*. Retrieved from www.africanreview.com/construction-a-mining/roads/eu-launches-road-project-in-eritrea.

Africa Star Railway Operation Company Limited. (May 2019). 'Mombasa-Nairobi SGR Operation Monthly Performance Report'.

Aglionby, J. (16 January 2017). 'Djibouti-Ethiopia Railway Carries Hope for Pan-African Trade'. *Financial Times*. Retrieved from www.ft.com/content/42d7af2e-d95a-11e6-944b-e7eb37a6aa8e.

Ahlquist, J. S., & Levi, M. (2011). 'Leadership: What It Means, What It Does, and What We Want to Know about It'. *Annual Review of Political Science*, 14, 1–24.

Akamatsu, K. (1962). 'A Historical Pattern of Economic Growth in Developing Countries'. *The Developing Economies*, 1, 3–25.

Akech, M. (2011). 'Constraining Government Power in Africa'. *Journal of Democracy*, 22(1), 96–106.

Alden, C., & Otele, O. M. (2022). 'Fitting China In: Local Elite Collusion and Contestation along Kenya's Standard Gauge Railway'. *African Affairs*, 121(484), 443–66.

Alves, A. C. (2013). 'China's "Win-Win" Cooperation: Unpacking the Impact of Infrastructure-for-Resources Deals in Africa'. *South African Journal of International Affairs*, 20(2), 207–26.

Angonotícias. (26 February 2013). 'SONIP vendeu 18.089 habitações nas centralidades em 15 dias'. *Angonotícias*. https://www.angonoticias.com/Artigos/item/37704/sonip-vendeu-18089-habitacoes-nas-centralidades-em-15-dias.

Angonotícias. (15 February 2016). 'Moradores das centralidades queixam-se ao governador'. *Angonotícias*. Retrieved from www.angonoticias.com/Artigos/item/49913/moradores-das-centralidades-queixam-se-ao-governador.

Angop. (22 September 2020). 'Benguela Railway: Cuito-Cuemba Section Cleared'. *Angop*. Retrieved from www.angop.ao/noticias-o/?v_link=www.angop.ao/angola/en_us/noticias/sociedade/2020/8/39/Benguela-railway-Cuito-Cuemba-section-cleared,669463a3-6558-4cc1-9f16-b6826d0ab535.html.

Anyanzwa, J. (19 June 2019). 'SGR Future in Doubt as Governments Revert to Old Metre Gauge Railways'. Retrieved from www.theeastafrican.co.ke/tea/business/sgr-future-in-doubt-as-governments-revert-to-old-metre-gauge-railways-1420522.

Arkebe O., & Kefale, D. (2020). 'A Strategic Approach to Industrial Hubs: Learnings in Ethiopia'. In O. Arkebe & J. Y. Lin (eds.), *The Oxford Handbook of Industrial Hubs and Economic Development*. Oxford University Press.

Atieno, W. (1 February 2018). 'Joho Threatens to Sue State, Alleges Plot to Shift Port Services to Naivasha'. *Business Daily*. Retrieved from www.businessdailyafrica.com/economy/Joho-to-sue-govt—transfer-of-port-services-to-Naivasha-/3946234-4287710-n8ls8rz/index.html.

Bach, J.-N. (2011). 'Abyotawi Democracy: Neither Revolutionary nor Democratic—A Critical Review of EPRDF's Conception of Revolutionary Democracy in Post-1991 Ethiopia'. *Journal of Eastern African Studies*, 5(4), 641–63.

Barry, A. (2013). *Material Politics: Disputes along the Pipeline*. John Wiley & Sons.

Bates, R. H. (1981). 'Food Policy in Africa: Political Causes and Social Effects'. *Food Policy*, 6(3), 147–57.

Bates, R. H. (2014). *Markets and States in Tropical Africa: The Political Basis of Agricultural Policies*. University of California Press.

Bayart, J.-F. (2000). 'Africa in the World: A History of Extraversion'. *African Affairs*, 99(395), 217–67.

BBC. (5 October 2016). 'Ethiopia-Djibouti Electric Railway Line Opens'. BBC. Retrieved from www.bbc.co.uk/news/world-africa-37562177.

BBC. (31 May 2017). 'Kenya Opens Nairobi-Mombasa Madaraka Express Railway'. BBC. Retrieved from www.bbc.co.uk/news/world-africa-40092600.

BBC. (2 December 2019). 'Letter from Africa: Is Kenya Building Bridges to Nowhere?' BBC. Retrieved from www.bbc.com/news/world-africa-50603137.

BBC. (29 June 2021). 'Ethiopia's Tigray War: The Short, Medium and Long Story'. BBC. Retrieved from www.bbc.com/news/world-africa-54964378.

Beerbohm, E. (2015). 'Is Democratic Leadership Possible?' *American Political Science Review*, 109(4), 639–52.

Bell, D. (2014). 'Political Leadership'. *Government and Oppositions*, 49(1), 139–58.

Bennett, A. (2010). 'Process Tracing and Causal Inference'. In D. Collier & H. Brady (eds.), *Rethinking Social Inquiry: Diverse Tools, Shared Standards*. Rowman & Littlefield.

Bennett, A., & Checkel, J. T. (2015). 'Process Tracing: From Philosophical Roots to Best Practices'. In A. Bennett & J. T. Checkel (eds.), *Process Tracing: From Metaphor to Analytical Tool* (pp. 3–38). Cambridge University Press.

Besley, T., & Case, A. (1995). 'Does Electoral Accountability Affect Economic Policy Choices? Evidence from Gubernatorial Term Limits'. *Quarterly Journal of Economics*, 110(3), 769–98.

Boone, C. (2011). 'Politically Allocated Land Rights and the Geography of Electoral Violence: The Case of Kenya in the 1990s'. *Comparative Political Studies*, 44(10), 1311–42.

Boone, C. (2012). 'Land Conflict and Distributive Politics in Kenya'. *African Studies Review*, 55(1), 75–103.

Booth, D., & Golooba-Mutebi, F. (2012). 'Developmental Patrimonialism? The Case of Rwanda'. *African Affairs*, 111(444), 379–403.

Branch, D. (2011). *Kenya between Hope and Despire: 1963–2011*. Yale University Press.

Branch, D., & Cheeseman, N. (2006). 'The Politics of Control in Kenya: Understanding the Bureaucratic-Executive State, 1952–78'. *Review of African Political Economy*, 33(107), 11–31.

Bräutigam, D. (2003). 'Close Encounters: Chinese Business Networks as Industrial Catalysts in Sub-Saharan Africa'. *African Affairs*, 102(408), 447–67.

Bräutigam, D. (2008). '"Flying Geese" or "Hidden Dragon"? Chinese Business and African Industrial Development'. In C. Alden, D. Large, & R. Soares de Oliveira (eds.), *China Returns to Africa: A Rising Power and a Continent Embrace*. Christopher.

Bräutigam, D. (2011). *The Dragon's Gift: The Real Story of China in Africa*. Oxford University Press.

Bräutigam, D., & Zhang, H. (2013). 'Green Dreams: Myth and Reality in China's Agricultural Investment in Africa'. *Third World Quarterly*, 34, 1676–96.

Bräutigam, D., Tang, X., & Xia, Y. (2018). 'What Kinds of Chinese "Geese" Are Flying to Africa? Evidence from Chinese Manufacturing Firms'. *Journal of African Economies*, 27(l), 29–51. https://doi.org/10.1093/jae/ejy013.

Bräutigam, D., Hwang, J., Link, J., & Acker, K. (2019). 'Chinese Loans to Africa Database'. Washington, DC: China–Africa Research Initiative, Johns Hopkins University School of Advanced International Studies.

Bräutigam, D., Bhalaki, V., Deron, L., & Wang, Y. (2022). 'How Africa Borrows from China: And Why Mombasa Port Is Not Collateral for Kenya's Standard Gauge Railway' (No. 2022/52). Working Paper.

Brødsgaard, K. E. (2017). *Chinese Politics as Fragmented Authoritarianism*. Routledge.

Brown, C. O. (2020). 'Economic Leadership and Growth'. *Journal of Monetary Economics*, 116, 298–333.

Brown, W., & Harman, S. (2013). 'African Agency in International Politics'. In W. Brown & S. Harman (eds.), *African Agency in International Politics* (pp. 1–16). Routledge.

Bueno de Mesquita, B., Smith, A., Siverson, R. M., & Morrow, J. D. (2003). *The Logic of Political Survival*. MIT Press.

Buire, C. (2017). 'New City, New Citizens? A Lefebvrian Exploration of State-Led Housing and Political Identities in Luanda, Angola'. *Transformation: Critical Perspectives on Southern Africa*, 93, 13–40.

Burgis, T., & Sevastopulo, D. (8 August 2014). 'China in Africa: How Sam Pa Became the Middleman'. *Financial Times*. Retrieved from www.ft.com/content/308a133a-1db8-11e4-b927-00144feabdc0.

Burgis, T., Anderlini, J., & Hornby, L. (14 October 2015). 'Queensway Tycoon Sam Pa Is Detained in Communist Probe'. *Financial Times*. Retrieved from www.ft.com/content/1a358d9c-725a-11e5-a129-3fcc4f641d98.

Burke, J. (10 August 2017). 'Kenya Election Monitors Urge Losing Candidates to Accept Poll Results'. *The Guardian*. Retrieved from www.theguardian.com/world/2017/aug/10/kenya-election-observers-urge-defeated-candidates-to-accept-result.

Cabestan, J.-P. (2020). *'African Agency and Chinese Power: The Case of Djibouti'*. South African Institute of International Affairs.

Cain, A. (2014). 'African Urban Fantasies: Past Lessons and Emerging Realities'. *Environment & Urbanization*, 26(2), 561–7.

Campos, I., & Vines, A. (2008). *'Angola and China: A Pragmatic Partnership'*. CSIS.

Carbone, G., & Pellegata, A. (2020). *Political Leadership in Africa*. Cambridge University Press.

Cardoso, F. H. (1977). 'The Consumption of Dependency Theory in the United States'. *Latin American Research Review*, 12(3), 7–22.

Cardoso, F. H., & Faletto, E. (1979). *Desarrollo y Dependencia en América Latina*. Siglo XXI.

Cardoso, R. V. (2015). 'The Crude Urban Revolution: Land Markets, Planning Forms and the Making of a New Luanda'. University of California, Berkeley: PhD Thesis.

Carmody, P. (2016). *The New Scramble for Africa*. Polity Press.

Carmody, P. (2020). 'Dependence Not Debt-Trap Diplomacy'. *Area Development and Policy*, 5(1), 23–31.

Carmody, P., & Kragelund, P. (2016). 'Who is in Charge? State Power and Agency in Sino-African Relations'. *Cornell International Law Journal*, 49, 1.

Carpenter D. P. (2001). *The Forging of Bureaucratic Autonomy: Reputations, Networks, and Policy Innovation in Executive Agencies, 1862–1928*. Princeton University Press.

CCECC. (April 2019). '**亚吉铁路运营维护项目工作简报2019年4月**'.

Centeno, M. A. (2003). *Blood and Debt: War and the Nation-State in Latin America*. The Pennsylvania State University Press.

Centeno, M. A., Kohli, A., & Yashar, D. J. (2017). *States in the Developing World*. Cambridge University Press.

Chabal, P. (2007). 'Introduction: E Pluribus Unum—Transition in Angola'. In P. Chabal & N. Vidal (eds.), *Angola: The Weight of History* (pp. 1–18). Hurst.

Chabal, P., & Daloz, J.-P. (2004). *Africa Works: Disorder as Political Instrument*. James Currey.

Cheeseman, D. B. (2010). 'Conclusion: The Failure of Nation-Building and the Kenyan Crisis'. In D. Branch, N. Cheeseman & L. Gardner (eds.), *Our Turn to Eat: Politics in Kenya since 1950* (pp. 243–56). Lit Verlag.

Chellaney, B. (2017). 'China's Debt-Trap Diplomacy'. *Project Syndicate*. Retrieved from www.project-syndicate.org/commentary/china-one-belt-one-road-loans-debt-by-brahma-chellaney-2017-01.

Chemouni, B. (2019). *'The Rise of the Economic Technocracy in Rwanda: A Case of a Bureaucratic Pocket of Effectiveness or State-Building Prioritisation?'* Effective States and Inclusive Development.

Chemouni, B. (2023). 'The Politics of State Capacity in Post-Genocide Rwanda: "Pockets of Effectiveness" as State-Building Prioritizations?' In S. Hickey (ed.), *Pockets of Effectiveness and the Politics of State-Building in Sub-Saharan Africa*. Oxford University Press.

Cheru, F., Cramer, C., & Oqubay, A. (2019). 'Introduction'. In F. Cheru, C. Cramer, & A. Oqubay (eds.), *The Oxford Handbook of the Ethiopian Economy* (pp. 3–16). Oxford University Press.

China–Africa Research Initiative. (2 April 2014). 'Chinese-Built Angolan "Ghost Town" Wakes Up?' China–Africa Research Initiative Blog. Retrieved from www.chinaafricarealstory.com/2014/04/chinese-built-angolan-ghost-town-wakes.html.

China Export and Import Bank (2019). 《2019年中国进出口银行绿色金融和社会责任白皮书》. Retrieved from www.eximbank.gov.cn/info/WhitePOGF/202001/P020200115377992690034.pdf.

China Road and Bridge Corporation. (2016). 'Social Responsibility Report 2016 on Mombasa-Nairobi Standard Gauge Railway Project'. CRBC.

China Road and Bridge Corporation. (2018). 'China Road and Bridge Corporation Social Responsibility Report 2016 on Mombasa Nairobi SGR Project'. CRBC.

China Road and Bridge Corporation. (2018). 'Kenya SGR Project Social Responsibility Report 2017/2018'. CRBC.

China's Bureau of Statistics. (n.d.). 中国国家统计局年度数据. Retrieved from https://data.stats.gov.cn/easyquery.htm?cn=C01.

Chinese Ministry of Foreign Affairs. (6 May 2014). 'Speech by H.E. Wen Jiabao, Premier of the State Council of the People's Republic of China, at the China-EU Investment and Trade Forum'. Retrieved from www.chinamission.be/eng/zt/t101949.htm.

Chome, N. (2015). 'Devolution Is Only for Development? Decentralisation and Elite Vulnerability on the Kenyan Coast'. *Critical African Studies*, 7(3), 299–316.

Clapham, C. (1985). *Third World Politics: An Introduction*. University of Wisconsin Press.

Clapham, C. (1996). *Africa and the International System: The Politics of State Survival*. Cambridge University Press.

Clapham, C. (2009). 'Post-War Ethiopia: The Trajectories of Crisis'. *Review of African Political Economy*, 36(120), 181–92.

Clapham, C. (2017). *The Horn of Africa: State Formation and Decay*. Hurst.

Collier, P. (16 October 2019). 'Ethiopia's Path to Prosperity is Opening Up under Abiy Ahmed'. *Financial Times*. Retrieved from www.ft.com/content/502dc8f4-ef62-11e9-a55a-30afa498db1b.

Cooper, F. (1996). *Decolonization and African Society: The Labor Question in French and British Africa* (no. 89). Cambridge University Press.

Corkin, L. (2016). *Uncovering African Agency: Angola's Management of China's Credit Lines*. Ashgate.

Cotterill, J. (11 November 2020). 'Angola Sharpens Fight to Recover Stolen Cash as Debt Pressure Mounts'. *Financial Times*. Retrieved from www.ft.com/content/5ebceb76-5e3f-4e08-98b8-3345b86a3482.

Council of Foreign Relations. (2019). 'China's Massive Belt and Road Initiative'. Retrieved from www.cfr.org/backgrounder/chinas-massive-belt-and-road-initiativeon.

CPCS. (2009). 'East African Railways Master Plan Study Final Report'. Retrieved from https://africog.org/wp-content/uploads/2017/06/The-East-African-Railways-Master-Plan.pdf.

CR20. (2020). 国家荣誉. 中国工人出版社.

Croese, S. (2016). 'State-Led Housing Delivery as an Instrument of Developmental Patrimonialism: The Case of Post-War Angola'. *African Affairs*, 116(462), 80–100.

Daily Nation. (26 June 2017). 'Jimi Wanjigi: Kenya's Most Feared Oligarch'. *Daily Nation*. Retrieved from www.nation.co.ke/news/State-capture—Kenya-s-most-feared-oligarch/1056-3987356-dek8hy/index.html.

Daily Nation. (27 November 2018). 'End of Rivalry Revives Hassan Joho's Businesses'. *Daily Nation*. Retrieved from www.nation.co.ke/news/politics/End-of-rivalry-revives-Hassan-Joho-s-businesses/1064-4870184-11jmsd1/index.html.

Data Commons. (n.d.). 'Data Commons: China'. Retrieved from https://datacommons.org/place/country/CHN?topic=Economics.

Davis, C. B., Wilburn, K. E., & Robinson, R. E. (1991). *Railway Imperialism*. Greenwood Pub Group.

Demony, C., & Cocks, T. (30 August 2022). 'Angola's Government Party Wins Divisive Election Extending Long Rule'. *Reuters*. Retrieved from www.reuters.com/world/africa/angolas-president-mpla-party-declared-winner-election-2022-08-29.

de Waal, A. (2013). 'The Theory and Practice of Meles Zenawi'. *African Affairs*, 112(446), 148–55.

de Waal, A. (2015). *The Real Politics of the Horn of Africa: Money, War and the Business of Power*. Polity Press.

Diário da República. (22 October 2004). I Series: No. 85, Decree-law 6/04. Luanda, Angola.

Diário da República. (11 March 2009). I Series: No. 45, Resolution 20/09. Luanda, Angola.

Dimitriou, H. T., Ward, J., & Wright, P. G. (2012). *'Mega Projects Executive Summary: Lessons for Decision-Maker: An Analysis of Selected International Large-Scale Transport Infrastructure Project'*. OMEGA Centre.

Dixit, A. (2002). 'Incentives and Organizations in the Public Sector: An Interpretative Review'. *Journal of Human Resources*, 37(4), 696–727.

Domínguez, J. I. (Ed.). (1997). *Technopols: Freeing Politics and Markets in Latin America in the 1990s*. Penn State Press.

Doner, R. F., Ritchie, B. K., & Slater, D. (2005). 'Systemic Vulnerability and the Origins of Developmental States: Northeast and Southeast Asia in Comparative Perspective'. *International Organization*, 59(2), 327–61.

Dreher, A., Fuchs, A., Parks, B., Strange, A. M., & Tierney, M. J. (2018). 'Apples and Dragon Fruits: The Determinants of Aid and Other Forms of State Financing from China to Africa'. *International Studies Quarterly*, 62(1), 182–94.

Duarte, A. (2010). 'The Real Transport System in the Post-Conflict Reconstruction of Angola: A Case Study of the Province of Benguela'. School of Oriental and African Studies, University of London: PhD Thesis.

Duarte, A., Pacheco, F., Santos, R., & Tjønneland, E. N. (2015). 'Diversification and Development, or "White Elephants?": Transport in Angola's Lobito Corridor'. CMI.

Dubois, E. (2016). 'Political Business Cycles 40 Years after Nordhaus'. *Public Choice*, 166(1–2), 235–59.

Dye, B. J. (2016). 'The Return of "High Modernism"? Exploring the Changing Development Paradigm through a Rwandan Case Study of Dam Construction'. *Journal of Eastern African Studies*, 10(2), 303–24.

Dye, B. J. (2022). 'Uneven Convergence in India's Development Cooperation: The Case of Concessional Finance to Africa'. *Third World Quarterly*, 43(1), 166–86.

East African Community. (n.d.). 'EAC Railways Sub-Sector Projects'. Retrieved from www.eac.int/infrastructure/railways-transport-sub-sector/92-sector/infrastructure/railways.

Ellis, R. E. (2009). *China in Latin America: The Whats and Wherefores*. Lynne Rienner Publishers.

Embassy of Ethiopia in Brussels. (10 September 2018). 'China Extends Debt Repayment for Ethiopia'. Retrieved from https://ethiopianembassy.be/china-extends-debt-repayment-for-ethiopia.

Emmenegger, P. (2021). 'Agency in Historical Institutionalism: Coalitional Work in the Creation, Maintenance, and Change of Institutions'. *Theory and Society*, *50*(4), 607–26.

Enriquez, E., & Centeno, M. (2012). 'State Capacity: Utilization, Durability, and the Role of Wealth vs. History'. *International and Multidisciplinary Journal of Social Sciences*, 1(2), 130–62.
EPRDF. (2006). *'Development, Democracy and Revolutionary Democracy'*. Adopted in the 4th General Assembly of the EPRDF.
Ethiopia Embassy in London. (22 July 2017). 'Hawassa Industrial Park Goes Fully Operational as Ethiopia Pushes to Become Manufacturing Hub'. Retrieved from www.ethioembassy.org.uk/hawassa-industrial-park-goes-fully-operational-as-ethiopia-pushes-to-become-manufacturing-hub.
Evans, P. (1992). 'The State as Problem and Solution: Predation, Embedded Autonomy, and Structural Change'. *The Politics of Economic Adjustment*, 3(3), 138–81.
Evans, P. (1995). *Embedded Autonomy: States and Industrial Transformation*. Princeton University Press.
Evans, P., & Rauch, J. E. (1999). 'Bureaucracy and Growth: A Cross-National Analysis of the Effects of "Weberian" State Structures on Economic Growth'. *American Sociological Review*, 64(5), 748–65.
Evans, P., Rueschemeyer, D., & Skocpol, T. (1985). *Bringing the State Back In*. Cambridge University Press.
Executive Research Associates (2009). *'China in Africa: A Strategic Overview'*. Executive Research Associates.
Fairfield, T., & Charman, A. E. (2017). 'Explicit Bayesian Analysis for Process Tracing: Guidelines, Opportunities, and Caveats'. *Political Analysis*, 25(3), 363–80.
Fairfield, T., & Charman, A. E. (2022). *Social Inquiry and Bayesian Inference: Rethinking Qualitative Research*. Cambridge University Press.
FAO. (2012). *'Reviewed Strategic Framework and Outline of the Medium Term Plan 2014–17'*. FAO.
Ferguson, J. (1991). *Expectations of Modernity: Myths and Meanings of Urban Life on the Zambian Copperbelt*. University of California Press.
Fetsum, B. (26 April 2017). 'Prime Minister Hailemariam Desalegn's Speech at the Railway Network in Adwa'. *Horn Affairs-Amharic*. Retrieved from https://hornaffairs.com/am/2017/04/26/pm-hailemariam-desalegn-speech-adwa-about-railway.
Fieldhouse, D. L. (1999). *The West and the Third World: Trade, Colonialism, Dependence, and Development*. Blackwell.
Fisher, J., & Gebrewahd, M. T. (2019). 'Game Over? Abiy Ahmed, the Tigrayan People's Liberation Front and Ethiopia's Political Crisis'. *African Affairs*, 118(470), 194–206.
Frank, A. G. (1998). *ReOrient*. University of California Press.
Fuiji, L. A. (2013). 'Working with Interpreters'. In L. Mosley (ed.), *Interviewing Research in Political Science*. Cornell University Press.
Fukuyama, F. (2013). 'What is Governance?' *Governance*, 26(3), 347–68.
Fyson, S. (2009). 'Sending in the Consultants: Development Agencies, the Private Sector and the Reform of Public Finance in Low-Income Countries'. *International Journal of Public Policy*, 4(3–4), 314–43.
Gallagher, K. P., & Porzecanski, R. (2010). *The Dragon in the Room: China and the Future of Latin American Industrialization*. Stanford University Press.
Gebre, S. (23 July 2018). 'Ethiopian Leader Calls for a Multiparty Democracy'. *Bloomberg*. Retrieved from www.bloomberg.com/news/articles/2018-07-22/ethiopian-pm-calls-for-multiparty-politics-in-electoral-reform.
Geddes, B. (1990). 'Building "State" Autonomy in Brazil, 1930–1964'. *Comparative Politics*, 22(2), 217–35.
Geddes, B. (1994). *Politician's Dilemma: Building State Capacity in Latin America*. University of California Press.
George, A. L., & Bennett, A. (2005). *Case Studies and Theory Development in the Social Sciences*. MIT Press.
Gill, B., & Reilly, J. (2007). 'The Tenuous Hold of China Inc. in Africa'. *Washington Quarterly*, 30(3), 37–52.
Goertz, G., & Mahoney, J. (2012). *A Tale of Two Cultures: Contrasting Qualitative and Quantitative Research*. Princeton University Press.

Goldstein, A., Pinaud, N., Reisen, H., & Chen, X. (2006). *The Rise of China and India: What's in it for Africa?* OECD Publications.

Gonzalez-Ocantos, E., & LaPorte, J. (2021). 'Process Tracing and the Problem of Missing Data'. *Sociological Methods & Research*, 50(3), 1407–35.

Greenhill, R., Prizzon, A., & Rogerson, A. (2013). *'The Age of Choice: Developing Countries in the New Aid Landscape'*. ODI.

Grindle, M. S. (1997). 'Divergent Cultures? When Public Organizations Perform Well in Developing Countries'. *World Development*, 25(4), 481–95.

Grindle, M. S. (2004). 'Good Enough Governance: Poverty Reduction and Reform in Developing Countries'. *Governance*, 17(4), 525–48.

Guguyu, O. (8 July 2020). 'G20 Derails Kenya's Push for China Debt Relief Deal'. *Business Daily*. Retrieved from www.businessdailyafrica.com/bd/economy/g20-derails-kenya-s-push-for-china-debt-relief-deal-2295320.

Guo, G. (2009). 'China's Local Political Budget Cycles'. *American Journal of Political Science*, 53(3), 621–32.

Hart, J. (2016). *Ghana on the Go: African Mobility in the Age of Motor Transportation*. Indiana University Press.

Hart, P., Kane, J., & Patapan, H. (2009). *Dispersed Democratic Leadership: Origins, Dynamics, and Implications*. Oxford University Press.

Harvey, P., & Knox, H. (2015). *Road: An Anthropology of Infrastructure and Expertise*. Cornell University Press.

Headrick, D. R. (1981). *The Tools of Empire: Technology and European Imperialism in the Nineteenth Century*. Oxford University Press.

Heaver, R. (2005). *'Strengthening Country Commitment to Human Development: Lessons from Nutrition'*. World Bank.

Helmke, G., & Levitsky, S. (2004). 'Informal Institutions and Comparative Politics: A Research Agenda'. *Perspectives on Politics*, 2(4), 725–40.

Helms, L. (2014a). 'Global Political Leadership in the Twenty-First Century: Problems and Prospects'. *Contemporary Politics*, 20(3), 261–77.

Helms, L. (2014b). 'Institutional Analysis'. In R. A. Hart (ed.), *The Oxford Handbook of Political Leadership*. Oxford University Press.

Hensengerth, O. (2011). *'Interaction of Chinese Institutions with Host Governments in Dam Construction: The Bui Dam in Ghana'*. German Development Institute.

Herbst, J. (2014). *States and Power in Africa: Comparative Lessons in Authority and Control*. Princeton University Press.

Herod, A. (1999). 'Reflections on Interviewing Foreign Elites: Praxis, Positionality, Validity, and the Cult of the Insider'. *Geoforum*, 30(4), 313–27.

Hickey, S. (2019). 'The Politics of State Capacity and Development in Africa: Reframing and Researching "Pockets of Effectiveness"'. ESID Working Paper No. 117. Effective States and Inclusive Development Research Centre, The University of Manchester.

Hickey, S. (2023). 'Comparative Analysis: PoEs and the Politics of State-Building and Development in Africa'. In S. Hickey (ed.), *Pockets of Effectiveness and the Politics of State-Building in Sub-Saharan Africa*. Oxford University Press.

Hickey, S., & Izama, A. (2020). 'The Politics of Governing Oil after "Best-Practice" Reforms: Can "Pockets of Effectiveness" Survive within Uganda's Political Settlement?' *The Extractive Industries and Society*, 7(4), 1200–10.

Hickey, S., & Mohan, G. (2023). 'Conceptualizing the Politics of PoEs'. In S. Hickey (ed.), *Pockets of Effectiveness and the Politics of State-Building in Sub-Saharan Africa*. Oxford University Press.

Hodges, T. (2004). *Angola: Anatomy of an Oil State*. Indiana University Press.

Holland, A. C. (2016). 'Forbearance'. *American Political Science Review*, 110(2), 232–46.

Holston, J. (2009). *Insurgent Citizenship: Disjunctions of Democracy and Modernity in Brazil*. Princeton University Press.

Human Rights Watch. (2002). *'The War is Over: The Crisis of Angola's Internally Displaced Continues—A Human Rights Watch Background Briefing Paper'*. Human Rights Watch.

Hyden, G. (2012). *African Politics in Comparative Perspective*. Cambridge University Press.
ICG. (16 December 2019). 'Keeping Ethiopia's Transition on the Rails'. Retrieved from www.crisisgroup.org/africa/horn-africa/ethiopia/283-keeping-ethiopias-transition-rails.
IDA and IMF. (2020). 'Joint World Bank-IMF Debt Sustainability Analysis May 2020'. Retrieved from https://treasury.go.ke/wp-content/uploads/2021/02/Joint-World-Bank-IMF-Review-May-2020.pdf.
IMF. (2003). '2003 Article IV Consultation—Staff Report'. IMF.
Instituto Nacional de Estatística. (2010). *'Inquérito Integrado sobre o Bem Estar da População 2008–2009: Principais Resultados Definitivos'*. Luanda.
Jackson, R. H., & Rosberg, C. G. (1982). *Personal Rule in Black Africa: Prince, Autocrat, Prophet, Tyrant*. University of California Press.
Jakobson, L. (2008). 'Does China Have an Energy Diplomacy? Reflections on China's Energy Security and Its International Dimensions'. In A. Marquina (ed.), *Energy Security: Visions from Asia and Europe*. Palgrave.
Jakobson, L., & Knox, D. (2010). *'New Foreign Policy Actors in China'*. Stockholm International Peace Research Institute.
Javernick-Will, A., & Scott, W. (2010). 'Who Needs to Know What? Institutional Knowledge and Global Projects'. *Journal of Construction Engineering Management*, 136(5), 546–57.
Johnson, C. (1982). *MITI and the Japanese Miracle: The Growth of Industrial Policy, 1925–1975*. Stanford University Press.
Joignant, A. (2011). 'The Politics of Technopols: Resources, Political Competence and Collective Leadership in Chile, 1990–2010'. *Journal of Latin American Studies*, 43(3), 517–46.
Jones, B. F., & Olken, B. A. (2004). 'Do Leaders Matter? National Leadership and Growth since World War II'. *The Quarterly Journal of Economics*, 120(3), 835–64.
Jones, L., & Hameiri, S. (2020). 'Debunking the myth of "debt-trap diplomacy"'. *Chatham House*, 19.
Jubilee Coalition. (2013). 'Transforming Kenya: Securing Kenya's Prosperity 2013–2017'. https://www.chathamhouse.org/2020/08/debunking-myth-debt-trap-diplomacy.
Kapiszewski, D., MacLean, L. M., & Read, B. L. (2015). 'Interviews, Oral Histories, and Focus Groups'. In D. Kapiszewski, L. M. MacLean, & B. L. Read (eds.), *Field Research in Political Science: Practices and Principles* (pp. 190–233). Cambridge University Press.
Karl, T. L. (1997). *The Paradox of Plenty: Oil Booms and Petro-States*. University of California Press.
Kelsall, T. (2013). *Business, Politics, and the State in Africa: Challenging the Orthodoxies on Growth and Transformation*. Zed Books.
Kenya Railway Corporation. (n.d.). 'Madaraka Freight Service'. Retrieved from https://krc.co.ke/madaraka-express-freight-service.
Keter, G. (17 July 2019). 'Matiang'i Takes Charge of Weekly Cabinet Meetings'. *The Star*. Retrieved from www.the-star.co.ke/news/2019-07-17-uhuru-delegates-weekly-cabinet-meetings-to-matiangi.
Khan, M. (2010). 'Political Settlements and the Governance of Growth-Enhancing Institutions'. https://eprints.soas.ac.uk/9968/1/Political_Settlements_internet.pdf
Khan, M. (2018). 'Political Settlements and the Analysis of Institutions'. *African Affairs*, 117(469), 636–55.
Kulundu, M. (30 January 2016). 'Why Joho's Businesses Were Closed—KRA'. *The Kenyans*. Retrieved from www.kenyans.co.ke/news/why-johos-businesses-were-closed-kra.
Kurgat, P. (22 November 2021). 'SGR Passenger Trains Stop Midway over Safety Scare'. *The Kenyans*. Retrieved from www.kenyans.co.ke/news/70841-sgr-passenger-trains-stop-midway-over-safety-scare.
Kynge, J., Peel, M., & Bland, B. (17 July 2017). 'China's Railway Diplomacy Hits the Buffers'. *Financial Times*. Retrieved from www.ft.com/content/9a4aab54-624d-11e7-8814-0ac7eb84e5f1.
Lamarque, H. (2019). 'Profitable Inefficiency: The Politics of Port Infrastructure in Mombasa, Kenya'. *Journal of Modern African Studies*, 57(1), 85–109.
Lavers, T. (2018). 'Responding to Land-Based Conflict in Ethiopia: The Land Rights of Ethnic Minorities under Federalism'. *African Affairs*, 117(468), 462–84.
Lawson, A. (2012). *'Evaluation of Public Financial Management Reform'*. AfDB.
Le Billon, P. (1999). *'A Land Cursed by its Wealth? Angola's War Economy 1975–99'*. UNU/WIDER.

Lee, C. K. (2017). *The Spectre of Global China: Politics, Labor, and Foreign Investment in Africa.* University of Chicago Press.

Lefort, R. (2007). 'Powers—Mengist—and Peasants in Rural Ethiopia: The May 2005 Elections'. *Journal of Modern African Studies*, 45(2), 253–73.

Lefort, R. (2013). 'The Theory and Practice of Meles Zenawi: A Response to Alex de Waal'. *African Affairs*, 112(448), 460–70.

Lefort, R. (2015). 'The Ethiopian Economy: The Developmental State vs. the Free Market'. In G. Prunier & É. Ficquet (eds.), *Understanding Contemporary Ethiopia: Monarchy, Revolution and the Legacy of Meles Zenawi.* Hurst.

Lefort, R. (2016). 'Ethiopia's Crisis. Things Fall Apart—Will the Centre Hold?' *Open Democracy.* Retrieved from www.opendemocracy.net/en/ethiopia-s-crisis.

Leonard, D. E. (2010). '"Pockets" of Effective Agencies in Weak Governance States: Where Are They Likely and Why Does It Matter?' *Public Administration and Development: The International Journal of Management Research and Practice*, 30(2), 91–101.

Levkowitz, L., Ross, M. M., & Warner, J. (2009). *'The 88 Queensway Group: A Case Study in Chinese Investors' Operations in Angola and Beyond'.* U.S.–China Economic & Security Review Commission.

Lewis, T. (2013). *Divided Highways: Building the Interstate Highways, Transforming American Life.* Cornell University Press.

Leys, C. (1996). *Underdevelopment in Kenya.* East African Publishers.

Li, C. (2015). *China's Centralized Industrial Order: Industrial Reform and the Rise of Centrally Controlled Big Business.* Routledge.

Li, C. (2016). 'Holding "China Inc." Together: The CCP and the Rise of China's Yangqi'. *The China Quarterly*, 228, 927–49.

Lin, L.-W., & Milhaupt, C. J. (2013). 'We Are the (National) Champions: Understanding the Mechanisms of State Capitalism in China'. *Stanford Law Review*, 65, 696–759.

Liou, C.-S. (2014). 'Rent-Seeking at Home, Capturing Market Share Abroad: The Domestic Determinants of the Transnationalization of China State Construction Engineering Corporation'. *World Development*, 54, 220–31.

Lodge, M., & Wegrich, K. (2012). *Executive Politics in Times of Crisis.* Palgrave.

Lonsdale, J. (2000). 'Agency in Tight Corners: Narrative and Initiative in African History'. *Journal of African Cultural Studies*, 13(1), 5–16.

Low, S. P., & Jiang, H. (2003). 'Internationalization of Chinese Construction Enterprises'. *Journal of Construction Engineering and Management*, 129(6), 589–98.

Macauhub. (26 March 2012). *'Angola Prepares for Privatisation of Railroads'. Macauhub.* Retrieved from Macauhub.

Macauhub. (9 January 2015). 'Angola and China Open Atlantic to African Neighbours'. *Macauhub.* Retrieved from https://macauhub.com.mo/feature/angola-and-china-open-atlantic-to-african-neighbours.

Macauhub. (30 August 2017). 'Angola Contracts Chinese Companies to Maintain Railway Network'. *Macauhub.* Retrieved from http://archive.ipim.gov.mo/en/portuguese-speaking-countries-news/2017-08-30-angola-contracts-chinese-companies-to-maintain-railway-network.

Mahoney, J. (2012). 'The Logic of Process Tracing Tests in the Social Sciences'. *Sociological Methods & Research*, 41(4), 570–97.

Markakis, J. (2011). *Ethiopia: The Last Two Frontiers.* James Currey Eastern African Studies.

Marques de Morais, R. (26 September 2011). 'The Ill-Gotten Gains behind Kilamba Housing Development'. *Maka Angola.* Retrieved from www.makaangola.org/2011/09/the-ill-gotten-gains-behind-the-kilamba-housing-development.

Marques de Morais, R. (2011). 'The New Imperialism: China in Angola'. *World Affairs*, 173(6), 67–74.

Marques de Morais, R. (2012). *'The Angolan Presidency: The Epicentre of Corruption'. Maka Angola.*

Meles, Z. (2006). 'African Development: Dead Ends and New Beginnings'. Retrieved from www.ethiopiantreasures.co.uk/meleszenawi/pdf/zenawi_dead_ends_and_new_beginnings.pdf.

Meles, Z. (2012). 'States and Markets: Neoliberal Limitations and the Case for a Developmental State'. In A. Noman, K. Botchwey, H. Stein, & J. E. Stiglitz (eds.), *Good Growth and Governance in Africa: Rethinking Development Strategies* (pp. 140–74). Oxford University Press.

Mertha, A. (2009). '"Fragmented Authoritarianism 2.0": Political Pluralization in the Chinese Policy Process'. *The China Quarterly*, 200, 995–1012.

Messiant, C. (1992). *'Social and Political Background to the "Democratization" and the Peace Process in Angola'. Seminar on Democratization in Angola*. Leiden.

Messiant, C. (2001). 'The Eduardo dos Santos Foundation: Or, How Angola's Regime is Taking over Civil Society'. *African Affairs*, 100, 287–309.

Messiant, C. (2007). 'The Mutation of Hegemonic Domination: Multiparty Politics Without Democracy'. In P. Chabal & N. Vidal (eds.), *Angola: The Weight of History* (pp. 93–123). Hurst.

Meyersson, E. (2016). *'Political Man on Horseback: Coups and Development'*. Stockholm Institute for Transition Economics.

Mghenyi, C., & Mudi, M. (29 October 2018). 'The Good, the Bad and the Ugly of Kenya's SGR Cargo'. *The Star*. Retrieved from www.theeastafrican.co.ke/business/The-good-the-bad-and-the-ugly-of-Kenya-SGR-cargo-/2560-4827106-vdl4b4z/index.html.

Milkias, P. (2003). 'Ethiopia, the TPLF, and the Roots of the 2001 Political Tremor'. *Northeast African Studies*, 10(2), 13–66.

Ministry of Finance and Economic Development. (2010). *'Growth and Transformation Plan, 2010/11–2014/15'*. Federal Democratic Republic of Ethiopia.

Ministry of Foreign Affairs of the People's Republic of China. (n.d.). 'The Department of African Affairs'. Retrieved from www.fmprc.gov.cn/mfa_eng/wjb_663304/zzjg_663340/fzs_663828.

Ministry of Transport and Infrastructure. (2013). *'Ministerial Statement to the Parliamentary Committee on Transport, Public Works and Housing on the Construction of the Mombasa to Malaba SGR'*. Nairobi.

Mkandawire, T. (2001). 'Thinking about Developmental States in Africa'. *Cambridge Journal of Economics*, 25(3), 289–314.

MOFCOM. (28 November 2003). '中华人民共和国商务部与安哥拉共和国财政部关于两国经贸合作特殊安排的框架协议'. Retrieved from http://policy.mofcom.gov.cn/pact/pactContent.shtml?id=1150.

MOFCOM (16 January 2022). '亚吉铁路2021年运营收入同比增长37.5%'. Retrieved from http://dj.mofcom.gov.cn/article/jmxw/202201/20220103237349.shtml.

Mohamud, M., & Verhoeven, H. (2016). 'Re-engineering the State, Awakening the Nation: Dams, Islamist Modernity and Nationalist Politics in Sudan'. *Water Alternatives*, 9(2), 182–202.

Mohan, G., & Lampert, B. (2013). 'Negotiating China: Reinserting African Agency into China–Africa Relations'. *African Affairs*, 112(446), 92–110.

Monson, J. (2009). *Africa's Freedom Railway*. Indiana University Press.

Moon, C.-i., & Prasad, R. (1994). 'Beyond the Developmental State: Network, Politics, and Institutions'. *Governance*, 7(4), 360–86.

Morgan, P. (2021). 'Many Chinas? Provincial Internationalization and Chinese Foreign Direct Investment in Africa'. *Oxford Development Studies*, 49(4), 351–67.

Morgan, P., & Zheng, Y. (2019). 'Tracing the Legacy: China's Historical Aid and Contemporary Investment in Africa'. *International Studies Quarterly*, 53(3), 558–73.

Mosley, J. (2020). 'Ethiopia's Transition: Implications for the Horn of Africa and Red Sea Region'. SIPRI Working Paper.

MPLA. (n.d.). 'Comboio volta a apitar no Bié 33 anos depois'. *MPLA*. Retrieved from www.mpla.ao/imprensa.52/noticias.55/comboio-volta-a-apitar-no-bie-33-anos-depois.a109.html.

Mrázek, R. (2018). *Engineers of Happy Land: Technology and Nationalism in a Colony*. Princeton University Press.

Mueller, S. (2010). 'Government and Opposition in Kenya, 1966–69'. In N. Cheeseman & D. Branch (eds.), *Our Turn to Eat: Politics in Kenya since 1950* (pp. 77–106). Lit Verlag.

Muliba, M., & Yepes, T. (2017). 'Infrastructure and Rural Productivity in Africa'. In M. Ncube & C. L. Lufumpa (eds.), *Infrastructure in Africa: Lessons for Future Development* (pp. 137–54). Policy Press.

Musella, F., & Webb, P. (2015). 'The Revolution of Personal Leaders'. *Italian Political Science Review*, 45(3), 223–6.

Mutambo, A. (8 August 2016). 'Catch Thieves at Port, Says Uhuru'. *Daily Nation*. Retrieved from https://mobile.nation.co.ke/news/catch-thieves-at-port-says-uhuru/1950946-3336870-rkwobyz/index.html.

Mwita, M. (8 August 2020). 'Kenya Eyes Bigger Export Market in China'. *The Star*. Retrieved from www.the-star.co.ke/business/2020-08-08-kenya-eyes-bigger-export-market-in-china.

Ng, T. (19 August 2013). 'Kenya Looks East to "Sincere Friend" in China'. *South China Morning Post*. Retrieved from www.scmp.com/news/china/article/1297869/facing-icc-trial-kenyan-president-uhuru-kenyatta-welcomed-china-visit.

Nigatu, Y., & Abbink, G. J. (2019). *'Political Breakthrough in Ethiopia? Prime Minister Abiy Ahmed's Reformist Agenda'*. Annual Report 2018, African Studies Centre Leiden.

Nordhaus, W. D. (1975). 'The Political Business Cycle'. *The Review of Economic Studies*, 42(2), 169–90.

Nordlinger E. A. (1981). *On the Autonomy of the Democratic State*. Harvard University Press.

North, D. (1990). *Institutions, Institutional Change and Economic Performance*. Cambridge University Press.

Nye, J. (2008). *The Powers to Lead*. Oxford University Press.

OECD. (14 September 2020). 'Unprecedented Falls in GDP in Most G20 Economies in Second Quarter of 2020'. *OECD*. Retrieved from www.oecd.org/sdd/na/g20-gdp-growth-second-quarter-2020-oecd.htm.

Oketch, W., & Mwakio, P. (14 July 2018). 'Fight for Millions That Could Have Cost Ex-KPA Boss Her Job'. *The Standard*. Retrieved from www.standardmedia.co.ke/article/2001287989/fight-for-millions-that-could-have-cost-ex-kpa-boss-her-job.

Okoth, E. (5 May 2019). 'Official Spin on Status of Loan Adds to Doubts on Fate of SGR Project'. *Daily Nation*. Retrieved from www.nation.co.ke/news/spin-on-status-of-loan-adds-doubts-SGR-project-fate—/1056-5100794-9wkl29z/index.html.

Okoth, E. (1 September 2019). 'Joho Firm Set to Take over Lucrative Cargo Terminal Deal'. *Daily Nation*. Retrieved from www.nation.co.ke/news/Joho-firm-to-take-over-lucrative-cargo-terminal-deal/1056-5256142-15pojpo/index.html.

Olingo, A. (27 April 2019). 'Kenya Fails to Secure $3.6b from China for Third Phase of SGR Line to Kisumu'. *The East African*. Retrieved from www.theeastafrican.co.ke/tea/business/kenya-fails-to-secure-3-6b-from-china-for-third-phase-of-sgr-line-to-kisumu-1416820.

Omondi, G. (20 December 2018). 'Mombasa Port at Risk as Audit Finds It Was Used to Secure SGR Loan'. *The East African*. Retrieved from www.theeastafrican.co.ke/tea/business/mombasa-port-at-risk-as-audit-finds-it-was-used-to-secure-sgr-loan-1408886.

Onis, Z. (1991). 'Review: The Logic of the Developmental State'. *Comparative Politics*, 24(1), 109–26.

Ostheimer, A. (2000). 'Aid Agencies: Providers of Essential Resources?' In J. Cilliers & C. Dietrich (eds.), *Angola's War Economy: The Role of Oil and Diamonds* (pp. 115–40). Institute for Security Studies.

Otieno, B. (15 May 2018). 'Uhuru Extends SGR Cargo Fees Promotion'. *Business Daily*. Retrieved from www.businessdailyafrica.com/economy/Uhuru-extends-SGR-cargo-fees-promotion/3946234-4563616-3gjyjjz/index.html.

Otieno, B. (18 December 2018). 'I Don't Oppose SGR, But Our People Lost Jobs, Joho Tells Handshake Team'. *The Star*. Retrieved from www.the-star.co.ke/news/2018-12-05-i-dont-oppose-sgr-but-our-people-lost-jobs-joho-tells-handshake-team.

Otieno, R. (31 May 2017). 'Raila: We Will Jail Those Who Inflated SGR Cost'. *The Standard*. Retrieved from www.standardmedia.co.ke/politics/article/2001241751/raila-we-will-jail-those-who-inflated-sgr-cost.

Oya, C., & Schaefer, F. (2019). *'Chinese Firms and Employment Dynamics in Africa: A Comparative Analysis'*. IDCEA Research Synthesis Report.

Pachirat, T. (2018). *Among Wolves: Ethnography and the Immersive Study of Power*. Routledge.

Parker, S., & Chefitz, G. (30 May 2018). 'China's Debtbook Diplomacy: How China Is Turning Bad Loans into Strategic Investments'. *The Diplomat*. Retrieved from https://thediplomat.com/2018/06/chinas-debtbook-diplomacy-how-china-is-turning-bad-loans-into-strategic-investments.

Patrick Musimba v. National Land Commission & 4 others, Petition No 613 of 2014 (2014).

Pearce, J. (2015). *Political Identity and Conflict in Central Angola, 1975–2002*. Cambridge University Press.

Phillips, J. (2018). 'Who's in Charge of Sino-African Resource Politics? Situating African State Agency in Ghana'. *African Affairs*, 118(470), 101–24.

Pilling, D., & Barber, L. (21 February 2019). 'Ethiopia's Abiy Ahmed: Africa's New Talisman'. *Financial Times*. Retrieved from www.ft.com/content/abe678b6-346f-11e9-bb0c-42459962a812.

Pilling, D., & Feng, M. (4 April 2017). 'Kenya's $4 Billion Railway Gains Traction from Chinese Policy Ambitions'. *Financial Times*. Retrieved from www.ft.com/content/d0fd50ee-1549-11e7-80f4-13e067d5072c.

Pitcher, A., Moran, M. H., & Johnston, M. (2009). 'Rethinking Patrimonialism and Neopatrimonialism in Africa'. *African Studies Review*, 52(1), 125–56.

Pitcher, M. A. (2017). 'Varieties of Residential Capitalism in Africa: Urban Housing Provision in Luanda and Nairobi'. *African Affairs*, 116(464), 365–90.

Pollack, D. L. (2001). 'Let Us Now Praise Great Men: Bringing the Statesman Back In'. *International Security*, 25(4), 107–46.

Price, R. (1974). 'Politics and Culture in Contemporary Ghana: The Big-Man, Small-Boy Syndrome'. *Journal of African Studies*, 1(2), 173–204.

Public Investment Committee. (2014). 'Special Report on the Procurement and Financing of the Construction of Standard Gauge Railway from Mombasa to Nairobi (Phase 1)'. National Assembly.

Railway Technology. (2016). 'Mombasa-Nairobi Standard Gauge Railway Project'. *Railway Technology*. Retrieved from www.railway-technology.com/projects/mombasa-nairobi-standard-gauge-railway-project.

Rauch, J. E., & Evans., P. B. (2000). 'Bureaucratic Structure and Bureaucratic Performance in Less Developed Countries'. *Journal of Public Economics*, 75(1), 49–71.

Ray, R., Gallagher, K., López, A., & Sanborn, C. (2017). *China and Sustainable Development in Latin America: The Social and Environmental Dimension*. Anthem Press.

RedeAngola. (23 August 2014). 'IMOGESTIN assumirá vendas nas centralidades'. *RedeAngola*. Retrieved from www.redeangola.info/imogestin-assumira-vendas-nas-centralidades/#disqus_thread.

Relógio, A. T., Tavares, F. O., & Pacheco, L. (2017). 'Importância do Caminho de Ferro de Benguela para o Desenvolvimento Regional'. *Cadernos de Estudos Africanos*, 33, 9–30.

Reuters. (19 August 2013). 'Kenya Signs Infrastructure, Energy Deals Worth $5 bln with China'. *Reuters*. Retrieved from www.reuters.com/article/kenya-china/kenya-signs-infrastructure-energy-deals-worth-5-bln-with-china-idUSL6N0GK2MT20130819.

Reuters. (31 May 2017). 'Kenya Inaugurates Chinese-Built Railway Linking Port to Capital'. *Reuters*. Retrieved from www.reuters.com/article/china/idUKKBN18R2UF?edition-redirect=uk.

Reyes, V. (2018). 'Ethnographic Toolkit: Strategic Positionality and Researchers' Visible and Invisible Tools in Field Research'. *Ethnography*, 21(2), 220–40.

Rhodes, R. A., & Hart, P. (2014). *The Oxford Handbook of Political Leadership*. Oxford University Press.

Rode, P., Terrefe, B., & da Cruz, N. F. (2020). 'Cities and the Governance of Transport Interfaces: Ethiopia's New Rail Systems'. *Transport Policy*, 91(7), 76–94.

Roll, M. (2014). *The Politics of Public Sector Performance: Pockets of Effectiveness in Developing Countries*. Routledge.

Ronoh, F. (4 January 2014). 'Nandi Hills MP Alfred Keter Vows to Continue Speaking the Truth'. *The Standard*. Retrieved from www.standardmedia.co.ke/article/2000101449/nandi-hills-mp-alfred-keter-vows-to-continue-speaking-the-truth.

Roque, P. C. (2009). 'Angola's Facade Democracy'. *Journal of Democracy*, 20(4), 137–50.

Rotberg, R. (2012). *Transformative Political Leadership*. University of Chicago Press.

Sanusi, L. (11 March 2013). 'Africa Must Get Real about Chinese Ties'. *Financial Times*. Retrieved from www.ft.com/content/562692b0-898c-11e2-ad3f-00144feabdc0.

Schatz, E. (2013). 'Ethnographic Immersion and the Study of Politics'. In E. Schatz (ed.), *Political Ethnography: What Immersion Contributes to the Study of Power*. University of Chicago Press.

Shinn, D. H. (2015). 'The Environmental Impact of China's Investment in Africa'. *Cornell International Law Journal*, 49(1), 25–65.

Singh, A. (2020). 'The Myth of "Debt-Trap Diplomacy" and Realities of Chinese Development Finance'. *Third World Quarterly*, 42(2), 239–53.

Skocpol, T. (1979). *States and Social Revolutions: A Comparative Analysis of France, Russia and China*. Cambridge University Press.

Skocpol, T. (1985). 'Bringing the State Back In: Strategies of Analysis in Current Research'. In P. Evans, D. Rueschemeyer, & T. Skocpol (eds.), *Bringing the State Back In* (pp. 3–37). Cambridge University Press.

Skowronek, S. (1982). *Building a New American State: The Expansion of National Administrative Capacities, 1877–1920*. Cambridge University Press.

Soares de Oliveira, R. (2007). 'Business Success, Angola-Style: Postcolonial Politics and the Rise of Sonangol'. *Journal of Modern African Studies*, 45(4), 595–619.

Soares de Oliveira, R. (2008). 'Making Sense of Chinese Oil Investment in Africa'. In C. Alden, D. Large, & R. S. Oliveira (eds.), *China Returns to Africa: A Superpower and A Continent Embrace* (pp. 83–110). Hurst.

Soares de Oliveira, R. (2015). *Magnificent and Beggar Land: Angola since the Civil War*. Hurst.

Soifer, H., & vom Hau, M. (2008). 'Unpacking the Strength of the State: The Utility of State Infrastructural Power'. *Studies in Comparative International Development*, 43(3), 219–30.

Solomon, S., & Frechette, C. (13 September 2018). 'Corruption Is Wasting Chinese Money in Africa'. *Foreign Policy*. Retrieved from https://foreignpolicy.com/2018/09/13/corruption-is-wasting-chinese-money-in-africa.

Sommerville, K. (1986). *Angola: Politics, Economics and Society*. Lynne Rienner Publishers.

Soreide, T. (2011). *'Ten Challenges in Public Construction'*. CEIC-CMI Public Sector Transparency Study.

Soulé-Kohndou, F. (2019). 'Bureaucratic Agency and Power Asymmetry in Benin-China Relations'. In C. Alden & D. Large (eds.), *New Directions in Africa–China Studies* (pp. 189–204). Routledge.

Stallings, B. (2020). *Dependency in the Twenty-First Century? The Political Economy of China–Latin America Relations*. Cambridge University Press.

State Council. (2021). 'China's International Development Cooperation in the New Era'. Retrieved from https://english.www.gov.cn/archive/whitepaper/202101/10/content_WS5ffa6bbbc6d0f72576943922.html.

State Council Information Office (2022). '蒙内铁路通车运营五年来——为肯尼亚铺就一条幸福路'. Retrieved from www.scio.gov.cn/31773/35507/35510/Document/1728382/1728382.htm.

Strange, A. (2022). 'Symbols of State: China's Global Prestige Projects, 1950–2017'. Working paper.

Strange, A. M., Dreher, A., Fuchs, A., Parks, B., & Tierney, M. J. (2017). 'Tracking Underreported Financial Flows: China's Development Finance and the Aid–Conflict Nexus Revisited'. *Journal of Conflict Resolution*, 61(5), 935–63.

Tarrósy, I. (2020). 'China's Belt and Road Initiative in Africa, Debt Risk and New Dependency: The Case of Ethiopia'. *African Studies Quarterly*, 19(3–4), 9–28.

Taylor, I. (2016). 'Dependency Redux: Why Africa is Not Rising'. *Review of African Political Economy*, 43(147), 8–25.

Taylor, I. (2020). 'Kenya's New Lunatic Express: The Standard Gauge Railway'. *African Studies Quarterly*, 19(3–4), 29–52.

Taylor, I., & Zajontz, T. (2020). 'In a Fix: Africa's Place in the Belt and Road Initiative and the Reproduction of Dependency'. *South African Journal of International Affairs*, 27(3), 277–95.

Temin, J., & Badwaza, Y. (2019). 'Aspirations and Realities in Africa: VI. Ethiopia's Quiet Revolution'. *Journal of Democracy*, 30(3), 139–53.

Terrefe, B. (2018). 'The "Renaissance" Railway Infrastructure and Discourse in EPRDF's Ethiopia'. University of Oxford: MPhil Thesis.

Tesfa-Alem, T. (4 August 2021). 'Ethiopia, Djibouti Railway Link Restored after Protests'. *The East African*. Retrieved from www.theeastafrican.co.ke/tea/rest-of-africa/ethiopia-djibouti-railway-link-restored-after-protests-3498006.

The East African. (20 January 2014). 'Kenya Railway Project Starts Amid Controversy'. *The East African*. Retrieved from www.theeastafrican.co.ke/news/Kenya-railway-project-starts-amid-controversy/-/2558/2152714/-/item/1/-/urd8hvz/-/index.html.

The Economist. (13 August 2011). 'China International Fund the Queensway Syndicate and the Africa Trade'. *The Economist*. Retrieved from www.economist.com/briefing/2011/08/13/the-queensway-syndicate-and-the-africa-trade.

The Export and Import Bank of China. (2016). 'The Export-Import Bank of China Annual Report 2016'. The Export and Import Bank of China, http://english.eximbank.gov.cn/News/AnnualR/2016/.

Therkildsen, O. (2008). *'Public Sector Reforms and the Development of Productive Capacities in LDCs'*. UNCTAD.

Throup, D., & Hornsby, C. (1998). *Multi-Party Politics in Kenya*. James Currey.

Todayng. (15 August 2019). 'Angolan Ex-Minister Jailed 14 Years for Corruption'. *Todayng*. Retrieved from www.today.ng/news/africa/angolan-minister-jailed-14-years-corruption-242685.

Trading Economics. (n.d.). 'Angola Exports to China'. Retrieved from https://tradingeconomics.com/angola/exports/china.

Tronvoll, K., & Hagmann, T. (2012). 'Introduction Traditional Authorities and Multi-Party Elections in Ethiopia'. In K. Tronvoll & T. Hagmann (eds.), *Contested Power in Ethiopia* (pp. 1–29). Brill.

Tull, D. M. (2006). 'China's Engagement in Africa: Scope, Significance and Consequences'. *Journal of Modern African Studies*, 44(3), 459–79.

Tull, D. M., & Blasiak, R. (2011). *'Weak States and Successful Elites: Extraversion Strategies in Africa'*. Stiftung Wissenschaft und Politik, German Institute for International and Security Affairs.

Universidade Católica de Angola. (2018). *'Relatório Económico de Angola 2017'*. Luanda.

UNSA. (2002). *'Angola: The Post-War Challenges'*. United Nations Systems in Angola.

Verhoeven, H. (2002). 'The Politics of African Energy Development: Ethiopia's Hydro-Agricultural State-Building Strategy and Clashing Paradigms of Water Security'. *Philosophical Transactions of the Royal Society*, 371(2013), 1–16.

Vine, A. (2022). 'Climbing Out of the Chinese Debt Trap'. Retrieved from www.chathamhouse.org/publications/the-world-today/2022-08/climbing-out-chinese-debt-trap.

Vines, A., & Weimer, M. (2009). 'Angola: Thirty Years of Dos Santos'. *Review of African Political Economy*, 36(120), 287–94.

Waldner, D. (1999). *State Building and Late Development*. Cornell University Press.

Wang, Y., & Wissenbach, U. (2019). 'Clientelism at Work? A Case Study of Kenyan Standard Gauge Railway Project'. *Economic History of Developing Regions*, 34(3), 280–99.

Weber, M. (1968). *Economy and Society: An Outline of Interpretive Sociology*. University of California Press.

Weinberg, A. (2012). *The Psychology of Politicians*. Cambridge University Press.

Weis, T. (2015). 'Vanguard Capitalism: Party, State, and Market in the EPRDF's Ethiopia'. University of Oxford: DPhil Thesis.

Weiss, R. S. (1994). *Learning from Strangers: The Art and Method of Qualitative Interview Studies*. The Free Press.

Weldesilassie, A. B., Gebreeyesus, M., Abebe, G., & Aseffa, B. (2017). *'Study on Industrial Park Development: Issues, Practices and Lessons for Ethiopia'*. Ethiopian Development Research Institute.

Whitfield, L., & Fraser, A. (2009). 'Negotiating Aid'. In L. Whitfield (ed.), *The Politics of Aid: African Strategies for Dealing with Donors*. Oxford University Press.

Whitfield, L., Therkildsen, O., Buur, L., & Kjær, A. M. (2015). *The Politics of African Industrial Policy: A Comparative Perspective*. Cambridge University Press.

Wikileaks 07LUANDA1015_a. (3 October 2007). 'Angola-Benguela Railroad Construction in Abeyance' (Cable: 07LUANDA1015_a). Retrieved from Wikileaks.

Wikileaks 09LUANDA51_a. (27 January 2009). 'New China Credit Line under Consideration'. Retrieved from Wikileaks.

Wikileaks 10LUANDA84_a. (26 February 2010). 'Request for Information on Chinese Engagement in Angola and Potential Areas for Cooperation'. Retrieved from Wikileaks.

Wise, C. (2020). *Dragonomics: The Rise of China in Latin America*. Yale University Press.

Wissenbach, U., & Wang, Y. (2017). 'African Politicians Meets Chinese Engineers: The Chinese-Built Standard Gauge Railway Project in Kenya and East Africa'. Johns Hopkins University-SAIS Working Paper.

World Bank. (2014). *'The Economics of Rail Gauge in the East African Community'*. World Bank, African Transport Unit.

World Bank. (2018). *'The Open Budget Portal: Kenya'*. World Bank.

World Bank. (n.d.). 'Poverty Headcount Ratio at $1.90 A Day (2011 PPP) (% of population)'. Retrieved from https://data.worldbank.org/indicator/SI.POV.DDAY.

Wrong, M. (2009). *It's Our Turn to Eat*. Fourth Estate.

Xinhua News. (28 December 2017). 'Chinese-Built Railways Improve Transport in Africa'. *Xinhua News*. Retrieved from www.xinhuanet.com/english/2017-12/28/c_136857657.htm.

Xu, Y.-C. (2014). 'Chinese State-Owned Enterprises in Africa: Ambassadors or Freebooters?' *Journal of Contemporary China*, 23(89), 822–40.

Ye, M. (2019). 'Fragmentation and Mobilization: Domestic Politics of the Belt and Road in China'. *Journal of Contemporary China*, 28(119), 696–711.

Young, O. R. (1991). 'Political Leadership and Regime Formation: On the Development of Institutions in International Society'. *International Organization*, 45(3), 281–308.

Yu, H. (2014). 'The Ascendency of State-Owned Enterprises in China: Development, Controversy and Problems'. *Journal of Contemporary China*, 23(85), 161–82.

Yuan, L., Li, Q., & Wang, J. (2019). *Facilitating African Manufacturing Development: China–Africa Cooperation in Industrial Parks*. China Commerce and Trade Press.

Zajontz, T. (2022a). 'Debt, Distress, Dispossession: Towards a Critical Political Economy of Africa's Financial Dependency'. *Review of African Political Economy*, 49(171), 173–83.

Zajontz, T. (2022b). 'Railway Imperialisms in East Africa: Laying the Tracks for Exploitation'. In Z. Cope & I. Ness (eds.), *Oxford Handbook of Economic Imperialism*. Oxford University Press.

Zeitz, A. (2019). 'The Financial Statecraft of Debtors: The Political Economy of External Finance in Africa'. University of Oxford: DPhil Thesis.

Zeitz, A. (2021). 'Correction to: Emulate or Differentiate? Chinese Development Finance, Competition, and World Bank Infrastructure Funding'. *The Review of International Organizations*, 16(4), 933–8.

Zhang, H. (2021). 'Chinese International Contractors in Africa: Structure and Agency'. Working Paper No. 2021/47. China–Africa Research Initiative, School of Advanced International Studies, Johns Hopkins University, Washington, DC. Retrieved from www.sais-cari.org/publications.

Zhou, H. (2022). 'Western and Chinese Development Engagements in Uganda's Roads Sector: An Implicit Division of Labour'. *African Affairs*, 121(482), 29–59.

Zweig, D., & Bi, J. (September 2005). *'China's Global Hunt for Energy'*. Foreign Affairs.

Zwitter, A. (2012). 'The Rule of Law in Times of Crisis: A Legal Theory on the State of Emergency in the Liberal Democracy'. *ARSP: Archiv Für Rechts-Und Sozialphilosophie/Archives for Philosophy of Law and Social Philosophy*, 95–111.

中国中铁. (2015). 中国中铁股份有限公司 2015 年年度报告. 中国中铁.

中国交建. (2015). 中国交通建设股份有限公司 2015 年年度报告. 中国交建.

中国网. (5 April 2007). 中基公司:拿什么履行344亿天价合同. Retrieved from www.china.com.cn/economic/txt/2007-04/05/content_8071497.htm.

中国铁建. (2015). 中国铁建股份有限公司2015 年年度报告. 中国铁建.

Index

Page numbers in *italics* refer to figures and tables.